Knowledge in Organizations

Resources for the Knowledge-Based Economy

Knowledge in Organizations

Laurence Prusak
Editor

Butterworth-Heinemann
Boston Oxford Johannesburg Melbourne New Delhi Singapore

Copyright © 1997 by Butterworth–Heinemann

℞ A member of the Reed Elsevier group

All rights reserved.

Recognizing the importance of preserving what has been written, Butterworth–Heinemann prints its books on acid-free paper whenever possible.

Library of Congress Cataloging-in-Publication Data

Knowledge in organizations / Laurence Prusak, editor.
   p.   cm.—(Resources for the knowledge-based economy)
   Includes bibliographical references and index.
   ISBN 0-7506-9718-0 (pbk. : alk. paper)
   1. Organizational learning.   I. Prusak, Laurence.   II. Series.
   HD58.82.K58   1997
   658.4′06—dc21   96-47427
                                                    CIP

British Library Cataloguing-in-Publication Data
A catalogue record for this book is available from the British Library.

The publisher offers special discounts on bulk orders of this book.
For information, please contact:
Manager of Special Sales
Butterworth–Heinemann
313 Washington Street
Newton, MA 02158-1626
Tel: 617-928-2500
Fax: 617-928-2620

For information on all business publications available, contact our World Wide Web home page at: http://www.bh.com/bb

10 9 8 7 6 5

Printed in the United States of America

Table of Contents

Introduction to Series—Why Knowledge, Why Now?

Why is there such an upsurge of interest in Knowledge? In 1996 there will be at least six major conferences on the subject; there are plans to add three new journals focusing on Knowledge, sometimes loosely called Intellectual Capital or Organizational Learning) and many major firms in the United States and (more slowly) Europe, are adding positions such as Chief Knowledge Officer, or Organizational Learning, and even a few Vice Presidents for Intellectual Capital!

How come all this focus on a subject that, at some levels, has been around since the pre-Socratic philosophers? Is it yet another one of the multitudinous management enthusiasms that seem to come and go, with the frequency of some random natural phenomena? We don't think so! Many of us doing research on this subject have seen the rise and fall of many of these varied nostrums—all of which attempted to offer to firms a new road to achieving a sustainable competitive advantage. However, when much of the shouting dies down, we have concluded that, excluding mono polistic policies and other market irregularities, there is no sustainable advantage other than what a firm knows, how it can utilize what it knows, and how fast it can learn something new!

However this still does not answer the question, why Knowledge, why now? Let us try to list some very broad trends that seem to be playing a significant role in the playing current in Knowledge.

A) The Globalization of the economy which is putting terrific pressure on firms for increased adaptability, innovation, and process speed.

B) The awareness of the value of specialized Knowledge, as embedded in organizational processes and routines, in coping with above pressures.

C) The awareness of Knowledge as a distinct factor of production and its role in the growing book to market ratios within Knowledge based industries.

D) Cheap networked computing which is at last giving us a tool to work and learn with each other.

While many can argue for and against these trends we feel that the preponderance of the evidence points to the increasing substitution of brain for brawn within our organizations and our social lives. Yet we have delayed few conceptional tools to better work with "wetware."

It is with these forces in mind that we offer the following volume to you. While there are, as yet, few agreed upon standards and analytic frames and definitions, there are enough serious articles and books to help managers get some real traction in dealing with the crucial yet elusive subject of Knowledge.

After all, we have had about 500 years of thought concerning the other major factors of production e.g., land, labor, and capital. Let these volumes start the process of codifying knowledge about knowledge in order for us to better manage in the 21st century.

Laurence Prusak

Introduction to Knowledge in Organizations

Laurence Prusak

Here's an uncontroversial thought if ever you've heard one: a firm's competitive advantage depends more than anything on its knowledge. Or, to be slightly more specific, on *what it knows*—how it *uses* what it knows—and *how fast* it can know something new.

Think about it. Product innovations are the result of a group's knowledge of unserved markets and/or new technical possibilities; efficient operations come from shared knowledge of how things work and how they could work; market share grows with better knowledge of customers and how to serve them. All of this is obvious, and if you're a business executive who's encountered competition any time in the past fifty years or so, your response might be an emphatic "so what?"

So why is it that, in three years of talking about knowledge and its role in organizations, I have yet to hear that reaction? Not once has a speaker-evaluation form come back to me marked "been there, done that," or words to that effect. In fact, there is ample evidence that senior executives are just being struck with the notion that knowledge is a factor of production potentially greater than the traditional triad of land, labor, or capital.

The fact is that, while it's true that an organization's knowledge has always been critical to its competitive success, up to now it wasn't so much in need of explicit management. Yes, it was vital—so was oxygen. But you no more had to manage it than you had to manage how employees breathed; knowledge flowed naturally, informally, at a level sufficient to fuel a marketplace advantage. (At least, that was the assumption.) As a result, it wasn't even a topic of discussion. Try finding many references to knowledge—or key synonyms such as insight, understanding, or judgment—in any well-regarded business text or journal in the past 25 years (always making an exception for Peter Drucker).

Things have changed. Today, the firm that leaves knowledge to its own devices puts itself in severe jeopardy. At best, this extremely valuable asset remains underleveraged, isolated in pockets of the organization, trapped in individual minds and local venues. At worst, the knowledge of executives running the firm has become obsolete, and is pushing it into a downward spiral. To avoid that fate, innovative managers in a vanguard of firms are taking positive action. Recognizing the value of knowledge, they are explicitly working to build better environments for knowledge to be created and better methods of measuring and managing its outputs.

What's Forcing the Focus on Knowledge?

When I note that things have changed, I mean specifically that six things have changed. The pace of change itself is the first. The nature of goods and services is the second. Third, the scope of the typical firm and its market. Fourth, the size and attrition rate of employee bases. Fifth, the structure of organizations. And finally, the capabilities and costs of information technology. These forces—and the numerous other wheels they set in motion—are removing any question of "why knowledge?" and sending senior management in search of *how*. A few paragraphs devoted to each will clarify their impact.

Our accelerating world

It's become almost a cliché to talk about the accelerating pace of change in our business environment: every commentator on any business trend pays homage to it. But undeniably, today's organization seems to experience evolutionary change faster and revolutionary change more frequently. This has made it imperative for firms to manage knowledge actively.

In a relatively stable business environment, an organization's people tend to stay put and naturally become highly knowledgeable over time. Tacitly, they absorb and socialize knowledge about the company's products and services, its markets, customers, competitors, and suppliers—and once gained, that knowledge sustains them indefinitely. Knowledge becomes embedded in the firm's routines and culture. New recruits learn from old hands purely by working alongside them, and exposure and seasoning is a far more important learning mechanism than training. In such an environment it is safe to assume that sufficient knowledge and capabilities exist in the organization, or that incremental learning occurs fast enough, to deal with contingencies. Time, logic, and experiments solve most problems.

Now, rapid change means quicker knowledge obsolescence, and a need to scale new learning curves in unnaturally compressed time frames. Every week in a typical company brings news of some emerging market, some hot technology, some unexpected form of competition—opportunities all, if only the company had the knowledge base to deal with them. Trying to keep pace, management constantly introduces internal change. New strategies, new structures, new processes, new tools—all create a need for many people to learn new things at once.

Huge overhauls of knowledge bases don't happen naturally. So where they have happened, they have often brought trauma. The fastest way to change the knowledge of an organization, after all, is to replace the people. Unfortunately, it's a stupid way, because it only means that the same type of coup will have to occur the next time major change hits the business. And meanwhile, much that was valuable in the old knowledge base—but that was captured only in organizational stories and cultural artifacts—has been lost.

Smart products and service intensity

The need to manage knowledge actively becomes more obvious when what you sell is knowledge. For a research lab, a consulting firm, a software vendor not to manage knowledge would be equivalent to Wal-Mart not managing inventory, or Ford not managing production. Interestingly, though, it's not just the gurus who are selling knowledge these days. Firms from BP, which drills oil, to Senco, which makes nails, now routinely describe themselves as being "in the knowledge business."

This is because the make-up of today's products and the way in which they are delivered encapsulate an unprecedented amount of knowledge. In the extreme, this takes the form of "smart products"—things that can, for example, diagnose their own maintenance requirements or adapt to a particular owners' preference. More broadly, we are seeing a rise in R&D expense (one proxy for measuring knowledge investment) as a proportion of cost of goods sold. The price of a camcorder has fallen by about 80% in six years' time, yet today's models have more engineering expertise behind them than ever. Knowledge-intensity in products is also resulting from a trend toward "mass customization," which essentially builds greater knowledge of particular customers' needs into what used to be a standardized product. John Deere seeders roll efficiently off the production line, but given thousands of possible variants, each one is tailored to its individual buyer. Could anyone deny this is now a more knowledge-intensive product? (One wonders how they're going to keep them down on the farm . . .)

Finally, as firms increasingly bundle products with service in their pricing, they are increasing the knowledge component of what they sell. A seller of lighting fixtures quickly discovers that different levels of service are sought by Home Depot, Saks Fifth Avenue, and a interior design firm. The firm that is able to translate that knowledge into tailored offerings stands to increase its business with every account. And in what might otherwise be a commodity business, it will see its profit margin widened disproportionately by this knowledge component.

It's not a small world after all

Global integration of the economy lets more and more firms, globally run and sourced, produce more and more goods for each dollar of profit. In the US, our market share of global GDP went from 52% to 23% in my own lifetime. Even though the pie has grown much bigger, our share in it is fiercely contested. In fact, the challenges of globalization may be alerting more executives to the need for knowledge management than anything else.

As companies try to position themselves to expand within the global economy, their efforts are often stultified by clear deficiencies in knowledge. Their people simply do not know enough about how to spot global opportunities, or once an opportunity is spotted, how business is done in that part of the world. Worse yet, they may not understand the basic model by which the business succeeds, or how to replicate that success in new outposts.

The huge scope of the modern organization makes an important case for more deliberate knowledge management. Sheer numbers is one problem: at Ernst & Young, for example, a piece of intellectual capital (i.e., knowledge codified and distributed) that is important to only one-tenth of employees must still find its way into 7,000 heads! Geography brings additional challenges: if knowledge is only transferred through proximity and exposure, how long does it take for something that is known in Munich to make it to Michigan? This is the problem that inspired Hewlett-Packard's Lew Platt to say: "If only HP knew what HP knows, we could be three times more productive!"

One last point on the scope of today's organization: highly diversified or vertically integrated firms may have heightened needs for knowledge management because they do not choose to concentrate on core competencies. Where the variety of businesses and types of operations is great, the chances diminish that important knowledge will simply seep through the organization informally and naturally. As Dorothy Leonard-Barton points out, in a volatile world, core competencies can become core rigidities. It is more expedient to learn how to learn than to learn a specific subject.

Here today, gone tomorrow

Even those rare firms who have not seen their knowledge needs change dramatically—who perhaps operate in mature industries or rely little on innovation—recognize an increasing need for knowledge management. This is because, while they may require the same basic knowledge base, they are typically asking a smaller number of employees to house it. Downsizing, the scourge of the nineties, is a severe strain on organizational knowledge. By removing slack from a worker's day, it makes new knowledge generation or acquisition difficult. At worst, downsizing is the intellectual capital equivalent of strip-mining, since it usually begins by early-retiring a firm's most experienced people and driving away its most talented.

Whether due to firms' disloyalty to workers or vice versa, or other forces altogether, workforce mobility is a fact of modern life. No organization can take its knowledge base for granted—erosion occurs with every position that turns over. Recognizing this means understanding that continuous investment is necessary, and not just in the knowledge base of individuals, but in the shared knowledge base of the firm. Firms who do only the former may become exploited as training grounds: spend two years in their new management program, then cash in by taking that expertise elsewhere. Enlightened firms don't react by curtailing such development, but they do find ways to make knowledge transfer a two-way street. By setting out to manage knowledge, to represent what people know and make it accessible, they turn individual knowledge into a transferable asset.

The reduction of employee bases and growing attrition rate within them become, of course, even bigger problems when the firm does not have the luxury of stable knowledge needs, but in fact must advance rapidly in gaining new knowledge. It seems inconceivable that, without active management, a firm could hope to meet escalating knowledge needs with fluctuating—or fewer—knowledge workers.

The coming virtuality

Knowledge management is also being necessitated by the changing structure of organizations, and particularly the desire to integrate far-flung operations. Businesses that were once organized along geographic lines are now reorienting themselves according to markets, or products, or processes—or all of the above in complex matrices. Within organizations, people in widely dispersed locations combine efforts on "virtual" teams. At a higher level, virtual organizations are made up of complementary, allied entities. In their simplest forms, these are formerly integrated organizations which have outsourced parts of their operations. At the most abstract, there are businesses like Amazon.com, the Internet-based book store that has no physical facilities and owns no inventory, but orchestrates promotion, selling, and delivery of over a million titles.

Any organizational structure that is not based on geography places greater demands on knowledge management. Where casual and local networks sufficed before, deliberate networks must be established. These can be formed without too much investment or top-down control; they can simply be enabled, enhanced, and allowed to self-organize. Informal communications can be augmented by creative use of multimedia technologies. The challenge is to recognize what knowledge-sharing mechanisms existed, however informally, before and need to be replaced in the new, wired world. Put another way: If the water cooler was a font of useful knowledge in the traditional firm, what constitutes a virtual one? How do we manage the need for face-time, which is essential to establishing trust, in a firm of tens of thousands? The real challenge here is to use technology in the most creative way to create the widest bandwidth for communications.

Multiplying connections

With regard to the five forces noted so far, it would be fair to say that better knowledge management is as much a driver of them as it is a resulting need. Highly dispersed operations, global expansion, continual change—none of these things would be possible if it weren't possible to deploy knowledge formally and deliberately. What's brought us this far has been, undeniably, the ability to capture and utilize knowledge via cheap computing.

What's new about information technology is that it's now transparent to the user, ubiquitous, and more capable than ever of capturing knowledge, as opposed to mere data or words. Real, interactive networks are made possible by telecommunications and technologies like groupware, and can put knowledgeable people in touch with each other who could never find one another before. And, as these technologies become richer in their means of expression (through the integration of multiple media), computers will take on an even greater role in enabling the use of knowledge as a transforming agent.

Even Better Reasons for Managing Knowledge

The pace of change, the knowledge-intensity of goods and services, the growth in organizational scope, staff attrition, new structures, and information technology . . . All of these forces are leading executives to more formal knowledge management. There is a growing recognition of knowledge as an asset, which can be substituted for land, labor, or capital, and can be a greater force than any of those in the production of goods and services.

For those executives, however, who somehow remain untouched or unmoved by such underlying forces, there is an even more powerful argument for knowledge management: the success of the vanguard who have already taken on the challenge. Consider the team at Hoffman-LaRoche, which worked to make the knowledge requirements of new drug approval more explicit. By substantially reducing the time to market of their next new product, they earned the company millions. Or the architects of the several initiatives underway at Hewlett-Packard, improving how knowledge is generated, captured, and transferred around the organization. Or the group at Monsanto which has constructed a knowledge base to make new and important insights instantly accessible.

Successes like these began with a recognition that knowledge management is now possible and necessary in ways it hasn't been in the past. And they are just the beginning. After all, firms have been managing, analyzing, and measuring land, labor, and capital for several hundred years. By contrast, we have only just begun to understand and analyze the workings of knowledge in organizations.

It's no wonder that most executives are struggling to understand exactly what to do with knowledge. But the few who are figuring it out are showing us the way forward. Along the way, they're making it clear why the rest of the business world is turning its attention to knowledge, and why, if your management team hasn't, it should now.

Why This Reader?

Various analysts, philosophers, and practitioners have been studying the other factors of production (land, labor, and capital) since at least the fifteenth century. Not unnaturally, there are at this stage in our understanding few things we don't know about their management. However, it is only since the end of World War II that the systematic study of knowledge as an economic force has taken place. Therefore, it is not surprising that we still do not have thorough and robust models and approaches to aid us in making our knowledge bases more effective and efficient. And while some business people might question the value of academic analysis in this area, their work is essential to gaining a clear and comprehensive understanding of how knowledge "works" within an organization.

The following articles were chosen for their high conceptual and practical quality, as well as for their diverse "takes" on knowledge. Some see knowledge primarily as a strategic asset (Earl, Lyles, Schwenk), others in terms of learning (Starbuck, Nonaka), memory (Walsh), the content of networks (Krackhardt, Hanson), and technology (Kogut, Zander). There is a case study (Mann et al.), a cautionary tale (Marshall et al.), and two influential conceptual pieces (Polanyi, Weick).

All of these pieces make significant contributions to our growing understanding of knowledge, as well as being intrinsically interesting. We hope they will add to each reader's stock of knowledge and help them better utilize this critical and elusive resource.

1

Knowledge as Strategy: Reflections on Skandia International and Shorko Films[1]

Michael J. Earl

INTRODUCTION

It has been argued by Bell (1979) and others that knowledge is the key resource of the post-industrial era and that telecommunications is the key technology. Employment categories have been reclassified to accommodate knowledge-working (Porat, 1977) and some analysts have argued that knowledge workers already form the dominant sector of western work forces (OECD, 1981). Computer scientists are prone to suggesting that knowledge-based systems can yield abnormal returns. For example, Hayes-Roth, Waterman and Lenat (1983) claim that knowledge is a scarce resource whose refinement and reproduction create wealth and, further, that knowledge-based information technology is the enabler that turns knowledge into a valuable industrial commodity. It could be argued whether knowledge is scarce, particularly as it can be created, reproduced and shared with as much chance of multiplying value as depleting it. Indeed economists who are concerned with allocation and distribution of scarce resources—and also who make assumptions about availability of perfect or costless information—do recognize these unusual qualities, classifying knowledge as a public good (Silberston, 1967). What is of interest, therefore, as the information society unfolds, is whether we can learn anything about knowledge, its value and

[1]These two cases demonstrate other business and management issues not discussed here. For example, Shorko informs us about technology-strategy relationships and change management. Skandia informs us also about managing the IS function and about global information systems.

knowledge-working from companies who are exploiting information technologies in new domains which have the character of knowledge processing.

The two case studies—Shorko Films and Skandia International—presented elsewhere in this volume provide such an opportunity. *Ex post,* they can be seen as examples of firms who built knowledge-based strategies which were enabled by IT. In Skandia's case there is evidence that this was an explicit strategic intent in an information-intensive industry, namely reinsurance. In Shorko Films, the strategy could be better described as an emergent one, following the language of Mintzberg and Waters (1985), in the manufacturing sector, namely chemicals.

Skandia International built a risks/claims/premiums database to be shared and maintained worldwide and accessed by a corporate data communications network. Essentially they built an encyclopedia on all reinsurance business in niche sectors which was available to their underwriters anywhere who would use decision support tools and analysis and enquiry routines to explore patterns over time, work within parameters learnt and codified through experience and select profitable business taken at sensible prices. The explicit strategy, explained in the 1988 Annual Report, was the building of a platform of "know-how" and taking the lead in information and communications initiatives across the sector. Although in a somewhat esoteric industry, the Skandia case can be seen as an investment in product/market data or information or knowledge (a definitional conundrum to be discussed later). Knowledge-building through IT at Skandia International allowed them to pursue a niche strategy, specializing in those reinsurance classes which generated high information processing and required high analysis.

Shorko Films built a distributed process control system to try and optimize—or at least improve—factory efficiency in the plastic film-making business. Data was collected by a series of electronic nodes (in concept a network) on many parameters of the production process and optimization was pursued on-line and in-line. However, this crucially provided the opportunity to construct an historical database of product/process experience that could be analyzed to learn how to make further improvements in the process. Moreover, a better understanding of the interaction between process and product allowed Shorko to specify and develop new products, make product range profitability decisions and work out how to satisfy customers' specialized requirements. Knowledge-building through IT at Shorko Films allowed them to pursue a competitive strategy of differentiation, exploiting their better understanding of process and its relationship to product, with the intent of yielding premium prices. Previously they had been caught on a seemingly hopeless task of low cost production demanded by the parent.

Both cases can be seen as demonstrations of Zuboff's (1988) concept of "informating." Indeed Shorko is a replication (or technology transfer) of the early directions Zuboff traced in the paper and pulp industry, and the IT investments began with an automating scope before the value of informating was recognized. The process management database becomes the model or image of the firm's operation, the line operators become knowledge workers analyzing and manipulating information, the distinction between managers and workers becomes blurred and the nervous system is the distributed process control electronics. Skandia is not unlike Zuboff's description of her financial services research sites. The database is not here the source of product development, but it is the generator of product decisions. The underwriters have developed new information processing skills using IT tools and the worldwide network is a transmitter and receiver of knowledge. These characteristics will be examined later.

More than "informating," however, Skandia and Shorko can be seen as evolving cases of *knowledge as strategy*. This concept is not novel. After all, science and technology are a critical basis of competition in many industries, for example chemicals or electronics, and know-how is often the foundation in industries like engineering, contracting or consultancy. Indeed, innovation, today perceived as a generic need in all industries, can be seen as knowledge-dependent, whilst the concept of core competences, popularized recently by Prahalad and Hamel (1990) as an alternative strategic paradigm to conventional product-market thinking, is close to the construct of know-how. What perhaps is interesting is that as information technology becomes pervasive and embedded in organizational functioning, new opportunities for building competitive strategies on knowledge are becoming apparent. This chapter therefore seeks to develop by induction some thoughts on knowledge as strategy. The vexed question of what is knowledge is a good starting point and an attempt is made to analyze and classify information systems from a knowledge perspective. Some observations on the strategic value of knowledge are made and thereby on the relative value of different types of information system. The two cases also are suggestive of what is required if knowledge is to be managed as a strategic resource and so a model of knowledge management is proposed and developed.

The concept of "knowledge as strategy" invites theorizing. Case studies such as these allow us to explore ideas, describe emerging phenomena, examine experience and develop propositions. They are a useful means of developing grounded theory (Glaser and Strauss, 1967) in new areas of interest.

KNOWLEDGE

The possible need to distinguish between data, information and knowledge was suggested above. In the 1960s and 1970s, many workers devoted considerable time and energy trying to define information and proposing distinctions from data. Delineation was not always easy or helpful and different disciplines brought alternative characterizations. Where computer science and management science converged, data was (or were) perhaps seen as events or entities represented in some symbolic form and capable of being processed. Information was the output of data that was manipulated, re-presented and interpreted to reduce uncertainty or ignorance, give surprises or insights and allow or improve decision-making. However, it was perhaps for many, but not all, safer to leave conceptualization and definition of knowledge to philosophers and to recognize that knowledge was potentially an even more complex phenomenon than information.

This is not to say that workable definitions and taxonomies were beyond us. For example, mathematical theories of communication (Shannon and Weaver, 1962) were found to be helpful in delineating levels of information processing. Micro-economic analyses of uncertainty (Knight, 1921) were insightful in relating information to decision-making, and epistemology (Kuhn, 1970) potentially provided some discipline in thinking about knowing. And as data processing and MIS advanced, we at least became both conscious of, and largely comfortable with, the differences, similarities and ambiguities of data and information.

In the late 1970s and the 1980s developments in artificial intelligence, expert systems, intelligent knowledge-based systems and their complementary challenges of knowledge engineering and symbolic representation and manipulation have perhaps likewise stimulated us to reassess knowledge. Indeed the very hyperbole and confusion surrounding these technologies and techniques have demanded some conceptual classification. Now we are at least conscious of the difficulties as the challenges of these branches of computer science have become apparent and so again we can be tolerant of the conceptual murkiness.

This paper does not seek to resolve these mysteries! However, to propose knowledge as a strategic resource, some conceptualization is required. And these two case studies do perhaps demonstrate some interesting—or at least debatable—attributes of knowledge.

We should perhaps first separate knowledge from intelligence. At the everyday level we observe that knowledge can be acquired whereas intelligence is more elusive. The two are connected; intelligence is required to produce knowledge and in turn knowledge provides a foundation upon which intelligence can be applied. Those who have worked in the area of artificial intelligence (AI) generally argue—in the spirit of this lay observation—that AI is concerned with formal reasoning and thus needs to not only represent evidence symbolically but build inference mechanisms employing techniques from pattern recognition to heuristic search, presumably falling short at inspiration and serendipity. AI, like intelligence itself, is essentially generic, general purpose reasoning and easily hits constraints of physical and social complexity. In the context of this chapter, however, as suggested later, the concept of designing and building more intelligence into organizations is not rejected.

Knowledge in contrast—and to be equally "lay" or trite—is what we know, or what we can accept we think we know and has not yet been proven invalid, or what we can know. Expert systems developers have preferred often to talk of "expertise" which is commonly defined as knowledge about a particular (specialist) domain (Hayes-Roth, Waterman and Lenat, 1983). These workers point out that experts—and potentially expert systems—perform highly because they are knowledgeable. The appeal of expert systems is that they can codify both established public knowledge and dispersed, often private or hidden knowledge and make it available to a wider set of users. For example, a bank developed expert systems for lending in order to capture the hard-won credit and risk analysis capabilities admired of loan officers about to retire and thereby be able to disseminate it to young successors and collapse a 40-year training curve. Indeed at Skandia, the intent was the spreading of underwriting skills and experience from senior to junior underwriters and from country to country. Expert systems essentially codify and arrange such knowledge into if . . . then rules.

One source of knowledge for these rule-based systems is "science," the published, tested definitions, facts and theorems available in textbooks, reference books and journals. However, experts develop and use expertise which go beyond this. They develop rules of thumb, assimilate and cultivate patterns, conceive their own frameworks of analyses and make educated guesses or judgments. This is also the stuff of expertise and is another layer of knowledge, perhaps less certain than that we might call "science." It is more private, local and idiosyncratic; it is perhaps better called judgment. We often pay considerably more for judgment than science. Interestingly, we use analysis and enquiry tools, decision support systems and modeling techniques to develop this layer of knowledge. And these applications have some knowledge in them, based on science or previously discovered working assumptions. They are not performing reasoning in the strict sense because they are application-specific or use limited rationality. But they bring some measure of intelligence to bear on the generating of knowledge.

How does this discussion relate to Shorko and Skandia? We can imagine that the distributed process control system contained—or could contain—rules based on physics and the chemistry of polymer/copolymer relationships. Furthermore, statistical process control parameters were built in to recognize unacceptable deviations and variances together with signals to indicate where intervention or caution were required. There was science and there was judgment.

In Skandia, the core database contained no science. But the surrounding applications and decision support tools contained both rules based on actuarial science and judgment embodied in limits on acceptable risks and prices, or underpinning trends and patterns to indicate probable outcomes, plus procedural rules on data input and access. Indeed a second generation of expert systems was being generated to improve risk analysis. The core of the "platform of know-how," however, was quite simple; it was the capturing and archiving of all transactions in order not to lose experience from which learning could be gained. Indeed business was bought in order to build a comprehensive experience picture; the value of these in some sense undesirable business transactions was the information content.

We can see the same phenomenon in Shorko. The decision to buy further computer power and the process management system enabled the capturing and archiving not of 32 hours' data but of a year's experience for analysis. In other words, experience has value and experience is untapped knowledge. It can also be current, continually updated and often situation-specific. The same was true for Skandia's reinsurance database. Other companies can do the same thing, but the experience-base will reflect each firm's particular business strategy.

So we can posit three levels of knowledge: science (which can include accepted law, theory and procedure), judgment (which can include policy rules, probabilistic parameters and heuristics) and experience (which is no more than transactional, historical and observational data to be subjected to scientific analysis or judgmental preference and also to be a base for building new science and judgments). This allows us to postulate two models. The first is a hierarchy of knowledge (Table 1.1) where each ascending level represents an increasing amount of structure, certainty and validation. Each level also represents a degree or category of learning. Experience requires action and memory, judgment requires analysis and sensing, whilst science requires formulation and consensus. It will be proposed below that this hierarchy has strategic implications.

This classification could be argued to be synonymous with the distinctions between data, information and knowledge. The lowest level is the equivalent of transaction data (and transaction processing systems). The middle level is the equivalent of information in the classical sense of reducing uncertainty to make decisions (and thus equivalent also of decision support systems). The highest level is knowledge where use is constrained only by its availability or the intellect to exploit it (and thus approximate to the classical expert system or what some call intelligent knowledge-based systems). This mapping of one taxonomy on another allows us to derive another model, Figure 1.1, which attempts to describe the differences between data, information and knowledge.

In the cases of Shorko and Skandia the core systems could be seen as no more than data. Skandia's decision support system inventory and Shorko's reskilling of operators into data analysts were converting data into information. However, both businesses were basing their competitive strategy on understanding their operations on chosen territories better than their rivals. Their goal was a knowledge capability: for Skandia "the platform of know-how," for Shorko "we didn't know enough about the process."

Strategic Value of Knowledge

What do these two cases tell us about the strategic value of knowledge? Both investments yielded strategic advantage; in Skandia this strategy was intended, at Shorko it was discovered—or it emerged using Mintzberg and Waters' term (Mintzberg and Waters, 1985).

At Skandia, the value of their know-how has been put to the test in two ways. First they will buy business transactions to capture the potential knowledge

TABLE 1.1   Levels of Knowledge

Metaphor	Knowledge state	Typical components
Science	Accepted knowledge	Laws, theorems and procedures
Judgement	Workable knowledge	Policy rules, probabilistic parameters and heuristics
Experience	Potential knowledge	Transactions, history and observation

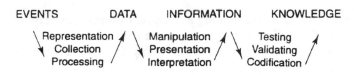

FIGURE 1.1   Towards Conceptualizing Knowledge

(or experience). Knowledge is not often free—it is bought or generated by transaction processing systems and decision support systems; it incurs production costs. Second, when approached to sell their reinsurance systems, Skandia has a clear policy. They might sell the transaction processing architecture but not the decision support and input/output routines, for these contain the second (workable) and perhaps eventually third (accepted) levels of knowledge. The transaction processing architecture gives the capability to capture potential knowledge, but it does not contain knowledge and the potential will be considerably firm-specific. A firm which buys this architecture will begin to collect data which reflects its chosen strategy not Skandia's. The only concern that Skandia might have is: will another firm be better at exploiting potential knowledge than they are? We can be sure, however, that Skandia would not sell the database, for this is their store of potential knowledge which could be valuable to a look-alike rival.

Such market tests have not yet been asked of Shorko, but here we can observe that whilst their new knowledge is not free, it did not cost much. The accepted level, the science, will have been in the public domain and is generally speaking a public good; costs here are low or zero. One could conceive of an application package being developed at this level if the market were strong enough. The workable level usually depends on IT and IS which are not large-scale and resource intensive; decision-support tools, for example, need not be too expensive. The potential level—in Shorko's case capturing experience—was not conceptually complex but it did require more infrastructure than the other levels. The final process management system (PMS) development was a low marginal cost and high marginal revenue investment, but it needed the prior investments as a foundation. (Equally setting up the worldwide transaction system SARA was the high cost investment for Skandia.) Fortunately the prior IS investments at Shorko yielded automation benefits and the transaction processing systems at Skandia had helped them be a low cost producer. The strategist, then, needs to be aware of the knowledge potential of automating and transaction processing systems.

Where does this lead us? We note that the cost of each level of knowledge is likely to diminish from potential through workable to accepted. Even in knowledge-based research and development, this seems to hold true. For example, pharmaceutical researchers might buy accepted knowledge bases relatively cheaply, but the cost of molecular modeling and the like, scanning available knowledge and analyzing experimental experience is high. This means the investor in knowledge as strategy must be confident of the returns if the knowledge required is not a public good. At the time of writing this essay, I heard of a board of a retailing firm who were continually postponing a decision to invest £24 million in electronic point of sale (EPOS) because it was not yet sure of the value—although the managers were eloquent about the need to know more about the customers and their buyer behavior.

Indeed the value question is interesting. Everybody can in principle tap and exploit the science or accepted level or at least they can if it is not under protection of patents, copyright or some similar mechanism. Of course, protected accepted knowledge may be extraordinarily valuable; the patent or copyright is a value-locking constraint. The potential level or experience level is also an investment strategy open to all, subject to affordability (which does mean that there are barriers to entry) but the more differentiated or niche is your competitive strategy, the more unique and thus value-holding the potential of experience becomes. In this sense what could be classified as ordinary transaction processing systems at Skandia and Shorko were strategic, not just because they respectively supported and created strategic thrusts (the outcome), but also because they created firm-specific valuable knowledge (the means).

The value of workable judgment knowledge is also potentially very high. It is this *use* of the databases at Skandia and Shorko which makes the difference. Of course, the necessary tools and skills can be developed by many firms. But without the databases such tools have no foundation. In this sense the underpinning infrastructure becomes the all important strategic capability. We further should note that expert systems—combining accepted and workable knowledge—which can be complex and costly to build, were in their infancy at Skandia and non-existent at Shorko. Much more modest decision-support systems and analyses and enquiry tools were the key weapon at Skandia. Screen-based analyses and the education of operators in information-based analysis and inference skills (with a vision of modeling and exploration work to follow) were the armory at Shorko. This is not expensive in IT terms; it is, however, demanding of human resource development. Indeed Skandia stressed the importance of complementary investment "in the personnel side" and Shorko were sending their operators to college to learn polymer science, computer science and mathematics.

A proposition therefore is that if strategy is based on knowledge, the value of each level in the classification of Table 1.1 increases downwards; so does the cost. However, the experience level—transaction processing systems—incurs joint costs; knowledge can often be the by-product of automation here. The potential value is only realized by investment in decision-support systems (or expert-support systems following Luconi, Malone and Scott-Morton, 1986) and judgment skills. The accepted knowledge level is the basis of human and organizational functioning. It is also a foundation upon which new industries have grown and existing ones adapt. However, without further development it is not a source of sustainable competitive advantage; conversely transaction processing systems which capture relatively more firm specific experience or potential knowledge can be; but only if exploited by decision-support systems at the workable knowledge level. This apparent value of transaction processing systems helps explain why many retailers have invested in EPOS, why they and financial service companies have launched credit and charge cards and why reservation systems are not just about channel warfare and inventory management. It also explains how American Express can grow a substantial insurance business, and banks develop ever more products.

Knowledge Management

This inductive analysis also suggests that knowledge-building is a multifaceted endeavor. At its simplest, it requires a combination of technological and social actions. Figure 1.2 is an attempt at a model of knowledge management. For a business to build a strategic capability in knowledge, the proposition is that at least four components are required. Knowledge systems, networks, knowledge workers and learning organizations.

The Skandia and Shorko cases demonstrate the *systems* that are required: SARA and the distributed process control system to capture experience; the corporate database and PMS archival database to store, steward and make accessible the experience; the decision-support tools and screen-based analyses to exploit it. In Skandia everyone had to use the system in underwriting to ensure all relevant data was captured; at Shorko this was in-line and automatic. In Skandia, the database had to be corporately managed—even though regions could manipulate subsets of it for their own use—to ensure its comprehensiveness and validity. At Shorko, the archive period had to be extended. Decision-support tools were already important at Skandia and were to become so at Shorko.

Capture systems can be concerned with product/markets (Skandia) or operations and processes (Shorko). We could also conceive of environmental data

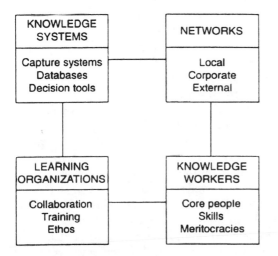

FIGURE 1.2 Knowledge Management

capture and should perhaps note that executive information systems increasingly serve this purpose by tapping into external databases, or by assembling environmental news, as described by Applegate (1988) at Phillips 66.

Networks appear to be significant in knowledge capture, knowledge-building and knowledge dissemination. At Skandia a corporate worldwide network both captured underwriting transactions to update the corporate database and disseminated knowledge-based parameters, knowledge-based trends and knowledge tools. In Shorko, the distributed process control system of 1000 nodes per line can be seen as an intensive local intelligence network. There is no evidence here of external networks. However, we can observe how in knowledge-intensive communities, such infrastructure is valued. The academic community is an exemplar. Possibly the most common and pressing demand in my own institution is faculty access to BITNET, JANET and related communications networks which transcend organizational boundaries. Knowledge-building is facilitated by networked interchange of papers, hypotheses, data and messages. And to draw on another case study company, Digital Equipment Corporation is renowned for its heavy use of Easynet—with 100,000 users and traffic doubling each year. This facilitates internal administrative efficiency but it also contributes to more creativeness through sharing of engineering problems and their solution, collaborative product development and building of alliances with third parties.

The *knowledge workers* component is the people challenge. First we note at Shorko that the automating phase of their IT investment displaced people. Those who remained, however, became core assets; their experience, their continuous knowledge acquisition and their skills arguably made them more valuable to the organization than before. We can observe at Skandia that, perhaps surprisingly, some of the IT professionals were being found to be peripheral (or surplus to requirements). The bulge needed to build their IT infrastructure was no longer necessary and they contributed only the fabric for knowledge as strategy. We would expect that those who remain will often be those with the skills to build the systems to support the judgment level of knowledge. Meanwhile the underwriters remain core not only as the selling and operations resource but as the analyzers, interpreters and exploiters of knowledge and contributors of experience.

The underwriters at Skandia and the operators at Shorko, however, have needed new skills. As proposed by Zuboff and discovered by Stymne (1989), those who *use* the new levels of information (or knowledge) provided by IT tend to be upskilled rather than deskilled. Computer mediated work requires a higher level of skill. In France, the operators went back to college. In Sweden, underwriters underwent "intensive internal and external training." We can note, from another case described by Nolan (1990), that as multimedia technology was used to train staff at Federal Express, the system also tested their competence. If the requisite level was met, the employees' remuneration was increased. This is illustrative of the trend to pay not for time or results or effort but for knowledge.

These tendencies then begin to suggest a move towards organizational meritocracy. De Pierrefeu at Shorko notes how workers became employees and foremen became managers. Blue collar workers became white collar workers, increasingly indistinguishable in their work and responsibility from managers. If workers whose self-respect and perhaps power was based on what they knew about a process now have to give up that knowledge to a system and thus to all, they are perhaps entitled to be treated on merit. The same principle could be "extrapolated" on Skandia. An underwriter who progressed by his private knowledge is now contributing to, and working on, systematic knowledge. We can see knowledge-based technology as not only a democratizing force, as in Shorko, but as an equalizing force where technical and knowledge-based skills entitle you to join the meritocracy and sharing knowledge entitles you to stay.

These trends at the individual level have their implications at the organizational level, for knowledge is only maximized if the organization can learn. There are several perspectives which could be drawn upon here from Argyris' research on organizational learning (Argyris and Schon, 1978) to Senge's (1990) more recent development work on enabling organizations to learn. The Shorko and Skandia cases give both weak and strong signals on what may be required in *learning organizations*.

First, we see indications of the need for collaborative organizational functioning. In Shorko, the operators had to work as a team to build the process knowledge (and the system) and to operate the new production lines environment. Furthermore, they were working with both technical specialists and management in these endeavors. In Skandia, there was a high degree of decentralization to offices and underwriters. However, the strategy depended on connecting these units and coordinating reinsurance business. The system and network forced this level of collaboration and Skandia already has resisted attempts to fragment it. We can look elsewhere for stronger signals of collaborative working where knowledge is strategy. Digital Equipment Corporation use skill-based virtual teams in product development and business projects by bringing key people across their Easynet network. Indeed, one of the images of the networked organization is the ability to cross internal and external organizational boundaries to exchange information, break down established positions and demarcation lines, locate relevant skills or experience and create synergies of shared talent. In another case I have examined, IKEA, the Swedish retailer, the decentralized, near to sources of supply, profit-center-evaluated buying managers use the data network to share knowledge about potential suppliers and product development.

Second, the skill requirements of knowledge-working noted earlier create demands for training and personal development. Dalborg at Skandia explained that "we are introducing powerful computer and communications systems in IT while making improvements on the personnel side."

Caillaud in Shorko says "you can't invest in technologies if you don't invest in people, especially in training." It is evident that the need is not just for technology-use training, but also for knowledge processing skills, such as analysis, reasoning and deduction. This may also mean "remedial" education on the accepted, scientific, knowledge level which underpins the business: risk and actuarial techniques for underwriters, polymer science for the Shorko operators. However, education is always remedial in a sense, for as potential knowledge becomes workable knowledge and perhaps becomes accepted knowledge, the implication is clear. Education in learning organizations is continuous.

Finally, a third requirement was hinted at earlier. There needs to be an ethos of knowledge as strategy. If organizational members are to share knowledge, collaborate and be willing to continuously learn, the incentive and support must be present. Indeed if we regard organizations as networks of contracts which govern exchange transactions between members having only partially overlapping goals—as described and analyzed by the transaction costs framework of economic organization (Williamson, 1975)—why should members in different locations, roles, levels and career stages subscribe to a knowledge-based strategy? The very uncertainty and complexity of knowledge domains, the information asymmetries built into organizations and the opportunism available to the informed would suggest that, in the mixed interest settings of firms, actors can selfishly withhold, distort or exploit knowledge.

One response is that information technology can help mediate this challenge, by lowering the costs of information processing required for coordination and control (Ciborra, 1987). This would include operational costs of knowledge acquisition, storage and sharing but also of management control processes required to implement knowledge-based strategies. The two cases suggest at least three other notable facets of knowledge as strategy when a transaction costs perspective is adopted.

In Shorko, the operators saw that the system was the summation of their very own collective and best knowledge and experience. However, they had a dramatic incentive to support the strategy—survival. Indeed, it also seems likely at Skandia that the bold vision which built the organizational and IT capabilities necessary for its platform of know-how was born out of the survival crisis that the international division faced in 1984. In short, we can posit the notion of the superordinate goal which can perhaps win over knowledge opportunism and "deviance." Of course, survival can be analyzed within the transaction cost framework—workers, all workers, are discounting their price in the short run either in the hope of reinstating the longer term employment contract or, for most of them, conceding in the short run to authority, in the hope of gains to come.

The second facet is that knowledge constructs combined with strategic change provide a rhetoric for managerial action and power. De Pierrefeu recalls in Shorko how "I explained that everything would change" and he and his team clearly spent considerable time in building a new ethos—personified in a physical way by making the process control center the new and bright hub of the factory. In Skandia, the new ethos was partly created or reinforced by the rhetoric of knowledge, namely the repeated references and tutorials in the annual reports and the use of the metaphor of "know-how."

Gowler and Legge (1983) have argued persuasively that rhetoric can be a powerful tool of management, both symbolically and more instrumentally. Earl too has demonstrated how the language, roles and rituals of specialist, technical endeavors and activities are one armory of management (Earl, 1983).

The third facet is more mundane. We can perhaps posit that the two cases show another potential of the experience and transaction processing level of knowledge in Table 1.1. Physical transaction data in Shorko and basic business transaction data in Skandia are less vulnerable to manipulation and withholding than the fabric of systems at the two higher levels. The data are structured, their collection is more automatable, there is less human intervention and quality control is easier. Of course the processing, interpretation and use of these data—at the judgment and science levels—bring opportunities for "games-playing," but there is an inherent visibility and robustness in experience level data upon which they may be built.

So a knowledge ethos seems necessary if knowledge-based strategies are to be pursued. The appeal of the superordinate goal and the management of rhetoric may be useful political devices to employ in this regard. IT may help by reducing the transaction costs of coordination and control required to buttress knowledge as strategy. Finally, transaction processing systems may have another source of knowledge value; they may have inbuilt properties of "objectivity" which limit the potential to subvert the knowledge ethos.

CONCLUSIONS

The Skandia and Shorko cases can be seen, respectively, as examples of IT supporting a competitive strategy and of IT creating a new strategic option. Underpinning them both, however, is investment in knowledge and the realization that knowledge can be a strategic resource. Information technology has made knowledge-based strategies much more feasible and these two cases indicate that databases and networks supported by decision-support tools are crucial enabling requirements.

It seems, however, that not all knowledge is the same. Three levels of knowledge, representing increasing degrees of certainty, structuredness and validation, can usefully be recognized: accepted knowledge or science, workable knowledge or judgment, and potential knowledge or experience. All of them rarely come free, but each level in that order seems to increase in cost—not in terms of discovery or cumulative investment over time, but more in terms of collation and exploitation by IT.

Expert systems and databases which codify or provide accepted knowledge are likely to be derivatives of a public good and useful but not often of firm-specific value. Decision-support tools which craft and make available workable knowledge are likely to be more private and thus competitively valuable. Transaction processing systems which capture potential knowledge and arrange it in databases are likely to be firm-specific and continuously providing a source of strategic value.

This classification could be alternatively expressed as data, information and knowledge. However, the earlier classification helps point out that "knowledge" exists at each level and that in a strategic—competitive—sense the direction of value is counter-intuitive. Data processing or transaction processing systems may contain potentially high knowledge value—in excess of either MIS and decision-support systems or expert systems and knowledge-based systems. Also transaction processing level systems may be the most expensive. Fortunately the cost bind implied by this analysis is often mitigated by the fact that data processing yields joint benefits of an automation kind and information processing joint benefits of a decision-making kind. Whilst therefore Zuboff's concept of "informating" can be seen as an alternative and more strategic option to "automating," we can note that often the IT infrastructure is common. The trick therefore is to recognize and pursue the knowledge opportunities in the firm's (current and planned) information technology and information systems infrastructure.

This leads on to the capabilities required of the firm if knowledge is to be a basis of strategy. They are both technological and organizational. Knowledge systems comprising capture devices, databases and decision tools are required. These are commonly built and used through communications networks local, corporate and external. The users become knowledge workers. These become core personnel through their knowledge and IT-mediated work. Their skills have to be enhanced and more meritocratic structures rebuilt. Accordingly at the organizational level, collaboration in knowledge development and use is essential, continuous training in knowledge and knowledge skills has to be provided and a knowledge-based ethos is required to lead, reward and support exploitation of knowledge as strategy.

The vision for this is particularly apparent in Skandia. The enactment is particularly apparent in Shorko. If Bell (1979) and others are right, these firms are not oddities; they are interesting prototypes of the firm in the post industrial or information or knowledge economy.

REFERENCES

Applegate, L.M. (1988) Phillips 66 Company. Executive Information System. Harvard Business School Case Study 9-189-006. Publishing Division, Harvard Business School.

Argyris, C. and Schon, D.A. (1978) *Organisational Learning: A Theory of Action Perspective*. Reading MA: Addison-Wesley.

Bell, D. (1979) Thinking ahead: communication technology—for better or for worse. *Harvard Business Review,* May–June 20–42.

Ciborra, C.U. (1987) Research agenda for a transaction costs approach to information systems. In Boland, R.J. Jnr and Hirscheim, R.A. (Eds.) *Critical Issues in Information Systems Research*. Chichester: J. Wiley & Sons.

Earl, M.J. (1983) Accounting and management. In Earl, M.J. (Ed.) *Perspectives on Management*. Oxford University Press.

Glaser, B.G. and Strauss, A.L. (1967) *The Discovery of Grounded Theory: Strategies For Qualitative Research*. Chicago, Ill: Aldine Publishing.

Gowler, D. and Legge, K. (1983) The meaning of management and the management of meaning: A view from social anthropology. In Earl, M.J. (Ed.) *Perspectives on Management*. Oxford University Press.

Hayes-Roth, F., Waterman, D.A. and Lenat, D.B. (1983) An overview of expert systems. In Hayes-Roth, F., Waterman, D.A. and Lenat, D.B. *Building Expert Systems*. Reading, Mass: Addison-Wesley.

Knight, F.H. (1921) *Risk, Uncertainty and Profit.* Chicago, Ill: University of Chicago Press.

Kuhn, T. (1970) *The Structure of Scientific Revolutions.* University of Chicago Press.

Luconi, F.L., Malone, T.W. and Scott-Morton, M.S. (1986) Expert systems and expert support systems: the next challenge for management. *Sloan Management Review,* Summer, 27, 4: 3–14.

Mintzberg, H. and Waters, J.A. (1985) Of strategies, deliberate and emergent. *Strategic Management Journal,* 6: 257–272.

Nolan, R.L. (1990) The knowledge work mandate. *Stage by Stage,* 10, 2, Nolan Norton & Co, pp. 1–12.

OECD. (1981) *Information Activities, Electronics, and Telecommunications. Technologies: Impact on Employment, Growth and Trade.* Paris: Organization for Economic Co-operation and Development.

Porat, M.U. (1977) *The Information Economy: Definition and Measurement.* Washington, DC: Office of Telecommunications, U.S. Department of Commerce.

Prahalad, C.K. and Hamel, G. (1990) The core competences of the corporation. *Harvard Business Review,* May–June, 79–91.

Senge, P.M. (1990) *The Fifth Discipline.* New York: Doubleday.

Shannon, C.E. and Weaver, W. (1962) *The Mathematical Theory of Communication.* University of Illinois.

Silberston, A. (1967) The patent system. *Lloyds Bank Review,* No. 84: 32–44.

Stymne, B. (1989) Information Technology and Competence Formation in the Swedish Service Sector. IMIT, Stockholm School of Economics.

Williamson, O.E. (1975) *Markets and Hierarchies: Analysis and Antitrust Implications.* New York: Free Press.

Zuboff, S. (1988) *In the Age of the Smart Machine.* New York: Basic Books.

2

Knowledge of the Firm. Combinative Capabilities, and the Replication of Technology

Bruce Kogut and Udo Zander

A fundamental puzzle, as first stated by Michael Polanyi (1966), is that individuals appear to know more than they can explain. That knowledge can be tacit has broad implications for understanding the difficulty of imitating and diffusing individual skills, a problem lying at the heart of artificial intelligence to the competitive analysis of firms. Though the idea of tacit knowledge has been widely evoked but rarely defined—as if the lack of definition is itself evidence of the concept, it represents a dramatically different vantage point by which to analyze the capabilities and boundaries of firms.

This article seeks to lay out an organizational foundation to a theory of the firm. To rephrase Polanyi's puzzle of tacit knowledge, organizations know more than what their contracts can say. The analysis of what organizations are should be grounded in the understanding of what they know how to do.

It is curious that the considerable attention given to how organizations learn has obscured the implication that organizations "know" something. In fact, the knowledge of the firm, as opposed to learning, is relatively observable; operating rules, manufacturing technologies, and customer data banks are tangible representations of this knowledge. But the danger of this simple characterization is that everything that describes a firm becomes an aspect of its knowledge. While this is definitionally true, the theoretical challenge is to understand the knowledge base of a firm as leading to a set of capabilities that enhance the chances for growth and survival.

In our view, the central competitive dimension of what firms know how to do is to create and transfer knowledge efficiently within an organizational context. The following article seeks to describe these capabilities by analyzing the contention put forth by Winter (1987) that technology transfer and imitation are blades of the same scissor. The commonality is that technology is often costly to replicate, whether the replication is desired by the firm or occurs by imitation and unwanted diffusion. Though the terminology may differ, the underlying phenomena impacting the costs of technology transfer and imitation share similarities, regardless whether the replication occurs within the firm, by contract, or among competitors.

That similar factors may determine both the costs of imitation and technology transfer presents an interesting dilemma to the firm. In the efforts to speed the replication of current and new knowledge, there arises a fundamental paradox that the codification and simplification of knowledge also induces the likelihood of imitation. Technology transfer is a desired strategy in the replication and growth of the firm (whether in size or profits); imitation is a principal constraint.

Our view differs radically from that of the firm as a bundle of contracts that serves to allocate efficiently property rights. In contrast to the contract approach to understanding organizations, the assumption of the selfish motives of individuals resulting in shirking or dishonesty is not a necessary premise in our argument. Rather, we suggest that organizations are social communities in which individual and social expertise is transformed into economically useful products and services by the application of a set of higher-order organizing principles. Firms exist because they provide a social community of voluntaristic action structured by organizing principles that are not reduceable to individuals.

We categorize organizational knowledge into information and know-how based, a distinction that corresponds closely to that used in artificial intelligence of declarative and procedural knowledge. To move beyond a simple classification, these types of knowledge are argued to carry competitive implications through their facility to be easily replicated within an organization but difficult to imitate by other firms. Following the suggestions of Rogers (1983) and Winter (1987), the characteristics of both types of knowledge are analyzed along the dimensions of codifiability and complexity. By examining first personal expertise and then social knowledge, the capabilities of the firm in general are argued to rest in the organizing principles by which relationships among individuals, within and between groups, and among organizations are structured.

But organizations serve as more than mechanisms by which social knowledge is transferred, but also by which new knowledge, or learning, is created. The theoretical problem is that if the knowledge of the firm is argued to be competitively consequential, learning cannot be characterized as independent of the current capabilities. To explore this dynamic aspect, we introduce the concept of a **combinative capability** to synthesize and apply current and acquired knowledge. This concept is, then, explored in the context of a competitive environment. By this discussion, we ground such concepts as localized learning to path dependence by developing a micro-behavioral foundation of social knowledge, while also stipulating the effects of the degree of environmental selection on the evolution of this knowledge.

To ground the abstraction of the argument in an example, we reexamine the empirical findings on the make-buy decision of firms. The importance of the ability to generate new knowledge suggests a different view on the "boundaries" of the firm, that is, what a firm makes and what it buys. Firms invest in those assets that correspond to a combination of current capabilities and expectations regarding future opportunities. Or, in other words, the knowledge of a firm can be considered as owning a portfolio of options, or platforms, on future developments.[1]

Figure 2.1 provides a roadmap to our argument. We begin by analyzing the knowledge of the firm by distinguishing between information regarding prices and the know-how, say, to divisionalize. This static portrait is the basis by which we explore how knowledge may be recombined through internal and external learning. An important limitation to the capability of developing new skills is the opportunity (or potential) in the organizing principles and technologies for further exploitation. Eventually, there are decreasing returns to a given technology or method of organizing, and there, consequently, results in an incentive to build new, but related skills. These investments in new ways of doing things, we suggest, serve as platforms on future and uncertain market opportunities.

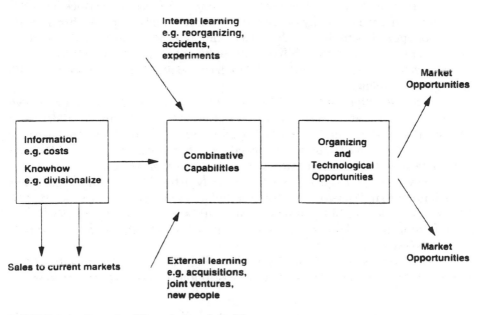

FIGURE 2.1 Growth of Knowledge of the Firm

---

[1]This notion of a platform is investigated in Kogut (1991) and Kogut and Kim (1991).

It is important to underline the presumption that the knowledge of the firm must be understood as socially constructed, or, more simply stated, as resting in the organizing of human resources. The issue of the organizing principles underlying the creation, replication, and imitation of technology opens a window on understanding the capabilities of the firm as a set of "inert" resources that are difficult to imitate and redeploy.[2] It is the persistence in the organizing of social relationships in which knowledge is embedded that is the focus of inquiry developed in this article.

Information and Know-How

There have been many suggestions as to how the knowledge of the firm might be categorized. Nelson (1982), for example, separates techno from logy, the former belonging to a firm, the latter to the public arena. A more common distinction is between research and development, or that between process and product.

For our purposes, we distinguish between two categories of knowledge as information and know-how.[3] By information, we mean knowledge which can be transmitted without loss of integrity once the syntactical rules required for deciphering it are known. Information includes facts, axiomatic propositions, and symbols. Nelson's idea of logy is, in fact, a recognition that within scientific communities, there exists a social agreement regarding the factual evidence by which to communicate the reliability of scientific findings. Similarly, public firms are required to report data to shareholders in a common format so as to facilitate analysis and appraisal. For the objective of public dissemination, information is standardized and released in order to be understood at minimal cost to those with the requisite training.

Of course, information is often proprietary. Firms maintain, as a rule, two sets of accounting data, one for external use, the other to aid managerial decisions and evaluation. Data can also be of competitive value. An obvious example is the value of information to traders of financial securities, but a more prosaic example is the data acquired by grocery stores on consumer expenditures.

Know-how is a frequently used, but rarely defined term. Von Hippel offers the definition that "know-how is the accumulated practical skill or expertise that allows one to do something smoothly and efficiently" (von Hippel 1988). The pivotal word in this definition is "accumulated," which implies that know-how must be learned and acquired.

Knowledge as information implies knowing what something means. Know-how is, as the compound words state, a description of knowing how to do some-

---

[2]See Lippman and Rumelt (1982), Wernerfelt (1984), Rumelt (1984), Barney (1986), and Kogut (1987), as well as the publications that appeared while this article was under review by Dierickx and Cool (1989) and Prahalad and Hamel (1990).
[3]Steve Kimbrough has pointed out in conversation that the terms are similar to Bertrand Russell's distinction between know-that and know-how.

thing. In economics, this distinction is, implicitly, preserved in the often made distinction between exchange and production economies, where the former consists of only traders responding to prices, and the latter to how inputs are transformed into outputs. To use a current example, the problems of the adoption economy in Eastern Europe consist not only of just finding the right prices, but also learning how to organize a market and a firm efficiently.

Though this distinction between information and know-how appears to be a fundamental element in the analysis of organizational knowledge, most efforts in this direction have tended, following March and Simon (1958) and Cyert and March (1963), to investigate the notion of routines in the context of organizational learning. Yet, this vantage point for the investigation of firm knowledge is ill-chosen. Learning has little significance in the absence of a theory of organizational knowledge.

A routine is in itself an insightful but incomplete characterization of knowledge. Because of the broad coverage of the term routine, an appeal is often made to the analogy of a blueprint, an analogy favored by a number of authors.[4] But a blueprint favors much more a description of information than know-how. Knowing how to do something is much like a recipe; there is no substantive content in any of the steps, except for their capacity to produce a desired end.[5] The information is contained in the original listing of ingredients, but the know-how is only imperfectly represented in the description.

It is revealing that this distinction between information and know-how as blueprints and recipes is similar to that made between declarative and procedural knowledge used in computer science. Declarative knowledge consists of a statement that provides a state description, such as the information that inventory is equal to a 100 books. Procedural knowledge consists of statements that describe a process, such as a method by which inventory is minimized. This distinction is robust to other phenomena than software, even to a furniture set where the inventory of parts is first described and then the recipe of assembly laid out.

Know-how, like procedural knowledge, is a description of what defines current practice inside a firm. These practices may consist of how to organize factories, set transfer prices, or establish divisional and functional lines of authority and accountability. The knowledge displayed in an organizational chart, as in any blueprint, is limited to providing information on personnel and formal authority. The know-how is the understanding of how to organize a firm along these formal (and informal) lines. It is in the regularity of the structuring of work and of the interactions of employees conforming to explicit or implicit recipes that one finds the content of the firm's know-how.

---

[4]See Nelson and Winter (1982); Hannan and Freeman (1977); March and Simon (1958).
[5]In light of the wide appeal genetics has for organizational analogies, it is of interest to refer to Dawkin's (1987) discussion of genes as recipes (and the phenotype as a blueprint). See also Simon (1962).

The Inertness of Knowledge

Firms differ in their information and know-how and these differences, when they are economically interesting, have persisting effects on relative performance. Thus, a central characteristic to be explained is the persisting difference in capabilities, that is, the difficulty in their transfer and imitation. The persistence of differentials in firm performance lies in the joint problem of the difficulty of transferring and imitating knowledge.

There is a need, therefore, to go beyond the classification of information and know-how and consider why knowledge is not easily transmitted and replicated. The transferability and imitability of a firm's knowledge, whether it is in the form of information or know-how, are influenced by several characteristics (Kogut and Zander 1990). Rogers (1983) and Winter (1987) have proposed that knowledge can be analyzed along a number of dimensions.

Consider the two dimensions of codifiability and complexity. Codifiability refers to the ability of the firm to structure knowledge into a set of identifiable rules and relationships that can be easily communicated. Coded knowledge is alienable from the individual who wrote the code. Not all kinds of knowledge are amenable to codification. Drafting a recipe for the manufacturing of a musical instrument is unlikely to capture the requisite skills of a craftsperson.

Nor is this limitation only applicable to know-how. It is not always possible to identify the relevant information which operates as the data to an actor or set of actions. There may be no 'theory' (in the sense used above) by which to identify the relevant information, such as drawing the blueprint. This argument bears similarities to the artificial intelligence debate on the obstacles to formalizing noncodified "background knowledge" to scientific theories (Dreyfus and Dreyfus 1988). Codifiability is a question of the degree that there exists an implied theory by which to identify and symbolically represent knowledge. A theory may be as lacking for information as for know-how.[6]

Though codifiability is a central characteristic, it does not capture other aspects of knowledge. Knowledge can vary in complexity. There are many ways to define complexity. From a computer science perspective, it can be defined as the number of operations (or CPU time) required to solve a task. Indeed, Simon's notion of nearly decomposable systems is closely related. An ordered system reduces the cost and necessity of complex communication patterns. Drawing upon information theory, Pringle (1951) draws the distinction between order and complexity, defining the latter as the number of parameters to define a system. Within any given ordering (or what we call a code), complexity can be accommodated, but at a cost.

These dimensions are not independent. Codifiability and complexity are related, though not identical. To return to Pringle's definition, it is obvious that the

---

[6]Contrary to Dreyfus' and Dreyfus' doubts, the organization behaviorists, Argyris and Schoen (1978, p. 11), believe it possible to derive the "theory-in-use" from "directly observable data of behavior ... to ground ... construction of the models of action theories which guide interpersonal behavior."

number of parameters required to define, say, a production system is dependent upon the choice of mathematical approaches or programming languages. For a particular code, the costs of transferring a technology will vary with its complexity. A change of code changes the degree of complexity.

Transformation of Personal to Social Knowledge

The final element in our characterization of the static properties of organizational knowledge is the distinction between the knowledge of an individual and that of the organization. Any discussion of firm knowledge confronts, ultimately, the problem of unit of analysis. We leave to the side the important task of specifying a more explicit integration of individual and organizational knowledge (such as via a shared culture, mechanisms of socialization, or an assumption of affiliative needs), but turn rather to laying out a description of the problem by distinguishing between personal, group, organizational, and network knowledge. The following discussion is summarized in Figure 2.2.[7]

Nelson and Winter (1982) have provided an important contribution by separating skills from routines. Individuals can be skilled in certain activities, such as driving a car or playing tennis. These skills may indeed be difficult to pass on. Variations in human intelligence alone may render difficult the transfer of technology, especially if intelligence is decomposed into aptitudes for solving differentiated tasks.

	Individual	Group	Organization	Network
Information	·facts	·who knows what	·profits ·accounting data ·formal & informal structure	·prices ·whom to contact ·who has what
Know-how	·skill of how to communicate ·problem solving	·recipes of organizing such as Taylorist methods or craft production	·higher-order organizing principles of how to coordinate groups and transfer knowledge	·how to cooperate ·how to sell and buy

FIGURE 2.2

[7]As a way of summarizing our argument, this figure was suggested to us by Gunnar Hedlund. See also Hedlund and Nonaka (1991).

It is, in fact, the problem of communicating personal skills that underlies Polanyi's (1966) well-known idea of tacit knowledge, an idea similar to the dimensions of noncodifiable and complex knowledge. As noted earlier, to Polanyi, the central puzzle is the following: why do individuals know more than they can express. An interpretation of his argument is that tacit knowledge consists of search rules, or heuristics, that identify the problem and the elements consisting of the solution (Polanyi 1966, pp. 23–24). The act of solving a problem rests on a sense of how the phenomena function; the formal expression of the solution is unlikely to capture fully this procedural knowledge, or even the data and information (or clues, as Polanyi describes it) leading to the solution. Thus, even in the arena of problem identification and solving, the know-how of heuristic search precedes the formal knowledge of the solution.[8]

The teaching of know-how and information requires frequently interaction within small groups, often through the development of a unique language or code. Part of the knowledge of a group is simply knowing the information who knows what. But it also consists of how activities are to be organized, e.g., by Taylorist principles.

It is the sharing of a common stock of knowledge, both technical and organizational, that facilitates the transfer of knowledge within groups. This view is widely held across a disparate literature. Arrow (1974) views one of the advantages of the organization as its ability to economize in communication through a common code. Piore (1985, p. xxv) likens the theory of internal labor markets to a "conception of production knowledge as being like a language" common to a particular group of workers. By shared coding schemes, personal knowledge can be transmitted effectively within close-knit groups (Katz and Kahn 1966). Personal knowledge can be transmitted because a set of values are learned, permitting a shared language by which to communicate (Berger and Luckman 1967). It is this language which provides a normative sanction of how activities are to be organized or what information is to be collected and evaluated.

But whereas the accumulation of small group interactions facilitate the creation of shared coding schemes within functions, a fundamental problem arises in the shifting of technologies from research groups to manufacturing and marketing (Dougherty forthcoming). At this point, the identification with a professional orientation conflicts with the need to integrate within the organization. The problems of different professional languages are attenuated when technology transfer is horizontal, that is, within the same function, as when a second plant identical to the first is built. To facilitate this communication, certain individuals play pivotal roles as boundary spanners, both within the firm as well as between firms (Allen and Cohen 1969; Tushman 1977).

The vertical transfer of technology, as when a product is moved from development to production, poses additional problems insofar that the shared codes of

---

[8]In the philosophy of the science, this distinction corresponds to the difference between the logic of discovery and the logic of demonstration. See also Dreyfus and Dreyfus (1988) for a discussion in relation to artificial intelligence.

functional groups differ. Leonard-Barton's (1988) finding that technology transfer success is dependent upon the mutual adaptation between the two parties highlights the critical transformation of personal and group knowledge in the process of codification. To facilitate this transfer, a set of higher-order organizing principles act as mechanisms by which to codify technologies into a language accessible to a wider circle of individuals. These principles establish how the innovation is transferred to other groups, the responsibility of engineers to respond to complaints, and the allocation of incentives to establish authority over decisions. These organizing principles, which we call higher-order as they facilitate the integration of the entire organization, are also supported by data regarding profitability, costs, or task responsibility (as represented in an organizational chart).

In this sense, a firm's functional knowledge is nested within a higher-order set of recipes that act as organizing principles. Complex organizations exist as communities within which varieties of functional expertise can be communicated and combined by a common language and organizing principles. To the extent that close integration within a supplier or buyer network is required, long-term relationships embed future transactions within a learned and shared code. In fact, the trading of know-how among firms often requires the establishment of long-term relationships (von Hippel 1988). In this wider perspective, a firm's knowledge consists also of the information of other actors in the network, as well as the procedures by which resources are gained and transactions and cooperation are conducted.

The Paradox of Replication

There is an important implication for the growth of the firm in the transformation of technical knowledge into a code understood by a wide set of users. An individual is a resource severely restrained by physical and mental limitations. Unless able to train large numbers of individuals or to transform skills into organizing principles, the craft shop is forever simply a shop. The speed of replication of knowledge determines the rate of growth: control over its diffusion deters competitive erosion of the market position.

For a firm to grow, it must develop organizing principles and a widely-held and shared code by which to orchestrate large numbers of people and, potentially, varied functions. Whereas the advantages of reducing the costs of intra- or inter-firm technology transfer encourage codification of knowledge, such codification runs the risk of encouraging imitation. It is in this paradox that the firm faces a fundamental dilemma.

The problems of the growth of the firm are directly related to the issues of technology transfer and imitation. Once organizing principles replace individual skills of the entrepreneur, they serve as organizational instructions for future growth. Technology transfer is, from this perspective, the replication of existing activities. The goal of the firm is to reduce the costs of this transfer while preserving the quality and value of the technology.

Because personal and small group knowledge is expensive to re-create, firms may desire to codify and simplify such knowledge as to be accessible to the wider organization, as well as to external users. It is an interesting point, with far-reaching implications, that such a translation rarely occurs without a transformation in the nature of the knowledge. Computer software packages not only reduce the complexity of the knowledge required to use a computer's hardware: knowing how to use software is, in fact, substantively different from knowing how the computer works.

The reason why software has been successful is that it is codified so as to demand a lower fixed cost on the part of the general user. The user is required to understand the function of the program without knowledge of the substantive technology. (A function is an attribute to the product; substantive technology is the knowledge by which the product is created or produced.) The cost of this transformation is that the user's choices are restricted to the expressed functions. The specificity of a software language cannot expand the capabilities of the hardware: rather, it can only reduce the costs of its accessibility. It is, in fact, the possibility to separate the expertise to generate the technology and the ability to use it that permits the nesting of a firm's knowledge, as described above. But it is also this separation, as discussed below, that facilitates the ease of imitation. Being taught the functional skills of how to do something is different than being taught how to create it. We turn to these static and dynamic considerations below.

Combinative Capabilities

The issue of being able to use and being able to create software reflects a distinction commonly made in the literature on technology transfer regarding know-how and know-why.[9] It is, in fact, this distinction between exploiting and developing capabilities that lies at the foundation of Rosenberg's (1976) observation that "reliance on borrowed technology (by developing countries) perpetuates a posture of dependency and passivity." For example, activities involved in a manufacturing production process can be codified and imitated without requiring the knowledge of how the machinery functions. A Japanese factory shop might, conceivably, be organized by rules for inventory management and these rules might be transferred to American operations. Yet, the knowledge that leads to the development of such practices is unlikely to be transferred as easily. Being taught the functional skills of how to do something is different than being taught how to create it.

---

[9]In the interest of avoiding a proliferation of terms, we would add the caveat that since formal science is characterized by recipes through which causal relationships are identified, this distinction may be simply a restatement of the question, identified in footnote 8, whether the methods of scientific discovery can be codified.

To return to the development of software as a problem in codifying knowledge, Papert (1979, p. 77) notes the paradox that some languages are simple to learn but become complex in application. He writes:

> *But what do we mean by 'simpler' and what do we mean by 'learn the language'? Indeed, the (user) . . . would learn its vocabulary very quickly, but they would spend the rest of their time struggling with its constraints. They would have to search for devious ways to encode even mildly complex ideas into this small vocabulary. Thus it is well-known that the programming language BASIC . . . is quickly learned, but its programs quickly become labyrinths.*

Papert's objection raises two important points. Some codes may be qualitatively better than others. They might facilitate certain technologies or practices better: the language of chemical pharmaceuticals may be inadequate for the development and transfer of biotechnologies. Even for the same technology, some firms may have evolved codes that differ in their efficacy.

The observation that some languages are more "easily learned" suggests, superficially, a contradiction in the argument. Basic is "simpler" but becomes quickly complex. But in what sense is it simpler other than through its familiarity to what the user already knows and through its design to address specific applications familiar to the user? Then why does it become a "labyrinth?" The implicit suggestion is that Basic does not provide an efficient capability to address a change in the required application.

Let us migrate the argument from the individual to the organizational level by sorting out the two issues of familiarity to the user and, as discussed later, of the capability to create new applications to address changes in the environment, such as changes in market demand. Creating new knowledge does not occur in abstraction from current abilities. Rather, new learning, such as innovations, are products of a firm's **combinative capabilities** to generate new applications from existing knowledge. By combinative capabilities, we mean the intersection of the capability of the firm to exploit its knowledge and the unexplored potential of the technology, or what Scherer (1965) originally called the degree of "technological opportunity."

In the technological literature, the determinants of "opportunity" are often regarded as physical in character: the speed of electrons is inferior to that of light. But since physical laws are eternally given, the critical question would then seem to be the social laws of their discovery and innovative application. Schumpeter (1968) argued that, in general, innovations are new combinations of existing knowledge and incremental learning.[10] He writes:

---

[10]The view that knowledge can be created only as combinations of what is already known has a long lineage, from Plato's Meno to Polanyi's (1966) idea of tacitness.

To produce other things, or the same things by a different method, means to
combine these materials and forces differently . . . Development in our sense
is then defined by the carrying out of new combinations (Schumpeter 1934,
pp. 65–66).

As widely recognized, firms learn in areas closely related to their existing
practice. As the firm moves away from its knowledge base, its probability of success converges to that for a start-up operation (as implicit in Lippman and Rumelt
1982). The abstract explanation for this claim is that the growth of knowledge is
experiential, that is, it is the product of localized search as guided by a stable set
of heuristics, or, in our terminology, know-how and information (Cyert and
March 1963, Nelson and Winter 1982). It is this local search that generates a condition commonly called "path dependence," that is, the tendency for what a firm
is currently doing to persist in the future.

It should be clear that individual limitations in learning new skills are not a
sufficient explanation. For even if mature individuals do not relearn—as psychological evidence suggests, an organization may reconstitute its knowledge by recruiting new workers with the requisite skills. The problem of the "inertness" of
what an organization knows is not reduceable to individuals, except for the de-
generate case of restrictions on the recruitment and retirement of human resources.

What makes the innovative search localized is that "proximate" technologies do not require a change in an organization's recipes of organizing research. If
current knowledge is inadequate, it may well be that a firm does not know what
changes are required in the existing principles and structure of relationships. Even
if identified, they may not be feasible, because the relational structure in the organization would be disturbed. Knowledge advances by recombinations because a
firm's capabilities cannot be separated from how it is currently organized.

Selection Environment

Up to now, we have been concerned with explaining the role of organizing
principles to facilitate the transfer of technology and ideas within the organization of the firm. The distinction between the ability to produce a product and the
capability to generate it is fundamental to broadening our perspective to the competitive conditions of imitation. The ability to build on current technology is instrumental in the deterrence of the imitation of a firm's knowledge by competitors.

Imitation differs from technology transfer in a fundamental sense. Whereas
technology transfer is concerned with adapting the technology to the least capable
user, the threat of imitation is posed by the most capable competitors. In abstraction from a particular technology, it is, *a priori,* impossible to state in general
what aspects of the transformation of ideas into marketable products will deter
imitation. No matter which factor, however, is the most important, imitation is
impeded by the possession of at least one bottleneck capability, as long as this ca-

pability is rewarded in the market.[11] This bottleneck can possibly arise through the benefits of reputation among consumers, patent protection, or the exercise of monopoly restrictions.

When these entry-deterring benefits are absent, competition switches from traditional elements of market structure to the comparative capabilities of firms to replicate and generate new knowledge. The nature of this competition is frequently characterized as a race between an innovator and the ability of the imitating firm either to reverse engineer and to decode the substantive technology. The growth of the firm is determined by a combination of the speed of technology transfer and of the imitative efforts of rivals.

Reverse engineering is often not a required response by competitors to new innovations. Incumbent competitors may simply respond to new product innovations by relying on other capabilities, such as brand labeling or distribution channels. Of more interest to our concerns, some competitors can imitate the function of the technology without necessitating reverse engineering of the substantive code. (As an example, many distinctive kinds of software can provide a spreadsheet function: the function is imitated, but not the underlying technology.) Many new products are only re-designs (i.e., recombinations) of existing components (Henderson and Clark 1990). In this kind of competition, the need to decipher the elements of the innovator's knowledge that generated the product can be simply bypassed.

In this on-going competition, there is a short-term consideration, i.e., at what speed and cost can a firm replicate its current technology and imitate others. In innovative industries, competition is frequently a question of the speed and efficiency by which diverse groups within a corporation cooperate, a problem exacerbated when multifunctional coordination is required in order to increase transfer times to the market (Dougherty forthcoming). Over time and across multiple products, small differences in efficiencies can generate significant variations in profitability and (as well established in evolutionary biology) survival.

Short-term competitive pressures can, however, draw from the investments required to build new capabilities. The direct effect of selection is on the acceptance and rejection of new products, but indirectly it is operating to reward or to penalize the economic merits of the underlying stock of knowledge.[12] Knowledge, no matter how resistant to imitation, is of little value if it results in products that do not correspond competitively to consumers' wants. Selection on product types acts to develop and retard the capabilities of firms.

The ability to indulge in a forward-looking development of knowledge is strongly contingent on the selection environment. Long-term survival involves a complex tradeoff between current profitability and investing in future capability. Future capabilities are of little value if the firm does not survive. In this sense, we

---

[11]This point is captured in empirical work using the survey results, whereby appropriability is defined as the item that indicates the maximum deterrence to imitation (Levin et al. 1987).

[12]This point, of course, lies at the heart of the genes versus phenotype controversy in biology. See, for example, Dawkins (1976).

have returned to Papert's concerns. Basic may be a poor language by which to address new applications or changes in the market. But for the student facing a deadline, programming in Basic may have clear survival value.

An important question, then, is the critical balancing between short-term survival and the long-term development of capabilities. A too strong reliance on current profitability can deflect from the wider development of capabilities (Stiglitz 1987). By their ability to buffer internal ventures from an immediate market test, organizations have the possibility to create new capabilities by a process of trial-and-error learning.

Thus luxury is often too exorbitant for companies or, for that matter, developing countries facing strong survival pressures. Yet, because investments in new ways of doing things are expensive, it is possible for a firm to continue to develop capabilities in ways of doing things which it knows, in the long run, are inferior (Arthur 1989). A too rigid competitive environment, especially in the early years of a firm's development, may impede subsequent performance by retarding a firm's ability to invest in new learning.

The Make Decision and Firm Capabilities

The merits of the above argument can be better evaluated by considering an example. An interesting application is the make-buy question, that is, whether a firm should source a component from the outside or make it internally. The examination of this problem throws into relief how an approach based on the knowledge of the firm differs from a contracting perspective.

It has become standard to argue that markets for the exchange of technology fail because of an appeal to a poker-hand metaphor: once the cards are revealed, imitation rapidly ensues since draws from the deck are costless. Because of the work of Teece (1977). Mansfield, Schwartz, and Wagner (1981), and Levin et al. (1987), it is widely recognized this argument is a shibboleth. Yet, the consequences of this recognition are scarcely to be seen in the literature on technology transfer.

In fact, the costliness of its transfer has often been reconstrued as market failure (Teece 1980). Because a buyer cannot ascertain its value by observation, technology cannot be priced out. Thus, markets fail for the selling of technology since it is costly to transact.

The problem of this market failure argument is not only that markets for technology do exist, but also that it is over-determined. The public good argument turns on the opportunism of the buyer: the costs of transfer do not necessitate a similar bahavioral assumption, though one can always throw it in for good measure. Opportunism is not a necessary condition to explain why technology is transferred within a firm instead of the market. Rather, the issue becomes why and when are the costs of transfer of technology lower inside the firm than alternatives in the market, independent of contractual hazards. The relevant market comparison, in this sense, are the efficiencies of other firms.

This issue extends to the more commonly studied case of contractual hazards affecting the make or buy decision, that is, whether to source from outside the firm. In the seminal empirical study of Walker and Weber (1984), evidence was found for the claim that the transaction costs of relying on outside suppliers lead to decisions to source internally. Yet, the most important variable is the indicator of differential firm capabilities, that is, whether the firm or the supplier has the lower production costs. Transaction cost considerations matter but are subsidiary to whether a firm or other suppliers are more efficient in the production of the component.

In the Monteverde and Teece (1982) paper that also supported the transaction cost argument, the most significant variable is the dummy for the firm. In other words, despite controls, the heterogeneous and unobserved firm effects were the dominant influence on the make-buy decision. Yet, both firms faced the same environment and transactional hazards.

While the boundaries of the firm are, unquestionably, influenced by transactional dilemmas, the question of capabilities points the analysis to understanding why organizations differ in their performance. The decision which capabilities to maintain and develop is influenced by the current knowledge of the firm and the expectation of the economic gain from exploring the opportunities in new technologies and organizing principles as platforms into future market developments. (See Figure 2.1.) We propose that firms maintain those capabilities in-house that are expected to lead to recombinations of economic value.

The evaluation of this economic gain rests critically upon a firm's ability to create and transfer technology more quickly than it is imitated in the market. Many investment decisions inside a firm do not include a make-buy calculation, for the presumption is that the new assets are extensions, or combinations, of the existing knowledge base.[13] Nor should it be surprising that there is a sense of ownership over the right to make and control the investment, for the physical assets are embedded within the replication of the existing social relationships and political structure of the firm. Because these relationships exist, an ongoing firm should have a greater capability to expand in current businesses than new entrants.

Path dependence is a rephrasing of the simple statement that firms persist in making what they have made in the past: for existing firms, knowledge advances on the basis of its current information and ways of doing things. To return to the Monteverde and Teece study, the finding that firms tended to produce internally those parts with high engineering content is a confirmation that auto companies specialize in engineering design and production. They make those parts that reflect their knowledge. (In fact, we should expect that they imitate those technologies which correspond closely to their knowledge.)

There are, of course, investment opportunities which are uncertain in terms of the applicability of a firm's current knowledge. Internal development, and imitation, are deterred because the organizing principles and information cannot be

---

[13]We would like to thank Gordon Walker for emphasizing that many new investment decisions entail only whether to and not to make internally; there is often no external evaluation.

easily identified. Thus, investments in new knowledge often have a characteristic of trial-and error learning, much like buying options on future opportunities.

Joint ventures frequently serve as options on new markets distantly related to current knowledge by providing a vehicle by which firms transfer and combine their organizationally-embedded learning. A common purpose of joint ventures is to experiment with new ways by which relationships are structured. That they frequently end by acquisition is a statement of their value as an ongoing entity of enduring social relationships which serve as platforms into new markets (Kogut 1991).

The decision to make or buy is, thus, dependent upon three elements: how good a firm is currently at doing something, how good it is at **learning** specific capabilities, and the value of these capabilities as **platforms** into new markets. To formalize the implications of these elements in terms of propositions, we would expect the following to hold:

1. Firms make those components that require a production knowledge similar to their current organizing principles and information.
2. The purchasing of technologies is carried out by the market when suppliers have superior knowledge which is complex and difficult to codify; by licensing when the transferred knowledge is close to current practice.
3. Firms develop internally projects that build related capabilities leading to platforms into new markets or rely on joint ventures (or acquisitions) when the capabilities are distantly related.
4. Immediate survival pressures encourage firms towards a policy of buying.

Similar propositions could be made in reference to other applications, such as acquisitions, the composition of a technology portfolio, and the sequence by which a firm invests in a foreign market.

CONCLUSIONS

The study of the knowledge of a firm raises issues, such as relatedness, technical core, or corporate culture, that are familiar to organizational theorists, but that have been hard to pin down. To a large extent, the theory of firm knowledge, as we have sketched it above, neglects the problem of individual motivation by focusing on organizing principles as the primary unit of analysis for understanding the variation in firm performance and growth. Because these principles are expressions of how a firm organizes its activities, they represent the procedures by which social relations are recreated and coordinated in an organizational context.

In contrast to a perspective based on the failure to align incentives in a market as an explanation for the firm, we began with the view that firms are a repository of capabilities, as determined by the social knowledge embedded in enduring individual relationships structured by organizing principles. Switching to new capabilities is difficult, as neither the knowledge embedded in the current relationships and principles is well understood, nor the social fabric required to support the new learning known. It is the stability of these relationships that generates the characteristics of inertia in a firm's capabilities.

Without question, there are issues, such as the creation of compatible incentives to induce behavior from individuals in accordance with the welfare of the organization, that can be fruitfully examined from a contracting perspective. But the transaction as the unit of analysis is an insufficient vehicle by which to examine organizational capabilities, because these capabilities are a composite of individual and social knowledge. After nearly two decades of research in organizational and market failure, it is time to investigate what organizations do.

ACKNOWLEDGEMENTS

We would like to thank Ned Bowman, Farok Contractor, Deborah Dougherty, Lars Hakanson, Gunnar Hedlund, Arie Lewin, and the anonymous referees for their comments. Partial funding for the research has been provided by AT&T under the auspices of the Reginald H. Jones Center of The Wharton School.

REFERENCES

Allen, Thomas and Stephen Cohen (1969). "Information Flow in Research and Development Laboratories." *Administrative Science Quarterly*, 14, 12–20.

Argyris, Chris and Donald Schoen (1978). *Organizational Learning: A Theory of Action Perspective*. Reading, MA: Addison-Wesley.

Arrow, Kenneth (1974). *The Limits of Organization*. New York: Norton.

Arthur, Brian (1989). "Competing Technologies, Increasing Returns, and Lock-in by Historical Events." *Economic Journal*, 99, 116–131.

Barney, Jay (1986). "Strategic Factor Markets Expectations, Luck, and Business Strategy." *Management Science*, 32, 1231–1241.

Cyert, Richard M. and James G. March (1963). *A Behavioral Theory of the Firm*. Englewood Cliffs, NJ: Prentice-Hall.

Dawkins, Richard (1976). *The Selfish Gene*. Oxford: Oxford University Press.

_____ (1987). *The Blind Watchmaker*. New York: Basic Books.

Dierickx, Ingemar and Karel Cool (1989). "Asset Stock Accumulation and Sustainability of Competitive Advantage." *Management Science*, 33, 1504–1513.

Dougherty, Deborah (1992). "Interpretative Barriers to Successful Product Innovation in Large Firms." *Organization Science*, 3, 2, 179–202.

Dreyfus, Hubert and Stuart Dreyfus (1988). "Making a Mind versus Modeling the Brain: Artificial Intelligence Back at a Branchpoint." In *The Artificial Debate*. Stephen Graubard (Ed.). Cambridge: MIT Press.

Hannan, Michael and John Freeman (1977). "The Population Ecology of Organizations." *American Journal of Sociology*, 82, 929–964.

Hedlund, Gunnar and Ikujiro Nonaka (1991). "Models of Knowledge Management in the West and Japan," mimeo, Stockholm School of Economics.

Henderson, Rebecca and Kim Clark (1990). "Architectural Innovation: The Reconfiguration of Existing Product Technologies and the Failure of Established Firms," *Administrative Science Quarterly,* 35, 9–31.

Kogut, Bruce (1987). "Country Patterns in International Competition: Appropriability and Oligopolistic Agreement," *Strategies in Global Competition,* N. Hood and J.-E. Vahlne (Ed.). London: Croom Helm.

_____ (1991). "Joint Ventures and the Option to Expand and Acquire," *Management Science,* 37, 19–33.

_____ and Dong Jae Kim (1991). "Technological Platforms and the Sequence of Entry," Working Paper, Reginald H. Jones Center, Wharton School.

_____ and Udo Zander (1990). "The Imitation and Transfer of New Technologies," mimeo.

Leonard-Barton, Dorothy (1988). "Implementations as Mutual Adaptation of Technology and Organization," *Research Policy,* 17, 251–267.

Levin, Richard, Alvin Klevorick, Richard Nelson and Sidney Winter (1987). "Appropriating the Returns from Industrial Research and Development," *Brookings Papers on Economic Activity,* 3, 783–831.

Lippman, Stephen and Richard Rumelt (1982). "Uncertain Imitability: An Analysis of Interfirm Differences in Efficiency Under Competition," *Bell Journal of Economics,* 13, 418–438.

March, James and Herbert Simon (1958), *Organizations,* New York: John Wiley.

Monteverde, Kirk and David Teece (1982)."Supplier Switching Costs and Vertical Integration in the Automobile Industry," *Bell Journal of Economics,* 13, 206–213.

Nelson, Richard (1982). "The Role of Knowledge in R & D Efficiency," *Quarterly Journal of Economics,* 96, 453–470.

_____ and Sidney Winter (1982). *An Evolutionary Theory of Economic Change,* Cambridge: Belknap Press.

Papert, Seymour (1979). "Computers and Learning," in M. Dertouzos and J. Moses (Eds.). *The Computer Age: A Twenty-Year View,* Cambridge, MA: MIT Press.

Piore, Michael (1985). "Introduction," in P. Doeringer and M. Piore. *Internal Labor Markets and Manpower Analysis.* New York: M. E. Sharpe Inc.

Polanyi, Michael (1966). *The Tacit Dimension,* New York: Anchor Day Books.

Prahalad, C. K. and Gary Hamel (1990). "The Core Competence of the Corporation," *Harvard Business Review,* (May–June), 79–91.

Pringle, J. W. S. (1951). "On the Parallel Between Learning and Evolution," *Behavior,* 3, 175–215.

Rogers, Everett (1983). *The Diffusion of Innovations,* (Third Ed.) (First Ed., 1962). New York: Free Press.

Rosenberg, Nathan (1976). *Perspectives on Technology.* Cambridge, UK: Cambridge University Press.

Rumelt, R. P. (1984). "Towards a Strategic Theory of the Firm." In *Competitive Strategic Management.* Robert Boyden Lamb (Ed.), Englewood Cliffs, NJ: Prentice-Hall, Inc.

Schumpeter, Joseph (1934). *The Theory of Economic Development.* Cambridge, MA: Harvard University Press, (First Published in 1911; republished 1968).

Simon, Herbert (1962). "The Architecture of Complexity." *Proceedings of the American Philosophical Society,* 106, 467–482.

Teece, David (1977), "Technology Transfer by Multinational Corporations: The Resource Cost of Transferring Technological Know-how." *Economical Journal,* 87, 242–261.

_____ (1980). "Economies of Scope and the Scope of an Enterprise." *Journal of Economic Behavior and Organization,* 1, 223–247.

Tushman, Michael (1977). "Special Boundary Roles in the Innovation Process." *Administrative Science Quarterly,* 22, 587–605.

von Hippel, Eric (1988). *The Sources of Innovation.* Cambridge: MIT Press.

Walker, Gordon and David Weber (1984). A Transaction Cost Approach to Make or Buy Decisions. *Administrative Science Quarterly,* 29, 373–391.

Wernerfelt, Birger (1984). "A Resource-Based View of the Firm." *Strategic Management Journal,* 5, 171–180.

Winter, Sidney (1987), "Knowledge and Competence as Strategic Assets," in *The Competitive Challenge—Strategies for Industrial Innovation and Renewal,* D. Teece (Ed.), Cambridge, MA: Ballinger.

3

Informal Networks:
The Company

David Krackhardt and Jeffrey R. Hanson

Many executives invest considerable resources in restructuring their companies, drawing and redrawing organizational charts only to be disappointed by the results. That's because much of the real work of companies happens despite the formal organization. Often what needs attention is the *informal* organization, the networks of relationships that employees form across functions and divisions to accomplish tasks fast. These informal networks can cut through formal reporting procedures to jump start stalled initiatives and meet extraordinary deadlines. But informal networks can just as easily sabotage companies' best laid plans by blocking communication and fomenting opposition to change unless managers know how to identify and direct them. Learning how to map these social links can help managers harness the real power in their companies and revamp their formal organizations to let the informal ones thrive.

If the formal organization is the skeleton of a company, the informal is the central nervous system driving the collective thought processes, actions, and reactions of its business units. Designed to facilitate standard modes of production, the formal organization is set up to handle easily anticipated problems. But when unexpected problems arise, the informal organization kicks in. Its complex webs of social ties form every time colleagues communicate and solidify over time into surprisingly stable networks. Highly adaptive, informal networks move diagonally and elliptically, skipping entire functions to get work done.

Managers often pride themselves on understanding how these networks operate. They will readily tell you who confers on technical matters and who discusses office politics over lunch. What's startling is how often they are wrong. Although they may be able to diagram accurately the social links of the five or six people closest to them, their assumptions about employees outside their immediate circle are usually off the mark. Even the most psychologically shrewd managers lack critical information about how employees spend their days and how they feel about their peers. Managers simply can't be everywhere at once, nor can they read people's minds. So they're left to draw conclusions based on superficial observations, without the tools to test their perceptions.

Armed with faulty information, managers often rely on traditional techniques to control these networks. Some managers hope that the authority inherent in their titles will override the power of informal links. Fearful of any groups they can't command, they create rigid rules that will hamper the work of the informal networks. Other managers try to recruit "moles" to provide intelligence. More enlightened managers run focus groups and host retreats to "get in touch" with their employees. But such approaches won't rein in these freewheeling networks, nor will they give managers an accurate picture of what they look like.

Using network analysis, however, managers can translate a myriad of relationship ties into maps that show how the informal organization gets work done. Managers can get a good overall picture by diagramming three types of relationship networks:

- The advice network shows the prominent players in an organization on whom others depend to solve problems and provide technical information.
- The trust network tells which employees share delicate political information and back one another in a crisis.
- The communication network reveals the employees who talk about work-related matters on a regular basis.

Maps of these relationships can help managers understand the networks that once eluded them and leverage these networks to solve organizational problems. Case studies using fictional names, based on companies with which we have worked, show how managers can bring out the strengths in their networks, restructure their formal organizations to complement the informal, and "rewire" faulty networks to work with company goals.

The Steps of Network Analysis

We learned the significance of the informal network 12 years ago while conducting research at a bank that had an 80% turnover rate among its tellers. Interviews revealed that the tellers' reasons for leaving had less to do with the bank's formal organization than with the tellers' relationships to key players in their trust networks. When these players left, others followed in droves.

Much research had already established the influence of central figures in informal networks. Our subsequent studies of public and private companies showed that understanding these networks could increase the influence of managers outside the inner circle. If they learned who wielded power in networks and how various coalitions functioned, they could work with the informal organization to solve problems and improve performance.

Mapping advice networks, our research showed, can uncover the source of political conflicts and failure to achieve strategic objectives. Because these networks show the most influential players in the day-to-day operations of a company, they are useful to examine when a company is considering routine changes. Trust networks often reveal the causes of nonroutine problems such as poor performance by temporary teams. Companies should examine trust networks when implementing a major change or experiencing a crisis. The communication network can help identify gaps in information flow, the inefficient use of resources, and the failure to generate new ideas. They should be examined when productivity is low.

Managers can analyze informal networks in three steps. Step one is conducting a network survey using employee questionnaires. The survey is designed to solicit responses about who talks to whom about work, who trusts whom, and who advises whom on technical matters. It is important to pretest the survey on a small group of employees to see if any questions are ambiguous or meet with resistance. In some companies, for example, employees are comfortable answering questions about friendship; in others, they deem such questions too personal and intrusive. The following are among the questions often asked:

- Whom do you talk to every day?
- Whom do you go to for help or advice at least once a week?
- With one day of training, whose job could you step into?
- Whom would you recruit to support a proposal of yours that could be unpopular?
- Whom would you trust to keep in confidence your concerns about a work-related issue?

Some companies also find it useful to conduct surveys to determine managers' *impressions* of informal networks so that these can be compared with the actual networks revealed by the employee questionnaires. In such surveys, questions are posed like this:

- Whom do you think Steve goes to for work-related advice?
- Whom would Susan trust to keep her confidence about work-related concerns?

The key to eliciting honest answers from employees is to earn their trust. They must be assured that managers will not use their answers against them or the employees mentioned in their responses and that their immediate colleagues will not have access to the information. In general, respondents are comfortable if upper-level managers not mentioned in the surveys see the results.

After questionnaires are completed, the second step is cross-checking the answers. Some employees, worried about offending their colleagues, say they talk to *everyone* in the department on a daily basis. If Judy Smith says she regularly talks to Bill Johnson about work, make sure that Johnson says he talks to Smith. Managers should discount any answers not confirmed by both parties. The final map should not be based on the impressions of one employee but on the consensus of the group.

The third step is processing the information using one of several commercially available computer programs that generate detailed network maps. (Drawing maps is a laborious process that tends to result in curved lines that are difficult to read.) Maps in hand, a skilled manager can devise a strategy that plays on the strengths of the informal organization, as David Leers, the founder and CEO of a California-based computer company, found out.

Whom Do You Trust?

David Leers thought he knew his employees well. In 15 years, the company had trained a cadre of loyal professionals who had built a strong regional reputation for delivering customized office information systems (see Figure 3.1). The field design group, responsible for designing and installing the systems, generated the largest block of revenues. For years it had been the linchpin of the operation, led by the company's technical superstars, with whom Leers kept in close contact.

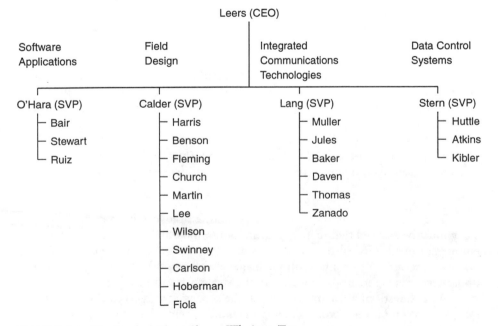

FIGURE 3.1 The Formal Chart Shows Who's on Top

But Leers feared that the company was losing its competitive edge by short-changing its other divisions, such as software applications and integrated communications technologies. When members of field design saw Leers start pumping more money into these divisions, they worried about losing their privileged position. Key employees started voicing dissatisfaction about their compensation, and Leers knew he had the makings of a morale problem that could result in defections.

To persuade employees to support a new direction for the company, Leers decided to involve them in the planning process. He formed a strategic task force composed of members of all divisions and led by a member of field design to signal his continuing commitment to the group. He wanted a leader who had credibility with his peers and was a proven performer. Eight-year company veteran Tom Harris seemed obvious for the job.

Leers was optimistic after the first meeting. Members generated good discussion about key competitive dilemmas. A month later, however, he found that the group had made little progress. Within two months, the group was completely deadlocked by members championing their own agendas. Although a highly effective manager, Leers lacked the necessary distance to identify the source of his problem.

An analysis of the company's trust and advice networks helped him get a clearer picture of the dynamics at work in the task force. The trust map turned out to be most revealing. Task force leader Tom Harris held a central position in the advice network—meaning that many employees relied on him for technical advice (see Figure 3.2). But he had only *one* trust link with a colleague (see Figure 3.3). Leers concluded that Harris's weak position in the trust network was a main reason for the task force's inability to produce results.

In his job, Harris was able to leverage his position in the advice network to get work done quickly. As a task force leader, however, his technical expertise was less important than his ability to moderate conflicting views, focus the group's thinking, and win the commitment of task force members to mutually agreed-upon strategies. Because he was a loner who took more interest in computer games than in colleagues' opinions, task force members didn't trust him to take their ideas seriously or look out for their interests. So they focused instead on defending their turf.

With this critical piece of information, the CEO crafted a solution. He did not want to undermine the original rationale of the task force by declaring it a failure. Nor did he want to embarrass a valued employee by summarily removing him as task force head. Any response, he concluded, had to run with the natural grain of the informal organization. He decided to redesign the team to reflect the inherent strengths of the trust network.

Referring to the map, Leers looked for someone in the trust network who could share responsibilities with Harris. He chose Bill Benson, a warm, amiable person who occupied a central position in the network and with whom Harris had already established a solid working relationship. He publicly justified his decision to name two task force heads as necessary, given the time pressures and scope of the problem.

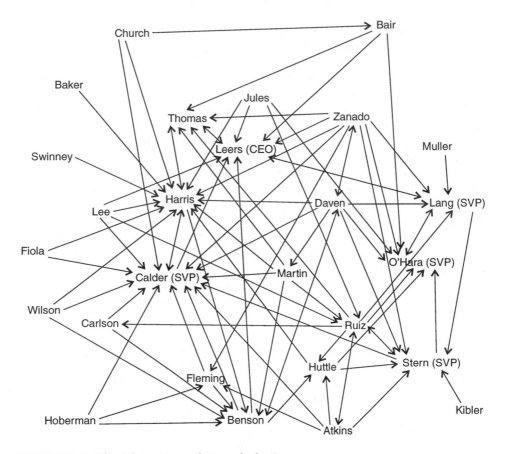

FIGURE 3.2 The Advice Network Reveals the Experts

Within three weeks, Leers could see changes in the group's dynamics. Because task force members trusted Benson to act in the best interest of the entire group, people talked more openly and let go of their fixed positions. During the next two months, the task force made significant progress in proposing a strategic direction for the company. And in the process of working together, the task force helped integrate the company's divisions.

A further look at the company's advice and trust networks uncovered another serious problem, this time with the head of field design, Jim Calder.

The CEO had appointed Calder manager because his colleagues respected him as the most technically accomplished person in the division. Leers thought Calder would have the professional credibility to lead a diverse group of very specialized design consultants. This is a common practice in professional service organizations: make your best producer the manager. Calder, however, turned out to be a very marginal figure in the trust network. His managerial ability and skills were sorely lacking, which proved to be a deficit that outweighed the positive ef-

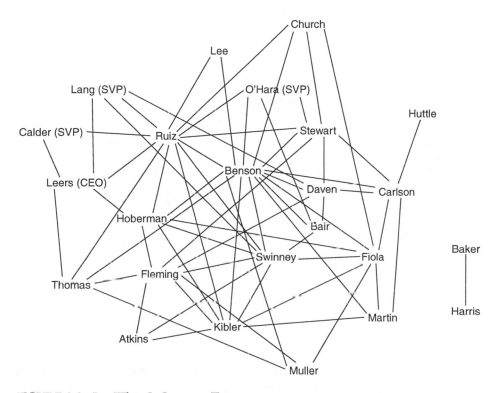

FIGURE 3.3 But When It Comes to Trust . . .

fects derived from his technical expertise. He regularly told people they were stupid and paid little attention to their professional concerns.

Leers knew that Calder was no diplomat, but he had no idea to what extent the performance and morale of the group were suffering as a result of Calder's tyrannical management style. In fact, a map based on Leers's initial perceptions of the trust network put Calder in a central position (see Figure 3.4). Leers took for granted that Calder had good personal relationships with the people on his team. His assumption was not unusual. Frequently, senior managers presume that formal work ties will yield good relationship ties over time, and they assume that if *they* trust someone, others will too.

The map of Calder's perceptions was also surprising (see Figure 3.5). He saw almost no trust links in his group at all. Calder was oblivious to *any* of the trust dependencies emerging around him—a worrisome characteristic for a manager.

The information in these maps helped Leers formulate a solution. Again, he concluded that he needed to change the formal organization to reflect the structure of the informal network. Rather than promoting or demoting Calder, Leers cross-promoted him to an elite "special situations team," reporting directly to the CEO. His job involved working with highly sophisticated clients on specialized

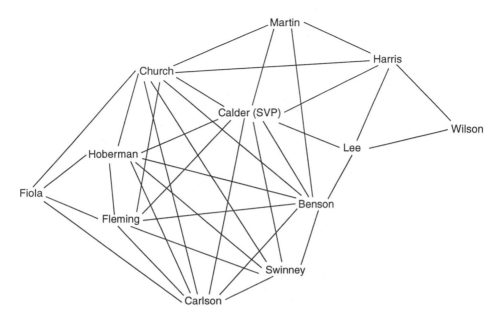

FIGURE 3.4 How the CEO Views the Trust Network

problems. The position took better advantage of Calder's technical skills and turned out to be good for him socially as well. Calder, Leers learned, hated dealing with formal management responsibilities and the pressure of running a large group.

Leers was now free to promote John Fleming, a tactful, even-tempered employee, to the head of field design. A central player in the trust network, Fleming was also influential in the advice network. The field group's performance improved significantly over the next quarter, and the company was able to create a highly profitable revenue stream through the activities of Calder's new team.

Fleming ————————————————————— Hoberman

FIGURE 3.5 The Trust Network According to Calder

Whom Do You Talk To?

When it comes to communication, more is not always better, as the top management of a large East Coast bank discovered. A survey showed that customers were dissatisfied with the information they were receiving about banking services. Branch managers, top managers realized, were not communicating critical information about available services to tellers. As a result, customers' questions were not answered in a timely fashion.

Management was convinced that more talking among parties would improve customer service and increase profits. A memo was circulated ordering branch managers to "increase communication flow and coordination within and across branches and to make a personal effort to increase the amount and effectiveness of their own interpersonal communications with their staffs."

A study of the communication networks of 24 branches, however, showed the error of this thinking. *More* communication ties did not distinguish the most profitable branches; the *quality* of communication determined their success. Non-hierarchical branches, those with two-way communication between people of all levels, were 70% more profitable than branches with one-way communication patterns between "superiors" and staff.

The communication networks of two branches located in the same city illustrated this point. Branch 1 had a central figure, a supervisor, with whom many tellers reported communicating about their work on a daily basis. The supervisor confirmed that employees talked to her, but she reported communicating with only half of these tellers about work related matters by the end of the day. The tellers, we later learned, resented this one-way communication flow. Information they viewed as critical to their success flowed up the organization but not down. They complained that the supervisor was cold and remote and failed to keep them informed. As a result, productivity suffered.

In contrast, Branch 2 had very few one-way communication lines but many mutual, two-way lines. Tellers in this branch said they were well-informed about the normal course of work flow and reported greater satisfaction with their jobs.

After viewing the communication map, top management abandoned the more-is-better strategy and began exploring ways of fostering mutual communication in all the branches. In this case, management did not recast the formal structure of the branches. Instead, it opted to improve relationships within the established framework. The bank sponsored mini-seminars in the branches, in which the problems revealed by the maps were openly discussed. These consciousness-raising sessions spurred many supervisors to communicate more substantive information to tellers. District managers were charged with coming up with their own strategies for improving communication. The bank surveyed employees at regular intervals to see if their supervisors were communicating effectively, and supervisors were informed of the results.

The communication network of a third branch surfaced another management challenge: the branch had divided itself into two distinct groups, each with its own culture and mode of operation. The network map showed that one group had evolved into the "main branch," consisting of tellers, loan officers, and administrative staff. The other group was a kind of "sub-branch," made up primarily of tellers and administrators. It turned out that the sub-branch staff worked during nonpeak and Saturday hours, while main-branch employees worked during peak and weekday hours. The two cultures never clashed because they rarely interacted.

The groups might have coexisted peacefully if customers had not begun complaining about the sub-branch. The main-branch staff, they reported, was responsive to their needs, while the sub-branch staff was often indifferent and even rude. Sub-branch employees, it turned out, felt little loyalty to the bank because they didn't feel part of the organization. They were excluded from staff meetings, which were scheduled in the morning, and they had little contact with the branch manager, who worked a normal weekday shift.

The manager, who was embedded in the main branch, was not even aware that this distinct culture existed until he saw the communication network map. His challenge was to unify the two groups. He decided not to revamp the formal structure, nor did he mount a major public-relations campaign to integrate the two cultures, fearing that each group would reject the other because the existing ties among its members were so strong. Instead, he opted for a stealth approach. He exposed people from one group to people from the other in the hopes of expanding the informal network. Although such forced interaction does not guarantee the emergence of stable networks, more contact increases the likelihood that some new ties will stick.

Previously planned technical training programs for tellers presented the opportunity to initiate change. The manager altered his original plans for on-site training and opted instead for an off-site facility, even though it was more expensive. He sent mixed groups of sub-branch and main-branch employees to programs to promote gradual, neutral interaction and communication. Then he followed up with a series of selective "staff swaps" whereby he shifted work schedules temporarily. When someone from the main branch called in sick or was about to go on vacation, he elected a substitute from the sub-branch. And he rescheduled staff meetings so that all employees could attend.

This approach helped unify the two cultures, which improved levels of customer satisfaction with the branch as a whole over a six-month period. By increasing his own interaction with the sub-branch, the manager discovered critical information about customers, procedures, and data systems. Without even realizing it, he had been making key decisions based on incomplete data.

Network Holes and Other Problems

As managers become more sophisticated in analyzing their communication networks, they can use them to spot five common configurations. None of these are inherently good or bad, functional or dysfunctional. What matters is the *fit,* whether networks are in sync with company goals. When the two are at odds, managers can attempt to broaden or reshape the informal networks using a variety of tactics.

Imploded relationships

Communication maps often show departments that have few links to other groups. In these situations, employees in a department spend all their time talking among themselves and neglect to cultivate relationships with the rest of their colleagues. Frequently, in such cases, only the most senior employees have ties with people outside their areas. And they may hoard these contacts by failing to introduce these people to junior colleagues.

To counter this behavior, one manager implemented a mentor system in which senior employees were responsible for introducing their apprentices to people in other groups who could help them do their jobs. Another manager instituted a policy of picking up the tab for "power breakfasts," as long as the employees were from different departments.

Irregular communication patterns

The opposite pattern can be just as troubling. Sometimes employees communicate only with members of other groups and not among themselves. To foster camaraderie, one manager sponsored seasonal sporting events with members of the "problem group" assigned to the same team. Staff meetings can also be helpful if they're really used to share resources and exchange important information about work.

A lack of cohesion resulting in factionalism suggests a more serious underlying problem that requires bridge building. Initiating discussions among peripheral players in each faction can help uncover the root of the problem and suggest solutions. These parties will be much less resistant to compromise than the faction leaders, who will feel more impassioned about their positions.

Fragile structures

Sometimes group members communicate only among themselves and with employees in one other division. This can be problematic when the contribution of several areas is necessary to accomplish work quickly and spawn creativity. One insurance company manager, a naturally gregarious fellow, tried to broaden employees' contacts by organizing meetings and cocktail parties for members of several divisions. Whenever possible, he introduced employees he thought should be cultivating working relationships. Because of his warm, easygoing manner, they didn't find his methods intrusive. In fact, they appreciated his personal interest in their careers.

Holes in the network

A map may reveal obvious network holes, places you would expect to find relationship ties but don't. In a large corporate law firm, for example, a group of litigators was not talking to the firm's criminal lawyers, a state of affairs that startled the senior partner. To begin tackling the problem, the partner posed complex problems to criminal lawyers that only regular consultations with litigators could solve. Again, arranging such interactions will not ensure the formation of enduring relationships, but continuous exposure increases the possibility.

"Bow ties"

Another common trouble spot is the bow tie, a network in which many players are dependent on a single employee but not on each other. Individuals at the center knot of a bow tie have tremendous power and control within the network, much more than would be granted them on a formal organizational chart. If the person at the knot leaves, connections between isolated groups can collapse. If the person remains, organizational processes tend to become rigid and slow, and the individual is often torn between the demands of several groups. To undo such a knot, one manager self-consciously cultivated a stronger relationship with the person at the center. It took the pressure off the employee, who was no longer a lone operative, and it helped to diffuse some of his power.

In general, managers should help employees develop relationships within the informal structure that will enable them to make valuable contributions to the company. Managers need to guide employees to cultivate the right mix of relationships. Employees can leverage the power of informal relationships by building both strong ties, relationships with a high frequency of interaction, and weak ties, those with a lower frequency. They can call on the latter at key junctures to solve organizational problems and generate new ideas.

Testing the solution

Managers can anticipate how a strategic decision will affect the informal organization by simulating network maps. This is particularly valuable when a company wants to anticipate reactions to change. A company that wants to form a strategic SWAT team that would remove key employees from the day-to-day operations of a division, for example, can design a map of the area without those players. If removing the central advice person from the network leaves the division with a group of isolates, the manager should reconsider the strategy.

Failure to test solutions can lead to unfortunate results. When the trust network map of a bank showed a loan officer to be an isolate, the manager jumped to the conclusion that the officer was expendable. The manager was convinced that he could replace the employee, a veteran of the company, with a younger, less expensive person who was more of a team player.

What the manager had neglected to consider was how important this officer was to the company's day-to-day operations. He might not have been a prime candidate for a high-level strategy team that demanded excellent social skills, but his expertise, honed by years of experience, would have been impossible to replace. In addition, he had cultivated a close relationship with the bank's largest client— something an in-house network map would never have revealed. Pictures don't tell the whole story; network maps are just one tool among many.

The most important change for a company to anticipate is a complete overhaul of its formal structure. Too many companies fail to consider how such a restructuring will affect their informal organizations. Managers assume that if a company eliminates layers of bureaucracy, the informal organization will simply adjust. It will adjust all right, but there's no guarantee that it will benefit the company. Managers would do well to consider what type of redesign will play on the inherent strengths of key players and give them the freedom to thrive. Policies should allow all employees easy access to colleagues who can help them carry out tasks quickly and efficiently, regardless of their status or area of jurisdiction.

Experienced network managers who can use maps to identify, leverage, and revamp informal networks will become increasingly valuable as companies continue to flatten and rely on teams. As organizations abandon hierarchical structures, managers will have to rely less on the authority inherent in their title and more on their relationships with players in their informal networks. They will need to focus less on overseeing employees "below" them and more on managing people across functions and disciplines. Understanding relationships will be the key to managerial success.

4

Top Management, Strategy and Organizational Knowledge Structures

Marjorie A. Lyles and Charles R. Schwenk

INTRODUCTION

A review of the strategic management literature reveals an increased emphasis on the top management team and its impact on the strategic behaviour and performance of the firm. One widely held perspective is that the top management team exerts influence over the members of the organization through its shared perspective of environmental events and organizational capabilities. Prahalad and Bettis (1986) suggest that this shared perspective can be described as a general knowledge structure that can store a shared dominant general management logic. Our purpose in this article is to expand the notion of organizational knowledge structures.

In the past decade, there has been extensive research on cognitive structures and processes and their impact on organizational behaviour. This research addresses such topics as decision-makers' frame of reference (Hambrick, 1981; Schwenk, 1988; Shrivastava and Schneider, 1984), assumptions (Mason and Mitroff, 1981), cognitive maps (Ford and Hegarty, 1984); schemas (Huff, 1983; Weick, 1979); belief systems (Dunbar *et al.*, 1982); scripts (Gioia and Manz, 1985; Gioia and Poole, 1984); organizational learning (Argyris and Schon, 1978; Fiol and Lyles, 1985; Hedberg, 1981; Jelinek, 1979; Levitt and March, 1988; Lyles, 1988; Shrivastava, 1983) and interpretive systems (Bartunek, 1984; Daft and Weick, 1984; Meyer, 1982).

Most of these studies focus on a single concept and its definition and impact. Less effort is devoted to the study of the more important issue of the linkages between individual-level cognitions, the development of shared understandings, and organizational action. This has led to a very fragmented view of these linkages.

Strategic management research has typically neglected the link between individual beliefs and cognitive structures, organization-wide beliefs and assumptions, and political processes. Hence, there are gaps in the research relating the interaction between individual-level understanding and organizational action. Some research assumes that organizations have knowledge structures as do individuals. Other research discusses the cognitions of key individuals but does not discuss the ways these are formed or modified by organizational events, or the extent to which understandings are shared by others in the organization.

This article reflects the growing need for a more developed theoretical foundation that may serve as the basis for future empirical studies aimed at testing the existence and linkages of organizational knowledge and strategic management. We hope to theorize beyond the current research base since a larger vision of the theory is needed, whereas experimentation has focused only on elements of the theory. We hope to present a theoretical construct and to raise questions that lend themselves to later experimentation. We do not intend to prove the existence of an organizational 'mind' or 'cognitive structures' (Sandelands and Stablein, 1987). However, we do intend to address two fundamental problems: What is an organizational knowledge structure? How might it develop and change?

In order to do this, we have had to set some limits on what we can consider and use as evidence. Our focus will be on the development of organizational knowledge and how knowledge structures might change. We rely on the literature of the cognitive psychologists and of the authors developing schema theory. Although we utilize this literature, we do not mean to imply that organizations have minds in the same sense that humans do. A basic assumption, however, is that there are shared understandings within organizations that influence organizational behaviour, though it is not necessary for knowledge to be shared in order to influence behaviour. These are stored over time and may be retrieved (Brunsson, 1985; Daft and Weick, 1984; Hedberg, 1981).

To help explain our theory we will use statements taken from interviews conducted with two senior executives of an international consulting firm that has just gone through a major strategic change. These interviews provide a means of illustrating the major issues. Our intent however is illustration—these sentences do not represent scientific research or deeper knowledge structures. Our objectives are to identify shared understandings through these statements.

This article examines three elements that influence the development of organizational knowledge. First, we will discuss the concept of schema and how key decision-makers' schemata influence the development of widely held cause-and-effect beliefs. The concept of 'schema' refers to individual-level knowledge while the term 'knowledge structure' refers to shared beliefs at the organizational level. Further, these beliefs have a *structure*.

Second, we argue that there are certain *core* features of the organization knowledge structure which remain invariant over long periods of time, while there are *peripheral* features which change. We will then discuss the process of organizational knowledge development. Since we are dealing with a social theory of knowledge development, bargaining, consensus and dissensus become important processes for communicating and integrating alternative schemas. Finally we explore the implications of our theoretical discussion and give propositions to guide future research.

ORGANIZATIONAL KNOWLEDGE STRUCTURES

Argyris and Schön (1978) suggest that an organization is, at its root, a cognitive enterprise and it learns and develops knowledge. The knowledge structure serves to define expected relationships, behaviours, and actions for organizational members.

The organizational knowledge structure is different from organizational culture and climate in at least two important ways. The concept of knowledge structures deals with goals, cause-and-effect beliefs, and other cognitive elements. Thus, it is narrower than culture and climate, both of which refer more to affective or emotional elements. Further, the knowledge structure is more clearly linked to an organization's strategy for survival and more subject to change than an organization's climate or culture, neither of which changes readily or provides specific strategies for action for an organization.

The schemata of top managers have an important influence on the development of the organization's knowledge structure. Alba and Hasher (1983) suggest that the information contained within a schema may be encoded, stored and retrieved. A subset of schemas, called scripts, contains information about particular, frequently experienced events (Schank and Abelson, 1977). In-depth discussion of schema properties can be found in such works as Alba and Hasher (1983); Anderson (1983); Bartlett (1932); and Schank and Abelson (1977).

By their very nature, organizational knowledge structures differ from personal schemata because they are socially constructed and rely on consensus or agreement (Daft and Weick, 1984; Hedberg, 1981; Weick, 1979). Weick and Bougon (1986, p. 109) suggest that in developing knowledge structures, there are three stages that people go through to reach agreement: (1) agreement on which concepts capture and abstract their joint experience; (2) consensus on relations among these concepts; and (3) similarity of view on how these related concepts affect each party. Some of the schema properties that are particularly relevant to organizational knowledge structures are encoding, storage, elaboration, forgetting, retrieval, modelling, modification of structures, adding new structures, and complexity of structures (Daft and Weick, 1984; Gioia and Manz, 1985; Lord and Foti, 1986).

Organizational researchers have shown that organizations develop shared frames of reference, recall of past events, the creation of stories and myths, vicarious learning, unlearning and memories (Dunbar *et al.*, 1982; Hedberg *et al.*, 1976; Huff, 1983; Jelinek, 1979; Lyles, 1988; Manz and Sims, 1981; Martin, 1982). It is important to draw together the concepts of earlier researchers to specify the elements of organizational knowledge structures and the way they interact. Figure 4.1 describes the ways knowledge structures may change over time.

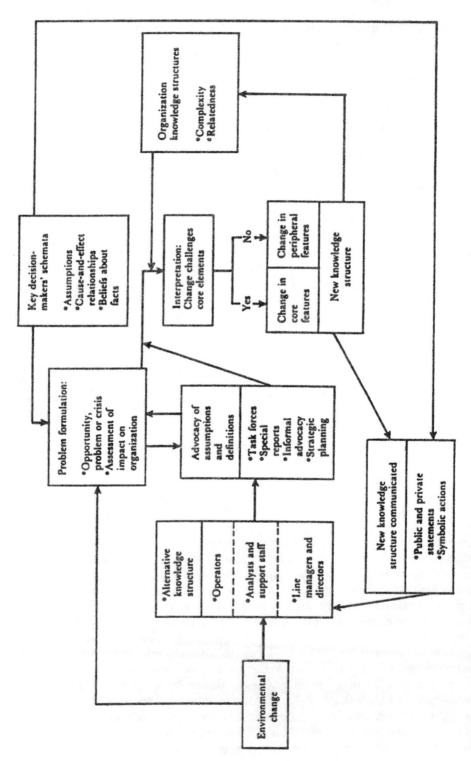

FIGURE 4.1 Changes in Organization Knowledge Structures

The process of developing the organizational knowledge structure is ongoing and continuous. As the figure shows, changes in a firm's environment may be perceived by many members and each may interpret it in different ways. However, when the change begins to affect company performance and when it cannot be adequately explained or predicted through the existing knowledge structure, it creates a challenge to that existing knowledge structure and creates an interactive effect among the organizational participants, the environment and behaviour (Bandura, 1977; Davis and Luthans, 1980).

Political processes are evoked when different coalitions (such as operators, managers, and analysts and support staff) within a firm who hold alternative schemas advocate their own positions through such mechanisms as task forces and special reports (Lord and Foti, 1986; Prahalad and Bettis, 1986; Taylor and Crocker, 1981). These different coalitions attempt to influence others and to gain the agreement of others about the coalition's interpretation of events (Lyles and Mitroff, 1985).

Changes in the organizational knowledge structure occur as a result of the impact of the interpretation of environmental events, results of past organizational actions, the influence of the key decision makers, and the advocacy position of coalitions within the firm. The political processes have to do with the negotiating and bargaining that takes place to gain support for alternative schemas. Sociopolitical themes, such as credibility and power, have been shown to influence the acceptance of particular views (Bower, 1970; Lyles and Mitroff, 1985; Mintzberg, 1983; Pfeffer, 1981). The degree of consensus about goals and about the means of achieving them influences the effectiveness of the firm (Bourgeois, 1980; Dess, 1987; Dess and Origer, 1987).

Once the key decision-makers sense and interpret changing environmental events, they frame them in the problem formulation process as problems, opportunities, or crises (Dutton and Jackson, 1987; Lyles and Mitroff, 1980; Mintzberg *et al.*, 1976). These decision-makers have a strong influence on the development of the organizational knowledge structures since it is primarily they who interpret the importance of environmental events and who communicate their view of the knowledge structure through speeches and statements. It seems likely that the key decision-makers' schemata closely reflect the 'core area' of the knowledge structure, and they influence the attitudes and beliefs of others in the organization by communicating and networking (Kotter, 1982; Tushman *et al.*, 1989; Zaleznik, 1977). Once the key decision-makers have determined that the change challenges the core elements of the knowledge structure, they make changes in the knowledge structure and communicate these changes to others in the organization.

A critical point in our model of changes in organizational knowledge structures is the distinction between core features of the knowledge structure and peripheral features. Environmental changes which challenge core features of the knowledge structure evoke more profound changes in the knowledge structure. Therefore, it is important that we discuss the differences between core and peripheral features.

Core Set of Knowledge Structures

Throughout the organization theory and philosophy of science literature are references to a core set of knowledge structures that explain beliefs and goals on which there is widespread agreement. These enable organizational members to understand the most basic purpose and mission of the firm. They provide a guide to expectations about organizational behaviour in the broadest sense of competitive situations. We suggest that this core set is similar to what Abelson (1981) calls a metascript: it is abstract and lacks detail but still provides a guide to the firm's business situations. It has widespread agreement and acceptance among the managers.

For example, Fayol (1949) describes an *'espirit de corps'* and a sense that 'union is strength.' Barnard (1938) suggests that organizations are cooperative systems that have a unifying purpose. It is the executive function to promote this widespread belief in the real existence of common purpose. It is belief that leads to co-operation, the development of a system of social action that overcomes the limitations of working alone. He suggests that it is the belief that is important, not necessarily the detailed understanding of the common purpose. Thompson (1967) refers to it as 'domain consensus.'

Even in other literatures, there is reference to core knowledge upon which there is widespread agreement. Kuhn (1962) suggests that in the development of science, there is a certain body of knowledge which provides a core upon which there is widespread agreement. Berger and Luckmann (1967) suggest that in 'secondary sociaiization,' when individuals become committed to an institution, there must be an immersion in and commitment to the new reality. It is the acquisition of knowledge that creates mutual identification. It is the internalization of the roles and attitudes of 'significant others' that creates knowledge about roles and language.

> *Proposition 1:* Firms are characterized by core elements of a generalized knowledge framework about which there is widespread agreement. The core facilitates understanding about the firm's general purpose, mission, and competitors.

For each organization there exists a *core* knowledge set about its mission, justification for its existence, and the basic business aim. This core would help to define the most basic of the repertoire of organizationally-relevant knowledge structures that describe the events and behaviours appropriate to the particular firm and the people within it. In order for the organization to exist, individuals and stakeholders must believe in the usefulness of the organization to serve some purpose and to carry out a mission. Barnard (1938), Cyert and March (1963) and Thompson (1967) develop this notion of a core set of values or beliefs that serve as motivating reasons for individuals to join together in an organization. Weick (1979) suggests that co-ordination within firms will be problematic until some agreement can be reached. It is necessary for sense-making. We propose that the core set provides the most basic elements of the organizational knowledge structure. It consists of the beliefs on which there is the most consensus among organizational members.

To illustrate these points, we use the consulting firm we studied. There was a core knowledge structure. The first element of this structure was the belief that the company should serve a wide range of client needs. This point was explained by one of our interviewees:

> *consulting . . . proliferated dramatically following World War II. The biggest firms were those that developed a working relationship with the senior management of a client company and advised on just about everything the client thought they needed advice on. The way in which you really sold the service was to maintain a close personal relationship with the people running divisions and then whenever they needed some outside assistance, they would call you to come and give it. So, firms tended to become all things to all clients.*

There was also agreement on who were the competitors.

> *Firms like McKinsey and Booz Allen, Arthur D. Little and some other smaller firms generally offered a variety of services. The CPA firms were somewhat more specialized, but they were big competitors.*

Lord and Foti (1986) suggest that scripts are basic elements that help to order events and causal relationships. Table 4.1 summarizes the basic elements of the knowledge structure as we interpret them from the two interviews. Our purpose is to illustrate how two members of an organization begin to define the perception of ambiguous information and how this interpretation may begin to shape expectations about actions and behaviours. The examples in Table 4.1 illustrate the basic elements of knowledge structures that are widely held in this particular firm.

To repeat briefly, this core set provides the initial knowledge structure through which the organizational members compare themselves to other organizations: it provides a basis for that comparison by providing knowledge about acceptable behaviour or actions for their firm. It can be used to show differences with what is acceptable behaviour in other organizations. This core is communicated and sponsored by top management in various ways including public and private statements, and symbolic actions. These actions are the means by which core knowledge structures are maintained.

Peripheral Structures

Proposition 2: Firms are characterized by elements of the knowledge structure that support the core set, but about which there may not be widespread consensus.

TABLE 4.1   Elements of the Firm's Knowledge Structure

	1960s
Firm-in-industry:	Provide consulting services 'Become all things to all people'
Firm-client script:	Develop close relationship with client Provide primarily 'manufacturing' expertise
Client script:	Client unsophisticated Loyal Heavy-industry, smokestack, manufacturing
Competitor script:	Provide broad base of services Big consulting firms Domestic
	1970s
Firm-in-industry:	Provide consulting services International Co-ordinated activities across regions
Firm-client script:	Purely business relationships Provide less manufacturing expertise
Client script:	Becoming sophisticated about buying services Disloyal Making decisions based on shopping around
Competitor script:	Becoming specialists Growing faster than 'us' International
	1980s
Firm-in-industry:	Moving away from 'manufacturing' consulting Equal domestic vs. international Independent regions
Firm-client script:	Provide client with best 'experts' 'Sell' them on us
Client script:	Sophisticated Many MBAs and ex-consultants in-house Few manufacturing
Competitor script:	Many small Niche strategies

Peripheral elements include knowledge about how to achieve the expectations established in the core set and how to interpret environmental and competitor signals—cause-and-effect beliefs that interrelate the core set to actions and environmental factors. The peripheral structures are open to much more debate and disagreement than is the core set. Astley *et al.* (1982) suggest that because of the division of labour within firms, a variety of perspectives develop and this would lead to the development of different knowledge structures at the peripheral level.

Thus, we propose that the peripheral knowledge structure may differ from the core knowledge structure in two ways: the content and the degree of consensus. The core set contains knowledge about the most basic of the firm's purposes and goals, while the peripheral set contains knowledge about subgoals and about the behaviour or steps necessary to achieve those goals. The core set and the peripheral set are related and linked together. Individuals apply their insights, heuristics, and schemas to attempt to achieve the subgoals that result in the accomplishment of the purpose of the firm.

In the case of our example firm, the peripheral set included beliefs about the clients and subgoals which would be served. One person stated:

Most partners thought that we needed to crystallize, clarify, and more precisely define our basic business strategy. I think most would agree with that, and they would probably need to make some changes in things that we see being done, but obviously not all agreeing on what those changes should be.

The clients were defined as 'the traditional smokestacks/heavy manufacturing businesses.' Expectations about appropriate organizational designs were also part of the peripheral knowledge structure.

We had been organized on a decentralized basis geographically. In our biggest office, we broke our consulting groups down into functional areas of activity. Within the regional organizations, they were not broken down that way.

The peripheral knowledge structure seems to contain knowledge about subgoals (*e.g.*, business-level goals or ends) and about behaviours appropriate for achieving them (means). A number of studies have appeared recently that address the linkages between environmental assessment, means-ends congruence, and consensus. Ends are defined as business-level goals (such as rate of sales growth, net profit over five years, *etc.*) and means are competitive methods within that particular business (such as new product development, customer service, *etc.*). Representative of this line of research are Bourgeois (1980), Dess (1987) and Dess and Origer (1987). While these studies do not consider knowledge structures directly, they make a contribution to this thinking by addressing consensus about means-ends and the impact on organizational performance. Although these studies do not address corporate level strategy (*e.g.*, what business do we want to compete in) and the results vary, they do seem to conclude that widespread consensus about means *and* ends does not lead to better performance.

Clearly the more agreement about the peripheral set and the core set, the more agreement there will be about specific courses of action necessary to ensure survival and the more single-minded will be the strategic thrust of the firm. This is the goal of congruity described by Barnard (1938) and Ouchi (1980). In this circumstance, the high level of consensus may lead to the development of strong scripts about behaviour in certain situations leading to poor adjustment or something similar to 'anchoring' (Kahneman *et al.*, 1982).

COMPLEXITY AND RELATEDNESS

We propose that there are two characteristics of organizational knowledge structures that become important to understanding how these structures work. Over time and as an organization learns, experience about certain events and instances is built up. The storage of these experiences becomes more complex and more abstract over time (Martin, 1982). Thus, the first characteristic of the knowledge structures is that of complexity. Complexity refers to the amount of information or the number of elements within a knowledge structure. The second characteristic, relatedness, refers to the linkages between elements in the knowledge structure, particularly the links between core and peripheral elements.

Proposition 3: The organizational knowledge structure is likely to become more complex over time.

Complexity

By complexity we mean the degree to which cognitive units are interrelated, creating a complex internal structure. Anderson (1983, p. 76) suggests that in knowledge representations, 'large knowledge structures must be encoded hierarchically, with smaller cognitive units embedded in larger ones.' In fact Anderson suggests that subhierarchies may become embedded within other hierarchies creating 'tangled hierarchies.' It is necessary to discuss the concept of hierarchy in connection with knowledge structures, since some elements of the structures (core) are more important than others (peripheral).

The complexity of the knowledge structure influences the ability of organizational members to retrieve elements that have become embedded in the hierarchical structure. This will influence their ability to respond to environmental changes and new situations. Levitt and March (1988) suggest that the memory of organizations is orderly but inconsistent. They suggest that knowledge becomes 'nested within' other knowledge, but not all events are recorded. Organizations do act as repositories which include the personnel, the rules of operation, stories, and computer bases.

Not all elements that are stored will be easy to retrieve. Which elements are retrieved depends upon the frequency of use, how recent they are, the usefulness, organizational proximity, preferences, self-interest and attention (Douglas, 1986; Levitt and March, 1988; March and Olsen, 1975; March *et al.*, 1991).

The more complex the structure, the more the simple units may become hidden or forgotten. The original element or experience may become lost because of employee changes, because of aversion to the topic, or because the direct relationships have become unclear (March and Olsen, 1975). More complex structures allow more diverse information to be recognized and processed. On the other hand, a simple structure may cause decision-makers to ignore many environmental signals and to reject them because they are not recognized (Walsh and Fahey, 1986).

The term 'experience' refers to an organization's contact with the environment which forms the basis for knowledge structures. The notion of complexity is based on the assumption that as a firm gains more experience and learns from it, it will become more expert at what it is doing. As it becomes more expert, the knowledge structure builds on the base established by the past experiences. As the knowledge structure becomes more complex, it is able to encompass a greater number of new situations and problems.

The literature on experts supports this notion of the development of complexity in the knowledge structure. McKeithen *et al.* (1981) suggest that schemas of experts contain more links among the elements and possibly more efficient hierarchies. Lurigio and Carroll (1985) suggest that expert schemas contain more information and become more complex. It would seem that this concept applies also to organizations that learn from their experiences and that this influences how they view their strategic options for the future (Hedberg, 1981; Shrivastava, 1983; Tushman *et al.*, 1989).

An alternative assumption about the notion of complexity is based on more sociological theories. These suggest that organizations may not learn *from* past experiences *per se*. Instead the firms may utilize the current experience, interpret it, and develop new views that influence future behaviour (March *et al.*, 1991). Hence, the current experiences may not lead to improved performance but to some changed behaviour. In fact March and Olsen suggest this may be 'superstitious' learning where 'organizational behaviour is modified as a result of an interpretation of the consequences, but the behaviour does not affect the consequences significantly' (1975, p. 139).

Some environmental events will have an impact, be retained and be included in the knowledge structure, thus causing a new association to be developed (Meyer, 1982). Simple structures may develop over time into complex ones by the inclusion of new experiences that tie into the knowledge of goals (Schank and Abelson, 1977). During this process of development, organizations with simple structures will attempt to find segments of the environment in which they can operate without being traumatized by too many jolts (Meyer, 1982); or they will ignore the jolts, remaining unaffected by them and maintaining the viability of their structure.

On the other hand a complex structure allows the recognition and interpretation of many signals. Organizations that are diversified face highly uncertain environments, or multinationals have more varied experiences than others. They may develop more complex structures that allow them to respond to a variety of environmental signals and that may even welcome periodic jolts (Tushman *et al.*, 1989).

Relatedness

Proposition 4: The organizational knowledge system is likely to have linkages between the core structure and the peripheral structure. The strength of this linkage is the degree of relatedness.

Relatedness represents the interrelationships between the core knowledge structure and the peripheral set. In cognitive psychology, the concept that lends some support to this notion is that of 'spreading activation.' Anderson suggests that activation measures the likelihood that a piece of knowledge will be useful at a particular time and also that 'spreading activation amounts to the process of bringing information into working memory' (1983, p. 88). The degree of relatedness will influence the rate at which knowledge is retrieved and also which knowledge is retrieved. As the knowledge structures become tightly linked or coupled, it reduces the need to process every element. This seems to correspond to the 'strong' and 'weak' ideology that Brunsson (1985) identifies.

If there is strong consensus among the organizational members regarding the core set and the peripheral set, we propose that they are tightly coupled. In this case there would be consensus not only about the basic mission of the firm, but also how to achieve it, and how to interpret environmental signals. On the other hand if there is consensus about the mission but disagreement about how to carry it out the core and peripheral elements would be loosely coupled. This point is illustrated by the following quote from one of the members of the consulting firm we studied:

> *We had organized in a very decentralized way and so some people thought that some of the suggestions that were being made would obviously lead to some changes in the organization structure. We had a lot of people who disagreed over our organization structure.*

We would characterize our sample firm as being loosely coupled. The degree of relatedness between the core and peripheral sets influences the firm's susceptibility to environmental change.

Proposition 5: When there is strong agreement about the core set and the peripheral set (tight coupling), the firm will need to maintain stability.

We propose that firms that have a structure that is tightly coupled need to maintain stability and to avoid jolts. Consequently these firms seek to maintain the *status quo* and to avoid change. They will be the forceful organizations Daft and Weick (1984) describe which attempt to change environmental factors. Top management in these firms avoids adapting their schemas to the environment. Nisbett and Ross (1980) suggest that when knowledge is embodied with strongly held values, people will attempt to discredit uncongenial evidence. In schema theory, this is known as the perseverence effect that suggests resistance to change even in the face of contradictory evidence (Fiske and Taylor, 1984). Instead the top management may attempt to change the environment.

Other firms which are tightly coupled attempt to enact their environment such that they seek or perceive the environmental conditions that fit their organizational structure. For example, a firm with a tightly coupled structure might search for the same market conditions in different countries so that it can use the same business methods over and over again. In other words it searches for the conditions that match its knowledge and past experiences, thus avoiding change. Lyles (1988) gives an example of a joint venture sophisticated firm that utilizes the same techniques for joint venturing in every country regardless of the local conditions.

Tightly coupled firms have the greatest rigidity in the sense that they do not have flexibility in responding to environmental changes. At the same time, because they attempt to maintain stability, they are most affected by rapidly changing environments. Their key decision-makers are interested in the reduction of debate or disagreement that might lead to views that contradict the tightly coupled relationships in the knowledge structure, and they promote stability in the structure. The key decision-makers in tightly coupled firms are interested in reducing disagreement because it could cause the 'uncoupling' of the knowledge structure and create trauma for the firm.

Proposition 6: When there is disagreement (loose coupling), it enhances the firm's ability to adjust to change and to be flexible.

Firms with a loosely coupled structure incorporate more disagreement and alternative interpretations of how best to carry out the firm's mission. Changes can be made more easily than in tightly coupled firms and there will be more flexibility in action taking and strategies. Environmental jolts do not affect such firms as greatly as tightly coupled firms (Weick, 1979). These firms can adjust their strategies to deal with changing environmental conditions and they can incorporate new information into their structures more easily.

Disagreement about the peripheral set and about the core-peripheral linkage may enhance the firm's ability to adjust to changes and to be flexible. Multiple views may exist and create the acceptance of diversity of action steps. These provide the basis for debate on alternative knowledge schemas about expectations of events and actions. Interestingly Prahalad and Bettis (1986) suggest that the recognition of the importance of strategic variety may be on the decline.

Relationship between Complexity and Relatedness

The relationship between complexity and relatedness is developed in Table 4.2. Each quadrant denotes a variation in strategic management determined by the organizational knowledge structure. Each also shows the areas of vulnerability.

Proposition 7: Loosely coupled firms with simple structures usually are young, emerging firms.

Quadrant I shows the conditions for a young, emerging firm in which there is widespread agreement about the basic mission, but little agreement about how to achieve it. It is open to different interpretations of the environment and because of its simple-loosely coupled relationship, it is resilient. It can be risk-taking, innovative, and experimental in its approach to strategic management as long as its actions are consistent with the simple core structure.

Proposition 8: Firms with a simple structure which is tightly coupled can be effective at strategic management if the environment is not rapidly changing or if they enact their environment.

In Quadrant II are firms that have a simple structure that is tightly coupled to subgoals and beliefs about how to achieve them. Standard operating proce-

TABLE 4.2   Maintenance of Knowledge Structure

| | | *Degree of relatedness* | |
		Loosely coupled	Tightly coupled
	Simple	Adaptation: incremental changes Environmental interaction: some inclusion, resilience Strategic orientation: innovative Example: typical new ventures	Adaptation: maintenance Environmental interaction: stimuli rejection enactment Strategic orientation: seeks single industry Example: Polaroid
Complexity of structure	Complex	Adaptation: continuous development Environmental interaction: inclusion, self-interested interpretation Strategic orientation: seeks opportunity frequently in diverse industries Example: The new General Motors	Adaptation: maintenance Environmental interaction: stimuli rejection enactmen Strategic orientation: seeks industry that fits requirements Example: US Gypsum (USG Corp.)

dures and/or a strong commitment to the right way of doing things develop—as does a strong emotional commitment. There is frequently a sense of 'knowing the right way of managing' that permeates the entire firm. Typical firms in this quadrant would have a single business orientation or would be in environmental niches. Up until recently, Polaroid fell into this quadrant with its strong, but simple, knowledge about its mission coupled with a strong belief about how to conduct its business.

> *Proposition 9:* A complex structure that is loosely coupled leads the firm to more easily adapt to environmental changes.

A complex structure that is loosely coupled as in Quadrant III can perhaps be best illustrated by large firms in diverse product areas with diverse internal management systems and procedures. Choices about strategic opportunities are debated, and there is no consensus about the right methods of achieving them. Consequently, we propose that environmental events are not filtered out but are likely to be recognized somewhere in the organization by fitting with the diverse structures. These are the firms that Prahalad and Bettis (1986) address as diversifiers.

> *Proposition 10:* In a firm with a complex structure that is tightly coupled, strategic management should focus on maintenance and control of the environment.

The essential point in the last quadrant is that external constraints and rapid changes in the structure can serve to threaten the firm's survival. The best illustration of this type might be IBM who must reject and filter environmental events while attempting to compete in the rapidly changing information services industry. It has a strong knowledge of how best to carry out its strategy and well-developed management systems that need to be protected from change. It enjoys being in the powerful position of being able to enact its environment.

In summary, the present argument proposes that strategic actions are partially determined by the knowledge structure. The degree of complexity may influence a firm's repertoire of the definitions and understandings of how to handle different situations and events. Relatedness will influence what is retrieved and how quickly: in tightly coupled firms there is no need for debate over things that everyone believes to be true. Because organizations are social systems, the degree of consensus is an important determinant of what is learned and stored in the organizational learning structure.

STRATEGIC CHANGE AND KNOWLEDGE STRUCTURES

The core elements remain relatively stable over time. The patterns of decisions and actions represent the interpretation by management of the relationship between the organizational knowledge structure and external reality. Interpersonal interactions partially determine the degree of consensus about the peripheral set.

Hence, the patterns of decisions, the amount of consensus and the organizational structure are management's translation of the knowledge structure (Ranson *et al.*, 1980). It provides them with an initial reference for assessing the environment and determining the meaning of environment cues. This view is supported by Weick whose selection process describes the superimposition of causal maps that provided meaning in the past to current puzzling situations such that the maps would 'provide a reasonable interpretation of what has occurred or they may confuse things even more. These maps are like templates that reveal configurations that may make sense or may not' (1979, p. 131). The relatively stable core set and the peripheral set determine the lens used by management for understanding environmental changes, interactions, and chains of events.

Although the core set of knowledge elements and cause-effect beliefs rarely change, it seems that the relationships represented in the knowledge structure do become more complex over time as more elements are incorporated (Narayanan and Fahey, 1982). When simple beliefs about cause-effect are not questioned and are strongly held, they remain unchallenged and widely accepted. They serve as a base for the development of more complex cause-effect elements. The simple relationships that form the foundation become buried and are rarely openly debated.

The more recent elements are the ones that serve as a focus for organizational debate. These usually do not initially address the relationships in the core. Thus the core set are usually unquestioned, embedded knowledge elements that remain unchallenged unless a major strategic event occurs. The peripheral set, on the other hand, is the area in which organizational debate and alternative viewpoints emerge. The more tightly coupled the core set and the peripheral set, the more difficult it will be for the firm to make changes in its knowledge structure.

IMPLICATIONS AND CONCLUSIONS

As we mentioned at the beginning of the article, strategic management researchers are showing increased interest in the cognitions of the top management team. The theoretical propositions in this article are meant to begin a discussion about the existence and maintenance of organizational knowledge structures. One of the crucial points about these and the difference between an individual's schema is that the organizational knowledge structure is built out of a social process. What we are trying to analyse is how the social process of creating organizational knowledge produces differences among firms. We think that Prahalad and Bettis (1986) began the discussion by addressing dominant logic in a very broad way. We have attempted to address the idea of collective knowledge more specifically in the hopes of identifying ideas to be tested.

Ours is not the only approach for understanding how organizations process information and take actions. More sociologically-oriented researchers have developed approaches which focus more on organizational behaviours and social processes. For example, Sandelands and Stablein (1987) in arguing for the 'concept of organization mind' have drawn analogies between the behaviour of individuals in an organization and neurons in an individual brain. They have also suggested that organizations are capable of parallel processing as is the human nervous system. Mary Douglas, in her book *How Institutions Think* (1986) has described the ways societies and the structure of institutions affect the cognitions of the individuals within them. She has provided examples of the ways organizational characteristics affect what their members remember and forget. Through an analysis of the textile and wine industries, she showed that changing technologies can affect the ways organizational participants classify information.

Though the sociologically-oriented approach certainly provides useful insights into the ways external factors may affect knowledge structures, we think our more psychologically-oriented approach may be more useful in understanding the *detailed features* of knowledge structures and how these features are related to each other. The approaches are complementary and we hope that future theoretical work will provide an integration.

There is a volume of research being developed that tests the relationships of cognitive elements and organizational behaviours. This research appears to support further work in the area of organizational knowledge structures. Future work may yield new ways of understanding such topics as strategic momentum (Miller and Friesen, 1980; Tushman *et al.*, 1989), organizational learning (Lyles, 1988), and dominant general management logic (Prahalad and Bettis, 1986).

One obvious shortcoming of the previous body of work is that it has dealt only with organizational behaviours, with no attempt at assessing how knowledge is retained or used. Our theoretical proposals about organizational knowledge structures assume that there is a representation of complex events and their interpretations are stored in the collective knowledge of the firm. These knowledge structures may not be complete or accurate. What is stored and what is retrieved may depend on the existing knowledge structure, the events triggering retrieval and/or the interaction of the people. The degree of complexity and relatedness will influence these. Strategic responses to new situations may be the result of generalizing from the existing knowledge structure (Anderson, 1983).

This article is only a first step towards understanding how shared collective knowledge structures develop and shape the strategic actions of the firm. We hope that it may stimulate further research which will one day make it possible to understand the ways that the cognitions of executives affect the relationship between environmental change and strategic response.

REFERENCES

Abelson, R. P. (1981). "Psychological status of the script concept." *American Psychologist*, 36, 715–29.

Alba, J. W. and Hasher, L. (1983). "Is memory schematic?." *Psychological Bulletin*, 93, 2, 203–31.

Anderson, J. (1983). *The Architecture of Cognition*. Cambridge, Mass.: Harvard University Press.

Argyris, C. and Schon, D. (1978). *Organizational Learning: A Theory of Action Perspective*. Reading, Mass.: Addison-Wesley.

Astley, W. G., Axelsson, R., Butler, R. J., Hickson, D. J. and Wilson, D. C. (1982). "Complexity and cleavage: dual explanations of strategic decision-making." *Journal of Management Studies*, 19, 4, 357–75.

Bandura, A. (1977). *Social Learning Theory*. Englewood Cliffs, N. J.: Prentice-Hall.

Barnard, C. I. (1938). *Functions of the Executive*. Cambridge, Mass.: Harvard University Press.

Bartlett, F. C. (1932). *Remembering: A Study in Experimental and Social Psychology*. Cambridge: Cambridge University Press.

Bartunek, J. M. (1984). "Changing interpretative schemes and organizational restructuring: the example of a religious order." *Administrative Science Quarterly*, 29, 355–72.

Berger, P. L. and Luckmann, T. (1967). *The Social Construction of Reality*. New York: Doubleday Anchor.

Bourgeois, L. J. III. (1980). "Performance and consensus." *Strategic Management Journal*, 1, 227–48.

Bower, J. L. (1970). *Managing the Resource Allocation Process*. Boston, Mass.: Graduate School of Business Administration, Harvard University.

Brunsson, N. (1985). *The Irrational Organization: Irrationality as a Basis for Organizational Action and Change*. New York: Wiley.

Cyert, R. M. and March, J. G. (1963). *A Behavioral Theory of the Firm*. Englewood Cliffs, N.J.: Prentice-Hall.

Daft, R. L. and Weick, K. E. (1984). "Toward a model of organizations as interpretation systems." *Academy of Management Review*, 9, 2, 284–95.

Davis, T. R. and Luthans, F. (1980). "A social learning approach to organizational behavior." *Academy of Management Review*, 5, 2, 281–90.

Dess, G. G. (1987). "Consensus on strategy formulation and organizational performance: competitors in a fragmented industry." *Strategic Management Journal*, 8, 3, 259–77.

Dess, G. G. and Origer, N. K. (1987). "Environment, structure, and consensus in strategy formulation: a conceptual integration." *Academy of Management Review*, 12, 2, 313–30.

Douglas, M. (1986). *How Institutions Think*. Syracuse, N.Y.: Syracuse University Press.

Dunbar, R. L. M., Dutton, J. M. and Torbert, W. R. (1982). "Crossing mother: ideological constraints on organizational improvements." *Journal of Management Studies*, 19, 1, 91–108.

Dutton, J. E. and Jackson, S. E. (1987). "Categorizing strategic issues: links to organizational action." *Academy of Management Review*, 12, 1, 76–90.

Fahey, L. and Narayanan, V. K. (1986). "Organizational beliefs and strategic adaptation." *Proceedings of the National Academy of Management*, Chicago, Ill., 7–11.

Fayol, H. (1949). *General and Industrial Management*, tr. C. Stours. London: Pitman.

Fiol, C. M. and Lyles, M. A. (1985). "Organizational learning." *Academy of Management Review*, 10, 4, 803–13.

Fiske, W. T. and Taylor, S. E. (1984). *Social Cognition*. Reading, Mass.: Addison-Wesley.

Ford, J. and Hegarty, H. (1984). "Decision makers' beliefs about the causes and effects of structure: an exploratory study." *Academy of Management Journal,* 27, 271–91.

Gioia, D. A. and Manz, C. C. (1985). "Linking cognition and behavior: a script processing interpretation of vicarious learning." *Academy of Management Review,* 10, 3, 527–39.

Gioia, D. A. and Poole, P. P. (1984). "Scripts in organizational behavior." *Academy of Management Review,* 9, 3, 449–59.

Hambrick, D. C. (1981). "Environmental strategy and power within top management teams." *Administrative Science Quarterly,* 26, 253–75.

Hedberg, B. L. T. (1981). "How organizations learn and unlearn." In Nystrom, Paul C. and Starbuck, William H. (Eds.), *Handbook of Organizational Design.* Oxford: Oxford University Press.

Hedberg, B. L. T., Nystrom, C. and Starbuck, W. H. (1976). "Camping on seesaws? prescriptions for a self-designing organization." *Administrative Science Quarterly,* 21, 41–65.

Huff, A. S. (1983). "Industry influence on strategy reformulation." *Strategic Management Journal,* 4, 3, 119–31.

Jelinek, M. (1979). *Institutionalizing Innovation: A Study of Organizational Learning Systems.* New York: Praeger.

Kahneman, D., Slovic, P. and Tversky, A. (1982). *Judgement Under Uncertainty: Heuristics and Biases.* Cambridge: Cambridge University Press.

Kotter, J. (1982). *General Managers.* New York: Free Press.

Kuhn, T. S. (1962). *The Structure of Scientific Revolutions.* Chicago: University of Chicago Press.

Levitt, B. and March, J. G. (1988). "Organizational learning." *Annual Review of Sociology,* 14, 319–40.

Lord, R. G. and Foti, R. J. (1986). "Schema theories, information processing, and organizational behavior." In Sims, Henry P. Jr., Gioia, Dennis A., and Associates, *The Thinking Organization.* San Francisco: Jossey-Bass, 20–48.

Lurigio, A. J. and Carroll, J. S. (1985). "Probation officers' schemata of offenders: content, development and impact on treatment decisions." *Journal of Personality and Social Psychology,* 48, 1112–26.

Lyles, M. A. (1988). "Learning among joint venture sophisticated firms." *Management International Review,* 28, 85–98.

Lyles, M. A. and Mitroff, I. I. (1980). "Organizational problem formulation: an empirical study." *Administrative Science Quarterly,* 25, 102–19.

Lyles, M. A. and Mitroff, I. I. (1985). "The impact of sociopolitical influences on strategic problem formulation." *Advances in Strategic Management,* 3, 69–81.

McKeithen, K. B., Reitman, J. S., Rueter, H. H. and Hirtle, S. C. (1981). "Knowledge organization and skill differences in computer programmers." *Cognitive Psychology,* 13, 307–25.

Manz, C. C. and Sims, H. R. Jr. (1981). "Vicarious learning: the influence of modeling on organizational behavior." *Academy of Management Review,* 6, 1, January, 105–14.

March, J. G. and Olsen, J. P. (1975). "Organizational learning and the ambiguity of the past." *European Journal of Political Research,* 3, 147–71.

March, J. G., Spoull, L. S. and Tamuz, M. (1991). "Learning from samples of one or fewer." *Organization Science,* 2, 1–13.

Martin, J. (1982). "Stories and scripts in organizational settings." In Hastorf, A. and Isen, A. (Eds.), *Cognitive Social Psychology.* New York: Elsevier-North-Holland, 225–305.

Mason, R. O. and Mitroff, I. I. (1981). *Challenging Strategic Planning Assumptions.* New York: Wiley.

Meyer, A. (1982). "Adapting to environmental jolts." *Administrative Science Quarterly,* 27, 515–37.

Miller, D. and Friesen, P. (1980). "Momentum and revolution in organizational adaptation." *Academy of Management Journal,* 23, 591–614.

Mintzberg, H. (1982). *Power in and Around Organizations.* Englewood Cliffs, N.J.: Prentice-Hall.

Mintzberg, H., Raisinghani, D. and Theoret, A. (1976). "The structure of 'unstructured' decision processes." *Administrative Science Quarterly,* 21, 246–75.

Narayanan, V. and Fahey, L. (1982). "The micro-politics of strategy formulation." *Academy of Management Review,* 7, 25–34.

Nisbett, R. E. and Ross, L. (1980). *Human Inference: Strategies and Shortcomings of Social Judgment.* Englewood-Cliffs, N.J.: Prentice-Hall.

Ouchi, W. G. (1980). "Markets, bureaucracies, and clans." *Administrative Science Quarterly,* 25, 129–41.

Pfeffer, J. (1981). *Power in Organizations.* Marshfeld, Mass.: Pitman.

Prahalad, C. K. and Bettis, R. A. (1986). "The dominant logic: a new linkage between diversity and performance." *Strategic Management Journal,* 7, 6, 485–501.

Ranson, S., Hinings, B. and Greenwood, R. (1980). "The structuring of organizational structures." *Administrative Science Quarterly,* 25, 1, March, 1–17.

Sandelands, L. and Stablein, K. (1987). "The concept of an organization mind." In Ditomaso, N. and Bacharach, S. (Eds.), *Research in the Sociology of Organizations.* San Francisco: JAI Press.

Schank, R. C. and Abelson, R. P. (1977). *Scripts, Plans, Goals, and Understanding: An Inquiry into Human Knowledge Systems.* Hillsdale, N.J.: Erlbaum.

Schwenk, C. (1988). "The cognitive perspective in strategic decision making." *Journal of Management Studies,* 25, 41–56.

Shrivastava, P. (1983). "A typology of organizational learning systems." *Journal of Management Studies,* 20, 7–29.

Shrivastava, P. and Schneider, S. (1984). "Organizational frames of reference." *Human Relations,* 37, 10, 795–809.

Smircich, L. and Stubbart, C. (1985). "Strategic management in an enacted world." *Academy of Management Review,* 10, 724–36.

Taylor, S. E. and Crocker, J. (1981). "Schematic bases of social information processing." In Higgins, E. T., Herman, C. P. and Zazza, M. P. (Eds.), *Social Cognition.* Hillsdale, N.J.: Erlbaum.

Thompson, J. D. (1967). *Organizations in Action.* New York: McGraw-Hill.

Tushman, M. L., Virany, B. and Romanelli, E. (1989). "Effects of CEO and executive team succession on subsequent organization performance." Columbia University Working Paper, February.

Walsh, J. P. and Fahey, L. (1986). "The rule of negotiated belief structures in strategy making." *Journal of Management,* **12**, 325–38.

Weick, K. E. (1979). *The Social Psychology of Organizing.* Reading, Mass.: Addison-Wesley.

Weick, K. E. and Bougon, M. G. (1986). "Organizations as cognitive maps." In Sims, Henry P. Jr., Gioia, Dennis A, and Associates (Eds.), *The Thinking Organization.* San Francisco: Jossey-Bass, 102–35.

Zaleznik, A. (1977). "Managers and leaders: are they different?" *Harvard Business Review,* **55**, 3, 67–78.

5

EPRINET: Leveraging Knowledge in the Electric Utility Industry

Marina M. Mann, Richard L. Rudman,
Thomas A. Jenckes, Barbara C. McNurlin

INTRODUCTION

Once, it was those with the most information who had the competitive edge. But in the the Information Age—when we are challenged by an explosion of unselected information—the edge belongs to those who have the right information;—and those who have it at the right time to apply it to their advantage.

As Peter Drucker (1989) puts it, "knowledge has become the real capital of a developed economy." But our vast, unapplied deposits of corporate knowledge and information have little power when they're tucked away in reports, file drawers, and databases. Organizations today do not lack information. They lack the tools to get the right information to the right people at the right time.

The Electric Power Research Institute (EPRI) is the research and development consortium for the U.S. electric utility industry. It is an organization whose prime mission today is to deliver research information and expertise to support its member utilities in their suddenly turbulent business environment. Originally, EPRI's mission extended only to the management of its R&D program. Delivery of its R&D results to the point of use is a new obligation. This simple, yet profound, shift is causing a major redefinition of the organizational structure, jobs, and ways of working at the Institute. Information technology is playing a central role in the unfolding scenario.

As an information provider, EPRI began to work with the concept of knowledge-as-capital early on. Its experience in managing the transition to that new economic reality may hold lessons for other organizations as they employ information technologies to meet the challenges of this increasingly competitive age.

Reprinted by special permission from the *MIS Quarterly*, Volume 15, Number 3, September 1991. Copyright 1991 by the Society for Information Management and the Management Information Systems Research Center at the University of Minnesota.

The Electric Power Research Institute

The Electric Power Research Institute is one of America's largest private research firms. Its 760 staff members are located at its Palo Alto, California, headquarters, in Washington, D.C., and at research sites around the country. The heart of EPRI is its six technical research divisions: Generation and Storage, Nuclear Power, Environment, Electrical Systems, Customer Systems, and Exploratory Research.

EPRI was formed in 1972 by the electric utility industry. At the time, the U.S. government was proposing to establish a federal agency to manage a national energy research program because of technical problems too large for any single utility or vendor to solve alone. The industry persuaded the Senate to allow it to establish its own industry-managed and industry-supported cooperative R&D program—EPRI.

To date, EPRI has invested $4.3 billion in research funds. These funds have come from the contributions of 700 member utilities, representing 70 percent of the total U.S. electricity sales (in kilowatt hours). In a recently initiated program, EPRI added its first international affiliate this spring—the British utility Power-Gen.

EPRI's business is information. Its product is knowledge. EPRI contracts with energy experts in 36 countries to research subjects of interest to its members. It is staffed with 450 scientists and engineers who manage some 1,600 R&D projects at a time. These projects, conducted by over 400 utility, university, commercial, government, and other R&D contractors, span many technologies—from electricity generation at the power station to electricity use in homes and businesses. Many of the issues they deal with are global—acid rain, the greenhouse effect, and superconductivity, to name just three.

As the hub—between the researching organizations and its members—EPRI must not only establish links among researchers and members but must also provide access to information and people across time and space.

EPRI's goal is to help its members compete successfully. As Gregory Reuger, senior vice president of Pacific Gas and Electric Co., one of the largest investor-owned gas and electric utilities in the United States, said in 1990,

We get our competitive edge by implementing new technologies more quickly than our competitors.

The Challenge

EPRI and its members urgently needed ways to compress the "information float"—from the findings of R&D projects, to the analysis of their results, to the application of those results in industry. Moreover, EPRI was suffering from "infosclerosis"—the hardening and clogging of its information arteries. The sheer volume and complexity of its scientific information made effectively moving that information in and out extremely difficult. In this respect, EPRI is at the "bleeding edge" of the Information Age, facing one of the major challenges of the 1990s—how to leverage its huge wealth of knowledge.

A staggering amount of information rolls off EPRI's R&D "production line." EPRI's databases contain over eight gigabytes of information from its 19 years of research—the equivalent of 2.7 million pages of text with diagrams and formulas. Last year alone it published 504 technical reports, distributed over 1.7 million two-page report summaries, shipped more than 12,000 copies of EPRI-developed software, held over 200 technical workshops and seminars, and answered over 13,000 hotline telephone inquiries.

Timeliness was an even more serious problem. Research results were *unavailable* for one to 24 months, while detailed reports were being produced. And then, when those sometimes massive technical reports made it out the door, members were expected to wade through them to find the nuggets of information they needed.

To unclog its information arteries, EPRI either had to expand staff significantly or leverage its efforts with information technology. Management chose the latter.

In a period of change, the timeliness of information is especially critical to competitive success. The electric utility industry has been in a period of severe change for more than a decade. Until passage of the U.S. Public Utility Regulatory Policies Act in 1978, individual utility service territories in the United States were defined and protected by federal regulation. Today, electric utilities compete for their large customers against independent power producers, gas utilities, other electric utilities (nearby or far away), and the large customers themselves, through cogeneration.

Furthermore, utilities must contend with a rising tide of environmental concern. Pacific Gas and Electric (PG&E), for example, like other utilities, today includes a commitment to the environment in its corporate goals. The utility is working on renewable energy sources, on bridging to these renewables, and in cooperation with many environmental groups.

The rate of change in this industry is likely to accelerate, so timely information will be increasingly critical to manage that change. Yet information overload presents growing obstacles to finding "the information needle in the haystack."

Solving the information delivery challenge for the present, as well as laying the groundwork for the future, is critical to EPRI's survival. Therefore, offering "value delivery" has become the focus of the information technology division. This means adding value to the research through new delivery mechanisms because the traditional delivery approaches no longer suffice.

As EPRI aims to fulfill its new dual mission—producing research and delivering knowledge—the corporate structure, business processes, and methods of work are changing.

The Vision

EPRI's vision for meeting today's challenge is to assist member utilities in exploiting EPRI's product (knowledge) as a strategic business resource, whenever and from wherever they choose. The goal is to assist them in increasing their efficiency, effectiveness, and competitiveness.

To accomplish this vision, EPRI is building state-of-the-art electronic information and communication services that (1) leverage its staff's time in creating knowledge and (2) leverage its members' time in acquiring that knowledge.

The delivery vehicle—the EPRINET communications and information network—is intended to transcend the boundaries of time, space, organization, and know-how by being available globally, around the clock. Its natural-language front end gives easy access to online information. Its expert system-based products tap the knowledge of energy experts. Its electronic mail opens up person-to-person communications. And its video-conferencing fosters small-group communication. Links between these various offerings expand information gathering and communication possibilities even more.

EPRINET is designed not only to deliver information to people but also to bring people together to pursue common interests, while leveraging EPRI scientists' time and knowledge.

In short, EPRI is applying information technology to the production, distribution, and consumption of knowledge. EPRI is in the sixth year of implementing this vision and the second year of seeing its members benefit from using EPRINET.

EPRINET

EPRINET is an electronic linkup to energy research information worldwide. It is based on the shopping center concept of having "anchor services" and "specialty services." Anchor services continually draw people into the network. The four anchor services are electronic mail, natural English language retrieval system, electronic directories and catalogs, and videoconferencing.

The specialty services are specialized to a kind of use (e.g., quick browsing), or a specific field (e.g., hydropower generation), or a job function (e.g., research engineer). They help people deal with information overload and help them find colleagues with similar interests. For descriptions of the current EPRINET services, see Figure 5.1.

These services must have enough breadth and depth for people to explore a subject, as they would in a conversation. If too narrowly defined, the services would be too limited to be helpful, and usage would cease after a short exploration. An example might be an on-line forum that discusses just one method of keeping biological organisms out of hydropower plant machinery. Engineers want to explore and compare various options, not read about only one.

The diversity in EPRINET is built-in, and growing, in order to satisfy the changing information needs of EPRI's diverse community.

Anchor Services

- Electronic Mail. EPRI uses the IBM PROFS electronic mail system as its basic communication mechanism—to bring people into EPRINET on a regular basis.
- Natural Language Retrieval System. The underlying information retrieval technology is natural language. Enter a few keywords in English and the system responds with the items in that database that contain those words. Users can search online directories, catalogs, abstracts, and papers with this mechanism.
- Electronic Directories and Catalogs. The main directory in EPRINET describes EPRI's technical staff—their names, positions, relevant publications, and recent projects by area of expertise. The network also contains catalogs of EPRI research work, including status reports of ongoing and completed projects, and abstracts and summaries of EPRI technical reports, papers, articles, videotapes, and speeches.

  In the future, EPRI will put its Technical Interest Profiles (TIPs) online. These profiles, filled out by member staff, identify the kinds of information they want to receive from EPRI. EPRI has used TIPS not only to feed the right information to members but also to brief its researchers on the areas members want researched.
- Videoconferencing. This service was introduced at EPRI in April and allows people to converse via voice and video, group-to-group. Used in conjunction with EPRINET, it can extend the types of person-to-person communications available.

  For example, suppose that participants in an online forum (an ongoing, electronic specialty service for exchanging information and discussion on a specific topic) decide they need the most up-to-date happenings on that subject. Rather than scan the research papers, they prefer a videoconference. They use EPRINET to identify the EPRI experts and then send a request to the appropriate EPRI program manager to make videoconferencing arrangements with those experts. An announcement is then posted telling forum members that at, say, 9:00 a.m. Tuesday there will be a point-to-point (evolving to point-to-multipoint) videoconference on topic X.

  The current goal in videoconferencing is to keep the groups small (five to six people at each site), to achieve a workshop environment, at low cost.

Specialty Services

Drawing on the anchor services, EPRI continues to add "knowledge packages"—products and services combined to make the technical nuggets in EPRI's knowledge fund easier to locate and use. They help members deal with information overload.

- Forums offer an electronic gathering place for information and discussion about a particular subject. Forums are usually on hot topics, such as EMF (electric and magnetic fields). Each forum can have its own news briefs, announcements, directory of forum participants, report database, and software models.
- News Briefs are just that: up-to-the minute industry news.
- Ask the EPRI Expert. Forums often include an *Ask the Expert* facility for answering questions online. In some cases, they list the names of the experts in that technical area. When the user selects a name, a template for sending an electronic message to that person appears. In other cases, the user can send a question to the *Ask the Expert* mailbox for review by an EPRI staff member who routes it to the appropriate expert.
- Bulletin Boards, where people can electronically post ideas and thoughts for others to see, allow participants to converse textually one-to-many or many-to-one.
- EPRIGEMS are interactive, diskette-based computer modules that use expert system technology to capture the results of EPRI research and the knowledge of EPRI staff. They are stand-alone EPRI products, some of which can combine with EPRINET.

(continued on next page)

FIGURE 5.1 EPRINET Services

- Each module works to solve a particular utility problem, such as boiler maintenance, stress corrosion cracking, or nuclear plant life extension. They present a new approach to packaging and delivering EPRI knowledge—to help utilities successfully apply EPRI technology in high-value situations.

  At a certain point in some EPRIGEMS, the product asks if the user wants to talk to an expert. If the answer is yes, the package displays a list of experts. When the user selects one or more experts, the system automatically logs the user onto EPRINET (assuming the PC is connected via modem to a telephone line) and the electronic mail system, so the user can type in a query.
- ElectriGuide™, an offline electronic directory, is a research catalog on CD-ROM. It contains three major databases, with abstracts of 7,000 EPRI technical reports, and descriptions of 1,000 EPRI products and 23,000 research projects. It also includes software packages and full texts of some technical documents, with illustrations. In addition it contains color slide presentations in areas such as demand-side management and end-user forecasting. After using the CD, users can log on to EPRINET and order published and audiovisual items online.

FIGURE 5.1   EPRINET Services (*Continued*)

Redesigning Business Processes

As EPRINET was first being conceived and built, starting in 1984, cultural change was also taking place as EPRI redefined its mission. At the time, management believed that the two efforts—EPRINET and cultural change—could be undertaken separately. However, in hindsight, it appears that the instability caused by the cultural redesign significantly affected the development of EPRINET.

Information systems executives who undertake similar, large, organization-changing projects in the midst of a general organizational change need to be aware of how to work through such instability. This section discusses not only what was done at EPRI but also the managerial lessons we learned from our experience.

Readying the organization for new ways of working

There were four aspects to readying the organization to work in new ways:

- Undertake intense automation
- Encourage cultural change
- Select strategic EPRINET products
- Market the new system

These aspects were not addressed in sequence, and they were not done just once. EPRI is currently in a second go-round, planning and implementing the next phases of EPRINET. This cycle will continue.

Intense Automation

Readying EPRI began with a period of intense automation from 1984 to 1987. The goal was to leverage EPRI's scientific staff resources with information technology. During this automation period, the information technology division concentrated, in large part, on:

1. Raising the level of computer literacy among the staff
2. Establishing connectivity among four internal computer environments
3. Developing external connectivity
4. Building a core of strategic databases

At that time, the utilities were experiencing similar developments as well. For the specifics of the automation effort, see Figure 5.2.

Encouraging Cultural Change

Accompanying the technical changes were cultural changes. The magnitude of those human changes becomes apparent when one considers that the average age of the EPRI scientific staff was over 45 years. The staff had not been raised during the computer age.

Moreover, EPRI staff had to accept real changes in their roles. For one thing, they were now responsible for delivering the results of their R&D research projects to members. They found themselves at the front line of the new emphasis—from research production to "value delivery." They learned to travel with laptop computers, retrieve information electronically, and "talk" to contractors and colleagues by electronic mail rather than telephone or face-to-face.

Many EPRI staff members changed reluctantly. But the time savings they realized made converts. As John Scheibel, of the Generation and Storage Division, reported:

> *I used to call my contractors every day, with only a 50/50 chance of making contact. With EPRINET, I have cut my telephoning by two-thirds.*

After using EPRINET, the R&D managers began to consider their workstations essential. By 1988, the transformation had advanced to the point that when EPRI's president announced EPRIGEMS (expert systems for diagnosing and solving specific utility problems) more than enough managers volunteered to prepare the first set. In fact, many pursued the idea on their own, with guidance from the core EPRIGEMS team. Today, 12 EPRIGEMS are available and a dozen more are in development.

1. Raising the Level of Computer Literacy

   • Created a State-of-the-Art Data Center. The center is equipped with enough processing throughput, storage, and communications capabilities to position EPRI for the 1990s.
   • Introduced Electronic Mail. IBM's PROFS electronic mail system was implemented in 1985 as a strategic product for raising the computer literacy of the staff. Persuading staff to use it required its active use by EPRI's president, senior executives, and project managers, so that usage would trickle down from senior management and up from project managers.
   • Installed PCs on Virtually Every Desk. In 1984, there were only 25 PCs in EPRI. Today there are more than 600. In fact, there is more processing power on EPRI desktops now than in the data center. And a cooperative processing environment is evolving, to share processing among machines.
   • Established a Lending Library of Laptop PCs. These menu-driven loaners support the traveling technical staff. On average, EPRI project managers spend 15–30% of their time traveling. If they carry a laptop, the "out of office experience" wastes far less time.
   • Created New Systems for Managing R&D Projects. A suite of programs was written to help project managers use computers to administer research projects. All the programs are menu-driven, are linked to databases, and are supported by both printed and online instructions.
   • Formed a Broad User Support Service. A general telephone help line operates 8 hours a day supporting in-house and commercial software. A 24-hour walk-in center was established for two years, until it was no longer required. A software lending library with more than 200 commercial programs was also established. All, of course, are protected by regular virus-protection programs.
   • Began an Intensive Computer Training Program. In-house computer training initially concentrated on introductory one to two-hour classes in the most commonly used software programs. In late 1988, training was expanded by placing members of the information technology division "on the floor" in the R&D divisions. And in 1991, more advanced classes became the emphasis.

2. Establishing Internal Connectivity. In 1988, EPRI began addressing text and file transfer among its four computer environments—IBM mainframe, IBM PCs and clones, Macintosh, and NBI word processors. The goal was to enable the staff to electronically move documents *in revisable format* from machine to machine, using PROFS and a translation program among word processing packages.

3. Developing External Connectivity. Management selected the IBM Information Network (IIN), supplemented by Tymnet, for high-speed, secure, global transmission of data and large files. (About 40% of the U.S. electric utilities lease lines to that network.)

   Then, PROFS was extended through IIN, so the technical staff could manage EPRI research and communicate with contractors operating at EPRI off-site research projects. PROFS was also customized to transparently send and receive messages from two other international networks: BITNET (now Internet) and MCI Mail.

4. Building a Core of Strategic Databases. As noted in Figure 5.1, these databases constitute catalogs and directories of EPRI technical staff, projects, technical reports, and products as well as status reports, software, videotapes, and speeches.

FIGURE 5.2   Intense Automation to Leverage EPRI Scientific Staff, 1984–1987

Selecting Strategic Products

At the same time, EPRI information technology management was analyzing the information flows and information needs within EPRI as well as among its members, its R&D contractors, universities, and industry organizations. They used the information linkage methodology developed by Kenneth Primozic and Edward Primozic (Primozic, et al., 1990) of IBM to identify the services and products that would offer strategic business advantages to EPRI's members. EPRI and utility staff employed the methodology in a three-day brainstorming workshop led by the methodology's creator, Kenneth Primozic, to distill the vision of the EPRINET venture. The objective: to focus the EPRINET effort to achieve competitive advantage for EPRI members.

Senior management began by stating: *Our goal is to leverage knowledge as a strategic resource. EPRI will be both an R&D organization and a knowledge provider.* Primozic responded: *To whom is EPRI linked in creating and distributing knowledge?*

The group identified contractors, research organizations, universities, government agencies, and technology as the key *inputs* to the knowledge base. It identified the utility industry, universities, research labs, government regulation/policy, and knowledge-as-capital as the *outputs*. The diagram in Figure 5.3 defines EPRI's "extended enterprise."

Within each of these organizations, the team identified different audiences—executives, middle management, research engineers, design and construction engineers, and operations people. Then the team looked at the present and future power relationships, asking: *Who is the buyer and who is the seller in each link?*

In discussing these links and relationships and how they might change, the management team saw that some of their suppliers and customers might become their competitors, if EPRI did not make a sustained effort to retain its position as the hub of research in the industry.

Primozic then asked: *In what ways can EPRI leverage knowledge?* Once the group had enumerated many ways, they studied each one to answer the question: *What is the most important way you can leverage this knowledge?*

Their answer (after much discussion): "reintegrate, synthesize, package, and distribute knowledge among the 1,600 contracts (on the input side) and the 700

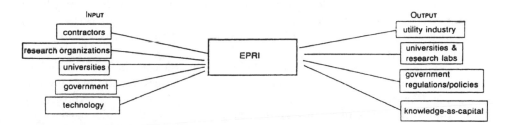

FIGURE 5.3 Information Linkage Analysis

member utilities (on the output side)." Thus focused, the group went on to define the kinds of information packages that needed to flow along the linkages for EPRI to be effective, the required timeframes, and the depth of information in each package.

EPRI also established the EPRINET Utility Advisory Group (UAG) to involve its member utilities in its information technology planning right from the start. The group was unusual for EPRI in that it represented a utility in microcosm. That is, unlike EPRI's many specialized advisory committees and task forces, the UAG represented the range of utility responsibilities, including technology transfer, power plant operations, R&D engineering, and design. One of the group's first assignments was to describe the utility engineer of the future and what information technologies he or she would need.

On the basis of these analyses, management defined several critical success factors that would give EPRINET a sustainable competitive advantage:

- Establish the "right" mix of product offerings
- Maintain the perspectives of the several market segments—that is, the types of people who would be using it (executives, planners, research engineers, and operations people)
- Use expert system technology and natural-language interfaces to make the system easy to use and easy to access by infrequent users
- Distill the mountains of information into practical "packages," such as report summaries, R&D project status reports, news of hot topics, and EPRIGEMS
- Build a timely, reliable, secure, global distribution channel

From July to October 1988, EPRINET was piloted internally by EPRI staff. In October, it was released for beta testing to 60 utility representatives in a forum on EMF (electric and magnetic fields)—a hot topic in the industry. This pilot is detailed in Figure 5.4.

Marketing EPRINET

The EPRINET team is taking a two-pronged approach to marketing the network. One group of three promotes use of the network internally among EPRI project and program managers. Another similar-size sales and marketing team deals with member utilities and with non-utility participants such as research contractors.

The first production version of EPRINET was released in May 1990. The marketing campaign began soon after. The number of users has climbed monthly since then (Figure 5.5). The steep rise beginning in September 1990 is directly attributable to the work of the marketing teams. By April, EPRINET participants represented 258 utilities, along with 248 private contractors, vendors, universities, and government and industry organizations. Virtually every EPRI employee was connected, as well. The marketing activities are described in Figure 5.6.

As the world's major supporter of electric and magnetic fields (EMF) research, EPRI is a prime source of information on the possible health effects of EMF. As a consequence, in the 1980s, Institute staff was devoting more and more time to fielding inquiries, providing documents, and explaining concepts to members, the public, the press, government agencies, and researchers.

EPRI had developed EMDEX, an EMF monitoring device that could be worn for extended periods to gather and store exposure data for later retrieval and analysis. In late 1988, the EMF project manager was establishing a project to test this device. He talked to the EPRINET team about using the network as the communication link among the volunteers wearing and using the device.

The three-month EMDEX test would therefore have a dual challenge: (1) to provide information about the rapidly evolving EMF topic, and (2) to evaluate EPRINET. A special-interest EMF forum was established on EPRINET to provide electronic mail, news, EMF information retrieval, and a service called Ask EMF, for asking questions of experts.

The study participants, who were geographically dispersed, were mostly new to online information systems. In their assessments of EPRINET, the majority described it as very useful, saying they got fast-breaking EMF news, had convenient access to EPRI staff and project colleagues, and saved time in sending messages. Electronic mail alone proved beneficial.

Such interutility communication is rising slowly, according to interviews with heavy users of EPRINET. They realize that by exchanging information with other utilities working on the same problems, they can avoid reinventing the wheel and more effectively use their research money.

FIGURE 5.4   The EMF Forum Pilot

Lessons on managing business change

As mentioned, EPRINET's development took place at the same time top management was redefining EPRI's mission. Building a communication system of this magnitude, during a time of such significant change, yielded several lessons on managing business redesign:

- Work "underground" for as long as practical
- Build support from many quarters simultaneously
- Get a corporate sponsor early
- Listen carefully to the corporate naysayers
- As the systems executive, be the change agent
- Do not have the same lead person during the entire project
- Underpromise and overdeliver
- Bet on people, not ideas

Work "Underground" for as Long as Practical

A new idea is fragile and must be carefully nurtured. Publicity triggers the corporate immune systems, as Gifford Pinchot III (1988) says in *The Intrapreneur's Ten Commandments*. So, until an idea can survive on its own, it must be protected.

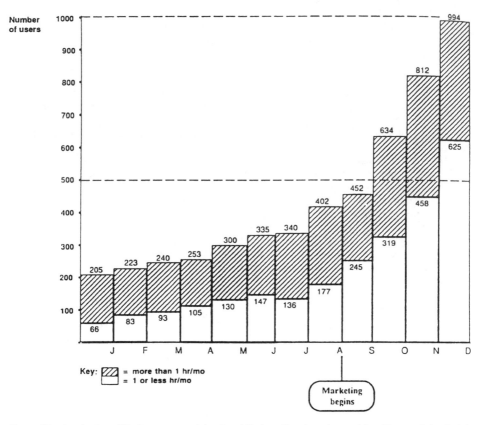

Note: Number in the white bar area pertains to white bar. Number above striped bar pertains to total for both bars.

FIGURE 5.5 Member Utility Staff Using EPRINET, 1990

To "grow" the EPRINET concept, a few people at EPRI spent half a day discussing how it would work, what kinds of problems it would solve, and which types of electronic tools people would need. They conceived the analogy of a shopping mall, combining a few "anchor tenants" with a variety of more-specialized services.

The team initially worked underground to put some "meat" on the ideas. The goal was to determine whether the concept of EPRINET really addressed the main problems facing EPRI—the collection, synthesis, and dissemination of massive amounts of information. EPRI also drew on the expertise of the consultants at Strategic Decisions in San Francisco to help create the system's framework.

Working underground, a team can make great progress. But, once the project becomes public, the review cycle—with its reports to committees and management—slows the pace significantly. During the underground period, the

- Promote It Internally. When EPRINET was introduced, the project team found some of the R&D staff reluctant to support the network. They did not want R&D money diverted from other projects. Only by demonstrating EPRINET's value—in leveraging staff and member time to produce research and transfer the results—were these staff won over. Now the converts rely on the system.

  The job of internal marketing is twofold: (1) encourage EPRI's managers to get others to sign up for EPRINET, and (2) put as much of their project work as possible onto the system. As the hubs of EPRI's research, these managers must spearhead use and continually put more of their project work online for EPRINET to become a way of life.

- Learn From and Use the Pilot. The successful pilot project proved to be an important contributor to kicking off the internal and external marketing efforts. Because few people like to be first to use a new product, the pilot provided an example others could follow.

  The pilot also provided user feedback. The EPRINET team discovered from the pilot, for example, that more understandable installation instructions were needed. The pilot group told them that getting started was the hardest part of using EPRINET. The team took that problem to heart and developed more materials for new users—including a pocket guide and quick-reference card.

- Lay Out a Launch Plan. With the new user materials in hand, the marketing manager laid out a launch plan. The first stage was to make the major target market—member utilities—aware of EPRINET's existence. The marketing team initiated an orientation program, with a standard script, slides, and handouts to be used initially at the largest 60-member utilities. The team worked with the manager of EPRI technology transfer at each of these utilities to schedule the presentations. In the presentations, they used such marketing techniques as pointing out competitive utilities that were signing up more employees.

- Begin the Promotion Campaign. Promotion began with a product announcement, using the traditional EPRI channels—memos, announcement sheets, and so forth. The team put together a shrink-wrapped introductory package, including the user manual and diskette. To start promotion off with a bang, they offered free sign-up for users, from mid-1990 to year end.

  The marketing team used every available opportunity to increase awareness of EPRINET. In addition to on-site visits, they had booths at industry trade shows (to increase name recognition) and spoke at conferences.

- Perform Market Research. Ideally, market research to uncover target audiences and their needs is done while a product is in development. The EPRINET project did not initiate such a study until late 1990.

  The findings of a study by the research firm of Kearns & West provided the driving force for EPRINET's external marketing campaign in 1991. The study identified utility engineers as the primary initial audience, followed by research and development staff, and then planning and forecasting staff. Last on the list was senior management, because they ranked online services as not directly valuable to them. They are an important indirect audience, however.

  Upon distributing the survey results throughout EPRI, the marketing team was pleasantly surprised to see certain project managers become more involved in EPRINET. These managers saw in the report that their projects had high user interest. So the survey had the unexpected result of spurring interest among these information providers, because it gave them feedback that their work was important.

(continued on next page)

FIGURE 5.6 Marketing EPRINET

- Define the 1991 Marketing Campaign. Based on the Kearns & West study, the 1991 marketing program stressed the theme of delivering value to customers, with two thrusts: encourage new customers and retain current customers. The month-by-month program was laid out, with about 30 activities in each area.

  To encourage new customers, telemarketing is being used to follow up with people who have seen the demonstration. The caller asks if the attendee received the promotion materials and whether they have ordered the product, and, if not, why?

  The team also initiated "targeted group" marketing to people with a common interest within a utility or among utilities—stressing the group communication and coordination benefits. The first targeted group was the 200 managers of technology transfer who encourage EPRI's use within their utilities.

  The marketing group also prepared materials for special interest groups, such as customer systems staff, who deal with end-use systems (electric cars, alternative generation, and other consumer areas). Most recently, they began promoting the system to non-utilities, significantly broadening their potential market.

  To retain existing customers, the team initiated a letter-writing campaign, because it is cheaper to retain a customer than to find a new one. This campaign appears to be effective in getting users to remember to use EPRINET. The first letter—to new users—welcomes them onto the system and encourages them to establish the EPRINET habit by logging on to the system at least once a week for two months. This letter asks for their impressions of the system. The second letter—to active users who have not logged on for one month—tells them what they missed. The third letter—to users who have ordered the package but have not logged on—tells them the benefits they will receive and how to find help getting started.

  The external marketing campaign started in mid-1990, and the effects are beginning to show up. The largest growth has been among low-usage participants (see Figure 5.5).

FIGURE 5.6 Marketing EPRINET (*Continued*)

EPRINET team created a crude design, developed a business plan, defined phase 1 and phase 2 products, involved people from all technical divisions and some customers, and sought out sponsor-mentors and pockets of support.

Build Support From Many Quarters Simultaneously

Project teams must spend a great deal of time creating an environment where an idea can survive on its own. Once the project is released to general scrutiny, it is hit with a barrage of reasons why it is a poor idea. If it has not been thoroughly fleshed out and if it does not have pockets of support around the organization to counter those arguments, it will die from lack of commitment. The best places to find initial supporters are among the organization's innovators. Everyone knows who they are. They like new ideas. They are familiar with computers. They give the best seminars to help people understand new technology. They are highly productive and are always looking for new ways to work. And they want the project to succeed. These people befriend the project. They provide feedback, and they make sure the project team is not thinking in isolation and that influence moves back and forth between them and the team.

As the EPRINET concept was unfolding, the team members tested their ideas by discreetly talking to small pockets of people—people they trusted and who liked new ideas. In particular, they talked to:

1. Prudent lovers of new ideas who thoughtfully adopted new ways of operating, to provide feedback to the team.
2. Influential EPRI researchers who taught the team how to politically move the concept through the organization.
3. The two most influential executives on the information strategy advisory committee—the chairman and the only technical vice president. This committee allocates the information technology budget at EPRI. These executives nurtured the concept, forged the corporate support at the highest levels to get the project funded, and protected the team from organizational burnout. Together with the information system executive, they became the sponsoring team for EPRINET.
4. The EPRINET Utility Advisory Group, which provided advice and guidance from EPRI's customers—the member utilities.

To demonstrate the viability of the idea, the information technology division proposed a small research and development project—the EMF Forum. This pilot was the project's introduction to the political arena, where its worth, viability, and shortcomings were openly debated. Because the concepts had been well thought out by this time, they were able to withstand the criticisms of people who believed the money should go for research work.

The project team learned that the more support they garnered from around the organization while operating underground, the more likely the project was to succeed, once released to others' scrutiny. But they also learned, from the numerous delays they encountered, the value of a corporate sponsor.

Get a Corporate Sponsor

A sponsor is a corporate champion who stands behind the project as it matures. This top-level executive preferably comes from outside the information systems department—ideally, from the heart of the enterprise. In EPRI's case, the heart is the R&D staff.

The most desirable sponsors are executives whose success depends on the success of the project. Also desirable are those who naturally counsel well with large numbers of people and can integrate diverse opinions. They must also listen well, because they need to "synergize" opinions.

At EPRI, this ideal sponsor was not available at the time, because the Institute was in the midst of its transition. A full-functioning, corporate-level technology transfer entity had not yet been formed, so there was no single executive leading that function—that work was diffused among the technical divisions. Such a group is just emerging now.

The EPRI environment has been the most difficult type of environment in which to champion a major project—one where the entire organization is in transition. In such cases, the information technology director generally must become the lead sponsor. At EPRI, the project "sponsor" was the coalition of three executives. Although not ideal, this team sponsor concept did work; and it was the only viable option.

The project team came to appreciate how important its two line-organization sponsors were, in marshaling advocates throughout the organization, reducing day-to-day stress on the project team, funneling money to the project, and reducing the cost—in time and dollars—of gaining acceptance of the new ideas.

Although life on the EPRINET project was difficult, in retrospect, those involved much preferred taking a low-profile route rather than being a highly visible skunkworks. A high profile would have triggered the corporate immune system too early for the project to survive the criticism. It was wise to plan the "coming-out party" carefully, they learned.

Listen Carefully to Corporate Naysayers

When a project emerges, the team must listen to the naysayers carefully. Just as visionaries help people visualize the future, corporate naysayers see every pothole along the way. Take note of these potholes. Make sure the project plans account for them, to minimize corporate risk. But keep moving, do not allow them to discourage the team or slow its pace.

At first, the EPRINET project team avoided the naysayers, for fear they would thwart the project's purpose. Outspoken naysayers are usually powerful people. But as time went on, the team realized they were acquiring an immense number of suggestions from these opponents. The pitfalls the critics identified were very real, so the team learned to draw them out. For example, the naysayers asked:

- "Without licensing agreements, how are you going to be able to move software electronically and still protect it legally?"
- "How are you going to protect EPRI from distributing virus-infected software over the network?"
- "If you make questions easier to ask, you will open up the floodgates, and EPRI staff will be inundated with electronic questions. They will be turned into automated secretaries answering the mail rather than traveling, teaching, and researching."
- "When you create large databases, you will be taking money away from advanced research projects in order to maintain those databases."

Using their concerns, the team created contingency plans and added mechanisms to EPRINET to handle those issues.

As the Systems Executive, Be the Change Agent

When an organization is in transition, the most appropriate executive to lead a major systems effort may be the head of information systems. This job differs from that of other senior executives because system executives must often step forward as champions of change. They are actually well suited for this role, because their careers have centered around technology-induced change.

But changing an organization requires courage. As an agent of change, the system executive must be prepared to lay his or her job on the line. The risk can be managed, however—by looking for and creating opportunities to demonstrate that one is an objective, cost-effective manager. A good guide for navigating the turbulent waters of change is to have integrity with the project; that is, to give first priority to the organization rather than to one's own career. When people come from this integrity, it shows.

There are times when the information system executive struggles with whether the project is extracting too high a personal price. Integrity says, "If you do not believe in this project, do not stay involved with it." This perspective helps guard against mental, physical, and political burnout.

Do Not Keep the Same Lead Person During the Entire Project

Information system executives must also realize that (like everyone else) they gain and lose political power. When they have the power, they can be effective spokespeople. At other times, they need to share the role.

Furthermore, it is not wise for a project to be associated with one individual too long, lest the project's vision and momentum become lost in that person's personality. The team must guard the project against a buildup of distrust against any one person over time. For survival, the project needs to "belong" to the organization, not an individual.

On the EPRINET project, the spokesperson's baton was passed among the top systems executive, the project leader, and the two members of the information strategy committee. All of them were sensitive to the fact that their personal power diminished when they were "out there" too much. Therefore, when one person's effectiveness waned, he or she was given a period of relief. But each of them knew they could draw on the others for support when needed.

Underpromise and Overdeliver

Develop an internal marketing plan that shows potential users—very clearly, in their own language—how the tool under development will benefit them. And release a very conservative rollout plan. Then proceed to deliver increased functionality, smashing deadlines along the way.

Information systems groups are always in a precarious situation when it comes to managing expectations, because the technology changes so fast. They will be criticized when they deliver a project, no matter how well they do, because expectations will have advanced all on their own.

With EPRINET, for example, Microsoft's Windows 3.0 was announced just as the system was delivered. All at once, people were expecting a windowing environment. But there had been no practical way to create such a graphical user interface for their IBM PCs prior to that announcement.

Be aware of such expectations, and do not build on them if they are unattainable. The EPRINET people made no promises, but in the background they were prototyping a windowed environment. Once Windows became available, they announced that the next release of EPRINET would have Windows at the end of 1991.

Bet on People, Not Ideas

Few things turn out as planned, but good people make them work anyway. If anything has been demonstrated over the past few years on the EPRINET project, it has been that people working in a synergistic mode achieve superior results. There are not many hotshots for hire these days, especially in the new cooperative systems environment, because that expertise is just now developing.

But that's OK. With the right working environment, it is not necessary to have driven people to be successful. A project only needs committed people. When they are following a vision and have clear expectations, they can and will do extraordinary things.

Impacts of EPRINET

How can we know whether we are successful? Well, if Peter Drucker is correct in declaring that knowledge is the new capital, then we can judge our success in terms of whether we are providing an effective learning environment—one that facilitates the creation and sharing of knowledge. Such an environment offers:

- Easy access to experts
- Stores of past research
- Insights into work in process
- Peer-group problem-solving
- Windows on world issues
- Participation in new ventures
- Freedom from time, geographic, and technical boundaries

Such an environment brings people, ideas, and information together in ways that facilitate collaboration and assimilation of knowledge. In interviews this spring, heavy users of the network signaled the emergence of such an environment.

With EPRINET, they said:

- People feel more informed
- People can expand their potential
- Responsibility can be put at the most appropriate level
- EPRINET provides a collaborative environment
- Task forces and committees can operate more effectively
- Business can be streamlined
- Members gain more benefit from EPRI membership

People Feel More Informed

Universally, the heavy users (people who use the system more than 5.5 hours per month) mentioned that they felt more informed by participating in EPRINET. Those who "network" and communicate with many colleagues said they could stay in touch with many more people, more frequently using the electronic mail system.

Jim Ray of Bonneville Power Administration (BPA) in Portland, Oregon, for example, works with a large network of people—BPA program managers, other utilities, and EPRI—in his job as the manager of technology transfer. He says,

I don't know how I would get this job done if I didn't have EPRINET to get communications out. And it would be impossible to call this many people to talk to them and get their input on various items.

Researchers say that the ease of finding and retrieving both "hot" and in-depth information on EPRINET keeps them more up-to-date on research work. Walt Myers, also of BPA, cites a recent incident where the chief engineer returned from a meeting and wanted a staff engineer to look into a subject. BPA did not have an engineer who knew the area, so Myers first searched the EPRINET database of EPRI report abstracts. He pulled out the relevant ones for the engineer assigned to the job—to provide him with background material on the topic. Says Myers,

This search gave me a feel for how widely studied that area was, before we spent a lot of time on it. The search gave me a gauge of activity and background on the subject. It worked very well.

Both types of EPRINET users—networkers and researchers—also seem to appreciate the quickly browsed news items, the EPRI announcements, and the interim project status reports. They believe they see more information for the time they spend, which they perceive as enabling them to stay better informed.

People Can Expand Their Potential

As the manager of EPRI technology transfer (METT) at one California utility expressed it, EPRINET has expanded his working potential. He is responsible for keeping up to date with 40 departmental coordinators, 20 regional technology transfer coordinators, and 30 R&D coordinators, not to mention the 200 METTs in other utilities around the United States. He says there is no way he could telephone or talk to this many people regularly. But he has been able to stay in touch with most of them electronically.

The information retrieval facilities can have a similar effect. Kam Joshi, of Texas Utilities Electric Company in Dallas, had the following experience:

I found in three minutes what had taken several weeks to find in the past.

Oliver Gildersleeve, of EPRI, wrote when using a laptop computer:

It's 11:47 p.m. in Phoenix. I'm selecting information to present to a planning committee here tomorrow. The committee chose the topics today, so there was no way to prepare before leaving Palo Alto. I found the information I needed on EPRINET.

The electronic medium expands what people can do, because access to people and information is easier.

Responsibility Can Be Put at the Most Appropriate Level

Use of both the information retrieval facilities and the electronic mail system has taken out the middlemen, allowing the right person to perform a job, as illustrated by the two examples below.

At Pacific Gas and Electric Co., a power plant executive wanted to hold a workshop featuring the new tools and research on fossil power plant activities. He drew up an agenda and his chief engineer then searched EPRINET's databases on the 15 listed topics. After reviewing the pertinent reports and projects, the engineer identified the authors and researchers of most interest to PG&E. They were invited to speak. The workshop was a big success, with over 100 attendees, because it was so tailored to the utility's needs.

Walt Myers of Bonneville Power Administration provides an example from the mail system. When he sends a question electronically and he knows the recipient will need to confer with others before responding, he generally sends a copy to those other people. By using the electronic copy function, he receives answers faster, because the people who need to make the decision are aware of the issues from the outset.

EPRINET Provides a Collaborative Environment

On EPRINET, people are forming "intellectual neighborhoods" by means of tailored distribution lists and bulletin boards. By creating distribution lists of people who share their interests, they can keep them all informed with a single message. Similarly, with bulletin boards, all comments are seen by everyone who chooses to participate. These neighborhoods are breeding grounds for collaboration and synergy, where people "bump into" others they might not normally encounter.

At Wisconsin Public Service Corporation, in Green Bay, for example, one EPRINET user told us:

If it hadn't been for EPRINET, Eric [from New Zealand] wouldn't have visited us. When the message was posted on the electronic [bulletin board] about his interest in seeing certain equipment, we invited him to come to Wisconsin.

A similar synergy occurred among people in the Northeast, the West Coast, and the Southeast United States. An EMF Forum member in Georgia read an article in *City Manager* magazine recommending certain protective measures against electric and magnetic fields from transmission lines. He used EPRINET to alert EMF Forum members to the article. The EPRI project manager sponsoring the forum passed the information along to his boss in Palo Alto, who prepared a response that was posted on the forum's news board. A forum participant in the Northeast who had not read the *City Manager* article read the news board. He relied on that EPRINET commentary when a worried customer of his utility called to ask about the article. All this took place within two days' time. The scanning was done in the Southeast, the response came from the West Coast, and the information was used in the Northeast.

And in a recent request, broadcast on EPRINET, for collaborators on a hydropower project, Bonneville Power Administration in Portland, Oregon, received one reply from Wisconsin—an unexpected quarter.

In essence, EPRINET is creating an "electronic water cooler" for the electric utility industry, where people can gather and swap thoughts without regards to time or location.

Task Forces and Committees Can Operate More Effectively

Those who have used the distribution lists on EPRINET generally use them to maintain lists of the task forces and committees they participate in. (EPRI and its members make significant use of task forces to do their work.)

EPRINET has helped several committees and project teams work more effectively. One such committee consists of 200 managers of EPRI technology transfer (METTs), who are responsible for encouraging the use of EPRI technology in their utilities.

When organizing a METT workshop or conference, the planning committee distributes draft agendas and solicits comments on EPRINET. For a recent conference, the committee received 12 pages of suggestions from METTs online.

This organizing committee holds weekly telephone conference calls. It now expects participating callers to access EPRINET simultaneously, so that they are all looking at the same version of the information while conversing. The information is better organized online than on their desks, and they can always find it.

On one project task force, EPRINET changed how EPRI conducted its research—testing the EMDEX monitoring device to record EMF levels (Figure 5.4). Using EPRINET, EPRI was able to broadcast a request for volunteers and then have those geographically dispersed volunteers submit their EMF data and discuss the subject from their offices. EPRI did not need to send its staff around the country testing the device at different sites, nor hold a conference to bring the interested researchers together. EPRI performed more thorough research and held more in-depth discussions for less money using the network.

With the growing emphasis on task forces in today's business world, an electronic communication system can make an important contribution by helping such groups operate more effectively.

Business Can Be Streamlined

Many EPRINET users told us that the fast turn-around from electronic mail significantly speeds up business. They expect answers sooner—often in one day's time—whereas, before, they might not have received the answer to a paper memo in less than two weeks. Consequently, says Walt Myers, of BPA.

I have fewer "in progress" files on my desk, because they get completed sooner.

In December 1989, Long Island Lighting Company, in Hicksville, New York, had many customers asking the utility to perform readings in their homes to determine whether the electric and magnetic fields were at safe levels. Although EMF safety levels were (and still are) in question, the utility needed to respond. Their technical information coordinator used EPRINET to ask participants of the EMF Forum for advice. Within two weeks, he had received 14 replies. He said:

No letter between CEOs of those same firms could have generated as quick and effective a response.

Another streamlining factor is that there are fewer social conventions attached to electronic mail so people feel freer to deal directly with others. As one engineer put it:

I probably would not feel as free about contacting the EPRI project manager if I had to write or call him. But with e-mail, I feel as if the office door is always open.

So, electronic mail streamlines business because it allows work-in-progress to be completed sooner, more people to be contacted more quickly, and people more opportunity to deal with others directly.

Members Gain More Benefit From EPRI Membership

Finally, several users noted that EPRINET increases their use of EPRI's research. Says Bruce LaMar, of Northern States Power, in Eau Claire, Wisconsin:

Before, I used journals and books. These would include some EPRI material, but I could not get the full benefit of what EPRI had done.

And David Morris, of Southern Company Services, in Birmingham, Alabama, reports,

During planning, we call up descriptions of new projects, industry news summaries, and past project reports. We fold all these EPRINET resources into our long-term planning, which helps us decide what issues we need to address. They give us a broader perspective of where we fit in the national picture.

Over the years, member utilities and collaborators have used EPRI's knowledge to save money, develop new products, and increase revenue. The following three examples come from many cited in the 1990 annual report (EPRI, 1990):

- Analysis from BLADE, EPRI's 3-D finite-element code, helped Tennessee Valley Authority decide to install titanium L-1 turbine blades in its Cumberland plant. TVA expects these longer-life blades to save $15 million over the next 20 years.
- The EPRI-Lennox dual-fuel heat pump was introduced to the commercial market as a replacement for conventional gas units. The DFHP pairs an electric heat pump for high efficiency with a gas furnace for supplemental heating.
- Commonwealth Edison estimates that use of EPRI's industrial market information system (IMIS) software is increasing its revenues from the industrial sector by $2 million a year. IMIS's market-targeting capability was responsible for eight megawatts of new process-heating sales in one year alone.

With access to EPRI's vast knowledge storehouse made easier through EPRINET, members who use the network will be more likely to encounter information they can use to their benefit. Therefore, the value of their membership will increase.

Future Directions

The challenge for EPRI—as for most organizations in today's time-driven, data-swamped information Age—is to skillfully use the power of information technology to select, shape, and transfer to our customers the information they need to maintain leadership in the global marketplace.

With the EPRINET system now linking member utilities and their industry colleagues nationwide. EPRI has established the essential connectivity. And it is now delivering EPRI's knowledge capital quickly to the desktop. The culture at EPRI and in the industry is changing, as well. As its people adopt the technology, they are evolving new, more-productive methods of organizing and presenting knowledge.

As we go forward, EPRI and its members—like the rest of the business community—will be managing increasingly complex information with a less-skilled workforce. With this in mind, while EPRI continues to improve its ability to use technology to integrate, synthesize, and deliver knowledge, it must turn its attention more fully to the end point—toward making the information it delivers easier and faster for its customers to assimilate.

Moreover, as EPRI keeps refining the network technically and enriching the delivered content, it will also continue to incorporate emerging technologies that will provide new opportunities to facilitate the creation and assimilation of information. For example, right now EPRI is exploring the virtual reality technology, which may have significant potential for the design and modeling of complex power plant systems, and for helping utilities transcend the training and experiential limits of tomorrow's workforce.

The world will change, and our organizations must manage that change. As information technologies hold keys to doing so, the challenges for information systems executives will also continue. Since information technologies lead into uncharted territories, we must enter these territories with enterprise—failing, succeeding, and learning as we proceed, and sharing our experience with colleagues.

ACKNOWLEDGMENT

Thanks to Judith Quinn, energy research writer, for her contributions to this article.

REFERENCES

Drucker, P. "The Post Business Knowledge Society Begins," *Industry Week,* April 17, 1989.

Electric Power Research Institute. *1990 Annual Report,* Palo Alto, CA, 1990.

Primozic, K., Primozic, E., and Leben, J. *Strategic Choices,* McGraw-Hill, New York, NY, 1990.

Pinchot, G., III. *The Intrapreneur's Ten Commandments,* Pinchot & Co., New Haven, CT, 1988.

6

A New Organizational Structure

Ikujiro Nonaka and Hirotaka Takeuchi

The previous chapter introduced middle-up-down as the management style most conducive to organizational knowledge creation. But for middle-up-down management to work effectively, we need an organizational structure that supports the management process. Knowledge creation has implications not only for the management process; it also has profound implications for organizational structure. This chapter develops the theoretical and practical bases of a new organizational structure, referred to as a "hypertext" organization, that enables an organization to create knowledge efficiently and continuously.

As knowledge and innovation become more central to competitive success, it should come as no surprise that there has been growing dissatisfaction with traditional organizational structures. For most of this century, organizational structure has oscillated between two basic types: bureaucracy and task force. But when it comes to knowledge creation, neither of these structures is adequate. What is necessary is some combination or synthesis of the two.

We discover in this chapter that there is a surprising model for such a synthesis. It is the U.S. military, which is bureaucratic in peacetime but highly task force-oriented in wartime. We view the U.S. victory against Japan in World War II as an "organizational" victory of the synthesized structure (U.S. military) over a purely bureaucratic structure (Japanese military).

The military case is a prelude to two case studies of Japanese companies attempting to carry out the synthesis of bureaucracy and task force. We introduce Kao as an "in transition" model of the new synthesized structure and Sharp as a "more perfected" model. But before we move on to describe this new organizational structure, which we refer to as "hypertext," a quick look is in order at the two traditional structures—bureaucracy and task force—that form the basis of the new structure.

Reprinted by permission, Ikujiro Nonaka, "A Dynamic Theory of Organizational Knowledge Creation," ORGANIZATIONAL SCIENCE, Volume 5, Number 1, February 1994. Copyright 1994, The Institute of Management Sciences (currently INFORMS), 290 Westminster Street, Providence, RI 02903 USA.

Critique of Traditional Organizational Structures

The oscillation between bureaucracy and task force goes back to the nineteenth century, when Max Weber asserted that the most rational and efficient organizations in modern society have bureaucratic characteristics (Gerth and Mills, 1972, pp. 196–198).[1] A bureaucratic structure works well when conditions are stable, since it emphasizes control and predictability of specific functions. Bureaucratic structure, which is highly formalized, specialized, centralized, and largely dependent on the standardization of work processes for organizational coordination, is suitable for conducting routine work efficiently on a large scale. It is common in stable and mature industries with mostly rationalized, repetitive type of work.

However, bureaucratic control can come at the cost of hobbling individual initiative and can be extremely dysfunctional in periods of uncertain and rapid change.[2] Bureaucracy can generate other dysfunctional characteristics, such as intra-organizational resistance, red tape, tension, shirking of responsibility, means becoming objectives, and sectionalism (Merton, 1940; Selznik, 1949; Gouldner, 1954). It can also hinder the motivation of organizational members. Many social psychologists have argued that a participation-oriented and organic organizational structure can be more effective than bureaucracy in impelling motivation (McGregor, 1960; Likert, 1961; Argyris, 1964).

The task force is an organizational structure designed precisely to address the weakness of bureaucracy. It is flexible, adaptable, dynamic, and participative. In business organizations, the task force is an institutionalized form of team or group that brings together representatives from a number of different units on an intensive and flexible basis, in many cases to deal with a temporary issue.[3] People in a task force work within a certain time frame, and focus their energy and effort on achieving a certain goal. In this way, the task-force organization often succeeds in making quantum leaps in fields such as new-product development.

However, the task-force model has its limits as well. Because of its temporary nature, new knowledge or know-how created in the task-force teams is not easily transferred to other organizational members after the project is completed. The task force is therefore not appropriate for exploiting and transferring knowl-

---

[1]According to Weber, modern bureaucracy has the following characteristics: (1) fixed and official order by laws or administrative regulations; (2) hierarchy, that is, levels of graded authority; (3) management based upon written documents; and (4) operation based on specified/specialized work.
[2]Burns and Stalker (1961) initiated contingency theory describing a bureaucratic structure as a mechanical system that works well only in a stable environment. On the other hand, an organic management system with a nonbureaucratic structure is more appropriate to an unstable environment. See Thompson (1967), Perrow (1967, 1973), Nonaka (1972), Galbraith (1973).
[3]The concept of the task force evolved from that of the military operation. The "task-force principle" is used by the Navy and Marines to organize forces for specific purposes, while preserving a separate administrative organization for training and housekeeping. A task organization can function in a variety of organizational magnitudes, from campaigns of entire fleets throughout a war to a single ship on a one-time mission.

edge continuously and widely throughout entire organizations. When composed of many different small-scaled task forces, the organization becomes incapable of setting and achieving its goals or vision at the corporate level.

In recent years, a myriad of new organizational models, basically versions of the task-force model, have been proposed. These include an "adhocracy," an "infinitely flat organization," a "spider's web (network)," and "inverted pyramid," a "starburst (satellite)," and an "internal market."[4] Proponents of these models argue that the bureaucratic structure is too sluggish in responding to uncertain environments. When properly conceptualized, these new models can focus attention away from authority in order to eliminate costly administrative structures and support the rapid execution of strategies. These organizational forms have forced a complete rethinking of the relationships among top executives, middle management, and the lower level.

All of these new organizational concepts share certain common characteristics. These new organizations: (1) tend to be flatter than their hierarchical predecessors; (2) assume a constant dynamic rather than a static structure; (3) support the empowerment of people in building intimacy vis-à-vis customers; (4) emphasize the importance of competencies—unique technologies and skills; and (5) recognize intellect and knowledge as one of the most leverageable assets of a company.

Although these new organizational models have often been touted as cures for almost any management ill, they are not a panacea. Each model is useful in certain situations, but not in others. Each requires a carefully developed

---

[4]Mintzberg (1989, chap. 6) has proposed the "adhocracies," which contain "project structures" that can fuse the contributions experts have drawn from different specialties in order to form smoothly functioning creative teams.

D. Quinn Mills (1991) has claimed that what has always been accepted as formal hierarchy is actually disappearing in many larger, formerly bureaucratic settings. These institutions are shifting toward what he calls "cluster" organizations.

Another example of new organization concepts is an "infinitely flat" organization, an organization with innumerable outposts guided by one central "rules-based" or "computer-controlled inquiry" system (Quinn, 1992).

The "network" organization operates essentially without—or with only minimal—formal authority or "order-giving" hierarchies (Imai and Itami, 1984). This organization mode is sometimes described as a "spider's web" because of the lightness yet completeness of its interconnected structure (Quinn, 1992).

For some companies, the person having direct contact with the customer is so important that, rather than operate merely in a flat or network mode, they will literally invert their organizations, making all line executives, systems, and support staff in the company "work for" the front-line (Quinn, 1992).

Some highly innovative companies have found a special form of disaggregation—best described as a "starburst" or "satellite" organization—to be very effective. These companies constantly "split off" and "sell off" units, like shooting stars peeled from the core competencies of their parents (Sakakibara, Numagami, and Ohtaki, 1989).

Recently, some scholars have proposed the concept of internal market organization that internalizes market mechanism, as the transition from hierarchy (Halal, Geranmayeh, and Pourdehnad, 1993).

infrastructure—culture, style, and reward system—to support it. When configured improperly, they can be less effective than the old-fashioned bureaucracy.

In fact, these newly developed managerial models merely recapitulate a very
old and by now somewhat stale debate over the dichotomy between bureaucracy
and task force. But from the viewpoint of knowledge creation, this debate may
represent a false dichotomy. Indeed, one might argue that it is a product of some
peculiarly Western tendency toward dichotomous thinking. We should consider
the traditional bureaucracy and the task force as complementary rather than mutually exclusive approaches to organizations.

A business organization should be equipped with the strategic capability to
exploit, accumulate, share, and create new knowledge continuously and repeatedly in a dynamic and spiral process. From that point of view, bureaucracy is effective in bringing about combination and internalization, while the task force is
suitable for socialization and externalization. In other words, the former is the
more appropriate structure for the exploitation and accumulation of knowledge,
while the latter is effective for the sharing and creation of knowledge. The business organization should pursue both the efficiency of a bureaucracy and the flexibility of a tasks-force organization; some combination or synthesis of the two is
needed to provide a solid base for knowledge creation.

An Attempt at Synthesis—Case of the Military Organization

Before describing such a synthesis within the business organization we take
a look at military structures of the United States and Japan during World War II.
Although the Japanese military stuck to bureaucracy, the U.S. military made a
clear-cut attempt to synthesize bureaucracy and the task force. We contend that
the Japanese military adapted itself to past successes that were achieved under bureaucracy. In contrast, the U.S. military evolved into a more flexible structure with
a focus on the task-force organization, and eventually won the war.

While organizational theory has often addressed the dichotomy between bureaucracy and task force, military organizations have historically been concerned
with the task of how a bureaucracy could have maintained in a dynamic and flexible manner. Military organization certainly maintain a typical bureaucratic structure in peacetime. However, in wartime, they must also demonstrate mobility. A
look at the confrontation of the Japanese and U.S. militaries during World War II
provides a unique case study of the synthesis we have been discussing

Bureaucracy under the Japanese Imperial Military

The central feature of the Japanese military organization was its conformity
to bureaucracy. The Japanese Imperial Army and Navy were set up as organiza-
tionally separate entities under the direct control of the Emperor, as shown in Figure 6.1. The rigid bureaucracy the Japanese military became a major obstacle

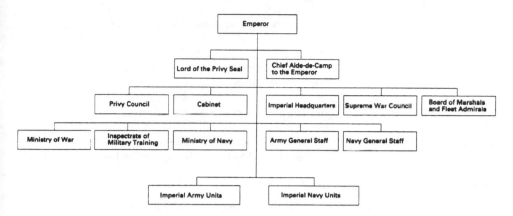

FIGURE 6.1 The Japanese Imperial Army and Navy: Organizational Structure

during World War II, when it was confronted with a totally new and dynamic environment. Structure directed strategy in the case of the Japanese military.

The strategies of both the Japanese Army and Navy were strongly dominated by paradigms that were formed from successful experiences during the Russo-Japanese War and the China Incident. These experiences and subsequent successes eventually ingrained certain paradigms or models of operation that became treated almost as "sacred" within the Japanese military. The paradigm prevalent within the Imperial Army, for example, revolved around the concept of hand-to-hand fighting. The key to victory on the battlefield, according to the Imperial Army, was thought to be the last great bayonet charge and the resulting hand-to-hand combat. This paradigm was articulated in the "Basics of Training for Warfare," issued by the Imperial Army Training Headquarters in 1908. The technique proved to be more than adequate for defeating the Chinese and the British-Indian Army in a number of battles during the war in Asia.

The Imperial Navy's model of operation was to focus on a battle of cannon fire with enemy warships. Victory was to be decided by the great salvos between giant battleships. This paradigm was formed during the Battle of Tsushima in the Russo-Japanese War. The victory of the Imperial Navy over the Russian Baltic Fleet on May 27 and 28, 1905, was the first complete triumph in world naval history, and had a strong influence on the Imperial Navy's strategic thinking. From that point forward, the Japanese Navy believed that the result of a battle between opposing fleets would have a great influence on the eventual outcome of the war.

The Japanese military's organizational characteristics reinforced these models or paradigms. Its structure, control system, promotion system, and leadership style were designed to conform to its paradigms. Table 6.1 shows the pattern of environmental adaptation of the Japanese military. Note that the organizational characteristics under the "hand-to-hand battle" paradigm of the Army and the "battle between warships" paradigm of the Navy were internally consistent. The

TABLE 6.1   Organizational Characteristics of the Japanese Imperial Forces

Characteristics	Army	Navy
Paradigm	Hand-to-hand battle	Battle between warships
Resource priority	Priority on the number of forces	Priority on individual warships
Organizational structure	Separation of soldiers from artillery	Fleet-dominant structure
Promotion system	Biased in favor of infantry	Biased in favor of gunnery
Leadership	Embodied in hand-to-hand combat	Embodied in battle between fleets
Heroes	Maresuke Nogi	Heihachiro Togo
Technology	Light and medium tanks to follow infantry	Big battleships, e.g., Musashi and Yamato

Source: Tobe et al. (1984).

heroes who eventually emerged and the technology employed were consistent with the respective paradigms as well.

The rigid paradigms worked well within a particular environment. The Army's paradigm of the bayonet charge and the resulting hand-to-hand battle was actually a great success, at least in battles in East Asia. From Manchuria and China to Hong Kong and Singapore, successes based on the existing paradigm gave the military confidence in their model, and led to the elevation of this pattern of success to the level of a behavioral norm for the organization.

However, it became difficult to abandon what had worked well in the East even when the environment changed. Not long after their general success, the Japanese military confronted the American military at Guadalcanal Island. They faced the U.S. Marines, who had developed a new fighting technique combining ground, sea, and air warfare. Against the U.S. Marines, the Japanese Army made three attempts to attack at night, on each occasion using a bayonet charge. This strategy resulted in heavy losses.

Despite recognizing the importance of firepower after the Battle of Guadalcanal, the Imperial Army was unable to break away from the main concept of hand-to-hand battle, epitomized by the bayonet charge. And although the Imperial Navy attempted to strengthen its aircraft carriers, it believed up to the very end that the destructive force of the 46-cm guns of the Yamato and the Musashi— which were embodiments of the principle of the big gun—would be the key to naval success.

The theory of organizational evolution points out that "adaptation precludes adaptability." In other words, there is a danger of overadaptation past success. The dinosaur is a case in point. At one point, this animal was both physiologically and morphologically suited to a particular environment. But it overadapted itself to that environment and could not adjust to eventual changes in the climate and food supply. The Japanese bureaucratic military fell into the same trap. It overadapted itself to past success and failed to "unlearn" those success factors within a new and changing environment.

A Synthesis under the U.S. Marines

Unlike the Japanese military, the U.S. military developed a flexible organizational structure in addition to a bureaucracy during World War II.[5] Among its various organizational innovations, we look at its introduction of the task-force organization, with particular attention paid to amphibious (combining both land and sea) operations.[6] The U.S. military developed an amphibious operation through actual landings on 18 Pacific islands during the war against Japan. The landing on the island of Guadalcanal was the first U.S. offensive, as well as the first actual use of an amphibious operation by the U.S. Marines.

While an amphibious operation had some characteristics in common with the usual land or sea battle, it required the simultaneous integration of many activities that were usually conducted separately by ground, sea, and air forces. Under an amphibious operation, soldiers traveled on battleships for a long distance, changed to landing ships at the landing point, and forced a landing on an enemy shore with neither heavy equipment nor direct support from the artillery. To protect the landing soldiers, therefore, both battleship bombardment and air attack had to be provided at the same time. This operation led to the formation of a task-force team, which was composed of members of the different bureaucracies.

The U.S. victory at Guadalcanal is regarded as the turning point of World War II, and the beginning of the "organizational" victory of the U.S. military over the Japanese. While the bureaucratic Japanese military continued its use of the bayonet charge and hand-to-hand battle, the flexible U.S. military developed a new task force organization, the Fleet Marine Force, to carry out landings on islands across the Pacific. Having established a base in the southern Pacific through

---

[5]As for the structure of its fighting forces, the Japanese Imperial Navy, along with its air force, instituted an air force-led task force prior to the U.S. military's formation of one, but did not discard the conventional battleship-oriented structure and strategy until the end of the war. The Nagumo task force which was formed to attack Pearl Harbor, for example, arranged the battleships in a regular square style, with scattered warning ships outside the battleship perimeter. This system, however, was unable to defend the aircraft carrier from enemy fighters by anti-air guns and machine guns. Without a radar system, the aircraft carrier's only option was self-defense. The Japanese Imperial Army did not integrate the infantry, artillery, and aircraft, either. The infantry, conducting hand-to-hand combats, dominated the structure as its core, and the infantry and artillery were used separately in many battles.

[6]For example, the U.S. Navy developed a circular anti-aircraft defense system in which nine warships, including battleships, cruisers, and destroyers, were located at regular intervals on the periphery. The formation had a radius of 1,500 meters, with an aircraft carrier at its center. The enemy planes rushing at the aircraft carrier were attacked from their sides and dive-bombers were shot when they came in at low altitude in order to launch torpedoes at a point of 1,500 meters from the targeted aircraft carrier.

the use of the Marines, the U.S. military started to carry out the bombing of main-
land Japan by the Army's large bombers, which flew out from the occupied island
bases.

In Search of a Synthesis—The Hypertext Organization

Just as the American military created a task force in addition to the traditional hierarchical structures of the Army and the Navy. A business organization
should have a nonhierarchical, self-organizing structure working in tandem with
its hierarchical formal structure. This point is particularly important for organizational knowledge creation. As business organizations grow in scale and complexity, they should simultaneously maximize both corporate-level efficiency and local
flexibility.

In this section, we present an organizational design that provides a structural base for organizational knowledge creation. The central requirement for this
design is that it provide a knowledge-creating company with the strategic ability
to acquire, create, exploit, and accumulate new knowledge continuously and repeatedly in a cyclical process. The goal is an organizational structure that views
bureaucracy and the task force as complementary rather than mutually exclusive.
The most appropriate metaphor for such a structure comes from a "hypertext,"
which was originally developed in computer science.[7]

A hypertext consists of multiple layers of texts, while a conventional text basically has only one layer—the text itself. Texts on a computer screen may be
paragraphs, sentences, charts, or graphics. Under a hypertext, each text is usually
stored separately in a different file. When a text is needed, an operator can key in
a command that pulls out all the texts on the computer screen at one time in a
connected and logical way. A hypertext provides an operator with access to multiple layers. This feature allows anyone looking into the computer screen not only
to "read through" the text, but to go down "into" it for further degrees of detail
or background source material. He or she may even go "into" a different medium,
such as video. For example, a hypertext version of, say, *Hamlet* might include
video clips of different actors interpreting the "To be or not to be" speech in different ways. The essential feature of a hypertext is this ability to get "in" and
"out" of multiple texts or layers.

These layers should be interpreted as the different "contexts" that are available. The layers put the knowledge of the hypertext document into a different
context. To continue with the *Hamlet* example, the play itself is one context. The
scholarly literature on the psychology of the character of Hamlet is another context, which enables the reader to interpret the play in a different light. Video clips
of actors performing the "To be or not to be" speech provide yet another context,
which helps the reader to transform her or his understanding of both the play and

---

[7]For further discussion, see Nonaka et al., 1992.

the scholarly literature. Thus, in terms of knowledge, each layer is really a different context.

Like an actual hypertext document, hypertext organization is made up of interconnected layers or contexts: the business system, the project team, and the knowledge base, as shown in Figure 6.2. The central layer is the "business-system" layer in which normal, routine operations are carried out. Since a bureaucratic structure is suitable for conducting routine work efficiently, this layer is shaped like a hierarchical pyramid. The top layer is the "project-team" layer, where multiple project teams engage in knowledge-creating activities such as new product development. The team members are brought together from a number of different units across the business system, and are assigned exclusively to a project team until the project is completed. At the bottom is the "knowledge-base" layer, where organizational knowledge generated in the above two layers is recategorized and recontextualized. This layer does not exist as an actual organizational entity, but is embedded in corporate vision, organizational culture, or technology. Corporate vision provides the direction in which the company should develop its technology or products, and clarifies the "field" in which wants to play. Organizational culture orients the mindset and action of every employee. While corporate vision and organizational culture provide the knowledge base to tap tacit knowledge, technology taps the explicit knowledge generated in the two other layers.

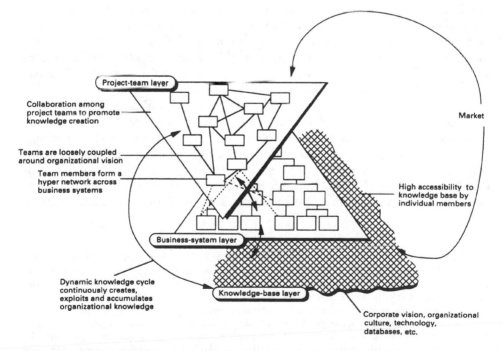

FIGURE 6.2 Hypertext Organization. *Source: Nonaka and Konno (1993)*

What is unique about a hypertext organization is that three totally different layers or contexts coexist within the same organization. As with the *Hamlet* example, knowledge can reside within the business- system context, which may be analogous to the play itself. The project team provides another context, which may allow organizational members to view the traditional organizational context in a totally different light. As such, it may be analogous to the scholarly literature on Hamlet himself. The knowledge base is the third context in which knowledge can reside. It is here that knowledge created inside the two other contexts is stored and recontextualized. The knowledge base may be analogous to the video clips of speeches performed by different actors. The key characteristic of the hypertext organization is the ability of its members to shift contexts. They can move among the three contexts in order to accommodate the changing requirements of situations both inside and outside the organization. This ability offers the same flexibility as a computer operator moving easily through a hypertext document.

The process of organizational knowledge creation is conceptualized as a dynamic cycle of knowledge traversing easily through the three layers. Members of a project team on the top layer, who are selected from diverse functions and departments across the business-system layer, engage in knowledge-creating activities. Their efforts may be guided by the corporate vision presented by top management. Once the team completes its task, members move down to the knowledge-base layer and make an inventory of the knowledge created and/or acquired during their time with the project team. This inventory includes both successes and failures, which are documented and analyzed. After recategorizing and recontextualizing the new knowledge acquired, team members return to the business-system layer and engage in routine operations until they are called again for another project. The ability to switch among the different contexts of knowledge swiftly and flexibly, so as to form a dynamic cycle of knowledge, ultimately determines the organizational capability for knowledge creation.

A hypertext organization, which is the dynamic synthesis of both the bureaucratic structure and the task force, reaps benefits from both. The bureaucratic structure efficiently implements, exploits, and accumulates new knowledge through internalization and combination, while the task force is indispensable for generating new knowledge through socialization and externalization. The efficiency and stability of the bureaucracy is combined with the effectiveness and dynamism of the task force in a hypertext organization.[8] Moreover, it adds another

---

[8]It should be noted here that another critical factor for realizing this dynamic combination is the total coordination of time, space, and resource within an organization. A bureaucratic organization coordinates "requisite variety" and generates a "natural frequency" by "orchestrating" various rhythms (Jacques, 1979). As we have mentioned in Chapter 3, each task force team creates its own "natural frequency" by synchronizing various rhythms brought into the field by members from diverse positions in a bureaucratic organization. The hypertext organization is an organizational structure that enables the orchestration of different rhythms, or "natural frequencies" generated by various product teams and hierarchical organization. It coordinates allocation of time, space, and resource within the organization so as to compose an organizational rhythm that makes organizational knowledge creation most effectively and efficiently. In this sense, a hypertext organization is

layer, the knowledge base, that serves as a "clearinghouse" for the new knowledge generated in the business-system and the project-team layers.

Needless to say, the knowledge content accumulated within the business-system layer is distinct from that generated in the project-team layer. To use the terminology developed in Chapter 3, bureaucracy is more adept at accumulating operational knowledge (via internalization) and systemic knowledge (via combination), while the project team generates conceptual knowledge (via externalization) and sympathized knowledge (via socialization). The role of the knowledge-base layer is to "mix" these different contents of knowledge and re-categorize or recontextualize them into something more meaningful to the organization at large. A hypertext organization has the organizational capability to convert continuously and dynamically the different knowledge contents generated by the bureaucracy and the project team.

A hypertext organization should not be confused with a matrix structure, which is used to achieve two or more different types of tasks in a conventional hierarchical organization.[9] Compared with the conventional matrix structure, a hypertext organization can be distinguished as follows:

1. In the matrix structure, an organization member must belong or report to two structures at the same time. In contrast, an organization member in a hypertext structure belongs or reports to only one structure at one point in time. He or she is assigned to the project team during the project period or to the business system during "normal" times. Project members can therefore focus their attention solely on the ongoing project.
2. Organizational knowledge creation flows naturally from a hypertext organization, since each structure generates and accumulates new knowledge differently, while a matrix structure is not primarily oriented toward knowledge conversion.
3. In a hypertext organization, knowledge contents are combined more flexibly across layers and over time.
4. Since deadlines are set for the projects, the resources and energy of the hypertext organization can be used in a more concentrated manner to fulfill the goal of the project during the project period.
5. Since projects are placed under the direct control of top management, communication time and distance across top, middle, and lower management in the formal hierarchy can be compressed, resulting in a more thorough and in-depth dialogue across management levels. In a sense, a hypertext organization fosters middle-up-down management.

a structural device to build "requisite variety," which is not secured solely by the middle-up-down management, into the organization.

[9]The matrix-structure concept is a balance between two or more bases of grouping, for example, functional with market (or for that matter, one kind of market with another, say, regional with product). This is accomplished by the creation of a dual-authority structure—two or more managers, units, or individuals are made jointly and equally responsible for the same decisions.

In addition, a hypertext organization has the organizational capability to convert knowledge from outside the organization. A hypertext organization is an open system that also features continuous and dynamic knowledge interaction with consumers and companies outside the organization. It is equipped with the capability to collect customer response to new products, find new trends in consumer needs, or generate new-product concept ideas with other companies.

The key characteristic of a hypertext organization is the ability of its members to shift contexts, moving easily in and out of one context into another. In the next section we will illustrate the hypertext organization by using two Japanese companies as examples. The first is Kao, which is still "in transition" from a matrix organization to a hypertext organization. At Kao, project members engage in specific projects while at the same time reporting to the business-system layer. They are not assigned exclusively to a project team. In contrast, Sharp represents a "more perfected" form of hypertext structure. An organization member stays in only one layer at any one time and shifts to another layer when the need arises.

Kao: An "In Transition" Case of a Hypertext Organization

We analyze Kao, Japan's leading household and chemical products maker, as an example of a hypertext organization still in transition. Having been established in 1887, Kao's businesses have expanded from toiletry products into cosmetics and floppy disks.[10] From the perspective of our theory, Kao qualifies as a hypertext organization because it utilizes three different layers, but is considered in transition because it is still structured as a matrix organization, with its project-team members reporting to two structures at the same time.

Kao's business-system layer is structured as flat as possible, which encourages active information sharing and direct employee interaction. It also utilizes a project-team approach to develop new products and solve organizational problems within the division structure, although the project team is not yet considered a stand-alone unit that employees can enter and leave. It also has the technological (explicit) and philosophical (tacit) knowledge bases that work to support and promote organizational knowledge creation. We shall now turn to describing each of these layers, with particular focus on the knowledge-creation process within each layer.

Business-System Layer: A Division System with Fluidity

Kao's business-system layer consists of a divisional system made up of 18 divisions, including the Home Product Division, Sanitary Product Division, and Chemical Division. Kao believes that direct communication among the employees

---

[10]Moreover, the company is currently planning to enter the food and printing markets.

of different divisions becomes limited in the conventional division system, and is thus striving to achieve active interaction among its employees. Kao also believes that direct interaction among employees generates creative ideas. But organizational members cannot interact equally when holding different amounts of information. Thus "information sharing" is regarded as the principle tenet that defines Kao's organization. Kao has built various mechanisms and support systems that assure the sharing of information within the business-system layer. They include "free access to information," "open floor allocation," "open meetings," and "fluid personnel change." These mechanisms and systems become the basis upon which tacit knowledge is shared or converted to explicit knowledge, and vice versa. We shall briefly describe each information-sharing mechanism below.

To assure "free access to information," computer systems have been introduced throughout the Kao organization, with all information being filed in a database. Through this system, anyone at Kao can tap into databases included in the sales system, the marketing information system (MIS), the production information system, the distribution information system, and the total information network covering all of its offices in Japan. The unique feature of this system is that any member, no matter what his or her position or to what section she or he belongs within the business system, has full access to the database (except for a limited amount of personnel information). In other words, anyone can get access to the rich base of explicit knowledge that exists within the business system through this "free access to information" system.

In the "open floor allocation" system, the divisions and functional groups within Kao are all configured around a large open space. Half of the executive floor space, for example, is occupied with an open space called the "decision-making room." In fact, executives rarely stay in their own offices. Divisional heads hold meetings at the round table located in one of the large open spaces. In the laboratories, researchers do not have their own desks, but share big tables. President Fumikatsu Tokiwa, a former researcher, explains the aim of this system as follows:

> *R&D members have a natural tendency to gather into small groups, and isolate themselves from others. To interact, it does not even help to speak loudly if the offices are separated. So we tried to remove both the physical and mental walls at the same time.*[11]

This kind of floor setup allows employees to share their tacit knowledge with others, or may trigger an externalization mode in the middle of a dialogue.

Information sharing and employee interaction are also accelerated throug "open meetings." Any meeting at Kao is open to any employee, and top-management meetings are no exception. Any employee can attend the relevant portion of the meeting and make his or her opinion known. Through this practice,

[11]Interviewed on May 21, 1991.

top management can acquire insights from those most familiar with the issues at hand, while employees can gain a better understanding of the general corporate policy. This kind of hands-on experience helps to mobilize all four modes of knowledge conversion.

What is known within Kao as the R&D conference is typical of these "open meetings." Through this conference, which is held every quarter, top management learns about research projects directly from the researchers, while research members gain an opportunity to voice their opinions directly to top management. This conference, which again is open to anyone outside of R&D, is regularly attended by some 1,800 people (out of a total of 7,000 employees).

Interaction among members with different experiences is also enhanced through the "fluid personnel change" system. For instance, researchers in one division are often transferred to other divisions or to other functional areas, such as sales or finance, on a "whoever is needed, wherever he or she is needed" basis. As a personnel director explains, "Ceaseless change is the basic way. Any member should experience at least three different positions in her or his first ten years within the company." This kind of active job-rotation system, especially among R&D people, enhances the accumulation and sharing of tacit knowledge and promotes interdisciplinary product development within the company. For example, Kao entered the cosmetics market in the mid-1980s with the introduction of a skin-care product called "Sofina" that resulted from the cooperative effort of people working in surface-active science and those in biological skin care.

As we have seen, Kao's organizational structure can be explained as a division system equipped with various mechanisms for active information sharing and direct employee interaction. Although it is a bureaucracy, the structure is flat, with all members of the organization being placed on equal footing and creating new knowledge through direct interaction of their respective functions. Its business system is sometimes described as a Japanese-style paperweight, which is shaped liked a large, circular coin with a small handle in the middle. The metaphor connotes the equal footing of all organizational members, with top management serving as the handle.

Project-Team Layer: Horizontal, Cross-Divisional Project Teams

Although Kao's organizational structure is basically a traditional division system structure, with daily work organized division by division, fast decision making and efficient resource allocation are achieved by treating each division as an independent profit center. However, when it comes to new-product development, marketing innovation, and human resource management issues, the divisions cooperate in a horizontal manner. Besides the vertical product divisions, Kao organizes three "horizontal" committees to deal with cross-divisional strategic issues. They are the Division Strategy Committee, Marketing Innovation Committee, and Human Resource Management Committee. We call Kao's organizational structure "in transition" because these committees are not totally outside of the business system. In other words, an organizational member is never solely committed to a project team; he or she is in both the business system and the committee at the same point in time.

The Division Strategy Committee, which meets twice a year and is attended by the vice presidents and division heads, determines which new products need to be developed by cross-divisional teams (see Figure 6.3). Ongoing cross-divisional projects, for example, include a hair treatment project for controlling hair hardness, a new cosmetics project for men's use, and an ultrathin paper products project for such products as diapers and sanitary napkins. Members of these teams come from the various divisions as well as from the R&D and production departments.

Kao's project-team activities are not limited to new-product development; they are applied widely throughout the entire organization, as in the case of the Marketing Innovation Committee. This committee meets two or three times a month and is attended by the product division's marketing-staff members as well as graphics engineers and market researchers, who operate outside the division. The committee examines common marketing issues across divisions, including effective market-research techniques, the appropriate advertising media mix, and environmentally conscious packaging. The committee forms Marketing Innovation Projects, which tackle these issues and develop appropriate recommendations.

The Human Resource Management Committee is another horizontal, cross-divisional committee, which meets once a month and is attended by division heads. This committee reviews the overall status of human resource development across divisions, and is also responsible for selecting the appropriate members from each division for new-product and marketing-innovation projects.

Kao applies the idea of horizontal, cross-divisional team activities even to its corporate staff operation. Each "center" specialized in public relations, legal affairs, accounting/finance, or human resources carries out normal staff functions, but cross-center project teams are formed in order to deal with corporatewide

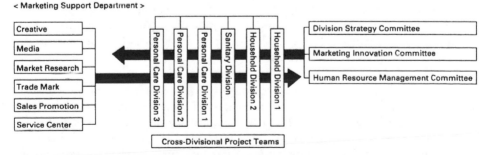

FIGURE 6.3 Cross-divisional Project Teams at Kao. *Source: Kao Corp.*

issues, such as the reduction of fixed cost, risk management, working-hour reduction, and the simplification of corporate staff operation. In trying to reduce fixed cost, for example, the accounting/finance staff people work together with their colleagues in human resources and legal affairs.

Explicit and Tacit Knowledge Bases at Kao

The knowledge-creating activities conducted within the business-system and the project-team layers are captured and recontextualized in the corporatewide knowledge base. Explicit knowledge is captured and recontextualized under the "Five Scientific Areas," which provide Kao with a sense of direction regarding which new markets Kao should enter in the future. In addition, tacit knowledge generated in the two layers is accumulated and reconceptualized along the philosophical principles proposed by top management. This recontextualization fosters a unique organizational culture within Kao, which reorients the mindset of every employee.

"Five Scientific Areas" as an explicit knowledge base

Kao believes that there are five key scientific areas vital to their current technology—fat and oil science, surface science, polymer science, biological science, and applied physics (see Figure 6.4). These five scientific fields are closely related to Kao's historical development. The first, fat and oil science, dates back to Kao's soap production in 1923. The second scientific area was initiated after World War II, with the production of surface-active agent, such as a detergent, from fatty acids. The third area, polymer science, was established as a result of its studies on surface-active agents. Since these agents are applied to fiber and fiber is made from polymers, these two technologies are closely related. Biological science and applied physics have been developed recently as key scientific areas for the future.

Knowledge created in the business-system and project-team layers can be recategorized into these five scientific areas, allowing Kao to move into markets that at first glance may seem distant from its core business. These markets may seem far removed at the "product" level, but they may have very clear commonalities at the level of "basic science." This focus on science is what allows Kao to be in cosmetics and, at the same time, in computer floppy disks. As President Tokiwa explains, recontextualizing Kao's business along basic sciences has helped the company to move into new markets:

> To develop products, we used to categorize technological cores by products. But we found that it gave us a much wider vision if we regard technological cores as scientific knowledge. For instance, surface science is the study of surface tension. Surface-active agents are used in shampoos and detergents in order to activate surface tension. However, surface science is not only applicable to surface-active agents. For instance, skin cream can be looked at

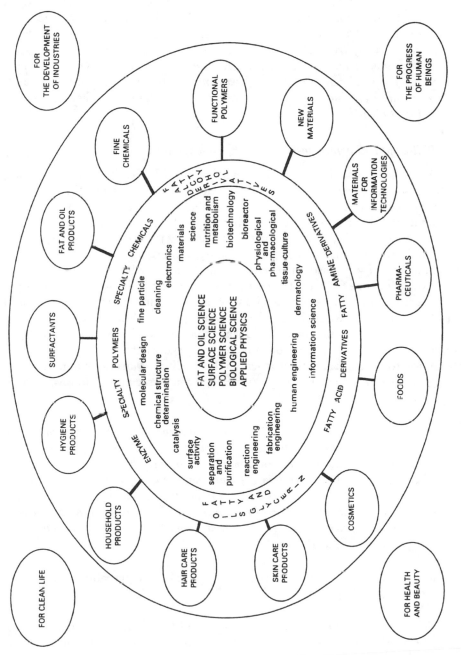

FIGURE 6.4 Kao's Five Scientific Domains. *Source: Kao Corp.*

from a surface-science point of view as the surface between oil and skin. In that sense, skin cream is no longer a cosmetic. Another example is the floppy disk. It is a plastic film coated with magnet powder. We regard it as a type of surface and applied results from surface studies. Our business areas have expanded widely by shifting our approach from that of surface-active agents to the study of surfaces as a science. Although some say that Kao has entered mutually unrelated markets, different market segments do not necessarily mean different businesses. They are naturally related businesses from our point of view.[12]

Philosophical principles as a tacit knowledge base

At Kao, top management is very conspicuous. CEO Yoshio Maruta is called the "philosopher executive" because he is a devout student of Buddhism and expresses his philosophy openly. He insists that what executive management needs is not managerial theory, but rather a philosophy on how to guide an organization. Maruta's philosophy can be summarized in accord with three principles: (1) contribution to the consumer; (2) absolute equality of humans; and (3) the search for truth and the unity of wisdom. These philosophical principles, in turn, form the tacit knowledge base for Kao. They provide the context under which Kao's corporate culture is defined. Its strong corporate culture, in turn, affects the behavior of every Kao employee. We shall describe each of Maruta's philosophies below.

"Contribution to the consumer" means that the primary purpose of the corporation is not to receive profit or to increase market share, but to offer joy and satisfaction to consumers with products as the medium. Maruta's commitment to serving the customers better through knowledge can be seen in the following comment.

The final goal of Kao is to utilize our knowledge into consumers' products. Increasing market share through competition is not the purpose. Kao will keep on contributing to the consumer according to the laws of the universe. There may usually be a certain gap between the knowledge we wish to provide and what the consumers wish to have. It happens because we usually see consumers' lifestyles from the corporate point of view, and cannot conceive actual consumer needs. Kao always has to stand from a consumers' viewpoint. (Maruta, 1988a, p. 5)

Maruta also believes that every human being has "equal ability" as long as restrictions are not imposed:

Everyone in this world is equal in his capability. But those abilities are often restricted in society by others. That is the origin of the separation of people

---

[12]Interviewed on May 21, 1991.

into those who control and those who are controlled. . . . This idea is applicable to a modern organization. Each person has equal creativity. If one member cannot give full play to his or her ability, there is something wrong with the organization or the individual's supervisor. . . . Management's task is to organize different individual's creative strengths. (Maruta, 1988b, p. 61)

Maruta argues that information differentials among employees should not become the source of authority or power. Since creative ideas result from interaction, information sharing becomes the fundamental basis of management. It is for this reason that information regarding Kao is available on computers on each floor, with every employee having access to this database.

Seeking "truth and the unity of wisdom," the third pillar of Maruta's philosophy, shows Kao's attitude toward knowledge creation. He says:

The intelligence of a corporation does not come from the president nor top management. That must come from the gathering of all knowledge of all members. A big organization is separated into many sections. If that organization does not have the system to integrate the knowledge of each section, the newly created knowledge would be poor. Each section's knowledge does not mean the knowledge of the head officer. For example, a line operator can give a great idea for rationalization. The long-run prosperity of a corporation depends on whether it can integrate and accumulate these ideas as one.[13]

The knowledge gathered from organizational members is stored within Kao's tacit knowledge base, which is strongly influenced by Maruta's philosophical principles. This tacit knowledge base guides the behavior of Kao employees and serves as the key driver for its unique corporate culture.

Interaction with the Outside—Kao's ECHO System

As we have seen, Kao is in the process of moving into a hypertext form of organization, in which various forms of knowledge are converted among the three layers inside its organization. At the same time, Kao is equipped with mechanisms that allow knowledge interaction with customers outside the organization. Kao's ECHO System is one such example (ECHO stands for "Echo of Consumer's Helpful Opinion"). The ECHO System processes and analyzes customers' questions and complaints about Kao's products. Kao's operators all over Japan answer customers' phone calls using three subsystems—ECHO/Entry System, ECHO/Support System, and ECHO/Analytical System (see Figure 6.5).

---

[13]Interviewed on March 27, 1991.

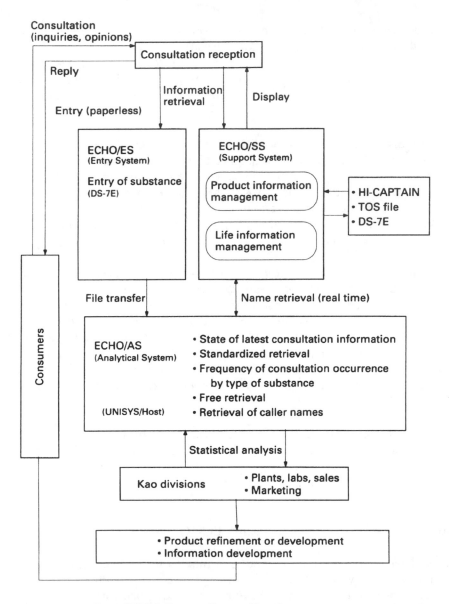

FIGURE 6.5 Kao's ECHO System. *Source: Kao Corp.*

The ECHO/Entry System enables an operator to input customers' questions and complaints according to predesignated key words and, in some complicated cases, in the form of sentences. Kao's operators handle up to about 250 phone calls a day, and over 50,000 phone calls a year.

The ECHO/Support System enables Kao's operators to respond to customers' questions quickly. For example, a mother may call in an emergency situation, asking what to do about a child who has swallowed detergent. In such a case, the Kao operator can reference the ECHO/Support System for a quick pictorial answer. Operators can also reference pictures of similar problems that have occurred in the past, such as the fading of clothes, staining of bathtubs, greasy stains on kitchen fans, and so on.

The ECHO/Analytical System enables the information collected through this system to be used anywhere throughout the Kao organization by the next morning. More than 350,000 consumer questions and complaints stored in the system can be analyzed and recalled, using 8,000 key words—for example, by customer name, by product, by department/division, by date, or by area. Information that may be useful in solving problems is often compiled into reports and sent to the relevant departments, including R&D, production, marketing, and sales.[14]

Sharp as a "Perfected" Hypertext Organization

In this section, we see how Sharp built a "perfected" form of hypertext organizational structure in order to create new knowledge at the organizational level.[15] Although knowledge creation takes place in different layers or contexts within Sharp, an organizational member stays in either the business-system layer or the project-team layer. It differs from the transitional structure at Kao in that the project-team layer is fully developed and completely independent from the business-system layer. At the same time, Sharp is similar to Kao in that it has both an explicit knowledge base and a tacit knowledge base that serve as the third layer of a hypertext structure.

Since its foundation in 1912, Sharp has had a reputation for creating new products—from a self-adjusting belt buckle and Sharp pencil in the early years to liquid crystal projection TVs and electronic organizers today.[16] This reputation has been captured in the slogan of the company's founder, "Don't imitate." Its constant pursuit of creativity and originality led Sharp to formulate its R&D activities along the hypertext organizational structure. Our case study will focus on

---

[14]Kao has a comprehensive Strategic Information System (SIS), which is one of the most advanced in Japan, of which the ECHO System is only a part. Kao considers tacit information as important as information generated by the computer. For example, when sales of a local wholesale subsidiary drop, the head of the Sales Division and his staff will visit and observe the stores in the area to find out the causes of the sales decrease and jointly develop measures to overcome it.

[15]This case study is based on Numagami, Nonaka, and Ohtsubo (1991).

[16]The history of Sharp dates back to 1912, when an inventor and tinkerer Tokuji Hayakawa founded a small metal works in Tokyo. Hayakawa was an inventive person and always encouraged his employees to pursue creativity by saying, "Don't imitate. Make something that others will want to imitate." Today, Sharp is positioned uniquely within the consumer electronics industry in Japan.

how knowledge is created within Sharp's R&D function through effective use of the three layers—business system, project team, and knowledge base.

The Business-System Layer: A Typical Hierarchy

Sharp's day-to-day R&D activities are organized in a typically traditional and hierarchical manner. The actual structure consists of the Corporate R&D Group, Business Group labs, and Business Division labs (see Figure 6.6). These three structures are separated on the basis of the time frame required for technological/product development. The Corporate R&D Group deals with long-term (3 or more years in the future) R&D themes; Business Group labs with mid-term (around 1.5 to 3 years) R&D themes; and Business Division labs with short-term (1.5 years or shorter) themes.

But these three structures are aligned as a traditional hierarchy, with research findings passed down the structures in a top-down fashion. Research findings at the Corporate R&D Group are transferred to the research laboratories of the nine Business Groups, then to the labs of each Business Division. During the product development process, rough prototypes are prepared in advance. Researchers at both the Business Group and the Business Division labs, who receive the prototypes, sometimes relocate to the Corporate R&D Group for a few months to improve their understanding of the research findings from the Corporate R&D Group. When research findings have to be utilized quickly for product commercialization, the Corporate R&D Group's researchers, in turn, sometimes move down to either the Business Group labs or the Business Division labs. Explicit knowledge concerning R&D is transferred efficiently and combined effectively under this kind of hierarchical structure.

Various meetings or conferences are used to coordinate the activities of the laboratories at the three levels (see Figure 6.7). They allow R&D members at Sharp to share knowledge not only within each level but also across the different levels. The first is the General Technology Conference, which is held once a month and is attended by the president, vice presidents, executive directors, and managers of the nine Business Group laboratories. They discuss what sort of R&D activities should be conducted at each laboratory for the upcoming one-year period. These discussions, which deal with the grand design of corporate R&D, often become heated and last as long as six hours, with a break for lunch. The second is the Laboratory Directors' Conference, which is held once a month and is attended by managers of both the Business Group and the Business Division labs, the director of the Corporate R&D Planning Office, and the director of the Intellectual Property Office. The Laboratory Directors' Conference makes specific and detailed decisions, including when and how to transfer certain technology to the business groups and which collaborations are needed with an outside party. The third is the Technology Development Strategy Conference, which is held once a month in each Business Group. Participation in this conference is not necessarily limited to lab members of the Business Group, but can include members of the

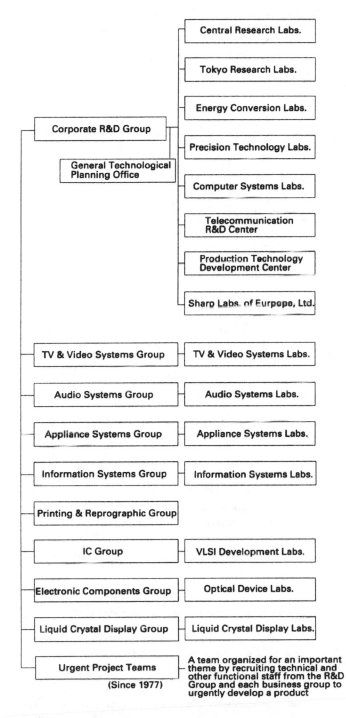

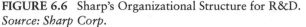

FIGURE 6.6 Sharp's Organizational Structure for R&D.
Source: Sharp Corp.

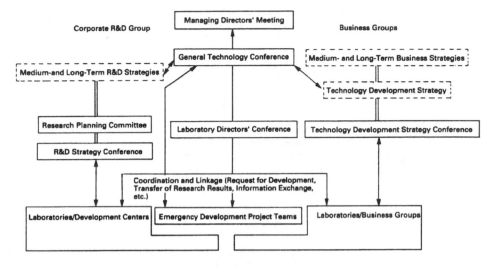

FIGURE 6.7   R&D Conferences Within Sharp. *Source: Sharp Corp.*

Product Planning Department and the Engineering Department, as well as selected individuals from the Corporate R&D Group. The Technology Development Strategy Conference is not merely a place for receiving technology from the
Corporate R&D Group, but a place for deliberating actively on what kind of key
technologies should be developed by each Business Group.

Project-Team Layer: The Urgent Project System

Sharp's R&D operations may have a traditional hierarchical structure, but
when it comes to new-product development the company utilizes the task-force
organization, which is a completely independent, parallel organizational structure. While normal product-development activities are carried out within each
Business Division,[17] the strategically important product development projects are
conducted under the "Urgent Project System."[18] Unlike the "in transition" hy-

---

[17]In the case of product development within the business divisions, numerous meetings are held for
product planning as a means to ensure cooperation and linkage among the engineering, marketing,
and production sections. To begin with, the Product Planning Committee has been established to
strengthen the link between marketing and product planning in the Business Division. The committee's aims are to refine the product concepts of the planning side by reviewing them from the marketing point of view. At the same time, the committee works to enhance marketing's sense of
participation and involvement. The Plans and Programs Promotion Meeting, on the other hand, has
been established to coordinate the efforts of the planning section with those of the production section. During these meetings, consideration is given to ways and means to convert product concepts
into concrete products.

[18]The Urgent Project System was developed based on the "734 Project," which was installed to de-

pertext structure at Kao, where project members retain their posts in their respective functional departments, the members of the Urgent Project System are relocated from their original departments and work exclusively for the project team.

The Urgent Project System gives its members, who could be recruited from any section or department within the company, the same "gold-badge" authority as corporate directors during the project period. The gold badge, which is a gold-colored nameplate, was called "kin-badge" ("kin" means "gold") in Japanese. "Kin" has the same sound as the first syllable of the word "urgent," which is "kin-kyu" in Japanese. Wearing the gold badge carries special significance not only for project members but for other employees at Sharp as well. Urgent Project members develop a priority product or technology within a year or two. But since it is managed directly under the president, the project budget is unlimited. People with the gold badge and their project are given top priority in using company facilities or equipment and in procuring materials. One Business Division manager describes the system as follows:

The members are given the freedom to do whatever is necessary for development. There is always the possibility that they might fail, but they put their heart and soul into research and that's what produces products close to the innovative concept. (Numagami et al., 1991, p. 16)

In addition, members of the Urgent Project can be taken from anywhere in the company at any time. A department may be deprived of its best people for over a year. Needless to say, management has to make every effort during the initial stages to ensure that the system is enforced as originally intended. Each Business Division proposes projects that require companywide development efforts and completion in a brief period of time. These proposals are either adopted or rejected, or "justified," at the above-mentioned General Technology Conference, the highest decision-making meeting at Sharp.

To date, many successful products have been commercialized under the Urgent Project System. Examples include the electronic organizer, the liquid crystal

velop the EL-805 calculator during the "calculator war" of the 1970s. Thanks to this project, Sharp won the "war" and became a leader in the industry (Sasaki, 1991).

In addition, some point out that the Urgent Project System is fashioned after Sharp's original development style. For instance, a member of the electronic organizer development team made the following comments:

Ordinarily, our approach is to specialize in something first, and then have it backed up by an ordinary organization, rather than first establishing an organization to make things. There is, of course, the approach of setting up an organization first and then giving it some themes, but as we are working with a small number of people, it would be impossible to try to do everything. So, what we have done is to decide on the domain in which we want to specialize. Planning or engineering must run first. Only then does the product image begin to take form. If demand can be expected, then we make manpower increases. That is our pattern of approach. The Urgent Project just happens to openly manifest the above-described way of product development (Numagami, Nonaka, and Ohtsubo, 1991, p. 16).

projection TV, magneto-optical discs, and inverter-controlled air conditioners. Later we will take an in-depth look at how the electronic organizer was developed. This story brings the inner workings of a hypertext organization to life. Some 20 teams are involved in Urgent Projects today.[19]

The success of the Urgent Project System led to changes in Sharp's business system. Sharp recently started two strategy meetings—New Life Strategy Meeting and NEWING Product Strategy Meeting—in order to diffuse the Urgent Project idea widely within the entire organization. In the New Life Strategy Meeting, held once a month and attended by the president, vice presidents, and managers of the Business Group and the Business Division, the division managers explain new-product development plans. "Super Excellent (SE) Products" are selected as a result of this meeting. The requirements for an SE product are stringent. It should (1) be able to create a new market trend, (2) represent a completely new technology, (3) use completely new materials, and (4) employ completely new manufacturing methods.

The NEWING Product Strategy Meeting is also held monthly and is attended by 20 people, including the president, vice presidents, and managers of the Business Group and the Business Division. The word "NEWING" is an original coinage interpreted within Sharp to mean "efforts to create a new market." The candidates for new-product concepts are proposed by each Business Group or Business Division manager and reviewed for their originality and marketability. According to President Tsuji, the basic guideline of the meeting is that "we start with saying 'yes' rather than 'no'" to the suggested new ideas and concepts. This positive stance encourages new ideas and motivates development efforts. Attendees at the meeting describe it as "a really practical meeting; you get extremely exhausted after the meeting." Every meeting reviews two proposals, with discussions sometimes lasting more than six hours.

Once a product development plan is recognized as an SE product or a NEWING product, development work starts within the division. The authority given to the development team is similar to that given the Urgent Project, since development-team members receive direct support from the president and have the right to ask for whatever cooperation they need from within the firm. However, it differs from the Urgent Project in that the members basically stay "in" their original business-system layer and conduct other work during the development process.

---

[19]The idea of an Urgent Project System has more recently been expanded into the product development system called "concurrent engineering." While each Urgent Project is accomplished with the completion of product development, concurrent engineering involves not only a product development team, but also design, production, and testing, teams even before product commercialization. This system aims to shorten the development time as well as to prevent product defects and to increase productivity after the developed product has been commercialized. Examples of products developed under this system are Liquid Crystal View Cam (video camcorder) and Eco-A-Wash (washing machine using less water and detergent) (*Nikkei Sangyo Shimbun*, October 25, 1993; *Nikkei Information Strategy*, December 1993).

Explicit and Tacit Knowledge Base at Sharp

Given the importance of both tacit and explicit knowledge, we need to think of the knowledge base in a far broader way than is traditional with most Western companies. In the case of Sharp, its explicit knowledge base can be described with the grand concept of "optoelectronics," which serves as a template for identifying useful and relevant new knowledge. Optoelectronics defines the field of research and resultant products in which Sharp wants to play. Sharp's tacit knowledge base can be symbolized with the slogan, "Don't imitate," which again serves as a template. Imbued with a tacit understanding of the imperative not to imitate, researchers at Sharp learn to distinguish what is really a "new product" from one that is not.

Optoelectronics as an explicit knowledge base

Optoelectronics designates the technological field in which Sharp wants to put its stakes. Sharp believes that it should create its own field, combining "opto" (light, or photo vision) technology with microelectronics. Sharp wants to become a company uniquely positioned in this field.[20] Optoelectronics, in other words, is its corporate vision. (See Figure 6.8 for an illustration.)

Every knowledge generated in the business-system and project-team layers is recategorized and recontextualized with the corporate vision of optoelectronics in mind. It represents the image of the world that Sharp wants to live in, and is one of the key concepts describing what Sharp ought to be. Although its impact is felt throughout the company, it has a special bearing on researchers and engineers within Sharp. For example, Vice President Atsushi Asada comments on how the vision affects researchers and engineers:

> *There is definitely a limit to what comes out spontaneously from one particular technology. Trying to bring a certain technology to a product limits the range of the researcher's view. Showing a concept in a more macroscopic way gives the researcher a greater degree of freedom. . . . All at once their mental horizon widens, and triggers a series of new proposals. A wider mental horizon immediately results in greater freedom for technology development.*[21]

---

[20]For example, the electronic organizer with a liquid crystal display was commercialized by Sharp based on its original ideas, and is still unmatched in terms of both product concept and component technologies. In the home telephone market, Sharp was the first in the industry to release a cordless telephone with an answering machine function. The CJ-A300 was released in September 1989 and sold 250,000 sets in four months. By virtue of this product, Sharp was able to double its market share from 9.5 percent in the previous year to 18.7 percent.

[21]Interviewed on December 18, 1990.

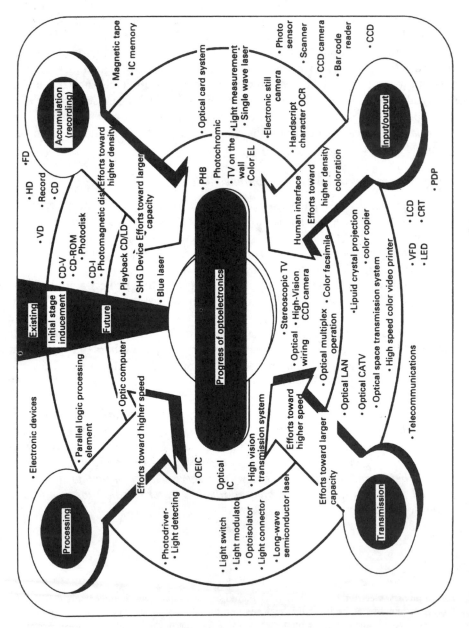

FIGURE 6.8 Development of Optoelectronics Technologies. *Source: Sharp Corp.*

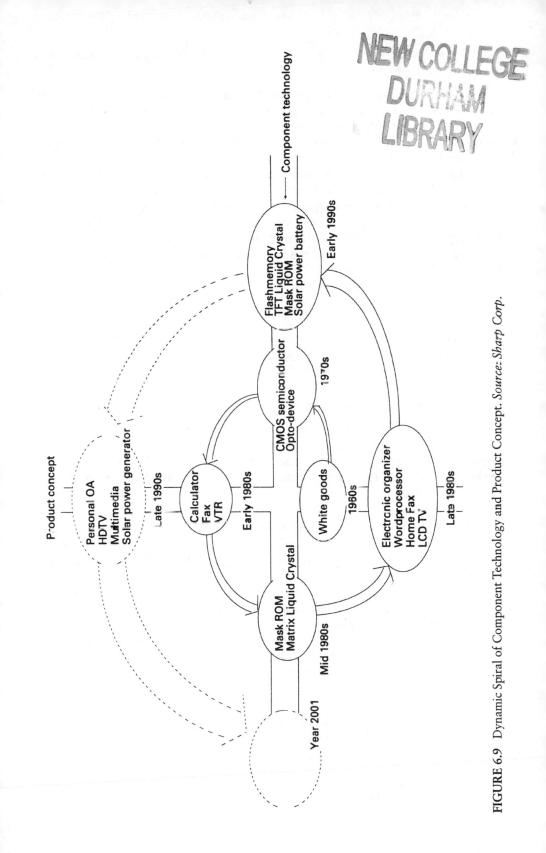

FIGURE 6.9 Dynamic Spiral of Component Technology and Product Concept. *Source: Sharp Corp.*

Much of the knowledge accumulated in the form of optoelectronics consists of knowledge created through the dynamic conversion of various knowledge contents. The essence of Sharp's strategy based on optoelectronics could be described as a dynamic conversion of component technologies and product concepts, as we can see in Figure 6.9. To use our terminology introduced in Chapter 3, component technologies can be interpreted as systemic knowledge (generated via combination) and product concepts as conceptual knowledge (created via externalization). By combining explicit knowledge (i.e., systemic knowledge) and by converting tacit knowledge into explicit knowledge (i.e., conceptual knowledge), Sharp has been successful in developing new technologies and products.

Optoelectronics also affects the tacit understanding of the imperative not to imitate, as described by President Tsuji:

> *In narrowing down fields, optoelectronics and microelectronics became our priorities, and we started to think about how the component technologies originating from them could be merged into the "opto" business. . . . Being a manufacturer, we do all sorts of things, but if we are average in everything we do, we wouldn't be able to make an outstanding product. . . .* [22]

"Don't imitate" as a tacit knowledge base

The founder's principle, "Don't imitate," represents Sharp's corporate culture. The principle forms the tacit knowledge base for Sharp, or a tacit understanding of the imperative not to imitate. President Tsuji explains that the purpose of the company since its foundation has always been the creation of unique product fields and concepts:

> *Ever since the company's foundation, it has been our understanding that our major mission as a manufacturer was to develop our own technology and to make products based on that technology. I am the third president, but Mr. Hayakawa, who was the first, kept saying that we must make products that others will want to imitate. I think this thinking has taken root in the minds of our employees. My predecessor, President Saeki, has also said, "We can't contribute to society by making products just like those of other companies." The meaning of this was more or less the same, but it had a slightly different angle than what Mr. Hayakawa had advocated. I think this thinking has permeated the minds of the executives and employees over the years.* [23]

The "Don't imitate" principle also serves as a guideline for Sharp's human resource development. President Tsuji considers the 1990s as a time period that

---

[22]Interviewed on January 29, 1991.
[23]Interviewed on January 23, 1991.

will require a different kind of workforce, dominated by those equipped with creativity:

> *What I keep telling the top managers is to manage employees in such a manner as to allow them to develop their own ideas. I tell them they mustn't push ideas from the top down. . . . In my beginning-of-the-year address last year, I told the employees, "You know the saying, 'the nail that sticks out gets hammered down.' But what if the nail doesn't stick out, what do you think would happen? It would rot inside. So even if you might get struck, it's better to stick out than rot." . . .*
>
> *And in my beginning-of-the-year address this year, I told them that they should all become* dragonflies. *A dragonfly has complex eyes, and it even has wings. I told them to absorb information with compound eyes and to experiment. I told them never to become a* flatfish *which has large eyes but only looks upwards. Our future tasks will be difficult tasks, but what is of great importance now is how to develop as many creative employees as possible. . . . These creative employees will challenge new things, and new entrepreneurs of a kind unknown before will arise from them. From all this, I believe that the image of a creative company will spontaneously emerge. . . .*
>
> *I also said one more thing to our key personnel, and that was, "When you are driving a car, you may have to look into your rear-view mirror sometimes. But if you are speeding and on a winding road, it's more important to look ahead."*[24]

As the words of President Tsuji indicate, "Don't imitate" has become a template for emphasizing the need to be creative. This tacit knowledge base fosters Sharp's corporate culture and influences the behavior of every employee at Sharp.

Interaction with the Outside—Sharp's Creative Lifestyle Focus Center

As we have seen, Sharp has nearly perfected a hypertext organization that allows knowledge to be converted among the three layers inside the company. In addition, it is equipped with an organizational mechanism for carrying out knowledge interaction with outside customers and companies. The Creative Lifestyle Focus Center, established in April 1985, is a case in point.[25] The center col-

---

[24]Interviewed on January 23, 1991.

[25]The beginning of this organization dated back to the oil crisis of the 1970s. The crisis triggered a change in consumer buying behavior. The baby boomers were already beginning to pick up on the "new family" style of living, but it was the oil crisis that converted the latent changes in their awareness into concrete changes in buying behavior. In view of this, in 1975, Masaki Seki, who was then executive director and had overall responsibility for the home electric appliance business, decided to reorient the business toward the development of differentiated products that were suggestive of a

lects consumer opinions, interprets market data, and creates new-product concepts, which it disseminates to the planning sections of the various business divisions, as well as to the R&D sections.

The Creative Lifestyle Focus Center started various activities that enable Sharp to create new concepts based on inputs from consumers. One such example is the "Trend Leader System," which brings together about 600 "leading consumers," ranging from junior high school students to senior citizens in their seventies. Depending on the nature of the information needed for developing new products, relevant people clustered into "focus groups" are called into the center. Skilled interviewers elicit information from them that may remain tacit otherwise. This system, which started in 1985, enables Sharp to predict consumer trends ten years into the future.

A second example is the "Life Creator System," which was initiated in early 1990. It sets up an actual "living experiment" in which consumers are asked to touch and use potential new products in their still-incomplete stage. For instance, the center will hand over the lens-related parts of a video camera to children as well as to representatives of different industries, including a toy dealer, in hopes that they will cooperate and come up with a new-product concept. These and other living experiments are carried out under the "Life Creator System."

A Hypertext Organization in Action: Sharp's Electronic Organizer

The development story of the electronic organizer brings out the inner workings of the hypertext organization. The significance of this story is the process by which the project shifts from the business-system layer to the project-team layer and back again into the business-system layer. As this criss-crossing takes place, organizational members involved in developing the electronic organizer also shift "in" and "out" of the two layers or contexts.

The origin of the electronic organizer, which started within the business-system layer, dates back to January 1985. Toshio Honda, the product development manager of the Calculator Division at that time, faced an urgent need to develop a new product:

> *I strongly felt a sense of crisis about both the domestic and overseas calculator market at that time. In the mid-1980s, annual domestic production reached 20 million units and the Japanese market was almost saturated. In*

new lifestyle, in order to cope with the changes in consumers' sense of value. The idea was not only to stress the technical functions of a product but also to differentiate the product by adding some emotional value to it. Based on this idea, in 1976 Sharp began to put the "new life strategy" into practice. Numerous product groups, consisting of products in which color, shape, and function were comprehensively coordinated for use by the "new families" to whom they were targeted, were created under the "new life strategy."

the overseas market, many NIES companies emerged as a competitive threat to Sharp. Given this situation, I came across the idea that Sharp should seek a market-creating product with the various technologies related to the calculator. (Komiya, 1988, p. 127)

Honda first promoted the product as a "calculator with an IC card for multipurpose use" and called it a "small information-management machine." His idea was based on the "system notebook," like Filofax, with pages that were replaceable as needed, that was popular among businessmen at that time. To bring his idea to fruition, Honda had to utilize technologies from outside the division—the new liquid crystal display technology and LSI technology—in addition to calculator technology. He also had to bring together many engineers from different fields within the company, which meant that the project plan needed the approval of the General Technology Conference, the highest R&D decision-making body within Sharp.

Honda developed the initial product concept so as to persuade top managers attending the meeting. He positioned the product as more than a successor to the calculator and called it "the tool to unite office automation and personal automation," which enabled information stored within the electronic organizer to be transferred to a computer through an IC card or telecommunication line. Honda pointed out that users of the electronic organizer would become potential customers for Sharp's computers and word processors.

Getting the gold badge

These efforts resulted in approval of the project plan at the General Technology Conference. A gold badge and a document stating an "official announcement of urgent directive" were given to eight members of "Urgent Project A1107" on June 1, 1985. This somewhat exaggerated announcement signified that a new-product development project, which would later introduce the world's first electronic organizer, officially started on that day under Sharp's Urgent Project System. The deadline for development was set at one year, and sales of the product were expected to start in October 1986.

The team, led by Hiroshi Nakanishi, then the engineering section manager at the Personal Machinery Division (the former Calculator Division), was composed of five members from the Personal Machinery Division, one engineer from the IC division, and one engineer from the Liquid Crystal Division of the Electronic Devices Group. The average age of the team members was 32, young relative to those working on other projects. As a result of the official announcement, these eight members were now officially "out" of the ordinary business-system layer and engaged exclusively "in" the Urgent Project team activity.

The interdivisional makeup of the team came in handy during the development process. The technology for incorporating LSI into a 2mm-thick IC card, for example, was developed by the member from the IC Division, while development of the clear panel touch-key was conducted mostly by the member from the

Liquid Crystal Division. Nakanishi exercised his gold-badge power to develop the LSI necessary for the liquid crystal panel operation.

A year later, Urgent Project A1107 was completed as scheduled and a proto-type machine was presented to top management at the General Technology Conference. President Tsuji examined the prototype at the meeting and rejected its commercialization without giving any detailed explanation. Urgent Project A1107 was officially over, and the young team members went back to their original business-system layers in disappointment.

Development process continues within the "business system"

The team leaders, however, never gave up. Honda and Nakanishi put their heads together to analyze why the project was rejected. They found that the main reason for the rejection was the fact that Japanese characters, or *kanji*, could not be used on the product. Honda reflected:

> The results of the market research clearly backed up the need for using kanji. . . . However, we thought the product would become prohibitively expensive with such a function. (Komiya, 1988, p. 133)

Nakanishi made a similar comment:

> We were plagued by the concern that we would have serious trouble with a large number of specs and high power consumption if we incorporated kanji processing. (Komiya, 1988, p. 133).

Although the necessary corrective action was widely known, there was no kanji-processing expert within Nakanishi's division (Personal Machinery). And without the mighty gold badge, he could not request the assistance of engineers from other divisions. It was Nakanishi who came up with the idea of forming an intradivisional development team composed of 14 division members, including one *kanji*-processing expert recruited from the Computer Division through the intrafirm position-offering system.[26]

Even without the authority of the gold badge, the intradivisional development team succeeded in developing an electronic organizer with a *kanji*-processing function in two months. The product, which was called PA 7000, was introduced to the market in January 1987. It became a big success, selling over 5 million units

[26]Under the intrafirm position-offering system, a researcher at some Business Division labs can apply for a position offered by other division labs in which he or she is interested. The researcher can send application to Sharp's human resource development (HRD) department by mail, and then go through several interviews with managers of the HRD department and the designated division. This whole process will never be made public, except for the initial notice of the position offered and the subsequent announcement of the researcher named to the position. This system contributes to promoting motivation among researchers at Sharp along their own lines of interest.

by 1991 and taking more than a 70 percent share of the domestic market the same year.[27]

The product development of the electronic organizer illustrates the mechanisms by which Sharp continuously launches itself into new products and markets. It also shows how the Urgent Project System allowed its developers to take advantage of the Sharp system for key technologies.

We argued in this chapter that the hypertext organization is the ideal structure to bring about continuous organizational knowledge creation. A hypertext organizational structure enables an organization to create and accumulate knowledge efficiently and effectively by transforming knowledge dynamically between two structural layers—those of the business system, which is organized as a traditional hierarchy, and of the project team, which is organized as a typical task force. The knowledge generated in the two layers is then recategorized and recontextualized in the third layer, the knowledge base. We presented two case studies—Kao as an "in transition" and Sharp as a "perfected" hypertext organization—to illustrate how the new organizational structure we are proposing provides the best fit for creating knowledge continuously at the organizational level.

---

[27]*Nikkei Business,* August 19, 1991, pp. 10–23.

7

The Tacit Dimension

Michael Polanyi

Some of you may know that I turned to philosophy as an afterthought to my career as a scientist. I would like to tell you what I was after in making this change, for it will also explain the general task to which my present lecture should introduce us.

I first met questions of philosophy when I came up against the Soviet ideology under Stalin which denied justification to the pursuit of science. I remember a conversation I had with Bukharin in Moscow in 1935. Though he was heading toward his fall and execution three years later, he was still a leading theoretician of the Communist party. When I asked him about the pursuit of pure science in Soviet Russia, he said that pure science was a morbid symptom of a class society; under socialism the conception of science pursued for its own sake would disappear, for the interests of scientists would spontaneously turn to problems of the current Five-Year Plan.

I was struck by the fact that this denial of the very existence of independent scientific thought came from a socialist theory which derived its tremendous persuasive power from its claim to scientific certainty. The scientific outlook appeared to have produced a mechanical conception of man and history in which there was no place for science itself. This conception denied altogether any intrinsic power to thought and thus denied also any grounds for claiming freedom of thought.

I saw also that this self-immolation of the mind was actuated by powerful moral motives. The mechanical course of history was to bring universal justice. Scientific skepticism would trust only material necessity for achieving universal brotherhood. Skepticism and utopianism had thus fused into a new skeptical fanaticism.

It seemed to me then that our whole civilization was pervaded by the dissonance of an extreme critical lucidity and an intense moral conscience, and that this combination had generated both our tight-lipped modern revolutions and the tormented self-doubt of modern man outside revolutionary movements. So I resolved to inquire into the roots of this condition.

My search has led me to a novel idea of human knowledge from which a harmonious view of thought and existence, rooted in the universe, seems to emerge.

I shall reconsider human knowledge by starting from the fact that *we can know more than we can tell.* This fact seems obvious enough; but it is not easy to say exactly what it means. Take an example. We know a person's face, and can recognize it among a thousand, indeed among a million. Yet we usually cannot tell how we recognize a face we know. So most of this knowledge cannot be put into words. But the police have recently introduced a method by which we can communicate much of this knowledge. They have made a large collection of pictures showing a variety of noses, mouths, and other features. From these the witness selects the particulars of the face he knows, and the pieces can then be put together to form a reasonably good likeness of the face. This may suggest that we can communicate, after all, our knowledge of a physiognomy, provided we are given adequate means for expressing ourselves. But the application of the police method does not change the fact that previous to it we did know more than we could tell at the time. Moreover, we can use the police method only by knowing how to match the features we remember with those in the collection, and we cannot tell how we do this. This very act of communication displays a knowledge that we cannot tell.

There are many other instances of the recognition of a characteristic physiognomy—some commonplace, others more technical—which have the same structure as the identification of a person. We recognize the moods of the human face, without being able to tell, except quite vaguely, by what signs we know it. At the universities great efforts are spent in practical classes to teach students to identify cases of diseases and specimens of rocks, of plants and animals. All descriptive sciences study physiognomies that cannot be fully described in words, nor even by pictures.

But can it not be argued, once more, that the possibility of teaching these appearances by practical exercises proves that we can tell our knowledge of them? The answer is that we can do so only by relying on the pupil's intelligent cooperation for catching the meaning of the demonstration. Indeed, any definition of a word denoting an external thing must ultimately rely on pointing at such a thing. This naming-cum-pointing is called "an ostensive definition"; and this philosophic expression conceals a gap to be bridged by an intelligent effort on the part of the person to whom we want to tell what the word means. Our message had left something behind that we could not tell, and its reception must rely on it that the person addressed will discover that which we have not been able to communicate.

Gestalt psychology has demonstrated that we may know a physiognomy by integrating our awareness of its particulars without being able to identify these particulars, and my analysis of knowledge is closely linked to this discovery of Gestalt psychology. But I shall attend to aspects of Gestalt which have been hitherto neglected. Gestalt psychology has assumed that perception of a physiognomy takes place through the spontaneous equilibration of its particulars impressed on the retina or on the brain. However, I am looking at Gestalt, on the contrary, as the outcome of an active shaping of experience performed in the pursuit of knowledge. This shaping or integrating I hold to be the great and indispensable tacit power by which all knowledge is discovered and, once discovered, is held to be true.

The structure of Gestalt is then recast into a logic of tacit thought, and this changes the range and perspective of the whole subject. The highest forms of integration loom largest now. These are manifested in the tacit power of scientific and artistic genius. The art of the expert diagnostician may be listed next, as a somewhat impoverished form of discovery, and we may put in the same class the performance of skills, whether artistic, athletic, or technical. We have here examples of knowing, both of a more intellectual and more practical kind; both the *"wissen"* and *"können"* of the Germans, or the "knowing what" and the "knowing how" of Gilbert Ryle. These two aspects of knowing have a similar structure and neither is ever present without the other. This is particularly clear in the art of diagnosing, which intimately combines skillful testing with expert observation. I shall always speak of "knowing," therefore, to cover both practical and theoretical knowledge. We can, accordingly, interpret the use of tools, of probes, and of pointers as further instances of the art of knowing, and may add to our list also the denotative use of language, as a kind of verbal pointing.

Perception, on which Gestalt psychology centered its attention, now appears as the most impoverished form of tacit knowing. As such it will be shown to form the bridge between the higher creative powers of man and the bodily processes which are prominent in the operations of perception.

Some recent psychological experiments have shown in isolation the principal mechanism by which knowledge is tacitly acquired. Many of you have heard of these experiments as revealing the diabolical machinery of hidden persuasion. Actually, they are but elementary demonstrations of the faculty by which we apprehend the relation between two events, both of which we know, but only one of which we can tell.

Following the example set by Lazarus and McCleary in 1949, psychologists call the exercise of this faculty a process of "subception."[1] These authors presented a person with a large number of nonsense syllables, and after showing certain of the syllables, they administered an electric shock. Presently the person showed symptoms of anticipating the shock at the sight of "shock syllables"; yet, on questioning, he could not identify them. He had come to know when to expect a shock, but he could not tell what made him expect it. He had acquired a knowledge similar to that which we have when we know a person by signs which we cannot tell.

Another variant of this phenomenon was demonstrated by Eriksen and Kuethe in 1958.[2] They exposed a person to a shock whenever he happened to utter associations to certain "shock words." Presently, the person learned to forestall the shock by avoiding the utterance of such associations, but, on questioning, it appeared that he did not know he was doing this. Here the subject got to know a practical operation, but could not tell how he worked it. This kind of subception has the structure of a skill, for a skill combines elementary muscular acts which are not identifiable, according to relations that we cannot define.

These experiments show most clearly what is meant by saying that one can know more than one can tell. For the experimental arrangement wards off the suspicion of self-contradiction, which is not easy to dispel when anyone speaks of things he knows and cannot tell. This is prevented here by the division of roles between the subject and the observer. The experimenter observes that another person has a certain knowledge that he cannot tell, and so no one speaks of a knowledge he himself has and cannot tell.

We may carry forward, then, the following result. In both experiments that I have cited, subception was induced by electric shock. In the first series the subject was shocked after being shown certain nonsense syllables, and he learned to expect this event. In the second series he learned to suppress the uttering of certain associations, which would evoke the shock. In both cases the shock-producing particulars remained tacit. The subject could not identify them, yet he relied on his awareness of them for anticipating the electric shock.

Here we see the basic structure of tacit knowing. It always involves two things, or two kinds of things. We may call them the two terms of tacit knowing. In the experiments the shock syllables and shock associations formed the first term, and the electric shock which followed them was the second term. After the subject had learned to connect these two terms, the sight of the shock syllables evoked the expectation of a shock and the utterance of the shock associations was suppressed in order to avoid shock. Why did this connection remain tacit? It would seem that this was due to the fact that the subject was riveting his attention on the electric shock. He was relying on his awareness of the shock-producing particulars only in their bearing on the electric shock. We may say that he learned to rely on his awareness of these particulars for the purpose of attending to the electric shock.

Here we have the basic definition of the logical relation between the first and second term of a tacit knowledge. It combines two kinds of knowing. We know the electric shock, forming the second term, by attending to it, and hence the subject is *specifiably* known. But we know the shock-producing particulars only by relying on our own awareness of them for attending to something else, namely the electric shock, and hence our knowledge of them remains *tacit*. This is how we come to know these particulars, without becoming able to identify them. Such is the *functional relation* between the two terms of tacit knowing: *we know the first term only by relying on our awareness of it for attending to the second.*

In his book on freedom of the will, Austin Farrar has spoken at one point of *disattending from* certain things for attending *to* others. I shall adopt a variant of this usage by saying that in an act of tacit knowing we *attend from* something for attending *to* something else; namely, *from* the first term *to* the second term of the tacit relation. In many ways the first term of this relation will prove to be nearer to us, the second further away from us. Using the language of anatomy, we may call the first term *proximal,* and the second term *distal.* It is the proximal term, then, of which we have a knowledge that we may not be able to tell.

In the case of a human physiognomy, I would now say that we rely on our awareness of its features for attending to the characteristic appearance of a face. We are attending *from* the features *to* the face, and thus may be unable to specify the features. And I would say, likewise, that we are relying on our awareness of a combination of muscular acts for attending to the performance of a skill. We are attending *from* these elementary movements *to* the achievement of their joint purpose, and hence are usually unable to specify these elementary acts. We may call this the *functional structure* of tacit knowing.

But we may ask: does not the *appearance* of the experimental setting—composed of the nonsense syllables and the electric shocks—undergo some change when we learn to anticipate a shock at the sight of certain syllables? It does, and in a very subtle way. The expectation of a shock, which at first had been vague and unceasing, now becomes sharply fluctuating; it suddenly rises at some moments and drops between them. So we may say that even though we do not learn to recognize the shock syllables as distinct from other syllables, we do become aware of facing a shock syllable in terms of the apprehension it evokes in us. In other words, we are aware of seeing these syllables in terms of that on which we are focusing our attention, which is the probability of an electric shock. Applying this to the case of a physiognomy, we may say that we are aware of its features in terms of the physiognomy to which we are attending. In the exercise of a skill, we are aware of its several muscular moves in terms of the performance to which our attention is directed. We may say, in general, that we are aware of the proximal term of an act of tacit knowing in the appearance of its distal term; we are aware of that *from* which we are attending *to* another thing, in the *appearance* of that thing. We may call this the *phenomenal structure* of tacit knowing.

But there is a significance in the relation of the two terms of tacit knowing which combines its functional and phenomenal aspects. When the sight of certain syllables makes us expect an electric shock, we may say that they *signify* the approach of a shock. This is their *meaning* to us. We could say, therefore, that when shock syllables arouse an apprehension in us, without our being able to identify the syllables which arouse it, we know these syllables only in terms of their meaning. It is their meaning to which our attention is directed. It is in terms of their meaning that they enter into the appearance of that *to* which we are attending *from* them.

We could say, in this sense, that a characteristic physiognomy is the meaning of its features; which is, in fact, what we do say when a physiognomy expresses a particular mood. To identify a physiognomy would then amount to relying on our awareness of its features for attending to their joint meaning. This may sound farfetched, because the meaning of the features is observed at the same spot where the features are situated, and hence it is difficult to separate mentally the features from their meaning. Yet, the fact remains that the two are distinct, since we may know a physiognomy without being able to specify its particulars.

To see more clearly the separation of a meaning from that which has this meaning, we may take the example of the use of a probe to explore a cavern, or the way a blind man feels his way by tapping with a stick. For here the separation of the two is wide, and we can also observe here the process by which this separation gradually takes place. Anyone using a probe for the first time will feel its impact against his fingers and palm. But as we learn to use a probe, or to use a stick for feeling our way, our awareness of its impact on our hand is transformed into a sense of its point touching the objects we are exploring. This is how an interpretative effort transposes meaningless feelings into meaningful ones, and places these at some distance from the original feeling. We become aware of the feelings in our hand in terms of their meaning located at the tip of the probe or stick to which we are attending. This is so also when we use a tool. We are attending to the meaning of its impact on our hands in terms of its effect on the things to which we are applying it. We may call this the *semantic aspect* of tacit knowing. All meaning tends to be displaced *away from ourselves,* and that is in fact my justification for using the terms "proximal" and "distal" to describe the first and second terms of tacit knowing.

From the three aspects of tacit knowing that I have defined so far—the functional, the phenomenal, and the semantic—we can deduce a fourth aspect, which tells us what tacit knowing is a knowledge of. This will represent its *ontological* aspect. Since tacit knowing establishes a meaningful relation between two terms, we may identify it with the *understanding* of the comprehensive entity which these two terms jointly constitute. Thus the proximal term represents the *particulars* of this entity, and we can say, accordingly, that we comprehend the entity by relying on our awareness of its particulars for attending to their joint meaning.

This analysis can be applied with interesting results to the case of visual perception. Physiologists long ago established that the way we see an object is determined by our awareness of certain efforts inside our body, efforts which we cannot feel in themselves. We are aware of these things going on inside our body in terms of the position, size, shape, and motion of an object, to which we are attending. In other words we are attending *from* these internal processes *to* the qualities of things outside. These qualities are what those internal processes *mean* to us. The transposition of bodily experiences into the perception of things outside may now appear, therefore, as an instance of the transposition of meaning away from us, which we have found to be present to some extent in all tacit knowing.

But it may be said that the feelings transposed by perception differ from those transposed by the use of tools or probes, by being hardly noticeable in themselves previous to their transposition. An answer to this—or at least part of an answer to it—is to be found in experiments extending subception to subliminal stimuli. Hefferline and collaborators have observed that when spontaneous muscular twitches, unfelt by the subject—but observable externally by a million-fold amplification of their action currents—were followed by the cessation of an unpleasant noise, the subject responded by increasing the frequency of the twitches and thus silencing the noise much of the time.[3] Tacit knowing is seen to operate here on an internal action that we are quite incapable of controlling or even feeling in itself. We become aware of our operation of it only in the silencing of a noise. This experimental result seems closely analogous to the process by which we become aware of subliminal processes inside our body in the perception of objects outside.

This view of perception, that it is an instance of the transposition of feelings which we found in the use of probes and in the process of subception, is borne out by the fact that the capacity to see external objects must be acquired, like the use of probes and the feats of subception, by a process of learning which can be laborious.

Modern philosophers have argued that perception does not involve projection, since we are not previously aware of the internal processes which we are supposed to have projected into the qualities of things perceived. But we have now established that projection of this very kind is present in various instances of tacit knowing. Moreover, the fact that we do not originally sense the internal processes in themselves now appears irrelevant. We may venture, therefore, to extend the scope of tacit knowing to include neural traces in the cortex of the nervous system. This would place events going on inside our brain on the same footing as the subliminal twitches operated by Hefferline's subjects.*

This brings us to the point at which I hinted when I first mentioned perception as an instance of tacit knowing. I said that by elucidating the way our bodily processes participate in our perceptions we will throw light on the bodily roots of all thought, including man's highest creative powers. Let me show this now.

Our body is the ultimate instrument of all our external knowledge, whether intellectual or practical. In all our waking moments we are *relying* on our awareness of contacts of our body with things outside for *attending* to these things. Our own body is the only thing in the world which we normally never experience as an object, but experience always in terms of the world to which we are attending from our body. It is by making this intelligent use of our body that we feel it to be our body, and not a thing outside.

I have described how we learn to feel the end of a tool or a probe hitting things outside. We may regard this as the transformation of the tool or probe into a sentient extension of our body, as Samuel Butler has said. But our awareness of our body for attending to things outside it suggests a wider generalization of the feeling we have of our body. Whenever we use certain things for attending *from* them to other things, in the way in which we always use our own body, these things change their appearance. They appear to us now in terms of the entities to which we are attending *from* them, just as we feel our own body in terms of the things outside to which we are attending *from* our body. In this sense we can say that when we make a thing function as the proximal term of tacit knowing, we incorporate it in our body—or extend our body to include it—so that we come to dwell in it.

The full range of this generalization can only be hinted at here. Indications of its scope may be seen by recalling that, at the turn of the last century, German

---

*Such a hypothesis does not explain how perceived sights, or any other state of consciousness, arise in conjunction with neural processes. It merely applies the principle that wherever some process in our body gives rise to consciousness in us, our tacit knowing of the process will make sense of it in terms of an experience to which we are attending.

thinkers postulated that indwelling, or empathy, is the proper means of knowing man and the humanities. I am referring particularly to Dilthey[4] and Lipps.[5] Dilthey taught that the mind of a person can be understood only by reliving its workings; and Lipps represented aesthetic appreciation as an entering into a work of art and thus dwelling in the mind of its creator. I think that Dilthey and Lipps described here a striking form of tacit knowing as applied to the understanding of man and of works of art, and that they were right in saying that this could be achieved only by indwelling. But my analysis of tacit knowing shows that they were mistaken in asserting that this sharply distinguished the humanities from the natural sciences. Indwelling, as derived from the structure of tacit knowing, is a far more precisely defined act than is empathy, and it underlies all observations, including all those described previously as indwelling.

We meet with another indication of the wide functions of indwelling when we find acceptance to moral teachings described as their *interiorization*. To interiorize is to identify ourselves with the teachings in question, by making them function as the proximal term of a tacit moral knowledge, as applied in practice. This establishes the tacit framework for our moral acts and judgments. And we can trace this kind of indwelling to logically similar acts in the practice of science. To rely on a theory for understanding nature is to interiorize it. For we are attending from the theory to things seen in its light, and are aware of the theory, while thus using it, in terms of the spectacle that it serves to explain. This is why mathematical theory can be learned only by practicing its application: its true knowledge lies in our ability to use it.

The identification of tacit knowing with indwelling involves a shift of emphasis in our conception of tacit knowing. We had envisaged tacit knowing in the first place as a way to know more than we can tell. We identified the two terms of tacit knowing, the proximal and the distal, and recognized the way we attend *from* the first *to* the second, thus achieving an integration of particulars to a coherent entity to which we are attending. Since we were not attending to the particulars in themselves, we could not identify them: but if we now regard the integration of particulars as an interiorization, it takes on a more positive character. It now becomes a means of making certain things function as the proximal terms of tacit knowing, so that instead of observing them in themselves, we may be aware of them in their bearing on the comprehensive entity which they constitute. It brings home to us that it is not by looking at things, but by dwelling in them, that we understand their joint meaning.

We can see now how an unbridled lucidity can destroy our understanding of complex matters. Scrutinize closely the particulars of a comprehensive entity and their meaning is effaced, our conception of the entity is destroyed. Such cases are well known. Repeat a word several times, attending carefully to the motion of your tongue and lips, and to the sound you make, and soon the word will sound hollow and eventually lose its meaning. By concentrating attention on his fingers, a pianist can temporarily paralyze his movement. We can make ourselves lose sight of a pattern or physiognomy by examining its several parts under sufficient magnification.

Admittedly, the destruction can be made good by interiorizing the particulars once more. The word uttered again in its proper context, the pianist's fingers used again with his mind on his music, the features of a physiognomy and the details of a pattern glanced at once more from a distance: they all come to life and recover their meaning and their comprehensive relationship.

But it is important to note that this recovery never brings back the original meaning. It may improve on it. Motion studies, which tend to paralyze a skill, will improve it when followed by practice. The meticulous dismembering of a text, which can kill its appreciation, can also supply material for a much deeper understanding of it. In these cases, the detailing of particulars, which by itself would destroy meaning, serves as a guide to their subsequent integration and thus establishes a more secure and more accurate meaning of them.

But the damage done by the specification of particulars may be irremediable. Meticulous detailing may obscure beyond recall a subject like history, literature, or philosophy. Speaking more generally, the belief that, since particulars are more tangible, their knowledge offers a true conception of things is fundamentally mistaken.

Of course, tacit reintegration of particulars is not the only way to recover their meaning, destroyed by focusing our attention on them. The destructive analysis of a comprehensive entity can be counteracted in many cases by explicitly stating the relation between its particulars. Where such explicit integration is feasible, it goes far beyond the range of tacit integration. Take the case of a machine. One can learn to use it skillfully, without knowing exactly how it works. But the engineer's understanding of its construction and operation goes much deeper. We possess a practical knowledge of our own body, but the physiologist's theoretical knowledge of it is far more revealing. The formal rules of prosody may deepen our understanding of so delicate a thing as a poem.

But my examples show clearly that, in general, an explicit integration cannot replace its tacit counterpart. The skill of a driver cannot be replaced by a thorough schooling in the theory of the motorcar; the knowledge I have of my own body differs altogether from the knowledge of its physiology; and the rules of rhyming and prosody do not tell me what a poem told me, without any knowledge of its rules.

We are approaching here a crucial question. The declared aim of modern science is to establish a strictly detached, objective knowledge. Any falling short of this ideal is accepted only as a temporary imperfection, which we must aim at eliminating. But suppose that tacit thought forms an indispensable part of all knowledge, then the ideal of eliminating all personal elements of knowledge would, in effect, aim at the destruction of all knowledge. The ideal of exact science would turn out to be fundamentally misleading and possibly a source of devastating fallacies.

I think I can show that the process of formalizing all knowledge to the exclusion of any tacit knowing is self-defeating. For, in order that we may formalize the relations that constitute a comprehensive entity, for example, the relations that constitute a frog, this entity, i.e., the frog, must be first identified informally by tacit knowing; and, indeed, the meaning of a mathematical theory of the frog lies in its continued bearing on this still tacitly known frog. Moreover, the act of bringing a mathematical theory to bear on its subject is itself a tacit integration of the kind we have recognized in the use of a denotative word for designating its object. And we have seen also that a true knowledge of a theory can be established only after it has been interiorized and extensively used to interpret experience. Therefore: a mathematical theory can be constructed only by relying on *prior* tacit knowing and can function as a theory only *within* an act of tacit knowing, which consists in our attending *from* it to the previously established experience on which it bears. Thus the ideal of a comprehensive mathematical theory of experience which would eliminate all tacit knowing is proved to be self-contradictory and logically unsound.

But I must not rest my case on such an abstract argument. Let me finish this lecture, therefore, by presenting you with a most striking concrete example of an experience that cannot possibly be represented by any exact theory. It is an experience within science itself: the experience of seeing a problem, as a scientist sees it in his pursuit of discovery.

It is a commonplace that all research must start from a problem. Research can be successful only if the problem is good; it can be original only if the problem is original. But how can one see a problem, any problem, let alone a good and original problem? For to see a problem is to see something that is hidden. It is to have an intimation of the coherence of hitherto not comprehended particulars. The problem is good if this intimation is true; it is original if no one else can see the possibilities of the comprehension that we are anticipating. To see a problem that will lead to a great discovery is not just to see something hidden, but to see something of which the rest of humanity cannot have even an inkling. All this is a commonplace; we take it for granted, without noticing the clash of self-contradiction entailed in it. Yet Plato has pointed out this contradiction in the *Meno*. He says that to search for the solution of a problem is an absurdity; for either you know what you are looking for, and then there is no problem; or you do not know what you are looking for, and then you cannot expect to find anything.

The solution which Plato offered for this paradox was that all discovery is a remembering of past lives. This explanation has hardly ever been accepted, but neither has any other solution been offered for avoiding the contradiction. So we are faced with the fact that, for two thousand years and more, humanity has progressed through the efforts of people solving difficult problems, while all the time it could be shown that to do this was either meaningless or impossible. We have here the classical case of Poe's *Purloined Letter,* of the momentous document lying casually in front of everybody, and hence overlooked by all. For the *Meno* shows conclusively that if all knowledge is explicit, i.e., capable of being clearly stated, then we cannot know a problem or look for its solution. And the *Meno* also shows, therefore, that if problems nevertheless exist, and discoveries can be made by solving them, we can know things, and important things, that we cannot tell.

The kind of tacit knowledge that solves the paradox of the *Meno* consists in the intimation of something hidden, which we may yet discover. There exists another important manifestation of these mental powers. We are often told that great scientific discoveries are marked by their fruitfulness; and this is true. But how can we recognize truth by its fruitfulness? Can we recognize that a statement is true by appreciating the wealth of its yet undiscovered consequences? This would of course be nonsensical, if we had to know explicitly what was yet undiscovered. But it makes sense if we admit that we can have a tacit foreknowledge of yet undiscovered things. This is indeed the kind of foreknowledge the Copernicans must have meant to affirm when they passionately maintained, against heavy pressure, during one hundred and forty years before Newton proved the point, that the heliocentric theory was not merely a convenient way of computing the paths of planets, but was really true.

It appears, then, that to know that a statement is true is to know more than we can tell and that hence, when a discovery solves a problem, it is itself fraught with further intimations of an indeterminate range, and that furthermore, when we accept the discovery as true, we commit ourselves to a belief in all these as yet undisclosed, perhaps as yet unthinkable, consequences.

Since we have no explicit knowledge of these unknown things, there can also be no explicit justification of a scientific truth. But as we can know a problem, and feel sure that it is pointing to something hidden behind it, we can be aware also of the hidden implications of a scientific discovery, and feel confident that they will prove right. We feel sure of this, because in contemplating the discovery we are looking at it not only in itself but, more significantly, as a clue to a reality of which it is a manifestation. The pursuit of discovery is conducted from the start in these terms; all the time we are guided by sensing the presence of a hidden reality toward which our clues are pointing; and the discovery which terminates and satisfies this pursuit is still sustained by the same vision. It claims to have made contact with reality: a reality which, being real, may yet reveal itself to future eyes in an indefinite range of unexpected manifestations.

We have here reached our main conclusions. Tacit knowing is shown to account (1) for a valid knowledge of a problem, (2) for the scientist's capacity to pursue it, guided by his sense of approaching its solution, and (3) for a valid anticipation of the yet indeterminate implications of the discovery arrived at in the end.

Such indeterminate commitments are necessarily involved in any act of knowing based on indwelling. For such an act relies on interiorizing particulars to which we are not attending and which, therefore, we may not be able to specify, and relies further on our attending from these unspecifiable particulars to a comprehensive entity connecting them in a way we cannot define. This kind of knowing solves the paradox of the *Meno* by making it possible for us to know something so indeterminate as a problem or a hunch, but when the use of this faculty turns out to be an indispensable element of all knowing, we are forced to conclude that all knowledge is of the same kind as the knowledge of a problem.

This is in fact our result. We must conclude that the paradigmatic case of scientific knowledge, in which all the faculties that are necessary for finding and holding scientific knowledge are fully developed, is the knowledge of an approaching discovery.

To hold such knowledge is an act deeply committed to the conviction that there is something there to be discovered. It is personal, in the sense of involving the personality of him who holds it, and also in the sense of being, as a rule, solitary; but there is no trace in it of self-indulgence. The discoverer is filled with a compelling sense of responsibility for the pursuit of a hidden truth, which demands his services for revealing it. His act of knowing exercises a personal judgment in relating evidence to an external reality, an aspect of which he is seeking to apprehend.

The anticipation of discovery, like discovery itself, may turn out to be a delusion. But it is futile to seek for strictly impersonal criteria of its validity, as positivistic philosophies of science have been trying to do for the past eighty years or so. To accept the pursuit of science as a reasonable and successful enterprise is to share the kind of commitments on which scientists enter by undertaking this enterprise. You cannot formalize the act of commitment, for you cannot express your commitment non-committally. To attempt this is to exercise the kind of lucidity which destroys its subject matter. Hence the failure of the positivist movement in the philosophy of science. The difficulty is to find a stable alternative to its ideal of objectivity. This is indeed the task for which the theory of tacit knowing should prepare us.

NOTES

1. Lazarus, R.S., and McCleary, R.A., *Journal of Personality* (Vol. 18, 1949), p. 191, and *Psychological Review* (Vol. 58, 1951), p. 113. these results were called in question by Eriksen, C. W., *Psychological Review* (Vol. 63, 1956), p. 74 and defended by Lazarus, *Psychological Review* (Vol. 63, 1956), p. 343. But in a later paper surveying the whole field—*Psychological Review* (Vol. 67, 1960), p. 279—Eriksen confirmed the experiments of Lazarus and McCleary, and accepted them as evidence of subception.

2. Eriksen, C. W., and Kuethe, J. L., "Avoidance Conditioning of Verbal Behavior Without Awareness: A Paradigm of Repression," *Journal of Abnormal and Social Psychology* (Vol. 53, 1956), pp. 203–09.

3. Hefferline, Ralph, F., Keenan, Brian, and Harford, Richard A., "Escape and Avoidance Conditioning in Human Subjects Without Their Observation of the Response," *Science* (Vol. 130, November 1959), pp. 1338–39. Hefferline, Ralph, F., and Keenan, Brian, "Amplitude-Induction Gradient of a Small Human Operant in an Escape-Avoidance Situation," *Journal of the Experimental Analysis of Behavior* (Vol. 4, January 1961), pp. 41–43. Hefferline, Ralph F., and Perera, Thomas B., "Proprioceptive Discrimination of a Covert Operant Without Its Observation by the Subject," *Science* (Vol. 139, March 1963), pp. 834–35. Hefferline, Ralph F., and Keenan, Brian, "Amplitude-Induction Gradient of a Small Scale (Cover) Operant," *Journal of the Experimental Analysis of Behavior* (Vol. 6, July 1963), pp. 307–15. See also general conclusions in Hefferline, Ralph F., "Learning Theory and Clinical Psychology—An Eventual Symbiosis?" from *Experimental Foundation of clinical Psychology*, ed. Arthur J. Bachrach (1962).

4. Dilthey, W., *Gesammelte Schriften* (Vol. VII, Leipzig and Berlin, 1934–36), pp. 213–16; [Translation by H. A. Hodges, *Wilhelm Dilthey* (New York, Oxford University Press, 1944), pp. 121–24].

5. Lipps, T., *Asthetik* (Hamburg, 1903).

8
Learning By Knowledge-Intensive Firms

William H. Starbuck

DISCOVERING EXPERTISE

The General Manager of the Garden Company (a pseudonym) invited John Dutton and me to advise him about what he called their 'lot-size problem.' He was wondering, he said, whether Garden was making products in economically efficient quantities.

We had no idea what a strange but memorable experience this would be!

The General Manager proposed that we start with a tour of their largest plant, and assigned someone to guide us. Our guide took us first to the model shop, which produced jigs and patterns for use in the main plant. In the model shop, a skilled craftsman would start with a raw piece of metal, work on it with several different machine tools, and end with a finished component. Each successive component differed from those produced before and after, and each craftsman's tasks were shifting continually.

Then our guide took us into the plant itself. To our amazement, we found little difference from the model shop. Many workers were using several different machine tools in succession. Since each worker had several machines, most of the machines were idle at any moment.

Some workers chose to decorate castings' non-functional insides with patterns such as one sees on the doors of bank vaults, each worker inscribing his personal pattern. Quality standards were incredibly high, for the workers saw themselves as artisans who were putting their personal signatures on their products.

In the middle of the plant stood a wooden shack. Nails on the wall of this shack represented the distinct areas of the plant. Hanging on each nail were the production orders awaiting work in one area. We saw workers enter the shack, leaf through the orders, and choose orders to work on. Our guide said orders got

Reprinted by permission of Blackwell Publishers. From The Journal of Management Studies 29 (1992) 713–740. Copyright 1992 by Blackwell Publishers.

processed promptly if they called for tasks the workers enjoyed, whereas orders might hang on the nails for weeks if they called for tasks the workers disliked.

Hoppers of partly finished components jammed the aisles. This, our guide explained, reflected raw-materials shortages, misplaced jigs and patterns, and missing components. After work began on an order, a worker would discover that needed raw material was out-of-stock—the order would have to wait while purchasing got the raw material. Or, a worker would be unable to find a needed jig, and a search would reveal that a subcontractor had borrowed the jig and not returned it—the order would have to wait while the jig was retrieved or replaced. Or, a product would be partly assembled and then the assemblers would discover that a component was missing—the incomplete assemblies would have to wait until the missing component emerged from production. Any of these problems might arise more than once during production of a single order. As one result, Garden was taking an average of nine months to deliver standard products that incorporated only a few hours of direct labour.

The plant tour left John and me rolling our eyes in wonder. We could not have imagined less efficient methods or greater disorder. It was hard to believe that Garden could even be making a profit! Yet the main building appeared in good condition, the office areas looked clean, and the General Manager's office had luxurious furnishings.

We told the General Manager that the plant had no lot-size problem, but we wondered whether he would not prefer to have one. A lot-size problem implied that machines would be set up for mass production and that workers would repeat specialized tasks. We suggested, however, that Garden would gain more direct benefit from production and inventory control than from mass production. A computer-based control system could keep raw materials in stock, monitor the progress of production, reduce delays, and make sure that jigs and patterns were available. Inventories could be much lower, machine usage could be much higher, and customers could receive their orders much more quickly.

The General Manager asked for estimates. We told him a control system would have a payback period of roughly two years and the inventory savings alone would cut production costs by at least ten percent. To this, he responded, 'Why should we want to do that? Ten percent of our production costs is only one percent of our revenues.' He then produced Garden's financial statements for the previous year. After-tax profits had been $40 million on sales of $83.5 million. 'And that,' he crowed, 'was a year in which we had a strike for ten months!'

He went on to explain that Garden made every effort to avoid direct competition. Over a third of Garden's personnel were engineers who were good at designing new products that no other firm was producing. Garden's policy was to continue making a product only as long as its gross margin exceeded 75 percent of sales. When competition drove a gross margin below 75 percent, Garden would stop offering that product for sale. The average gross margin across all products exceeded 90 percent.

Allowing for the corporate tax rate of 52 percent, we surmised that Garden employed expert tax accountants as well as expert engineers.

John and I had received several lessons in business . . . and the General Manager had not even charged us tuition!

Garden's high profits did not arise from fine steel, unusually skilled craftsmen, or exceptional capital equipment. Its marketing was ordinary. Although Garden delivered high quality, it used no esoteric production technologies, and it often subcontracted production to a broad array of machine shops. It was this subcontracting that had enabled Garden to earn high profits despite a long strike. The profits also did not come from managerial competence of the sort most production firms cultivate. In that domain, Garden appeared utterly incompetent.

The remarkable profits sprang from technical and strategic expertise. The key labour inputs came not from the machinists in the plant, but from the engineers and managers in the office building. These people had created monopolistic opportunities for Garden over and over again. Garden was the only producer of many of its products, and the dominant producer of all of them.

Garden's key input was expertise. It was a knowledge- intensive firm (KIF).

Knowledge intensity has diverse meanings, partly because people use different definitions of knowledge. The next section of this article gives my conclusions about such issues. Two following sections then make empirically based observations about the activities inside KIFs. The first of these sections reviews the kinds of work experts do, and explains why experts find learning hard. The ensuing section then describes organizational learning: KIFs learn by managing training and personnel turnover, and by creating physical capital, routines, organizational culture, and social capital. To see the results of learning, the fifth section looks at KIFs' long-term strategic development, including multinational expansion.

WHAT IS A KIF?

The term *knowledge-intensive* imitates economists' labelling of firms as capital-intensive or labour-intensive. These labels describe the relative importance of capital and labour as production inputs. In a capital-intensive firm, capital has more importance than labour; in a labour-intensive firm, labour has the greater importance. By analogy, labelling a firm as knowledge-intensive implies that knowledge has more importance than other inputs.

Although the terms capital-intensive, labour-intensive and knowledge-intensive refer to inputs, capital, labour and knowledge also may be outputs. Why is it useful to classify firms by their inputs? A study of office-equipment or software companies groups firms by their outputs. Such a study emphasizes similarities and differences across customers and distribution channels, and it makes a good basis for analysing relations with customers or competitors. By contrast, a study of meat packers or machine shops groups firms by their inputs. By emphasizing similarities and differences across raw materials and personnel, such a study makes a good basis for analysing internal structure and operations. Input classes highlight the effects of resource availabilities, and their determinants, such as governmental policies. As well, Sveiby and Risling (1986) argued that KIFs call for new definitions of ownership and new ways of controlling the uses of capital. Traditional notions of ownership, they said, assume that financial or physical capital dominates labour, whereas human capital dominates in KIFs.

Assessing the importance of knowledge is harder than comparing capital and labour, however. Economists compare capital and labour by expressing them in monetary units, but market prices mainly reflect values that many firms share. At best, prices reflect those aspects of inputs that could transfer readily from one firm to another. Prices ignore inputs' importance for intrafirm activities or for activities that are idiosyncratic to a single firm. Since much knowledge has disparate values in different situations, monetary measures of knowledge are elusive and undependable.

Knowledge itself is almost as ambiguous an idea as value or importance, and it has many guises (Winter, 1987). During a dozen seminars aimed at research about knowledge-intensive firms, almost every speaker devoted time to his or her preferred definition of knowledge. Such discussions have led me to five conclusions.

1. *A KIF may not be information-intensive.* Knowledge is a stock of expertise, not a flow of information. Thus, knowledge relates to information in the way that assets relate to income (Machlup, 1962, took another view). Some activities draw on extensive knowledge without processing large amounts of current information—management consulting, for example. Conversely, a firm can process much information without using much knowledge. For instance, Automatic Data Processing (ADP) produces payroll cheques. ADP processes vast amounts of information, but it is probably more capital-intensive than knowledge-intensive. Producing a payroll cheque requires little expertise, and many people have this expertise.

The distinction between a KIF and an information-intensive firm can be hard to draw. From one perspective, ADP merely processes data for other firms, using mainly capital in the forms of computers and software. From another perspective, ADP succeeds because it does its specialized task better than its customers can do it themselves. This superior performance may come from both expertise and returns to scale, so expertise and large scale reinforce each other.

2. *In deciding whether a firm is knowledge-intensive, one ought to weigh its emphasis on esoteric expertise instead of widely shared knowledge.* Everybody has knowledge, most of it widely shared, but some idiosyncratic and personal. If one defines knowledge broadly to encompass what everybody knows, every firm can appear knowledge-intensive. One loses the value of focusing on a special category of firms. Similarly, every firm has some unusual expertise. To make the KIF a useful category, exceptional expertise must make an important contribution. One should not label a firm as knowledge-intensive unless exceptional and valuable expertise dominates commonplace knowledge.

Some forms of expertise may be hard to measure separately from their effects. Why, for example, does one attribute strategic expertise to the Garden Company? One might label Garden a KIF because it employed so many engineers. But many firms employ more engineers with less remarkable results, and Garden's products embodied no technological miracles. These engineers were unusual because they were using their knowledge in ways that gave Garden extraordinary strategic advantages.

Managerial expertise may pose special problems in this regard. It would make no sense to measure managerial expertise by the fraction of employees who are managers or by the wages paid to managers. To judge managers expert, one has to look either at the managers' behaviours or at the results of their behaviours. Do their firms produce unusually high profits? Do the managers show interpersonal skill?

3. *Even after excluding widely shared knowledge, one has to decide how broadly to define expertise.* One can define expertise broadly, recognize many people as experts, and see the expertise embedded in many machines and routines. This strategy makes KIFs less special, but it removes some blinkers caused by stereotypes about expertise, and it increases the generality of findings about KIFs. Alternatively, one can acknowledge only the legitimated expertise of people who have extensive formal education, and can emphasize high-tech machines and unusual routines. This second strategy makes KIFs appear more special, but produces findings that generalize only to the few firms that use such expertise intensively. It also accepts stereotypes about expertise.

These definitional strategies have political overtones. A broad definition of expertise obscures the influence of social class and social legitimacy, whereas a narrow definition highlights the influence of social class and social legitimacy. Legitimated expertise is normally an upper-middle-class possession. Legitimated experts usually earn salaries high enough to put them into the upper-middle class. They normally gain their expertise through formal higher education, which entails at least the expense of forgone income. Higher education also may give experts entry into recognized professions.

Even jobs widely regarded as unskilled may entail much knowledge (Kusterer, 1978). Skilled trades may be as esoteric and difficult to enter as the professions (Ekstedt, 1989). Yet, people put other labels—such as know-how or skill or understanding—on expertise learned through primary school or on-the-job experience.

Sweden has spawned much of the public discussion and research about KIFs. In 1983, Sveiby started writing about 'knowledge companies' in one of Sweden's most prominent periodicals, and Swedish business executives expressed strong interest in this topic. Sveiby and Risling followed in 1986 with a book that became a non-fiction best-seller. Probably this interest reflects Sweden's high incomes and high educational levels.

4. *An expert may not be a professional, and a KIF may not be a professional firm.* Professionals have specialized expertise that they gain through training or experience, and KIFs may employ people who have specialized expertise. Thus, KIFs may be professional firms.

Many KIFs are not professional firms, however. One reason is that not all experts belong to recognized professions. A profession has at least four properties besides expertise: an ethical code, cohesion, collegial enforcement of standards, and autonomy (Schriesheim *et al.*, 1977). Professionals' ethical codes require them to serve clients unemotionally and impersonally, without self-interest. Professionals identify strongly with their professions, more strongly than with their clients or their employers. They not only observe professional standards, they believe that only members of their professions have the competence and ethics to enforce these standards. Similarly, professionals insist that outsiders cannot properly supervise their activities.

Management consulting and software engineering, for example, do not qualify as recognized professions. Without doubt, those who do these jobs well have rare expertise. Nevertheless, the ultimate judges of their expertise are their clients or their supervisors, and their employers set and enforce their ethical codes and performance standards. Similarly, despite talk about professional management, managers do not belong to a professional body that enforces an ethical code and insists that its values and standards supersede those of managers' employers. Employers appoint managers without regard for the candidates' memberships in external bodies. Strong loyalty to a professional body would contradict managers' roles as custodians of their employing firms.

Sveiby and Lloyd (1987) divided 'knowhow companies' into categories reflecting their managerial or technical expertise. They pointed to law firms as examples of high technical but low managerial expertise. To illustrate firms with high managerial and low technical expertise, they cited McDonald's fast-food chain. On the other hand, Ekstedt (1988; 1989, pp. 3–9) contrasted 'knowledge companies' with industrial companies, high-technology companies, and service companies 'such as hamburger chains.' In his schema, both high-technology companies and knowledge companies have high knowledge intensity, but high-technology companies have a higher intensity of real capital than do knowledge companies.

Professional firms can exploit and must allow for all five properties of professions, not merely expertise. Health-maintenance organizations, for instance, must accept doctors' codes of ethics and must allow medical societies to adjudicate some issues. KIFs form a broader category, in which many issues reflect labour markets, interpersonal networks, and experts' individuality, self-interest, and social standing.

Yet, it could be that most KIFs have nearly all the properties that authors have assigned to professional firms. For example, Hinings *et al.* (1991, pp. 376, 390) wrote:

> *Bucher and Stelling (1969) suggested that organizations dominated by professionals had a number of special characteristics, including professionals building their own roles rather than fitting into preset roles, spontaneous internal differentiation based on work interests, competition and conflict for resources and high levels of political activity. . . . The distribution of authority has long been identified as unique in an autonomous professional organization because of its emphasis on collegiality, peer evaluation and*

autonomy, informality, and flexibility of structure (Bucher and Stelling, 1969; Montagna, 1968; Ritzer and Walczak, 1986).

Professionals are not the only experts who build their own roles, divide work to suit their own interests, compete for resources, or emphasize autonomy, collegiality, informality and flexible structures. Other occupations share these traditions, and some experts have enough demand for their services that they can obtain autonomy without support from a recognized profession.

There is another reason KIFs may not be professional firms.

5. *KIFs' knowledge may not be in individual people.* Besides the knowledge held by individual people, one can find knowledge in: (a) capital such as plant, equipment, or financial instruments; (b) firms' routines and cultures; and (c) professional cultures.

People convert their knowledge to physical forms when they write books or computer programs, design buildings or machines, produce violins or hybrid corn, or create financial instruments such as mutual-fund shares (Ekstedt, 1988; 1989). Conversely, people may gain knowledge by reading books, studying buildings, buying shares, or running computer programs.

People also translate their knowledge into firms' routines, job descriptions, plans, strategies and cultures. Nelson and Winter (1982) treated behavioural routines as the very essence of organizations—the means by which firms can produce predictable results while adapting to social and technological changes. Simultaneously, Deal and Kennedy (1982) and Peters and Waterman (1982) were saying it is cultures that perform these functions.

Describing McDonald's as a firm with low technical expertise overlooks the expertise in McDonald's technology and organization. McDonald's success stems from its ability to deliver a consistent quality in diverse environments and despite high turnover of low-skilled people. To get such results, the firm operates extensive training programmes and conducts research about production techniques and customers' tastes. Although training at Hamburger University may give McDonald's managers more skill than those at most restaurants, McDonald's managers may have no more skill than those in most production firms. Ceaseless expansion forces McDonald's to concentrate training on new managers. Also, McDonald's substitutes technology and routines for in-person management.

Professional cultures too carry valuable knowledge. For instance, lawyers live amid conflict. Lawyers' culture not only supports conflict, it shows them how to conflict to maximum effect and with minimum damage to their egos and reputations. Lawyers strive to advocate their clients' interests even when this might produce injustice, and they depend on conflict to foster justice by exposing all sides. Lawyers try to keep their roles as advocates for their clients separate from their interpersonal relations as members of the legal profession. They observe behavioural codes strictly and much of their conflict concerns interpretations of and conformity to behavioural codes. When lawyers cannot themselves resolve disagreements, they seek help from above—judges in courts or superiors in law firms. The legal profession also serves as micro environments in which lawyers

can cultivate long-term reputations. Some lawyers seek reputations as tough nego-
tiators who yield little and demand much. To nurture such reputations, they may
refuse to make concessions that their clients want to make.

A Starting Point

Debates about how KIFs differ from other firms persuaded me to focus on
firms that would be knowledge-intensive by almost anyone's definition. As a starting point, I defined an expert as someone with formal education and experience
equivalent to a doctoral degree, and a KIF as a firm in which such experts are at
least one-third of the personnel. Later, Lawrence Rosenberg pointed out that some
expertise takes non-human forms. Some KIFs may even hold most of their expertise in non-human forms, but I have not studied such firms.

I have not been distinguishing firms from other organizations because many
KIFs operate at the boundary between government and private enterprise. They
are not-for-profit firms that work mainly or exclusively for government agencies.

Although I have interviewed in eight firms satisfying the above criteria, three
stand out as excellent examples.

The Rand Corporation and Arthur D. Little are the two firms that came immediately to mind when I first began thinking about the *knowledge-intensive
firm*. The Rand Corporation is the prototypic think tank, located near the beach
in Santa Monica. Staffed by PhDs, Rand mainly makes policy studies: Rand's personnel evaluate current policies and generate policy alternatives. Rand holds long-
term contracts from the US Air Force and the US Army, and it receives short-term
grants or contracts from many federal agencies. Its reports are ubiquitous in
Washington, D.C.

On the other coast, in a wooded campus near Harvard and MIT, Arthur D.
Little is the oldest American consulting firm and an exemplary one. A. D. Little
has 21 offices and roughly 1500 consultants. In a typical year, they complete over
5000 projects in 60 countries. The project topics range from product technology,
to operations management, to economic development and strategic planning.

Partners in Wachtell, Lipton, Rosen and Katz make more money than those
in any other American law firm: it is to Wachtell, Lipton that other lawyers turn
when they need the very best and they do not care how much it costs. Moreover,
not only the partners do well at Wachtell, Lipton: surveys of junior lawyers have
repeatedly said Wachtell, Lipton is the best place to work.

Although quite unlike each other, all three firms share similarities, as do the
other firms I have studied. Large fractions of their people have advanced degrees.
They process information slowly in comparison to information-intensive firms.
Their capital equipment is mainly general-purpose office space, office machines
and computers, although A. D. Little also has laboratories.

My observations come mainly from interviews. Indeed, 'interview' seems an
inadequate label for fascinating conversations with very intelligent, perceptive, articulate people. I had only to point to a few issues that interested me, and they

would begin to extrapolate—telling me who else I should interview, what issues *ought* to interest me, where my assumptions seemed wrong, and how their worlds look to them. I often found myself discussing topics or trying frameworks I had not considered before walking into a room.

Are KIFs Peculiar?

One critic complained that all my examples describe peculiar firms that exist solely because their environments have uncorrectable problems. An answer to this charge has three parts.

First, all firms *are* peculiar: we should look for and celebrate their individuality. There are many ways to solve most problems, more opportunities than anyone can pursue, many criteria for judging what is best. It is as important to see how individuals differ—whether individual people, or individual organizations, or individual societies—as to see what they have in common. It is as important to understand complexities as simplicities.

Second, successful firms *cause* their environments to have uncorrectable problems. Firms and their environments change symbiotically. Not only must an environment be hospitable to a KIF, but the existence of a KIF induces its environment to assume that it exists. For example, US military services reassign personnel every two or three years. As a result, military personnel have little experience in their successive jobs, know little of tasks' histories or traditions, and cannot manage long-term projects effectively. Long-term projects would founder if they depended on military personnel. By providing civilian specialists who can have long tenures, the Rand Corporation and the Aerospace Corporation help the military to manage long-term projects, and they reduce the costs of retraining. Yet, having the services of Rand and Aerospace may have kept the military from developing other ways to manage long-term projects and other personnel policies.

Third, I have sought out the most successful firms, and all exceptionally successful firms exploit peculiarities. A modal firm in a competitive industry makes low profits, and it does not survive long. High profits and long survival come from monopolistic competition. Monopolistic competition arises from firms' developing distinctive competencies and mirroring their environments' unusual needs and capabilities.

Wachtell, Lipton shows how exceptional success may feed on peculiarities. The firm's founding partners had disliked their experiences in other law firms: they agreed to follow some unusual policies that would produce a better work environment. These policies have fostered collaboration and given the firm an edge in attracting new lawyers. The founding partners came from a less-well-known law school whose graduates had restricted job opportunities: much better than its reputation, this school supplied highly talented lawyers during the early years. A crisis during the firm's second year led the partners to adopt an unusual policy: Wachtell, Lipton never agrees to represent clients for long periods. This policy has had unforeseen long-term consequences for the types of cases the firm handles.

Success reinforces success, and excellence itself fends off competition. Today, with elegant offices on New York's Park Avenue, Wachtell, Lipton can choose among the top graduates from law schools across America. Potential clients offer the firm four to eight times as many cases than it can handle: it can pick the cases that look most interesting and best suit its abilities. The cases that potential clients bring are non-routine ones that involve large sums, and they often concern immediate threats. Such cases draw attention, as do Wachtell, Lipton's legal innovations.

EXPERTS' WORK

Interactions Between Creating, Applying, and Preserving

The experts in KIFs gather information through interviews or reading; they analyse and interpret this information; and they make written and oral reports to clients and colleagues (Rhenman, 1973, p. 161). An observer cannot overlook the strong, overt similarities across people, sites and projects.

Nevertheless, experts themselves describe their activities diversely. Some say that they are applying old knowledge to new problems, others that they are creating new knowledge, and still others that they are preserving knowledge that already exists. Experts who see themselves as producing new knowledge emphasize the recency or originality of their data and the differences between their findings and those of predecessors. They may classify such work either as basic scientific research or as applied research on markets, products, or processes. Other experts see their work mainly as applying existing knowledge to current problems. For instance, when most lawyers do research, they analyse and interpret previous cases and they emphasize the continuity over time of knowledge and its meaning. To gain acceptance of their rulings, most judges de-emphasize the innovative quality of their reasoning.

The distinction between creating knowledge and applying it is often hard to make. Lawyers may be more successful if they reinterpret precedent cases imaginatively, or if they conceive original strategies. The Garden Company's engineers were applying known techniques, but they were applying them to products no one else had imagined. Basic research may have direct applicability, and applied research may contribute fundamental knowledge. When it comes to systems as complex as a human body or an economy, people may only be able to create valid knowledge by trying to apply it (Starbuck, 1976, pp. 1100–3).

To my surprise, several experts described themselves as memory cells. They said their jobs are to preserve information that their clients have difficulty preserving. As mentioned above, because the US military services rotate assignments frequently, military personnel lack job experience and cannot manage long-term projects. Also, military wage scales are too low to attract and retain highly educated experts. To compensate, the military services sign contracts with KIFs that provide long-term continuity of management and expertise. These KIFs employ civilian experts who do not rotate assignments frequently and who either manage long-term projects directly or advise military managers. There may be enough of these KIFs to make up a distinct, long-term-memory industry.

Creating, applying and preserving intertwine and complement each other. At least over long periods, merely storing knowledge does not preserve it. For old knowledge to have meaning, people must relate it to their current problems and activities. They have to translate it into contemporary language and frame it within current issues. Effective preserving looks much like applying. As time passes and social and technological changes add up, the needed translations grow larger, and applying knowledge comes to look more like creating knowledge.

For new knowledge to have meaning, people must fit it into their current beliefs and perspectives; and familiarity with existing knowledge signals expertise. Evaluators assess completed research partly by its applicability and they judge research proposals partly by the researchers' mastery of past research. Thus, Rand Corporation, which depends on research grants for some of its income, makes elaborate literature searches before writing proposals. Rand also employs public-information staff, who highlight the relevance of research findings. Similarly, A. D. Little's executives believe that having credibility with clients requires their firm to specialize in certain industries, technologies and functions. They want new experts to have had several years experience in one of these industries and functions or technologies.

Ambiguity about the meaning of knowledge creation implies a weak tie, if any, between knowledge creation and knowledge intensity. Clearly, more input does not always produce more output. For example, Brooks (1975) pointed out how rare are the skills needed to create operating systems for computers. Adding more people to such a programming project does not accelerate it. On the contrary, more people may slow a project down, by forcing the experts with rare skills to spend more time co-ordinating, communicating and observing bureaucratic routines. An example of another kind concerns R&D by a large chemical firm. As Figure 8.1 shows, this firm has spent more and more on R&D but incremental dollars have yielded fewer and fewer patent filings.

Learning

Because experts are learned, one expects them to value learning highly. Nonetheless, many experts resist new ideas.

Such resistance has several bases. First, clients or even other experts may interpret experts' need to learn as evidence of deficient knowledge. Thus, experts find it risky to discuss their learning needs with clients or colleagues. Second, many experts get paid by the hour, and many others have to account carefully for their uses of time. Explicit learning reduces the time available for billable services. Third, expertise implies specialization, which reduces versatility and limits flexibility. To become experts, people must specialize and move into distinct occupational niches. Required years of education limit entry to these niches; and many

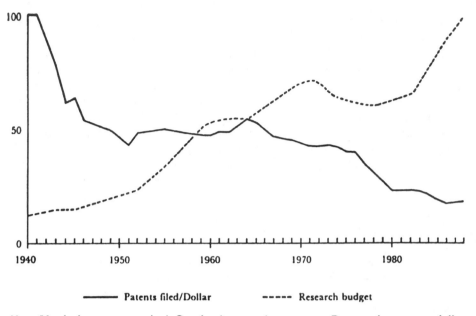

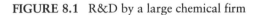

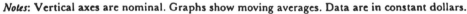

Notes: Vertical axes are nominal. Graphs show moving averages. Data are in constant dollars.

FIGURE 8.1   R&D by a large chemical firm

experts belong to recognized professions that restrict entrance through licenses and examinations. These niches, however, could become evolutionary dead-ends (Beyer, 1981). Fourth, experts' niches are partial monopolies. Like other monopolists, experts hold favourable positions that confer high incomes and social status. These positions also give experts much to lose from social and technological changes. Fifth, expertise entails perceptual filters that keep experts from noticing some social and technological changes (Armstrong, 1985; Starbuck and Dutton, 1973). Even while they are gaining knowledge within their specialities, experts may overlook exciting and relevant events just outside their domains.

Knowledge creation accelerates the social and technological changes in experts' domains (Wolff and Baumol, 1987). Because employers or clients often seek expertise to help them to understand rapid social and technological changes, experts tend to find employment in rapidly changing domains. Thus, most experts are all too aware that expertise needs updating: they have to seek a dynamic stability in which their apparent knowledge evolves while they retain their favourable positions.

Besides, experts' scepticism about new ideas can enhance their learning. Learning is not adaptation, and it requires more subtlety and complexity than mere change. People can change without learning, and too much readiness to discard current knowledge undermines learning. To learn, one must build up knowledge like layers of sediment on a river bottom. To learn effectively, one must accumulate knowledge that has long-term value while replacing the knowledge that lacks long-term value.

The key issue that experts, like other learners, confront is how to sift out knowledge that will have little value in the future. For this winnowing, expertise itself evidently confers no advantages. Studies of many fields have consistently found that renowned experts predict future events no more accurately than do informed people (Armstrong, 1985; Ascher, 1978; Camerer and Johnson, 1991). Still, few experts know about such studies, and many experts overestimate their abilities as oracles.

ORGANIZATIONAL LEARNING IN KIFS

Personnel Training and Turnover

Learning generally poses different issues for firms than for individual experts. For example, the need to update leads individual experts to spend time reading or attending conferences or courses. By contrast, senior people in a firm see updating as an activity to manage more than to do. Senior people may assign their juniors to take certain courses, or to read certain journals and to summarize what they read. Senior people sometimes deny certain juniors permission to attend conferences and tell others that they must attend and report what they heard.

What individuals find hard, firms may find easy, and vice versa. In particular, individual experts learn little from changing firms, whereas organizational learning readily takes the form of personnel changes. KIFs aggressively pursue new experts with wanted knowledge, and they limit the job security of continuing experts. Since most consulting or research projects have short terms, experts must repeatedly renegotiate their relations with their firms and adapt their knowledge and skills to current tasks. Some small consulting firms give new consultants just three months in which to start bringing in enough business to cover their salaries. A would-be consultant who does not meet this target has to seek other employment. Large consulting firms may not treat each consultant as a separate profit centre, but they do ask consultants to account strictly for their time. A. D. Little, for example, expects most consultants to spend 70–75 percent of their time on activities for which clients are paying, and 20–25 percent of their time on personal betterment or soliciting new business.

Such development and personnel policies keep expertise closely aligned with environmental opportunities, so rigidity and blind spots may be more troublesome for individual experts than for KIFs. Indeed, such policies make KIFs faddish; and efforts to stay on the cutting edges of rapid technological and social changes accentuate this faddishness.

The policies also make boundaries porous. Just as KIFs may hire experts from their clients or customers, KIFs' clients or customers may add expertise by hiring KIFs' personnel (Stinchcombe and Heimer, 1988). Experts at the forefront of social or technological change usually have many job opportunities. Replacing experts solely to update expertise weakens loyalty to the firm and adds variance to organizational culture. The social networks that make it easy to adopt new ideas also make in-house ideas accessible to other firms, as does the case of transmitting information. Thus, KIFs find it hard to keep unique expertise exclusive.

Stinchcombe and Heimer (1988) described successful software firms as 'precarious monopolies.' They are monopolies insofar as they exhibit unusual abilities. Niches evolve naturally as individuals and small groups concentrate on specific streams of innovation. The firms also strive explicitly to develop and maintain unusual abilities. Unusual abilities help the firms to market their services and to avoid head-on competition.

Stinchcombe and Heimer pointed out that these partial monopolies are constantly at risk, both because technological changes may make unusual abilities obsolete and because key experts may depart. Computer technology has been changing especially rapidly, and the software firms' relations with clients and computer manufacturers repeatedly expose their experts to job offers. To sell their services to clients, software firms have to publicize the talents of their key experts, and this publicity creates job opportunities for the touted experts.

Not all KIFs control distinctive domains of knowledge. Professional firms find it especially hard to sustain monopolistic positions. The recognized professions work at keeping their control of knowledge and at preserving their members' autonomy: firms would run into strong opposition if they would try to convert professional expertise to organizational property. Moreover, many products of professional firms are easy to imitate. For example, Martin Lipton invented the 'poison pill' defence against unfriendly corporate takeovers; but, after other law firms saw a few examples, Watchtell, Lipton was no longer the sole source for poison pills (Powell, 1986).

Several modes of organizational learning do convert individual expertise into organizational property. These conversion processes produce at least three types of organizational property: physical capital, routines and organizational culture. The creation of social capital, such as mutual trust with clients or customers, tends to convert organizational experience into the property of individuals.

Physical Capital

Both KIFs and individuals can gain new expertise by buying capital goods. Computer software affords obvious examples.

Not long ago, expertise was uneven across accountants who handled income taxes. Now, every accountant has low-cost access to software that makes no arithmetical errors, omits nothing, incorporates the latest changes in tax codes, and warns of conditions that might trigger audits by tax authorities.

Lawyers have recently begun to use a computer program, CLARA, to help them do legal research. CLARA helps small law firms to compete more effectively against large firms, and helps novice lawyers to produce results comparable to experienced lawyers (Laudon and Laudon, 1991, chapter 4). Although unfinished,

CLARA does research almost as well as law professors. On reading of this achievement, one practising lawyer sniffed: 'Too bad; maybe it will get better someday.'

In the short term, KIFs may be able to turn expertise into concrete capital. For instance, decades of experience enabled the large public accounting firms to create systematic auditing procedures. The firms then turned these procedures into checklists that novice accountants and clerical staff can complete. Similarly, Rand Corporation's research occasionally produces databases that have value beyond the projects that created them. Rand tries to exploit these databases by proposing new projects that would draw upon them.

Physical capital may be even harder to protect and retain than are people, however. Physical capital also may be less flexible than either the technologies it uses or the markets it serves. The auditing checklists created by firm A work just as well for firm B, so B can easily take advantage of A's experience.

IntelligenceWare wrote superior programs for artificial-intelligence applications. The firm has been seeking to exploit these programs by adapting them to diverse uses. Over the longer term, competing firms can analyse and imitate IntelligenceWare's programs. Also, because IntelligenceWare's programs are too complex for incremental evolution, experience will eventually force the firm to undertake a drastic rewrite.

Databases can be updated piecemeal, but they too gain or lose currency. At Rand Corporation, Brian Jenkins has compiled a database on terrorism. He began this on his own initiative, but the database became a more general asset when terrorist acts escalated and Rand began receiving enquiries about terrorism from the press. Although the press's interest in terrorism fluctuates with the incidence of terrorism, such a database requires continual maintenance.

Orlikowski (1988, pp. 179–267) detailed a consulting firm's efforts to capture its experience as software. Over ten years and many projects, consultants built various software 'tools' that help them plan projects and carry them out efficiently. The tools originated separately when consultants saw needs or opportunities, but the firm's general production philosophy implicitly guided these developments and rendered the tools mutually compatible. Also, at first, isolated people used these tools voluntarily, but informal norms gradually made their use widespread and mandatory. Thus, the tools both expressed the firm's culture in tangible form, and reinforced the culture by clarifying its content and generalizing its application. Generalization made the differences among clients' problems less and less important, and it weakened the contributions that clients could make to problem-solving. Generalization also reduced the influence of more-technical consultants and increased the influence of less-technical consultants. In their interviews, the consultants stressed the tools' strong influence on their perceptions of problems and their methods of solving them. Eventually, the firm started to sell the tools to other firms. At that point, the firm's culture, methods, and experience became products that other firms could buy.

The ease of distributing it makes physical capital an effective way to build organizational culture, and it offers firms opportunities to expand their markets.

Easy distribution also can cost firms their competitive advantages. Departing employees can easily take forms, manuals, or floppy disks with them. When firms turn physical capital into products that they sell to competitors, knowledge-intensive capital loses the character of being esoteric and advantageous. In this sense, a portable expert system is self-contradictory. Distributing an expert system renders its knowledge no longer esoteric, and thus no longer expert. It is not only tax accountants who now have low-cost access to programs for filing income taxes; millions of non-accountants are using these programs to file their business or personal taxes.

Routines

Firms also learn by creating routines (Nelson and Winter, 1982; Starbuck, 1983), but formalized routines look bureaucratic. Highly educated experts dislike bureaucracy: conflicts between professions and bureaucracies have attracted much research (Schriesheim *et al.,* 1977), and some of these conflicts apply to expertise in general. Most experts want autonomy, they want recognition of their individuality and they want their firms to have egalitarian structures.

Some experts derive independent power from their close ties with clients, so service KIFs with multiple clients look more like loose confederations than bureaucracies. Among the service KIFs, only those having long-term contracts with a very few clients seem able to bureaucratize. Even such KIFs must bureaucratize cautiously, for their expert employees have external job opportunities. Of course, a product KIF such as the Garden Company does not run into such problems because its experts have little contact with customers.

The KIFs that can enforce bureaucratic routines can draw benefits from them. Impersonal roles make programmes for personnel development possible, and they ease transfers of people to meet shifting tasks. Consistent quality is essential to keeping long-term clients or customers. Bureaucratic clients or customers expect the KIFs they hire to look and behave as they do. For example, the Aerospace Corporation has a seven-layer managerial hierarchy because this structure matches the hierarchy of the US Air Force.

Bhargava (1990) observed that the software firms in which developers interact closely with clients emphasize formalized documentation. These firms devote more effort to planning and systems analysis, to writing user manuals, and to recording the activities carried out and times spent on specific projects. These documents contribute to better client relations and reduce the firms' dependence on developers who might depart.

The Rand Corporation illustrates effective bureaucratization by a KIF. Rand's library staff watch for opportunities to submit proposals, and produce bibliographies to aid technical experts' proposal writing. Some of Rand's experts review others' proposals and reports to assure that they meet Rand's standards for data gathering and statistical analysis. Copy editors suggest ways to make proposals and reports more intelligible. These activities undoubtedly improve final reports' acceptability and the odds of proposals' winning funds. Rand's research proposals have a far-above-average success rate.

Larger KIFs are better able and more inclined to bureaucratize, and larger KIFs can better tolerate and balance the opposing forces in their work. For instance, Brooks (1975) argued that 'conceptual integrity' is the key to high quality in systems design. Attaining conceptual integrity, he said, probably requires centralized control by a few key experts, whereas programming and testing a designed system may require many experts. Such work can be troublesome for KIFs with experts who see themselves as equals and substitutes. Large KIFs mitigate these problems by dividing work into projects and allowing experts to specialize in either design or implementation (Bhargava, 1990). Creating routines requires persistence, and both persistence and learning may benefit from specializing with respect to technologies, markets, functions or locations.

On the other hand, large KIFs may lack knowledge intensity. KIFs are prone to grow by adding support staff instead of experts. Adding support staff promises to increase profitability per expert by using experts more efficiently, whereas growth by adding experts may use experts less efficiently. KIFs also grow by adding activities, products or services that promise to extract more value from the expertise already in-house. Thus, KIFs tend to lose knowledge intensity as they grow.

Some experts see this loss of knowledge intensity as desirable—a sensible way to get the maximum value from current staff. Other experts see growth as a necessity demanded by large clients or numerous customers. Still other experts see this loss of knowledge intensity as a danger to be combated—by avoiding growth, diversification and geographic dispersion.

Routinization helps to make knowledge intensity unstable. As with physical capital, converting expertise to routines is risky. Routines may become targets of imitation, spread, and gradually lose the character of being esoteric and advantageous. A routine used by many firms confers small comparative advantages on its users.

Organizational Culture

Cultures have to be built gradually because they are delicate and poorly understood. Building a special organizational culture takes much effort as well as imagination. Imitating another firm's culture is quite difficult, if even possible, because every culture involves distinctive traditions.

Maister (1985, p. 4) wrote admiringly of 'one-firm firms,' which stress 'institutional loyalty and group effort.' 'In contrast to many of their (often successful) competitors who emphasize individual entrepreneurship, autonomous profit centers, internal competition and/or highly decentralized independent activities, one-firm firms place great emphasis on firmwide co-ordination of decisionmaking, group identity, cooperative teamwork and institutional commitment.' According to Maister, one-firm firms:

take very seriously their missions (usually service to clients),
grow slowly while choosing clients and tasks carefully,
devote much effort to selecting and training personnel,
do R & D beyond the requirements of revenue-producing projects,
encourage free communication among personnel,
and
give information freely to their personnel, including financial information.

Maister also warned that one-firm firms may become complacent, lacking in entrepreneurship, entrenched in their ways of doing things, and inbred.

Orlikowski (1988, pp. 152–60) said Maister's idealization accurately describes the consulting firm she studied, except that her firm discourages R&D beyond the needs of current clients. The firm devotes seven percent of its revenue to a training programme and each consultant spends over 1500 hours in training during the first six years with the firm. Overtly technical in content, this training involves both self-study and classes at the firm's school. The consultants measure their career progress by their progress through this programme. Nevertheless, most consultants seem to agree with the one who said: 'The biggest advantage of the school is the networking and socializing it allows. It really is not that important as an educational experience.'

Alvesson (1991; 1992) too described a consulting firm that spent much effort on formal socialization. The top managers ran a 'project philosophy course.' They also sought 'to sell the metaphor *the company as a home* to the employees.' Designed to foster informal interaction, the building has a kitchen, sauna, pool, piano bar and large lounge area. The firm supports a chorus, art club and navigation course. All personnel in each department meet together every second week. Every third month, each department undertakes a major social activity such as a hike or a sailing trip. The firm celebrated its tenth anniversary by flying all 500 employees to Rhodes for three days of group activities.

Interviews with software developers convinced Bhargava (1990) that larger firms work harder to build cultures. They use their cultures to promote free communication, to make them less dependent on key experts and to ease personnel transfers. He found fewer communication problems and fewer personnel transfers in smaller firms.

Van Maanen and Kunda (1989) vividly described people's ambivalence toward culture-building efforts in a computer firm. Most people readily adopt corporate language and enjoy belonging to a supportive collectivity. Some embrace corporate values and rituals enthusiastically; more do so cynically. Most people also hold themselves aloof from group membership and protect their individual identities.

All the KIFs I have studied select experts carefully, they use teams extensively, they take their missions seriously, they manage growth cautiously and their people talk openly. Only Wachtell, Lipton, however, comes close to the one-firm model in discouraging internal competition, emphasizing group work, disclosing information, and eliciting loyalty to the firm. The other KIFs depart from the one-firm model in having multiple profit centres, assessing the productivities of individual experts, and revealing only the financial information that laws require. All the KIFs, including Wachtell, Lipton, depart from the one-firm model in decentralizing activities, encouraging entrepreneurship, and not involving everyone in decision-making.

KIFs do downplay formal structures, and they achieve co-ordination through social norms and reward systems instead of hierarchical controls (Nelson, 1988; Van Maanen and Kunda, 1989, pp. 70–93). One reason is experts' sense of their importance as individuals and their desires for autonomy: close control would induce exits. Another reason is common values and norms that result from many years of formal education. KIFs appear to derive some of their properties from universities, and some KIFs employ many who could be university faculty. Third, experts have to work independently because projects involve just a few people (Alvesson, 1992). The instability of projects and services provides a fourth reason: to absorb variations in demands for their services, KIFs need fluidity and ambiguity. Matrix structures are prevalent, and organization charts sketchy. Supervisors counsel non-directively. Experts form liaisons across formal boundaries. Indeed, the Rand Corporation designed its building to foster unplanned encounters.

Still, social norms and reward systems are not equivalent to cultures. KIFs confront serious obstacles to creating and maintaining unusual cultures, especially cultures that embody organizational learning. The attributes that make hierarchical controls troublesome—autonomy, mobility, professionalization, uncertain funding—also make it hard for KIFs to integrate people and to socialize them into unusual organizational cultures. When experts join new firms, they bring with them well-developed values, standards, habits, mental frameworks and languages. Although they have much in common with their colleagues, the culture they share is supra-organizational.

Social Capital

The Garden Company's customers can easily see whether Garden's products do what the maker claims. The customers do not buy Garden's expertise directly. One result is that Garden's relations with customers are impersonal. Another result is that these relations may be fleeting. The customers readily switch to other suppliers, and Garden itself cuts off relations with customers when it stops making products that are less profitable.

Buyers of expertise itself, by contrast, often have difficulty assessing their purchases. Clients often consult experts because they believe their own knowledge inadequate, so they cannot judge the experts' advice or reports mainly on substance. Clients may be unable to assess experts' advice by acting on it and watching the outcomes: the clients do not know what would have happened if they had acted otherwise and it is frequently obvious that outcomes reflect uncontrollable or unpredictable influences. Clients may not even understand what their expert advisers are saying. Many experts—with awareness—use jargon that obscures their meaning. As a result, clients have to base their judgments on familiar, generic symbols of expertise. Do the experts speak as persons with much education? Have the experts used impressive statistical computations? Are the experts well dressed? Did the experts use data of good quality? Do the experts' analyses seem logical and credible? Do the experts appear confident?

Successful service KIFs, therefore, pay attention to their symbolic outputs. For example, as mentioned above, the Aerospace Corporation uses seven managerial levels that match the Air Force's hierarchy. Aerospace also asks technical experts to practise briefings in-house before presenting them to Air Force officers, and it provides strong support for writing, graphics, and artwork.

Clients also hire experts to obtain legitimacy instead of expertise. In such circumstances, the client-expert relationship is a charade: the clients choose advisers who will give wanted advice. Such selection can be unconscious. For instance, when the Facit Company was in serious trouble, the board listened to presentations by several would-be advisers (Starbuck, 1989). They then hired McKinsey & Company because that proposal had sounded most sensible: McKinsey's proposal had endorsed the general strategy the board had been pursuing. One result was that the board found it easy to take McKinsey's advice. Another result was that following McKinsey's advice only made the situation worse.

Rhenman (1973, pp. 160–71) has commented perceptively from his experience:

> . . . there is in the consultant-client relationship an element of conflict. A game is played with all the usual trappings: negotiations, opposing strategies, etc. The client likes to 'sound out' the consultant. The client wavers between consultant A and consultant B. He also considers the cost of a particular consultant: will the organization really benefit? Has the consultant perhaps other purposes in mind, beyond his duty to the client? Perhaps he is seeking an opportunity for research or financial reward? The consultant may be particularly anxious to get this assignment. How can he persuade the client to engage him? Or he may be temporarily hard pressed for time. Can he persuade the client to postpone the assignment, or some particularly time-consuming part of it? And during the assignment the consultant is often sure to feel that the client is blind to his own best interests, or that he, as consultant, is becoming involved in internal conflicts. . . .
>
> We have already intimated that political groups may well try to use the engagement of the consultant for their own ends. Other groups may suspect and oppose the engagement on similar grounds; a long and heated struggle can easily develop. The consultant may be aware of what has been going on, or he may realize it only when he discovers that his engagement is tied to certain definite conditions. . . .
>
> But the political system is not simply a part of the background. Soon, whether he realizes it or not, the consultant will become a pawn in the political game: his presence will always have some effect on the balance of power, sometimes perhaps a good deal. If he is not politically aware, various interest groups will almost certainly try to use him for their own purposes.

Over the long term, service KIFs try to convert clients' satisfaction with specific projects into long-term relations. Even in contexts that are initially impersonal, repeated interactions between specific people create bonds. Firm-to-firm ties gradually evolve into person-to-person ties. An expert who repeatedly serves the same client begins to perceive 'my' client, and the client comes to think of 'my' expert.

Such personalizing can happen with any expert, but the experts having the strongest social skills are not normally those with the greatest technical expertise. Those with superb abilities in both dimensions are rare: one interviewee estimated that only ten people in the US are 'great technical lawyers who work well with colleagues, are effective with clients and show good judgment.'

Thus, KIFs use internal specialization, in which socially skilful experts work on building ties with a few specific clients, and technically superior experts provide specialized expertise to many clients. The KIFs offer clients familiar contact persons, who then draw upon *ad hoc* teams with expertise fitting specific projects. To a client, a KIF looks like a single source of diverse expertise that gives high priority to that client's problems.

Formally, American lawyers call the persons whom clients choose to contact 'originating attorneys.' Informally, they call them 'rainmakers.' Rainmaking is mysterious and magical, and rainmakers wield power. Their personal and lasting ties with clients give the contact persons divided loyalties as well as power. The divided loyalties serve a quality-control function that nurtures continuing ties between KIFs and clients. The power is a central fact-of-life that KIFs have to appreciate or risk losing long-term clients.

Keith Uncapher once worked at the Rand Corporation, designing information systems for the Defense Advanced Research Projects Agency (DARPA). Rand's top managers declared that the firm should no longer build hardware, but Uncapher believed that DARPA's goals demanded special-purpose hardware. He made a fifteen-minute oral proposal to DARPA, received an initial grant of $10 million, and started a new organization, the Information Science Institute.

As the foregoing implies they should, service KIFs favour client relations over technical expertise. If KIFs allow client relations to dominate too strongly, however, they may lose key technical experts. Instead of thinking that they work for firms, technical experts may think firms exist for their benefit and should be working for them. To remain stable, KIFs have to reconcile their client-relations specialists and technical specialists. Each of these needs the other over the long term, but their mutual dependencies may seem obscure at any one moment.

STRATEGIC DEVELOPMENT

This article's second section asserts: 'Knowledge is a stock of expertise, not a flow of information.' Ironically, firms' stocks of expertise come from the flows in complex input-output systems. Knowledge flows in through hiring, training and purchases of capital goods. Some knowledge gets manufactured internally, through research, invention and culture building. Knowledge flows out through personnel departures, imitated routines and sales of capital goods. Some knowledge becomes obsolete. Fluid knowledge solidifies when converted into capital goods or routines. The sequences of events resemble random walks, and the net outcomes are difficult to foresee. Thus, strategies do not evolve coherently (Greenwood *et al.*, 1990).

Diversification

For product KIFs, strategic development calls for regulating numbers of customers and numbers of product lines. Similarly, service KIFs need to regulate numbers of clients and numbers of topical foci. As with other specialization-diversification problems, high risks come from having very few clients or customers and very few topics or product lines. A KIF with very few topical foci must perform superbly in those areas, and a KIF with very few customers cannot afford customer dissatisfaction. The issues, however, do not all lie in the realms of expertise or social skills.

For a year and a half after Wachtell, Lipton began, one client accounted for 75 percent of its revenue. Then, this client asked Wachtell, Lipton to do something unethical. They replied that they could not take the wanted action. The client countered that Wachtell, Lipton must either do its bidding or lose its business. The partners refused . . . and gave up 75 percent of their revenue. At that point, unsure their firm could survive, the partners adopted a policy that has had profound consequences: Wachtell, Lipton would work only one-case-at-a-time. It would never again make a long-term commitment to a client.

If Wachtell, Lipton had been more ordinary, this policy might have been deadly. But the firm became one of the rare ones to which corporations turn when their normal legal resources seem inadequate—at least, when corporations don't want to find out whether their normal legal resources would be adequate. In this status, having no long-term clients becomes an asset, for Wachtell, Lipton can be hired by whoever calls first.

Some KIFs serve a few clients contentedly. Keith Uncapher said, 'I wouldn't know how to look good to two clients.' He designed the Information Science Institute to serve only DARPA, and no other client. The Aerospace Corporation derives 99 percent of its revenues from a single long-term contract and makes no effort to change this situation.

Most KIFs that begin with narrow foci try to diversify. Like Aerospace, the Rand Corporation initially served a single client, the US Air Force. At the Air Force's urging and with its help, Rand began making strenuous efforts to gain broader support and greater autonomy. These efforts have had partial success. Rand has raised an endowment exceeding $40 million, and it does research for over 80 sponsors annually. Nevertheless, three military sponsors still account for 70 percent of Rand's revenues, and 80 percent of its research deals with national security.

A. D. Little has attained broad diversification after developing incrementally for over a century. A. D. Little's precursor, Griffin & Little, began in 1886 as specialists in the chemistry of paper-making. In 1909, when the current firm incorporated, its expertise encompassed paper-making, forest products, textiles, plastics and sugar. These industries were central to the economy of New England, the firm's home.

Over the years, as the firm expanded its geographic reach, it added a wide range of physical and biological sciences and expertise on a wide spectrum of manufacturing technologies. A. D. Little first studied regional economics in 1916, began financial studies in the 1930s, and moved into management consulting broadly in the 1950s.

These expansions sprang partly from the firm's standards about conflict of interest. After advising a client about a topic, A. D. Little will not advise a different client from the same industry about the same topic. Future projects must change either the industry or the topic.

Just as diversification regarding clients may erode a KIF's ties with its long-standing clients, topical diversification may undermine a KIF's credibility. A few years ago, A. D. Little's senior managers concluded that their firm had become too amorphous. Hiring had become hard because the firm had so few experts in any single specialty. Covering too many specialties for too many dissimilar clients was yielding neither enough profit nor enough client satisfaction. A survey revealed that clients were turning to other consultants to get 'focused depth of resources.'

Thus, the firm went through a major planning effort, and began to focus on half-a-dozen functions in a handful of industries—mainly chemicals, financial services, health care and telecommunications. Alfred Wechsler explained, 'We try to define our expertise with verb-noun-adverb combinations. For example: we know how *to manufacture a paper cup inexpensively*.'

A. D. Little's strategic development has generally paralleled the developments in its client population—large industrial enterprises. Chandler (1962) described how single-product firms grew into multiple-product, divisionalized firms during the first half of the century: in the same period, A. D. Little was adding many product lines and decentralizing. In the 1970s and 1980s, conglomerates such as ITT decided to retrench into a few core businesses: A. D. Little was making analogous changes at the same time. After 1950, many American firms expanded overseas, and A. D. Little too became multinational.

Its initial foreign venture was an office in Zurich that opened in 1957 to serve American firms that were expanding into Europe. To their surprise, the consultants discovered that European firms also wanted their services. They now have offices in six European cities and in Mexico, Brazil, Venezuela, Saudi Arabia, Japan, Singapore, Hong Kong and Taiwan. In 1972, they added laboratories in England; these later expanded to Germany.

Multinational KIFs

For KIFs, multinationality poses challenging issues that differ from those facing industrial firms. Many industrial firms use authority and steep hierarchies, and they can often use formal controls or hardware technology to reach performance standards. Consulting firms and other KIFs dare not resort to authority or formal controls and they lack technological wonder pills. They have to depend on autonomous small teams to act ethically and to meet performance standards. This, in turn, means that they need cultural homogeneity.

Nonetheless, A. D. Little has found national differences to be minor problems. One reason may be careful selection of experts. Another reason may be the homogeneity arising from education. Haire *et al.* (1966) found that managers with similar education espouse similar values no matter what their nationalities. Wuthnow and Shrum (1983) discovered that education erases the ideological differences between managers and professional-technical workers. After much education, managers and professionals espouse similar values.

Perhaps because they use authority, formal controls and technology to produce homogeneity, many industrial firms have shown insensitivity toward local values or treated host-country personnel less well than home-country personnel. Yet, insensitivity and inequity have not prevented industrial firms from operating successfully in foreign lands. Consulting firms, on the other hand, would fail if they did allow for local values, and they are apt to treat host-country consultants more than equally.

For instance, A. D. Little is trying to deliver reliable quality across diverse sites, but its clients want services tailored to their individual needs and contexts. Tailoring calls for consultants to act differently, whereas reliable quality and teamwork call for them to act similarly. A. D. Little began its multinational expansion by exporting American experts. Experience promptly convinced the firm that a foreign office must hire primarily experts native to that country. First, devising effective solutions for problems usually requires thorough understanding of the contexts in which those solutions will be tried. Second, clients do not want to waste time explaining basic economic, sociological or political facts to expensive foreign consultants. Thus, the consultants who staff a foreign office tend to have strong social skills and close ties with their clients. These assets, in turn, tend to give the host-country consultants high status within the firm.

LOOKING BACK AND FORWARD

Summary

Because everyone defines knowledge differently, discussions of KIFs evoke debates about proper definition. Such debates have led me (a) to emphasize esoteric expertise instead of widely shared knowledge; (b) to distinguish an expert from a professional and a knowledge-intensive firm from a professional firm; (c) to differentiate a knowledge-intensive firm from an information-intensive firm, and (d) to see knowledge as a property of physical capital, social capital, routines, and organizational cultures, as well as individual people.

Highly successful KIFs exhibit uniqueness, and they reflect and exploit the peculiarities of their environments. Since they and their environments change symbiotically, their environments reflect and exploit these KIFs.

Whereas experts distinguish between preserving, creating, and applying knowledge, their daily work obscures these distinctions. Not only do preservers, creators, and appliers behave similarly, but preserving, creating and applying are interdependent. Furthermore, experts resist new ideas—even the experts who describe themselves as creators of knowledge. Such resistance arises from self-interest and narrow perspectives. Yet, it may improve learning—by both individual experts and their firms—by making people ask whether knowledge has lasting value.

KIFs learn by hiring, training and dismissing personnel. They also convert ideas into physical capital, routines, organizational culture and social capital. Personnel changes and purchases of capital goods generally offer fast ways to pick up new ideas. Training, physical capital, routines and organizational cultures can turn individuals' knowledge into collective property. Knowledge in people or in physical capital is easy to lose, and KIFs have difficulty using routines and building special cultures. Social capital transforms a series of successful relations with a client into a long-term relation, but it also converts collective successes into individual property. One consequence is that hierarchies within KIFs reflect social skills as well as technical expertise.

Three themes afford a framework for interpreting KIFs' strategic development. First, complex input-output systems for knowledge make KIFs' strategic development look erratic. Second, KIFs have to regulate numbers of customers or clients, and numbers of product lines or topical foci. Some KIFs focus on small numbers of clients, customers, product lines or topics, but most KIFs try to diversify. Third, service KIFs often mirror prominent characteristics of their clients. These similarities are loosely qualitative, however, for KIFs differ from their clients in many ways.

Post-Industrial Currents

One cliché prediction says: future societies will have ever higher proportions of service workers, because machines will replace blue collars much more often than white collars. Perhaps KIFs are also growing more prevalent. But the future is always moot, and more interesting than the general trends are the swirling currents within them.

First, KIFs tend to grow by becoming less specialized and by adding support staff rather than experts. It nearly always *seems* that additional support staff, products or services will extract more value from the experts already in-house. Individual experts, too, think about broadening their domains as they update their knowledge and see social and technological changes opening new opportunities. But when support staff come to outnumber experts greatly, or when KIFs claim expertise in too many domains, KIFs lose their halos of expertise and their credibility.

Second, all kinds of expertise become less profitable as they grow more prevalent. Esoteric expertise has monopoly power and this power erodes as expertise becomes less esoteric. Neither experts nor KIFs nor KIFs' industry associations should seek proliferation. Yet, experts resist control and they have strong penchants to start new firms. Very small firms can compete successfully if they take advantage of their peculiarities and the peculiarities of their environments. The Garden Company could easily lose out to competitors with better ideas.

Third, some kinds of expertise attract consumers even though their benefits are obscure. Examples include crisis intervention, economic forecasts, investment advice, psychotherapy . . . and management science. Some obscure-benefit expertise seems to have high value partly because the experts are unusual. Such expertise may lose value as the experts come to make up higher proportions of the work force. On the other hand, such an outcome is not obvious. Placebos make effective treatments although they are very common. Mystery can be routinized. People need help with their problems even when the problems have no solutions—perhaps, especially then.

Obscure-benefit domains may be either more or less stable than the domains in which expertise yields clear benefits. Obscure-benefit domains are stable if they satisfy perennial human needs and no alternatives appear. There were probably economic forecasters before there were humans; even in recent times, the demand for economic forecasts has mounted as organizations have grown larger and more rigid. Obscure-benefit domains can be unstable if beliefs change, if human needs shift, or if more effective substitutes appear. Astrology is a case in point. Clear-benefit domains may themselves wither—as dentists are discovering.

Fourth, physical capital will displace some of experts' activities. Similar changes are occurring across the economy, within firms, and in the work of individual experts. Several new industries are distributing expertise in the form of physical capital. Both firms and individual experts are creating databases and expert systems, and they are buying or building tools to amplify experts' productivity by replacing some of their activities.

These substitutions will enable fewer experts to serve more clients or customers or to invent more products. They also will mean that many clients or customers no longer need experts or that they can make the products they have been buying. Millions of people are already using software to do accounting, to file income taxes, to write wills, to construct leases, or to help them write articles. Computers are revolutionizing product design, manufacturing control and computer programming. Spiralling medical costs may yet compel the use of software that diagnoses diseases and issues medical prescriptions.

To appreciate such currents' beauty and intricacy, social scientists need to stop averaging across large, diverse categories. The average painting is flat grey, the average day is neither hot nor cold and has 12 hours of daylight, the average firm is mediocre and short-lived, and the average expert knows little about any field. In the social sciences, broad patterns over-simplify and capture only small fractions of what is happening. They leave scientists in worlds that look random. Broad patterns also tend to emphasize what is consistent with the past and to overlook subtle changes.

There is also a world of bright colours, sizzling days, exceptional firms, rare experts, and peculiar KIFs.

NOTE

*I owe thanks to many who contributed generously their time, ideas, insights, and contacts. This article reflects help from Mats Alvesson, Tora Bikson, Andrew Brownstein, Mark Chignell, Jess Cook, Joan Dunbar, Roger Dunbar, Tamara Erickson, James Fogelson, Charles Fombrun, Ari Ginsberg, John Jermier, Charles La Mantia, Kenneth Laudon, Martin Lipton, Henry Lucas, Louis Miller, Frances Milliken, Theodore Mirvis, Harold Novikoff, Paul Nystrom, Anthony Pascal, Lawrence Pedowitz, Fioravante Perrotta, Joseph Post, Lewis Rambo, Donald Rice, Harland Riker, James Ringer, Stephen Robinson, David Ronfeldt, Lawrence Rosenberg, Roberta Shanman, Lee Sproull, Serge Taylor, Jon Turner, Keith Uncapher, Mary Ann Von Glinow, Herbert Wachtell, Alfred Wechsler, Elliott Wilbur, Sidney Winter, and an anonymous referee.

REFERENCES

Alvesson, M. (1991). "Corporate culture and corporatism at the company level: a case study." *Economic and Industrial Democracy,* **12,** 347–67.

Alvesson, M. (1992). "Leadership as social integrative action. A study of a computer consultancy company." *Organization Studies,* **13,** 2, 185–209.

Armstrong, J. S. (1985). *Long-Range Forecasting: From Crystal Ball to Computer* (2nd Edn). New York: Wiley-Interscience.

Ascher, W. (1978). *Forecasting: An Appraisal for Policy-Makers and Planners.* Baltimore: Johns Hopkins University Press.

Beyer, J. M. (1981). "Ideologies, values, and decision making in organizations." In Nystrom, P. C. and Starbuck, W. H. (Eds.), *Handbook of Organizational Design Volume 2.* Oxford: Oxford University Press, 166–202.

Bhargava, N. (1990). "Managing knowledge bases in knowledge intensive firms: an empirical study of software firms." Manuscript, New York University.

Brooks, F. P., Jr. (1975). *The Mythical Man-Month: Essays on Software Engineering.* Reading, Mass.: Addison-Wesley.

Bucher, R. and Stelling, J. (1969). "Characteristics of professional organizations." *Journal of Health and Social Behavior,* **10,** 3–15.

Camerer, C. F. and Johnson, E. J. (1991). "The process-performance paradox in expert judgment: how can experts know so much and predict so badly?" In Ericsson, K. A. and

Smith, J. (Eds.), *Toward a General Theory of Expertises Prospects and Limits*. Cambridge: Cambridge University Press, 195–217.

Chandler, A. D. (1962). *Strategy and Structure*. Cambridge, Mass.: MIT Press.

Deal, T. and Kennedy, A. (1982). *Corporate Cultures*. Reading, Mass.: Addison-Wesley.

Ekstedt, E. (1988). *Human Capital in an Age of Transition: Knowledge Development and Corporate Renewal*. Stockholm: Allmänna Förlaget.

Ekstedt, E. (1989). "Knowledge renewal and knowledge companies." *Uppsala Papers in Economic History*, Report 22, Department of Economic History. University of Uppsala.

Greenwood, R., Hinings, C. R. and Brown, J. L. (1990). "'P²-Form' strategic management: corporate practices in professional partnerships." *Academy of Management Journal, 33*, 725–55.

Haire, M., Ghiselli, E. E. and Porter, L. W. (1966). *Managerial Thinking*. New York: Wiley.

Hinings, C. R., Brown, J. L. and Greenwood, R. (1991). "Change in an autonomous professional organization." *Journal of Management Studies, 28*, 375–93.

Kusterer, K. C. (1978). *Know-How on the Job: The Important Working Knowledge of "Unskilled" Workers*. Boulder, Col.: Westview Press.

Laudon, K. C. and Laudon, J. P. (1991). *Business Information Systems: A Problem Solving Approach*. Hinsdale, Ill.: Dryden.

Machlup, F. (1962). *The Production and Distribution of Knowledge in the United States*. Princeton, N.J.: Princeton University Press.

Maister, D. H. (1985). "The one-firm firm: what makes it successful." *Sloan Management Review, 27*, 1, 3–13.

Montagna, P. D. (1968). "Professionalization and bureaucratization in large professional organizations." *American Journal of Sociology, 73*, 138–45.

Nelson, R. L. (1988). *Partners with Power: The Social Transformation of the Large Law Firm*. Berkeley: University of California Press.

Nelson, R. R. and Winter, S. G. (1982). *An Evolutionary Theory of Economic Change*, Cambridge, Mass.: Harvard University Press.

Orlikowski, W. J. (1988). "Information technology in post-industrial organizations: an exploration of the computer mediation of production work." Doctoral dissertation, New York University.

Peters, T. J. and Waterman, R. H. (1982). *In Search of Excellence*. New York: Harper & Row.

Powell, M. J. (1986). "Professional innovation: corporate lawyers and private lawmaking." Manuscript, Department of Sociology, University of North Carolina, Chapel Hill.

Rhenman, E. (1973). *Organization Theory for Long-Range Planning*. London: Wiley.

Ritzer, G. and Walczak, D. (1986). *Working: Conflict & Change* (3rd Edn). Englewood Cliffs, N.J.: Prentice-Hall.

Schriesheim, F., J., Von Glinow, M. A. and Kerrs, S. (1977). "Professionals in bureaucracies: a structural alternative." In Nystrom, P. C. and Starbuck, W. H. (Eds.), *Prescriptive Models of Organizations*. Amsterdam: North-Holland, 55–69.

Starbuck, W. H. (1976). "Organizations and their environments." In Dunnette, M. D. (Ed.), *Handbook of Industrial and Organizational Psychology*. Chicago: Rand McNally, 1069–123.

Starbuck, W. H. (1983). "Organizations as action creators." *American Sociological Review,* 48, 91–102.

Starbuck, W. H. (1989). "Why organizations run into crises . . . and sometimes survive them." In Laudon, K. C. and Turner, J. (Eds.), *Information Technology and Management Strategy.* Englewood Cliffs, N.J.: Prentice-Hall, 11–33.

Starbuck, W. H. and Dutton, J. M. (1973). "Designing adaptive organizations." *Journal of Business Policy,* 3, 21–8.

Stinchcombe, A. L. and Heimer, C. A. (1988). "Interorganizational relations and careers in computer software firms." In Simpson, I. H. and Simpson, R. L. (Eds.), *Research in the Sociology of Work, Volume 4: High Tech Work.* Greenwich, Conn.: JAI Press, 179–204.

Sveiby, K. E. and Lloyd, T. (1987). *Managing Knowhow.* London: Bloomsbury.

Sveiby, K. E. and Risling, A. (1986). *Kunskapsföretaget—Seklets viktigaste ledarutmaning?* (The Knowledge Firm—This Century's Most Important Managerial Challenge?) Malmö: Liber AB.

Van Maanen, J. and Kunda, G. (1989). "Real feelings: emotional expression and organizational culture." *Research in Organizational Behavior,* 11, 43–103.

Winter, S. G. (1987). "Knowledge and competence as strategic assets." In Teece, D. J. (Ed.), *The Competitive Challenge: Strategies for Industrial Innovation and Renewal.* Cambridge, Mass.: Ballinger, 159–84.

Wolff, E. N. and Baumol, W. J. (1987). "Sources of postwar growth of information activity in the U.S." Manuscript, New York University.

Wuthnow, R. and Shrum, W. (1983). "Knowledge workers as a 'new class': structural and ideological convergence among professional-technical workers and managers." *Work and Occupations,* 10, 471–87.

9

Organizational Memory

James P. Walsh and Gerardo Rivera Ungson

If an organization is to learn anything, then the distribution of its memory, the accuracy of that memory, and the conditions under which that memory is treated as a constraint become crucial characteristics of organizing.
—Karl E. Weick (1979a: 206)

Despite the fact that memory remains one of the core concepts in information-processing theories (Johnson & Hasher, 1987; Richardson-Klavehn & Bjork, 1988; Shannon & Weaver, 1949), the understanding of this concept is limited, particularly in theories about organizations. Specific theories have depicted organizations to function as information-processing systems (Galbraith, 1977; Tushman & Nadler, 1978). To the extent that organizations exhibit characteristics of information processing, they should incorporate some sort of memory, although not necessarily resembling human memory. These theories, however, have not elaborated on the nature and function of any type of memory.

Even so, some researchers agree that information about the past can be stored in an organization (Douglas, 1986; Kantrow, 1987). Earlier theorists postulated that an organizational memory is embodied in standard operating procedures (March & Simon, 1958). Later theorists viewed organizational memory in terms of structural artifacts (e.g., roles) that, over time, lose their efficacy and become obstacles to change (Starbuck & Hedberg, 1977). A number of theorists have attempted to list its contents (Argyris & Schon, 1978; Daft & Weick, 1984; El Sawy, Gomes, & Gonzalez, 1986; Hall, 1984; March & Olsen, 1976). For example, March and Olsen (1976: 62–63) believed that "past events, promises, goals, assumptions, and behaviors" are stored in memory, whereas Argyris and Schon (1978: 19) asserted that "learning agents' discoveries, inventions, and

Reprinted by permission of *Academy of Management Review*, copyright 1991, Volume 16, Number 1, January 1991, pp. 57–91. The authors would like to thank Chris Argyris, Mary Ann Glynn, Alan Meyer, Craig Pinder, Lance Sandelands, Ralph Stablein, and Nic Van Dijk for their helpful comments on earlier versions of this manuscript. The financial support of the Tuck Associates Program is gratefully acknowledged.

evaluations must be embedded in organizational memory." Hall (1984) posited that an organization's memory is comprised of cause maps, architecture, strategic orientations, and standard operating procedures.

Although it has generally been recognized that organizational memory consists of mental and structural artifacts that have consequential effects on performance, these concepts have remained fragmented, and have not been synthesized into a more coherent theory. Such a synthesis is the principal task of this article. Because the idea of organizational memory is bound to raise possible problems of anthropomorphism, we begin by exploring concepts that might overcome these problems. Following this discussion, we define organizational memory and propose that memory's retention facility can be structured in terms of five retention "bins." We discuss the processes of information acquisition, retention, and retrieval from memory in the context of these structural bins and then elaborate on how organizational memory can be used, misused, and abused in organizations. Some current organizational theories are reformulated in terms of the memory construct, and emphases and predictions are reassessed. The article closes with a look at a preliminary research agenda for the study of organizational memory.

ORGANIZATIONAL MEMORY AND THE PROBLEM OF ANTHROPOMORPHISM

From Individual to Organizational Memory

Memory is "the faculty of retaining and recalling things past" (*American Heritage Dictionary,* 1969), and it is associated primarily with individuals. A widely recognized belief is that the acquisition, retention, and retrieval of knowledge and experience from retention repositories (i.e., memory) influence subsequent individual behavior (Anderson, 1980). Through chemical and neurophysiological investigations and related studies in individual problem solving (Newell & Simon, 1972), researchers have gained some understanding of how information is acquired, coded into short-term and long-term memories, and evoked in various contexts. Even though these definitions pertain mainly to individuals, some researchers have suggested that memory can reside in supraindividual collectivities as well. For example, Loftus and Loftus (1976: 1) argued that memory functions "as some kind of repository in which facts (information) may be retained over some period of time . . . memory is possessed not only by humans but by a great number of things as well."

The extension of these concepts to the organizational level, however, is fraught with ambiguity. Researchers disagree on the specific form of organizational memory and on what level it might reside in the organization. Opinions range from Argyris and Schon (1978: 11), who argued that organizational memory is only a metaphor (i.e., "organizations do not literally remember"), to Sandelands and Stablein (1987: 136), who raised the possibility that "organizations are mental entities capable of thought." Other opinions that fall some place between these rather divergent perspectives are unclear as to whether information is stored and processed by individuals who comprise the organization (Kiesler & Sproull, 1982; O'Reilly, 1983; Sims & Gioia, 1986; Ungson, Braunstein, & Hall, 1981), by the organization itself (Galbraith, 1977), or by the dominant coalition or upper echelon as a reflection of the organization (Hambrick & Mason, 1984).

Errors of Generalization

One reason for the difficulty in defining organizational memory is that it is unclear whether or not information-processing ideas that are derived primarily from work on biological organisms can be extended to social and organizational phenomena—that is, the proposition that organizations have memories raises questions about anthropomorphism. This is not a new problem. Theories that depict organizations as having to learn (Fiol & Lyles, 1985; Starbuck & Hedberg, 1977) or give birth, reproduce, and die (Miles & Randolph, 1980; Pondy & Mitroff, 1979) have been criticized for such extensions (Pinder & Bourgeois, 1982).

Krippendorff (1975) identified two errors associated with this process of generalization. Errors of commission occur when irrelevant information is imposed on the target domain. For example, when groups and organizations are described as having life and death properties that are similar to biological organisms, errors of commission may occur (i.e., How useful is it to talk about the pain that accompanies an organization giving birth?). Errors of omission appear when the information that is transferred is selective and, thus, an important part of what it pertains to is omitted. In the preceding example, omission errors also may occur (i.e., Why consider memories as central libraries when memories are actually distributional and transient in character?).

To overcome possible errors of omission and commission, theorists simply have avoided homomorphic extensions (i.e., establishing that two entities are similar in form and share common properties) in favor of less stringent functional extensions (i.e., establishing that two entities merely assume similar functions). Organizations have been compared to military units (e.g., line and staff functions), life cycles (e.g., birth, growth, reproduction, and death), information systems (e.g., acquisition, processing, and retrieval of information), and language systems (e.g., surface and deep structures). In these contexts, for example, it is not assumed that organizations take on the dispositional properties of birth, growth, reproduction, and death, but that akin to individual life cycles, organizations reveal similar patterns as they age. In doing so, the anthropomorphism problem is avoided.

Unfortunately, functional extensions also have the effect of merely relabeling well-known phenomena. For example, it is hardly debatable that organizations resemble information-processing systems in terms of having sensors, memories, and central processors. Although such analogies and metaphors may clarify and extend our thinking about organizations, they do not resolve issues that deal with *construct validity* (i.e., How is organizational memory different from individual memory?), *measurement* (i.e., How do individuals, for example, retrieve information from organizational memory?), and *consequentiality* (i.e., Of what consequence is it for organizations that they are able to preserve knowledge of past events and bring it to bear on present decisions?). The goal of this paper is to address all three of these issues.

Working Assumptions

Daft and Weick (1984) remind us that any approach to the study of organizations makes specific assumptions about the nature, the design, and the functions of organizations. Our discussion of organizational memory builds on three assumptions. The most basic assumption, already intimated, is that organizations functionally resemble information-processing systems that process information from the environment. As information-processing systems, organizations exhibit memory that is *similar in function* to the memory of individuals. Sensors act to receive information, information is processed with defined symbols in some processing capacity, and information is retrieved from memory. In both individual problem-solving and information-processing systems, sensors, processors, and memories are hypothesized to function in similar ways.

The second assumption extends the concept of organizations as information systems by also depicting them as interpretative systems (Burrell & Morgan, 1979; Daft & Weick, 1984; Weick, 1979a). Because interpretations about the environment vary considerably in terms of their uncertainty and complexity, organizations must develop processing mechanisms to scan, interpret, and diagnose environmental events (Duncan, 1972; Galbraith, 1977; Lawrence & Lorsch, 1967; Thompson, 1967). Varieties in organizational interpretational forms result from the differences in the ways managers form beliefs about their environments and the differences in their methods of intruding into these environments (Daft & Weick, 1984). This particular concept of organizations implies the existence and use of some form of memory.

The third assumption deals with the ontological basis of organizations that underlies Daft and Weick's (1984) concept of interpretation systems. For us an organization is a network of intersubjectively shared meanings that are sustained through the development and use of a common language and everyday social interactions (Burrell & Morgan, 1979). Taken in this context, *memory* is a concept that an observer invokes to explain a part of a system or behavior that is not easily observed (Krippendorff, 1975), rather than a variable that is interrelated with other variables to produce particular outcomes. Organizational memories, therefore, are not variables with dispositional properties that have discrete causal effects on, say, structure and technology.

A Definition of Organizational Memory

In general, an organization may exist independent of particular individuals, but it should be recognized that individuals acquire information in problem-solving and decision-making activities. This focus on individual cognitive activities as the central element in the organization's acquisition of information reflects an active construction of memory. However, interpretations of problems and solutions vary with individuals. The thread of coherence that characterizes organizational interpretations is made possible by the sharing of interpretations. Thus, through this process of sharing, the organizational interpretation system in part transcends the individual level. This is why an organization may preserve knowledge of the past even when key organizational members leave (Weick & Gilfillan, 1971). We will later argue that interpretations of the past can be embedded in systems and artifacts (e.g., structures, transformations, ecology), as well as within individuals. In this way, organizational memory is both an individual- and organizational-level construct.

Taken collectively, these arguments suggest several implications for a definition of organizational memory. The construct is composed of the structure of its retention facility, the information contained in it, the processes of information acquisition and retrieval, and its consequential effects. In its most basic sense, organizational memory refers to stored information from an organization's history that can be brought to bear on present decisions. This information is stored as a consequence of implementing decisions to which they refer, by individual recollections, and through shared interpretations. Following a formulation that we will develop later in the paper, information can be considered as decisional stimuli and responses that are preserved in particular storage bins and that have behavioral consequences when retrieved.

It is important to distinguish between decision information, which refers to cues perceived by individuals as reducing equivocality (Shannon & Weaver, 1949), and memory, which refers to stored information about a decision stimulus and response that, when retrieved, comes to bear on present decisions. This distinction is important because both information and memory can be mistakenly interchanged in the context of acquisition and retrieval. The difference between information and memory lies in their temporal qualities, as well as their uses in organizations.

This definition suggests three imperatives for considering organizational memory: (1) we need to more fully specify the locus of organizational memory (i.e., its retention structure); (2) we need to examine the processes by which information can be acquired, stored, and retrieved from this retention structure; and (3) we need to investigate precise ways by which the use of memory is consequential to organizational outcomes and performance. The first two perspectives are developed in the next section; the third is developed as part of a discussion on the utility of organizational memory.

DEFINING THE LOCUS OF ORGANIZATIONAL MEMORY

Acquisition

Information about decisions made and problems solved forms the core of an organization's memory over time. We will consider both the nature of this information and recognize which aspects of a decision may be acquired. First, information about the particular stimulus event that triggered the decision-making process is typically retained by individuals in the organization. Kiesler and Sproull (1982: 550) would call this stimulus a "problem," whereas Weick (1979a: 130) would call it an "ecological change." In any event, the origin of a particular decision can be encoded. Second, the organization's response to this stimulus is also acquired. In effect, interpretations about organizational decisions and their subsequent consequences constitute an organization's memory.

The journalist's six questions (who, what, when, where, why, and how of the attributes of both a particular decision stimulus and response) provide a useful way of characterizing the scope of information that may be acquired about a particular decision stimulus and organizational response. It is important to note that the "why" of an organizational response can be known only when both the various properties of the stimulus and response are considered concurrently. All of the other information can be known discretely. This distinction provides the basis for our next argument that organizational memory is not centrally stored, but distributed across different retention facilities.

Such an argument is not to imply, however, that all information pertaining to a decision stimulus and response will be part of an organization's memory in each event. In some cases, the information itself may be so equivocal that it is almost unknowable (Weick, 1979a). As such, individuals typically create a cognitive heuristic to reduce the uncertainty and equivocality in the information environment they confront. Bartlett (1932: 21), for example, introduced the concept of the schema (which is grounded in the "reactions and experiences which occurred some time in the past") as this cognitive heuristic. After Miller (1956) documented the finite storage capacity of human memory, the study of the a priori structuring of information environments burgeoned (see Brewer & Nakamura, 1984; Taylor & Crocker, 1981, for reviews). Even at the organizational level of analysis, Ranson, Hinings, and Greenwood's (1980) *interpretive scheme* and Shrivastava and Schneider's (1984) *organizational frame of reference* have been argued to filter information that is considered within an organization. These individual- and organization-level schemata, interpretive schemes, and frames of reference may block, obscure, simplify, or misrepresent some of the attributes of the decision stimuli and organizational responses. It is beyond the scope of this paper, however, to delineate precisely which aspects of a problem and its resolution will be filtered or encoded (see Jackson & Dutton, 1988; Kiesler & Sproull, 1982; Weick, 1979a; and the schematic information processing review papers identified above for an introduction to this topic). The point here is that it is theoretically possible for some, if not all, information relating to a decision stimulus and response to be part of an organization's memory. We will next consider where such information can be stored.

Retention

Decision information is thought to be stored in various physical locations (Simon, 1976); individuals (Argyris & Schon, 1978); accepted procedures (Cyert & March, 1963); and even standards of dress, protocol, and furniture arrangement (Smith & Steadman, 1981). Pondy and Mitroff (1979: 19) tried to simplify the discussion and argued that the storage facility is composed of "brains and paper." Borrowing the storage metaphor from individual-level memory processes (Cowan, 1988), we posit the existence of five storage bins or retention facilities that compose the structure of memory within organizations and one source outside of the organization (Figure 9.1). The argument has two fundamental elements: (1) patterns of retention vary according to how well decision stimuli and responses can be stored and (2) organizational memory is not stored in one location, but rather it may be distributed across different parts of an organization. After examining the nature of these facilities, we will discuss aspects of the decision information that most likely will be stored in each bin.

Individuals

Individuals have their own recollections of what has transpired in and about organizations. As Argyris and Schon (1978), Nystrom and Starbuck (1984), Sandelands and Stablein (1987), and others have recognized, individuals in an organization retain information based on their own direct experiences and observations. This information can be retained in their own memory stores (Cowan, 1988) or more subtly in their belief structures (Walsh, 1988; Walsh, Henderson, & Deighton, 1988), cause maps (Weick, 1979a), assumptions (Brief & Downey, 1983), values (Beyer, 1981), and articulated beliefs (Sproull, 1981). Briefly, individuals store their organization's memory in their own capacity to remember and articulate experience and in the cognitive orientations they employ to facilitate information processing. Moreover, individuals and organizations keep records and files as a memory aid. As Huber (1991), March and Olsen (1975), Simon (1976), Weick (1979a), and Yates (1990) observed, such information technologies help to constitute an organization's memory.

Culture

Organizational culture has been the subject of increasing interest (Allaire & Firsirotu, 1985; Smircich, 1983). It has been defined as a learned way of perceiving, thinking, and feeling about problems that is transmitted to members in the organization (Schein, 1984). The words *learned* and *transmitted* are central to this definition and our purpose. Culture embodies past experience that can be useful

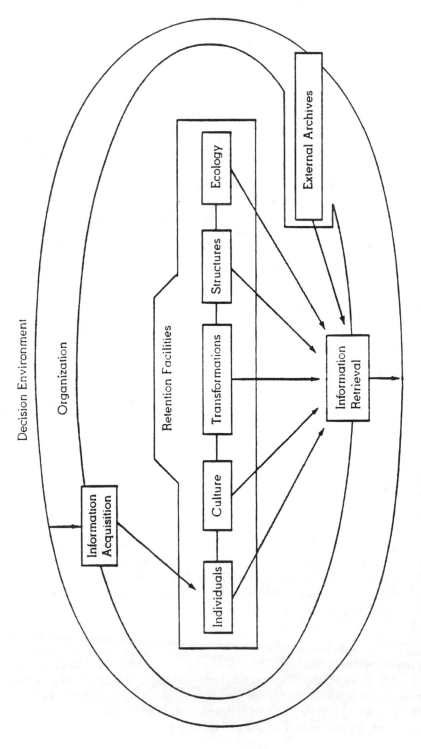

FIGURE 9.1   The Structure of Organizational Memory

for dealing with the future. It is, therefore, one of organizational memory's retention facilities. This learned cultural information is stored in language (Donellon, 1986), shared frameworks (Duncan & Weiss, 1979; Shrivastava & Schneider, 1984), symbols (Dandridge, 1983; Pfeffer, 1981a), stories (Martin, Feldman, Hatch, & Sitkin, 1983; Wilkins, 1983), sagas (Clark, 1972), and the grapevine (Davis, 1953). Because this information is transmitted over and over again, some of the detail and context of the various decisions are likely to be dropped or even altered to suit the telling. Just the same, the fact that this information is collectively retained in the transmission process (i.e., the sharing of interpretations) is an important aspect of the retention facility. Information, then, is housed in this supraindividual collectivity (Douglas, 1986; Halbwachs, 1950/1980).

Transformations

Information is embedded in the many transformations that occur in organizations. That is, the logic that guides the transformation of an input (whether it is a raw material, a new recruit, or an insurance claim) into an output (be it a finished product, a company veteran, or an insurance payment) is embodied in these transformations. Perrow (1979: 76), for example, argued that the analyzability of search behavior in the transformation process characterizes the nature of technology. This search behavior varies from analyzable (where there are known ways of solving a problem) to unanalyzable (where the residue of experience, judgment, knack, wisdom, and intuition directs problem solving). In either case, the retrieval of past information from past transformations guides current transformation processes. By way of summary, we would note that Weick's (1979a) discussion of the function of a standard operating procedure applies to all of the transformations that occur in organizations. He wrote, "A standard operating procedure is a schema that structures dealing with an environment. [It] is a frame of reference that constrains exploration and often unfolds like a self-fulfilling prophecy" (1979a: 156).

Transformations occur throughout the organization. Practices from the design of work itself (Taylor, 1923), to selection (Arvey, 1979) and socialization (Van Maanen & Schein, 1979), to budgeting (Wildavsky, 1979) and market planning (Cosse & Swan, 1983) inhabit transformations and build on past experience. Hedberg, Nystrom, and Starbuck (1976: 47) referred to these as "activity programs." Similarly, memory is preserved in a variety of procedures (Cyert & March, 1963), rules (March & Sevon, 1984), and formalized systems (Walsh & Dewar, 1987). As Jelinek (1979: 162) noted, "Administrative systems are the mechanisms for impounding and preserving knowledge."

Structures

Organizational structure must be considered in light of its implications for individual role behavior and its link with the environment. Individual roles provide a repository in which organizational information can be stored. As a sociological concept, roles involve the labeling of particular positions in society, based on societal expectations. For example, we expect particular behaviors from professors, lawyers, politicians, and law-enforcement officers. Merton (1968) noted that social interaction between persons is conditioned by mutual expectations attendant to their particular roles. For example, when students interact with faculty members, they encode a particular set of behavior based on their expectations, and they incorporate this behavior into their actions. Similarly, faculty members follow a related encoding process when they interact with their students (Schank & Abelson, 1977).

Thus, the concept of role provides one link between individual and organizational memories. Weber (1968) postulated that individual enactments are guided by collectively recognized and publicly available rules. Taken altogether, these rules represent formal and informal codifications of "correct" behavior that is conditioned by consensual agreement among the participants. In Walsh and Dewar's (1987) terms, this reflects the coding and channeling functions of an organization's rules. It is in this context that Krippendorff (1975: 23) suggested (perhaps anthropomorphically) that "the combination of roles in interaction memorizes an interaction sequence and thus constitutes a social memory of super-individual information."

To the extent that social roles become patterned over time to depict task differentiation and control, we can extend our argument about individual roles to apply to organizational structure as well. Particular theorists of organizational design acknowledge this premise. Meyer and Rowan (1977) characterized structure as reflecting the institutionalized myths of society that are sustained and legitimized by members of an organization. And, indeed, according to Douglas (1986: 112) an organization's memory serves to legitimate the maintenance of these myths. Finally, information-processing theorists (Duncan, 1972; Galbraith, 1977; Tushman & Nadler, 1978) have hypothesized that structure reflects and stores information about the organization's perception of the environment.

Ecology

The actual physical structure or workplace ecology of an organization encodes and thus reveals a good deal of information about the organization. Sommer's (1969) classic work illustrated the behavioral bases of physical design. In particular, the physical setting often reflects the status hierarchy in an organization. As a consequence, the workplace ecology helps shape and reinforce behavior prescriptions within an organization. Indeed, Oldham and Rotchford (1983) found that employees' interpersonal experiences were affected by their organization's physical layout. Specifically, employees who worked in a densely populated, dark office reported receiving low performance feedback in a setting that is marked by high interpersonal conflict and few opportunities to develop friendships. Not surprisingly, visitors' responses to an organization and its occupants have been shown to vary according to the nature of interior office design (Campbell, 1979; Morrow & McElroy, 1981). The workplace ecology, therefore, retains information about an organization and its membership.

External archives

It is important to observe that the organization itself is not the sole repository of its past. Just as when an individual's memory fails, he or she can turn to others to help recall a particular event, an organization is surrounded by others who follow its actions. Although they are not a part of an organization's memory per se, these other sources do house information that can be retrieved about the organization's past.

Basically, former employees retain a great deal of information about an organization. Regardless of whether these individuals resigned, were dismissed, or retired, they can retain a fairly accurate account of their former organization's history, especially the history that transpired during their tenure. Neustadt and May (1986: 241) referred to such sometimes invaluable people as "old hands."

A number of others in an organization's environment work to uncover and record its action and performance. Competitors often chronicle an organization's every move (Porter, 1980). The government requires all publicly held companies to record and report a good deal of information each year in their annual 10-K reports. Moreover, governmental regulatory bodies, agencies, task forces, and committees routinely compile data regarding a company's performance. Financial service firms also record an organization's activities to inform their own and others' investment decisions. Moreover, firms (e.g., Standard & Poor's Corporation) collect data on company performance and sell this information to interested parties (e.g., COMPUSTAT). The news media also follow organizations on a daily basis and record their observations in a variety of outlets. Finally, business historians will also chronicle an organization's past (Broehl, 1984).

Properties of retained information

Each of the five internal bins that comprise the retention facility of an organization's memory varies in its capacity to retain decision information. Table 9.1 summarizes these properties. We should note that only individuals by themselves or

TABLE 9.1 Properties of Decision Information Retained on Organizational Memory

	Who	What	When	Where	Why	How
Individuals	S/R	S/R	S/R	S/R	S/R	S/R
Culture	S/R	S/R	S/R	S/R	S/R	S/R
Transformations	R	R	R	R		R
Structures	R	R				
Ecology					R	R

Note: S = Decision Stimulus
      R = Organizational Response

as a part of a social collectivity have the ability to retain information about the events that triggered a decision response, as well as information about the organization's response.

Two points should be made about the role played by individuals in the retention of information. First, only individuals have the cognitive capability to fully understand the "why" of a decision in the context of an organization's history (Wong & Weiner, 1981). An understanding of why comes from an analytical assessment of the relationship between a cause and an effect (or in our terms, a decision stimulus and an organizational response). Whether they use this capability is another issue. We recognize that individuals' ambivalence about understanding cause-and-effect relationships (Bradley, 1978; Miller & Ross, 1975) suggests that the "why" in any decision is likely to distort and decay quickly. The "why" in a decision also will distort and decay as it is passed over time from person to person as a part of an organization's culture. As such, a culture may carry an interpretation of why a decision was made but this received wisdom from the past may or may not be accurate. This problem of inaccuracy is compounded by the fact that it is difficult if not impossible for a corporate culture to query itself in a way that might correct this problem.

Second, as an aggregation of individuals' shared beliefs, an organization's culture also reflects information about the who, what, when, where, and how of a decision stimulus and response. The idea that an aggregation of individuals can house such information has been considered in the social sciences for nearly a century. Early on, Durkheim (1895/1938: ivi) argued that there are "collective ways of acting or thinking [that] have a reality outside of the individuals who, at every moment of time, conform to it." Durkheim's student, Fleck (1938/1979: 38), developed this idea further and argued that "cognition is . . . not an individual process of any theoretical particular consciousness. Rather it is the result of a social activity, since the existing stock of knowledge exceeds the range available to any one individual." He argued that this stock of knowledge is housed in a "thought collective." Another of Durkheim's students. Halbwachs (1950/1980: 51), believed that "a man must often appeal to others' remembrances to evoke his own past." A group whose members help evoke those remembrances is said to have a "collective memory." Durkheim and his students were among the first in the social sciences to argue that groups of individuals can retain knowledge about issues in a way that transcends the cognitive facilities of any individual through the process of sharing. Contemporary scholars have conceptualized sharing in terms of a collective map (Axelrod, 1976), a hypermap (Bryant, 1983), an intersubjectivity (Eden, Jones, Sims, & Smithin, 1981), a collective memory (Schuman & Scott, 1989), a dominant logic (Prahalad & Bettis, 1986), and a negotiated belief structure (Walsh & Fahey, 1986). Consistent with all of such work, our point is that the retention of organizational memory is not just an individual-level phenomenon, but can apply to a supraindividual collectivity as well through a process of sharing.

Transformations, structures, and ecology, however, might not retain information about a decision stimulus but they inhabit an organization's response to such a stimulus. By definition, they embody the means to carry out an organization's objectives. Once established, transformational technologies establish recipes or formulas about what is to be done, how and when to do it, and where to do it, and they may also include implications for the skills and abilities required of a person to accomplish these tasks (i.e., who). Structures, defined as stable role definitions, are less precise about change, but can clarify who is to perform what tasks and duties. It is the transformation technology, however, that establishes the specific task requirements (i.e., the who, what, when, where, and how of task accomplishment). Finally, by its role in the channeling of behavior in organizations, the workplace ecology generally undergirds the where and to a lesser extent the how of a particular transformation.

Retrieval

Following work at the individual level of analysis, information processing that is based upon the retrieval of information from memory can vary along a continuum from automatic to controlled (Kahneman, 1973; Langer, 1983). Automatic retrieval covers cases whereby information about present decisions is drawn effortlessly and intuitively, partly as a function of the execution of some well-established or habitual sequences of action. At the organization level, one example of automatic retrieval occurs when present behaviors are based on previous practices and procedures that have been shared and encoded in transformations, role structures, culture, and workplace ecology. The theoretical antecedents of automatic retrieval in individuals are grounded in notions of limited attention (Posner, 1982), information-processing capacities (Miller, 1956), and the desire to reduce uncertainty and equivocality (Weick, 1979a). Indeed, individuals are hypothesized to employ heuristics and schemata (Abelson & Black, 1986; Nisbett & Ross, 1980) when solving problems. Schemata are formed from past experience to facilitate information processing in information-rich decision environments. As repositories of past experience, schemata not only facilitate information acquisition and encoding (Cohen, 1981), but they also facilitate retrieval (Anderson & Pichert, 1978; Cantor & Mischel, 1977). Discrepant information may be ignored, while gaps may be filled with historically relevant information. It is no wonder that schemata speed problem solving (Taylor, Crocker, & D'Agostino, 1978).

At an aggregate level of analysis (i.e., culture), supraindividual schemata have been argued to function in much the same way. Douglas (1986: 12) articulated how it is that all members of an organization are likely to automatically retrieve similar information from organizational memory. She argued that to establish legitimacy any institution must ground itself in nature and reason. It does so by "control[ling] the memory of its members; it causes them to forget experiences incompatible with its righteous image, and it brings to their minds events which sustain the view of nature that is complementary to itself." Douglas (1986: 92, 91) referred to this process as an "institutional grip" that serves to "squeeze each others' ideas into a common shape." It is in this same spirit that

Weick (1979a: 225) asserted that "retained information is sacred in most organizations." Such information is dismissed and distorted at one's peril. From this perspective, retrieval is motivated both by influence strategies and the implementation of past decisions.

Information also may be retrieved in an effortful and controlled manner. The ease with which this can occur varies across the five retention facilities. Individuals may retrieve information purposefully and consciously by making an analogy to a past decision (Neustadt & May, 1986). Individuals' recollections of experiences and decisions, once conceptualized by Halbwachs (1950/1980) as a *thought collective*, are constrained by the limits of their participation in the organization. Not only is there a greater coverage of past experiences in such a collective, but the individuals can prompt each other to help remember the past. In this sense, multiple and even conflicting individual memories enable a more comprehensive retrieval process. The work on autobiographical memory (Rubin, 1986) and, in particular, the work that examines the relationship between personal histories, life stage, and the ability to recall public events (Brown, Shevell, & Rips, 1986; Schuman & Scott, 1989) complements our understanding of these retrieval processes in individuals. Moreover, Ackerman and Malone's (1990) innovative ideas about growing an "answer garden" in an organization testify to the promise of information technology as a means to help retain and retrieve past experience in organizations. This work begins to answer Huber's (1990) call for the development of computer-based organizational memories. How decision makers choose to utilize this retrieved information is a matter that will be considered in the following section. The point here is that information about a past decision stimulus and response can be consciously retrieved, but only by an individual or a collection of individuals (with or without the aid of information technology).

For some firms, it is difficult, but not impossible, to consciously retrieve information from an organization's culture. It is difficult, in part, because organizational members do not always realize that their gossip, historical sagas, and stories constitute "data" and, in part, because it is very difficult to be a participant observer and maintain objectivity in the best of circumstances (Spradley, 1980). As a result, outside ethnographers might have to be employed by an organization to read its own culture.

The content of an organization's history that is retained in transformations, structures, and ecology is very difficult to decipher and not prone to effortful retrieval (March & Sevon, 1984). As we have discussed, the retrieval of information from these storage facilities may be largely automatic. The only way then to control the retrieval of decision information from them is to either dismantle or redesign the transformational technology, structure, or ecology. The controlled retrieval of decision information from these three sources is nearly impossible without changing the content of what is stored. A consideration of how controlled and automatic retrieval processes can be managed in organizations will be developed as propositions in the following section.

THE ROLE AND UTILITY OF ORGANIZATIONAL MEMORY

Of what consequence is it to organizations that they are able to preserve knowledge of past events and bring it to bear on present decisions? Business history is filled with examples of companies chastised for not forgetting their past, while others have been urged to remember their past. Starbuck and Hedberg (1977), for example, reviewed the problems the Facit Company faced in coping with the changing technology in the mechanical calculator industry. The company's near bankruptcy and subsequent takeover was attributed to Facit's top managers' inability to recognize the development of electronic calculators as a serious competitive threat. These managers' memory for their great successes in the mechanical market blinded them to the changes. Wilensky (1967), in contrast, reviewed the Ford Motor Company's experience with the Edsel failure. He attributed this failure, in part, to Ford's insensitivity to the increasing sales of foreign imports. Yates (1983) examined the Detroit auto makers' exact problem 25 years later and found little evidence of a lesson learned.

The role of organizational memory in the management of organizations seems to be unclear. In the following sections we will review the short history of work that has already been completed in this area, and then we will develop propositions about the use, misuse, and abuse of organizational memory in the management of organizations.

A Historical Perspective

As the Facit and Detroit auto maker examples illustrated, most of the early references to organizational memory generally have been raised in the context of a discussion of organizational adaptation or learning. Although there has been some appreciation for the fact that organizational memory can blind you if examined and mock you if not retrieved, these early theorists did not share the same vision of the role of memory in learning. Some underscored memory's negative effect upon organizational learning (e.g., March, 1972; Nystrom & Starbuck, 1984), whereas others emphasized the positive aspects of memory (e.g., Duncan & Weiss, 1979; Schon, 1983). It can be shown that the two perspectives are not necessarily mutually exclusive.

History is more or less bunk! . . . Henry Ford

There has been a great deal of concern at the individual level of analysis about the biases (Larwood & Whitaker, 1977), world views (Starbuck & Hedberg, 1977), and blind spots (Murray, 1978) of executive decision makers. Belief structures develop according to experience in an information environment to give it form and meaning (Walsh, 1988). These belief structures, however, can blind decision makers to aspects of these environments and thereby can compromise their organization's effectiveness (Walsh & Fahey, 1986). This same concern exists at the organizational level of analysis. At the organizational level, Nystrom and Starbuck (1984: 53) wrote, "Encased learning produces blindness and rigidity that may breed full-blown crises." The recognition of these potentially harmful encased learnings led March (1972) to conclude that memory is an enemy of organizations, an enemy that can reinforce a single-loop learning style that maintains the status quo (Argyris & Schon, 1978). In this view, it is not surprising to learn that Albert Speer was secretly pleased that the allied bombers destroyed the German factories' filing systems with their air raids. By destroying the files, the Allies were destroying many of the outmoded "traditions and procedures that had been the mainstays of those bureaucracies" (Weick, 1979b: 65).

In summary, those that worry about organizational memory's role in organizational learning are concerned that the information content of that memory will compromise organizational decision processes. They worry that a clear view of the past will obscure an accurate view of the present—that is, problem definition, alternative generation and evaluation, and decision choice can be constrained by what Kantrow (1987) called *corporate tradition*.

> *Those who cannot remember the past are condemned to repeat it!*—George Santayana

There are theorists, however, who celebrate the role that organizational memory can play in organizing. Cyert and March (1963), for example, observed that programming facilitates organizational learning. Successful organizations embed their adaptation activities in standard operating procedures. Success facilitates programming; programming, in turn, often breeds more success (Starbuck, Greve, & Hedberg, 1978). Since routine activities are handled best by these standard procedures, transactional costs associated with search and experimentation are reduced. Accordingly, the organization becomes more efficient. Indeed, in their review of the formalization literature. Walsh and Dewar (1987) found that most empirical investigations of formalization focused on its role in enabling these kinds of efficiencies. By reducing transactional costs, organizational memory helps to implement decisions that have been made (or need not be made again). Moreover, Kantrow (1987: 147) argued that new decisions are less likely to be rejected if they are imbued with the tradition and legitimacy of the past. He wrote, "Change that works by recapturing something that was there in the past has many resources on which to draw and a whole network of support on which to rely." Wilkins and Bristow (1987: 227) articulated a similar argument; they advised executives to "learn to change by honoring the past."

In contrast to those who decry organizational memory's constraining role in the early stages of decision making, some theorists argue that memory can facilitate problem definition, alternative generation and evaluation, and choice. Neustadt and May (1986: 32), for example, argued that "better decision making involves drawing on history to frame sharper questions." Similarly, Hedberg, Nystrom, and Starbuck (1976: 41) reasoned that "footholds in time are the appropriate components for assembling trajectones into the future." Even March

(1972), who argued that memory should be treated as an organization's enemy, acknowledged that "for most purposes, good memories make good choices." Duncan and Weiss (1979) agreed that the content of organizational memory does not always have to be seen as a constraint. Moreover, they believed that a facility must exist in an organization in order to store communicable, consensual, and integrated knowledge. This knowledge integrates and coordinates all organizational activities—even the transmission of new knowledge throughout the system. This facility, of course, is an organization's memory.

In summary, those who view organizational memory in a positive light do so for a number of reasons. While recognizing that a complete reliance upon the past can produce blinding encased learnings, they argue that a cautious appreciation for the past (reviewing the past decision's stimulus as well as the organizational response) can enhance the vision of a current decision situation. It is important to consider here our distinction between memory's retention structure and the content of the decision information stored in it. The structural facility is important for housing information, be it old or new. It is the content of this information that is sometimes decried for its role in hindering learning, not the storage facility itself. Finally, there is a belief that organizational memory can facilitate decision implementation. Beyond enhancing the ability to make a sound decision, memory helps to control and coordinate its implementation.

These distinctions between the structure of organizational memory and the nature of information stored in it and memory's role in both the formation and implementation of decisions are helpful when considering the ultimate utility of organizational memory in the management of organizations. The tension between the two historical perspectives rests on a fine distinction between a celebration of the efficiency born of automatic retrieval processes and the apprehension of not knowing it these efficiently produced routines and programs are out of step with the present circumstances. The resolution of this tension embodies the challenge in the use of organizational memory.

Use, Misuse, and Abuse of Organizational Memory

Any discussion of the use, misuse, and abuse of organizational memory naturally involves a discussion of the active management of organizational memory *by individuals*. This is a tricky conceptual issue because the discussion implies the purposeful use of memory by individuals when, in fact, misuses and abuses of memory can occur as a result of automatic retrieval processes (especially from transformations, structures, and ecology) of which individuals may not be as conscious. Therefore, the following discussion will focus on how decision makers may purposely and consciously employ organizational memory while recognizing that automatic retrieval may occur at both the individual and supraindividual levels of analysis.

A consideration of organizational memory reveals that it plays three important roles within organizations. First, it plays an informational role. The information content that is housed in memory's retention facilities can contribute to efficient and effective decision making (particularly in the prechoice decision stages). Second, organizational memory fulfills a control function. It can reduce the transaction costs that are often associated with the implementation of a new decision. The "whats" and "hows" that can be housed in many of the storage bins serve to efficiently shape desired behaviors without incurring expensive monitoring costs. Third, organizational memory can play a political role. Control of information creates a source of dependence with which individuals or groups in power are able to influence the actions of others. The filtering of particular information from memory that supports a particular agenda can serve as a means to enhance and sustain power. Acknowledging these broad roles, we now develop a number of propositions that deal with how organizational memory is used, misused, or abused in organizational life.

The use of organizational memory

Neustadt and May (1986: 251) pointed out that decision makers must recognize that "the future has no place to come from but the past." It is incumbent upon decision makers, therefore, to understand how the past will shape their present decisions. Because the present is not wholly derived from the past, an effective decision maker must balance an appreciation of history with an assessment of the present to achieve particular ends. In such a case, the use of organizational memory can facilitate these decisional processes.

Specifically, the retrieval of both decision stimulus and response information from the individual retention facility and other sources of memory can help to frame a particular problem or opportunity in its historical context. By and large, it is the controlled (i.e., purposeful and conscious) retrieval of information from the retention facilities that can be the most help in the decision formulation stages, when a person is assessing the similarities and differences between the past and the present (Neustadt & May, 1986). In Weick's (1979a: 221) terms, they should "treat memory as a pest" and attempt to discredit or doubt this retrieved information in the context of the present decision; that is, decision makers should work to establish the predictive validity of the past. Because past decisions are not entirely predictive of the future, nor are they necessarily applicable to the present, this use of past information should be examined with care. The uncontested use of past decisions can enhance the likelihood that errors will occur. As such:

> *Proposition 1:* Decisions that are critically considered in terms of an organization's history as they bear on the present are likely to be more effective than those made in a historical vacuum.

Once a decision has been made, decision makers turn their attention to its implementation within the organization (Janis & Mann, 1977). Overcoming resistance to change is one of the key tasks facing managers at this point (Kotter & Schlesinger, 1979). By communicating how the present decision (with its implications for the future) has its roots in the organization's collective experience, decision makers can imbue their choice with a sense of legitimacy that otherwise would be lost (Kantrow, 1987). This legitimacy can help foster a commitment to a chosen course of action, as opposed to a mere compliance with the new direction. This commitment not only enhances each individual's attachment to the organization (Reichers, 1985), it decreases monitoring and supervisory costs as well (Ray, 1986). As such:

> *Proposition 2:* Decision choices framed within the context of an organization's history are less likely to meet with resistance than those not so framed.

Organizational memory holds a second implication for the management of decision implementation. The decision response information that is housed in each of the storage facilities has been shown to have a powerful influence in shaping behavior. As we pointed out, much of this information is retrieved automatically. We recognize that individuals with their "encased learnings" may obstruct a change effort. In this light, Starbuck and Hedberg (1977: 256) argued that "top management heads will have to roll" because they cannot be trusted to move beyond their past encased learnings. Additional justification for replacing top managers was offered by Starbuck, Greve, and Hedberg (1978: 133). They observed that these managers "overestimate the generality of their past decision rules and their past analytic techniques, so they underestimate the speed with which their expertise becomes obsolete." Cangelosi and Dill (1965: 199) would support the view that management succession is likely to yield profound changes if for no other reason than the egotism of top managers usually prompts them to disregard past precedent entirely. Only a portion of only one of organizational memory's retention facilities is replaced, however, when top managers are dismissed.

Change agents must recognize that encased learnings and responses are stored in the other retention facilities and that this information is subject to automatic retrieval. Information in these other retention facilities also must be unlearned. The best way to unlearn or forget these past memories is to promote what the cognitive psychologists call retroactive interference. This is the phenomenon of forgetting that occurs when new learning inhibits the recall of old learning. The cultural, transformational, structural, and ecological facilities then must be filled with new behavioral prescriptions (responses) consistent with the new intended direction. In this light, it is no surprise to discover that the performance implications of management succession are so equivocal (Walsh & Seward, 1990). Accordingly:

> *Proposition 3:* Change efforts that fail to consider the inertial force of automatic retrieval processes are more likely to fail than those that do.

The misuse of organizational memory

Organizational memory can be misused in three contexts. First, the automatic retrieval of information may be allowed to shape a routine decision response when a nonroutine response is called for. Second, the controlled retrieval of information may contribute to a nonroutine response when a routine decision would have been appropriate. And third, a controlled retrieval process may be appropriately activated in an attempt to elicit a nonroutine response, but it may be employed poorly.

As the first proposition established, the critically evaluated controlled retrieval of information from organizational memory can enhance decision making. A problem arises when decision makers are unaware that the decision response information housed in their organization's memory is shaping behavior through an automatic retrieval process. In such a circumstance, the behavioral prescriptions that are encoded in organizational memory end up shaping a response to a situation when a more considered response may have been called for. Marcus (1988), for example, illustrated how rule-bound organizations have trouble responding innovatively to challenges. In this instance, the neglect of the powerful influence of organizational memory constitutes misuse. The decision consequences in this circumstance may be severe. Essentially, the decision makers commit a Type II error. They end up with a routine decision response when a non-routine response would be more appropriate. Accordingly:

> *Proposition 4:* The automatic retrieval of past decision information that fails to meet the requirements of more novel situations is likely to promote deleterious decision making.

Perhaps a fear of committing the kind of Type II decision error identified above leads decision makers to commit a Type I error. Analagously, Kerr (1975) reasoned that physicians would much prefer to diagnose a well person as sick, rather than a sick person as well. In the management arena, decision makers may employ a controlled retrieval process to formulate a nonroutine decision response when a routine response based on an automatic retrieval process would suffice. In this instance, the costs to be borne are largely opportunity costs. The decision makers could have engaged other problems with their time and talents. As such:

> *Proposition 5:* In inertial situations that call for routine solutions, the critical consideration of purposefully retrieved past decision information consumes a manager's time and energy and, thus, creates wasteful opportunity costs.

Many decision makers are well aware of the impact that the past has on the future. When confronted with a decision situation, they search for precedent. As such, they exhibit an effortful retrieval process and reason by analogy. Neustadt and May (1986), however, warned us of the limitations of such reasoning. In fact, they classified analogies according to the hold they have on our reasoning (i.e., irresistible, captivating, seductive, and familiar). Without stopping to consider the similarities and differences between the past and the present, decision makers can be blinded by past analogies. Ironically, such an awareness of history can promote a routine response to a situation, just when a nonroutine response is called for. In this instance, the decision makers appropriately engaged in a controlled retrieval process, but they did not critically evaluate the retrieved information. As such, they misused organizational memory. Indeed, Duhaime and Schwenk (1985) illustrated how reasoning by analogy may compromise an organization's acquisition and divestment strategy. Accordingly:

> *Proposition 6:* The controlled retrieval of decision information that is not examined in the context of novel situations is likely to promote deleterious decision making.

The abuse of organizational memory

Weber (1968) argued that any analysis of bureaucratic organizations must include how internal organization contributes to both efficiency and domination. Our discussion of the use of organizational memory was largely concerned with how it can promote efficiency; here we will consider how its abuse can promote domination in the extreme.

Perrow (1972: 16) observed that the "resources and goals of the organization are up for grabs, and people grab for them continually." The control function inherent in organizational memory marks it as a tempting tool that can be used by people when they grab for resources. Indeed, the management of information is useful for legitimating and consolidating power in organizations (Feldman & March, 1981). Information control creates a source of dependency with which individuals or groups in power are able to influence the actions of others (March & Simon, 1958; Pfeffer, 1981b). It follows then that individuals and groups can manage information to acquire power; once in power, they can selectively retain and retrieve information to consolidate it. By actively managing what information is acquired, retained, and retrieved, people in power can maintain, if not enhance, their standing in ways that correspond to their beliefs and ideology. Moreover, given that the decision stimulus information is lost as it is stored in the organization's transformations, structure, and ecology, retrieved information can be distorted and manipulated to serve self-aggrandizing ends. The point here is that retained decision information is not value free; its informational and control functions can serve either useful efficiency or abusive domination. As such:

> *Proposition 7:* The self-serving manipulation of organizational memory's acquisition, retention, and retrieval processes by an organization's members will enable their autocratic entrenchment and, thus, compromise the organization's sustained viability.

REASSESSING THEORIES OF ORGANIZATIONS USING MEMORY

We have advanced arguments for more specific representations of memory in our present theories. If such representations are indeed different from others, they should lead to different emphases, concepts, explanations, and even predictions in some areas of organizational theory. The hypothesized principles of the acquisition, retention, and retrieval of information in and out of organizational memory need to be assessed and then tied to other theories. We will elaborate on particular areas for which the concept of organizational memory may complement existing theories.

Individuals as Sources of Memory

The most fundamental issues to be addressed in the study of information acquisition are, "What information is acquired by the organization, and why?" It should be recognized that one of the most important keys to understanding acquisition, retention, and retrieval processes is to understand the nature of the individuals that compose the organization. Individuals are important not only because they, themselves, are a source of retained information, but also because they largely determine what information will be acquired and then retrieved from the other memory stores (see Figure 9.1 and Table 9.1). As such, an examination of the nature of the individuals that compose the organization can offer initial insights about the construct validity of organizational memory.

The most important individual attribute that is relevant to the study of organizational memory may be length of service in the organization. As Pfeffer (1983) noted, an understanding of an organization's practices and beliefs comes with tenure in the organization. Long-tenured individuals can facilitate the retrieval of information from organizational memory. However, Morris (1973) and Pfeffer (1983) also pointed out that an internal labor market dominated by employees of long-standing tenure is not attractive to younger, ambitious individuals who may embody or may be receptive to new ideas. In such circumstances, the organization is poised to purposefully retrieve information from memory, but it may no longer acquire information effectively. Pfeffer (1983) concluded that an organization that is marked by an unbroken distribution of length of service in its employees (i.e., no distinct tenure-based cohorts) is likely to be most effective. The perspective developed here would add that the range of the distribution is important to consider as well. The absolute length of service in the tenure profile of the organization is critical to the effective retrieval of information. Simply put, the organization needs a continuous link to its "old timers" to ensure adequate organization memory acquisition and controlled retrieval processes.

The Impact of Environmental Change on Memory

The principles of organizational memory are most in evidence when the organization's environment changes profoundly. Such a change might be thought to trigger change-based acquisition processes as well as possible retrieval processes. The study of an organization's responses to deregulation in an industry (Smith & Grimm, 1987) or to a technological discontinuity (Tushman & Anderson, 1986) might provide an opportunity to assess the various principles of memory or to explore some of their hypothesized ties to adaptation and change management. Smith and Grimm (1987), for example, investigated the relationship between strategic change and later firm performance following the deregulation of the railroad industry. According to these authors, firms that changed strategies outperformed firms that did not. It is quite possible that the effective use of organizational memory contributed to the successful strategic realignments.

To begin, we would predict that the companies who thrived following deregulation would be marked by a long-linked tenure profile; those that either failed or suffered performance problems would be managed by a demographically distinct cohort. Companies in the first instance would be more likely to attend to the full ramifications of the change (Starbuck et al., 1978). Second, we would predict that the companies who successfully reoriented their strategies would have managed organizational memory's retention and retrieval processes. Specifically, we would expect management turnover in the successful companies as some of their individual storage facilities are emptied of past recollections that, if uncritically or automatically retrieved, might impede the implementation of a new strategic direction. Similarly, attempts to control automatic retrieval processes by changing the corporate culture, transformations, structures, and ecology might be evidenced if the strategic change was "revolutionary" (Miller & Friesen, 1980). Finally, case studies across the successful and unsuccessful firms should demonstrate automatic and controlled retrieval differences. Consistent with Proposition 1, we predict that successful firms would have retrieved past instances of their company's responses to environmental shocks, evaluated their similarity or dissimilarity to deregulation, and then formulated a new strategy in this context. In keeping with Proposition 4, we expect that unsuccessful firms would not have considered past history thereby letting their automatic retrieval processes produce a routine response when a nonroutine response was appropriate. If these firms did consider the past, Proposition 6 would suggest that they reasoned uncritically by analogy to produce a response that was more consonant with the past than the present.

Memory as a Component in Organizational Design

An understanding of organizational memory may provide tools for enhancing our theories of organizational design. We argued previously that information-processing theories of organizational design (Galbraith, 1977; Lawrence & Lorsch, 1967; Thompson, 1967) have not been explicit in specifying the function of organizational memory, if any, in designing organizations. Two reasons might account for this omission.

First, it may have been assumed that memory is adequately reflected in organizational structure. Because organizational structure is typically represented as a product of historical forces and managerial choices (i.e., stable relationships between jobs over time), the tendency is to systematically trace changes in organizational structure over time and to assume that the decision information content of memory is reflected in such changes. Even though organizational memory is reflected a bit in organizational structure, we argue that it is not an isomorphic representation. Organizational memory includes other artifacts (i.e., ecology, transformations, etc.) that build on the historical interactions among members of the organization.

A second and related reason, initially suggested by Krippendorff (1975), is that many theories tend to deemphasize temporal interrelationships. Even when time is a key variable, the tendency is to emphasize formative changes in organizational structure (e.g., shifts from functional to multidivisional to matrix structures) in contrast to addressing changes in the firm's constitutive character (e.g., shifts in the meaning of organizational structure as constructed within the relevant contextual system). The restrictive focus on organizational structure as a product of historical forces or as a result of contemporaneous social interactions between organizational members precludes an active synthesis of organizational memory and organizational design.

One such application would be the management of clans (Ouchi, 1980) and networks (Miles & Snow, 1986). A *clan* is a specific governance structure that arises because of bureaucratic failure under conditions of high performance ambiguity. Conceivably, clans operate on the basis of trust and are regarded as having lower transactional costs due to sophisticated socialization (Ouchi, 1980). But what makes the organizing costs associated with clans lower than those of bureaucracies or markets? Wilkins and Ouchi (1983) have argued that all parties in any transaction have to view exchanges as equitable. This demand for equity leads to transaction costs, particularly when the value of goods and services is difficult to establish. Accordingly, the problem faced by organizations is this: How can a perception of equity be achieved among self-interested parties who are bounded-rational?

Unlike markets and bureaucracies, clans face more ambiguity in determining a fair and equitable transaction. Wilkins and Ouchi (1983) postulated that clan members have to believe that they will be dealt with equitably in the long run, particularly when present exchanges appear inequitable to them. In this context, we argue that a necessary condition for making this possible is the presence of organizational memory. Two premises are important here: (1) that the organization has the capability of recording decisions and (2) that the organization has the capacity to activate past decisions in present decision-making processes.

The management of memory also bears strongly on a new and emerging organizational form: the network. A *network* can be defined as a purposeful and conscious relationship between and among distinct organizations (Jarillo, 1988; Miles & Snow, 1986). Networks usually evolve to reduce external transactions, achieve economics of scale and scope, and facilitate the sharing of information (Park, 1990). Similar to clans, networks depend on truth (i.e., "fair sharing mechanisms" among members to sustain their viability and to discourage opportunistic behavior among them). In addition to any formal agreements that may bind them (e.g., joint ventures, strategic alliances), members of the network rely on trustworthy transactions (sustained by memory) to preserve and stabilize network relationships.

If a person accepts the possibility that past decisions are brought to bear on present events, then the person must postulate the existence of an organizational memory that enables the coexistence of the past and present. We argue that there are organizational consequences for managers who recognize the existence of memory and who manage it actively, as opposed to those who do not. As a design issue, the recognition of organizational memory entails understanding how past events are acquired, retained, retrieved, and even forgotten within the organization.

TOWARD A METHODOLOGY FOR STUDYING ORGANIZATIONAL MEMORY

The foregoing discussion of organizational memory suggests a general research agenda. Although the concept of memory makes much intuitive sense, particularly when used metaphorically to extend present concepts of organizations, it defies precise measurement and assessment. Even though issues about measurement and assessment are important, it is relevant to first delineate research phases in which a direct measurement approach may or may not be appropriate. Consistent with our concept of organizational memory, we argue that three research phases are necessary: (1) confirming the structure of organizational memory; (2) parsing the acquisition, retention, and retrieval processes into meaningful steps; and (3) assessing the consequentiality of memory for organizational performance. As Table 9.2 indicates, each phase can be viewed as a distinct step with its own methodological and analytic imperatives.

Phase 1: Assessing the Structure of Organizational Memory

The key epistemological question in this phase is conceptual: Does the concept of organizational memory have construct validity? We hypothesized that the structure of organizational memory is composed of a number of storage bins: individuals, culture, transformations, structures, ecology, and external archives. Underlying our hypothesis is a premise that memory is distributional in nature; that is, the repository of organizational information is not confined to one central location (as is the case of the brain in the individual body), but, rather, it is distributed throughout the entire organization (as might be the case of memory within the human brain). Within this conceptual definition, any attempt to directly measure or assess organizational memory is doomed to be partial and incomplete, unless one rigorously examines all the bins. Of course, this is a daunting task.

As such, we suggest that the appropriate strategy for examining memory in this context is not through verification or direct measurement, but rather by falsification (Bacharach, 1989). In his attempt to challenge inductive approaches to theory building, Popper (1959) argued that good theories result from a legitimate attempt to prove them wrong (i.e., falsify), rather than by an attempt to confirm them. This approach may be particularly meaningful when examining

TABLE 9.2 Research Issues in the Study of Organizational Memory

Conceptions of Organizational Memory	Conceptual Premises	Epistemological Questions	Suggested Research Strategies
Phase 1—Assessing the structure of organizational memory	Distributional: Arrayed in five bins: individuals, culture, transformations, structures, and ecology.	Conceptual: Does the concept of organizational memory have construct validity?	Test through falsification: inference about memory based on boundary conditions. Precedent: Transactional cost (no direct measures applied, but existence inferred from high information impactedness and asset specificity).
Phase 2—Parsing the information acquisition, retention, and retrieval processes	A focus on the properties of decision information, as well as the automatic and controlled retrieval processes.	Empirical: Can reliable and valid measures of the constructs be obtained?	Test through process verification: oral history methodologies and retrospective analysis, mapping parameters of memory, charting flows of action, identifying episodic scripts and stimulation. Methods: Protocol analysis; institutional mapping techniques.
Phase 3—Assessing the consequences of organizational memory	Contexts in which organizational memory is used, misused, and abused, particularly in organizing/design issues.	Analytical: What research measures will illuminate the hypothesized effects of organizational memory?	Test through statistical verification: counterposing of hypothesized effects versus predictions of rival theories. Precedent: Institutional theory (counterpositioning of two or more theories).

organizational memory. Its distributional nature suggests that most attempts to confirm the existence of memory are bound to be incomplete. The attempt to disconfirm the existence of decision information in each of these bins, for example, appears to be a better research strategy. Methods for falsifying theories entail specifying boundary conditions that are most likely to establish memory and testing the hypothesized effects against competing theories. This latter approach is discussed in more detail in the section on Phase 3.

Phase 2: Parsing the Process

In contrast to the first conceptual phase, the key epistemological question here is empirical: Can we obtain adequate measures of our concepts? Because the acquisition, retention, and retrieval of memory is an ongoing process, it is difficult to pinpoint exact boundaries between these processes. Even so, researchers must decide how to parse the process into ecologically meaningful stages that are subject to verification and measurement.

Previously we suggested that individuals are an excellent starting point for examining information acquisition, retention, and retrieval processes. A number of research methods are available to obtain such information. People can query themselves or others about past recollections. This can be on an ad hoc basis or through systematic oral histories (Vansina, 1985). In fact, Schuman and Scott (1989) used this very approach in their study of the collective memories of various generations of Americans. Individual beliefs, values, and assumptions are more difficult to uncover. The researchers can either ask the person to try to supply them or the theorist can use a variety of techniques which will reveal these beliefs (Bougon, Weick, & Binkhorst, 1977), values or goal orientations (Bourgeois, 1985), and assumptions (Mason & Mitroff, 1981). Individual recollection can also be aided by a reliance upon the organization's files and archives. With the passage of time, however, their sheer volume presents a daunting task of interpretation, as does an inability to recall the particular context of the various decisions. At that point, the in-house historian can become a helpful guide to the past (Smith & Steadman, 1981).

At the retention stage, we need to address issues of encoding. Specifically, we need to understand where information of various kinds is stored. The journalist's questions were invoked at the beginning of this article in an attempt to explicate how the content of retained information is likely to vary across the different retention facilities. These ideas need to be assessed. Moreover, we need to understand how retained information is affected by the passage of time. Does this information decay in some predictable fashion? How do retroactive interference processes affect the nature of the information that is being supplanted?

Finally, the retrieval and use of information from organizational memory await examination. What kinds of events or circumstances trigger the controlled search for information from memory? Moreover, how do various organizational attributes moderate the response to such triggering stimuli? With respect to use,

what factors prompt decision makers to engage in effortful retrieval and interpretation processes (i.e., examining similarities and differences between the past and
present), as opposed to employing a more automatic process wherein their reasoning is guided only by unexamined past analogies?

Even though there are many ways to record this information, we prefer
process methods of verification that are similar to those used when attempting to
chart an organization's institutions (Barley & Tolbert, 1988). Process methods include mapping the parameters of organizational memory, charting flows of actions, and identifying episodic scripts of information retention. Mapping the
parameters of memory involves identifying characteristics of retention in each of
the five bins. Because researchers ultimately will attempt to link these parameters
with use, assembling longitudinal indicators is of crucial importance—a process
that eventually should examine "why" information is stored in particular bins.
Charting flows of action results in a compilation of a detailed history of retention
activity among the various bins. When a sufficient history is compiled, researchers
might identify recurring patterns from which they can induce scripts or episodes
that characterize the retention and retrieval process. Therefore, we can begin to
better understand why particular aspects of decision information are stored in the
various bins. Understanding the purpose behind each script would provide the
first step in understanding the process by which information becomes stored in
various social and organizational contexts.

The archival study of organizational demography coupled with case studies
of organizational memory management practices in companies dealing with naturally occurring shocks represents but one approach to the study of organizational
memory. It might also be possible to employ some organizational experimentation
techniques. Salancik's (1979) ideas about the utility of organizational stimulation
have yet to be explored. It is quite possible to imagine a study of encoding and retrieval processes whereby organizations could be "stimulated" with varying types
of shocks. Subsequently, the firm could be queried about its recollections of these
stimulations. Such a study could provide insight on organizational attention processes, as well as on how the new information is encoded; that is, it would not be
difficult to assess attributes of how the "sent" stimulation varied from attributes
of the "received" recollections as a function of both the nature of the stimulation
and the organization's demographic profile.

Phase 3: Assessing the Consequences of Organizational Memory

The key epistemological question in this final phase is analytic: What research methods are appropriate for examining the hypothesized costs and benefits
of memory in organizations? The problem here is compounded by the fact that a
researcher may not be able to measure organizational memory at any one time
(see Phase 1), thus precluding the use of logical deduction and hypothesis testing.

We recommend a research strategy that counterposes the predictions of organizational memory with the predictions of one or more competing theories. In

such cases, it is important to specify the boundary conditions that develop, sustain, and activate organizational memory. Earlier, we suggested that there could be a long and stable history of tenured individuals, a standing tradition of cohort groups, and low turnover. We posit that such organizations will have a higher capacity to acquire, retain, and retrieve decision information relative to other organizations.

The above method has been used in a similar fashion to study the effects of organizations having high transactional costs (Wilkins & Ouchi, 1983). Similar to the organizational memory construct, transactional costs tend to be distributional and difficult to measure. Accordingly, researchers introduced boundary conditions that lead to high transactional costs (e.g., high asset specificity and bounded rationality) and then examined their hypothesized effects on governance structures. The same research strategy should be useful here.

CONCLUSIONS

Despite the general use of the term *organizational memory,* it is not clear that we have understood the concept or its implications for the management of organizations. To date, a myriad of unexamined conjectures has defined a concept that has even served as a basis for prescriptive management advice. This article examined the historical treatment of the concept, refined it, and defined it as a theoretical construct. Moreover, we discussed its role in organizing, and shaped an appreciation for the methodological challenges awaiting future researchers in this area. In so doing, we detailed the structure, content, and process attributes of organizational memory. Our goal has been to stir research interest on an important but often overlooked construct in the organizational sciences.

REFERENCES

Abelson, R. P., & Black, J. B. 1986. Introduction. In J. A. Galambos, R. P. Abelson, & J. B. Black (Eds.), *Knowledge structures:* 1–18. Hillsdale, NJ: Erlbaum.

Ackerman, M. A., & Malone, T. W. 1990. Answer garden: A tool for growing organizational memory. *Proceedings of the ACM Conference on Office Information Systems:* 31–39. Boston: Massachusetts Institute of Technology.

Aiken, M., & Hage, J. 1966. Organizational alienation: A comparative analysis. *American Sociological Review,* 31: 497–507.

Allaire, Y., & Firsirotu, M. E. 1985. Theories of organizational culture. *Organizational Studies,* 5: 193–226.

American heritage dictionary of the English language. 1969. New York: Dell.

Anderson, J.R. 1980. *Cognitive psychology and its implications.* San Francisco: Freeman and Company.

Anderson, R. C., & Pichert, J. W. 1978. Recall of previously unrecallable information following a shift in perspective. *Journal of Verbal Learning and Verbal Behavior.* 17: 1–12.

Argyris, C., & Schon, D. A. 1978. *Organizational learning: A theory of action perspective.* Reading, MA: Addison-Wesley.

Arvey, R. D. 1979. *Fairness in selecting employees.* Reading, MA: Addison-Wesley.

Axelrod, R. 1976. *The structure of decision.* Princeton: Princeton University Press.

Bacharach, S. B. 1989. Organizational theories: Some criteria for evaluation. *Academy of Management Review,* 14: 496–515.

Barley, S. R., & Tolbert, P. S. 1988. *Institutionalization as structurization: Methods and analytic strategies for studying links between action and structure.* Paper presented at the conference for Longitudinal Field Research Methods for Studying Organizational Processes. University of Texas, Austin.

Bartlett, F. C. 1932. *Remembering.* Cambridge: Cambridge University Press.

Beyer, J. M. 1981. Ideologies, values and decision making in organizations. In P. C. Nystrom & W. H. Starbuck (Eds.), *Handbook of organizational design,* vol. 2: 166–202. New York: Oxford University Press.

Blauner, R. L. 1964. *Alienation & freedom.* Chicago: University of Chicago Press.

Bougon, M., Weick, K., & Binkhorst, D. 1977. Cognition in organizations: An analysis of the Ulrecht jazz orchestra. *Administrative Science Quarterly,* 22: 606–639.

Bourgeois, L. J. 1985. Strategic goals, perceived uncertainty, and economic performance in volatile environments. *Academy of Management Journal,* 28: 548–573.

Bradley, G. W. 1978. Self-serving biases in the attribution process: A reexamination of the fact or fiction question. *Journal of Personality and Social Psychology,* 36: 56–71.

Brewer, W., & Nakamura, G. V. 1984. The nature and functions of schemas. In R. S. Wyer & T. R. Srull (Eds.), *Handbook of social cognition,* vol. 1: 119–160. Hillsdale, NJ: Erlbaum.

Brief, A. P., & Downey, H. K. 1983. Cognitive and organizational structures: A conceptual analysis of implicit organizing theories. *Human Relations,* 36: 1065–1090.

Broehl, W. G. 1984. *John Deere's company: A history of Deere & Company and its times.* Chicago: J. G. Ferguson.

Brown, N. R., Shevell, S. K., & Rips, L. J. 1986. Public memories and their personal context. In D. C. Rubin (Ed.). *Autobiographical memory:* 137–158. Cambridge: Cambridge University Press.

Bryant, J. 1983. Hypermaps: A representation of perceptions in conflicts. *Omega,* 11: 575–586.

Burrell, G., & Morgan, G. 1979. *Sociological paradigms and organizational analysis.* London: Heinemann Educational Books.

Campbell, D. E. 1979. Interior office design and visitor response. *Journal of Applied Psychology,* 64: 648–653.

Cangelosi, V. E., & Dill, W. R. 1965. Organizational learning: Observations toward a theory. *Administrative Science Quarterly,* 10: 175–203.

Cantor, N., & Mischel, W. 1977. Traits as prototypes: Effects of recognition memory. *Journal of Personality and Social Psychology,* 35: 38–48.

Clark, B. 1972. The organizational saga in higher education. *Administrative Science Quarterly,* 17, 178–184.

Cohen, C. E. 1981. Person categories and social perception: Testing some boundaries of the processing effects of prior knowledge. *Journal of Personality and Social Psychology,* 40: 441–452.

Cosse, T. J., & Swan, J. E. 1983. Strategic market planning by product managers—room for improvement? *Journal of Marketing,* 47: 92–102.

Cowan, N. 1988. Evolving conceptions of memory storage, selective attention, and their mutual constraints within the human information-processing system. *Psychological Bulletin,* 104: 163–191.

Cyert, R. M., & March, J. G. 1963. *A behavioral theory of the firm.* Englewood Cliffs, NJ: Prentice-Hall.

Daft, R. L., & Weick, K. E. 1984. Toward a model of organizations as interpretation systems. *Academy of Management Review,* 9, 284–295.

Dandridge, T. C. 1983. Symbols' function and use. In L. R. Pondy, P. J. Frost, G. Morgan, & T. C. Dandridge (Eds.), *Organizational symbolism:* 69–80 Greenwich, CT: JAI Press.

Davis, K. 1953. Management communication and the grapevine. *Harvard Business Review,* 4: 43–49.

Donnellon, A. 1986. Language and communication in organizations. In H. P. Sims & D. A. Gioia (Eds.), *The thinking organization:* 136–164. San Francisco: Jossey-Bass.

Douglas, M. 1986 *How institutions think.* Syracuse. NY: Syracuse University Press.

Duhaime, I. M., & Schwenk, C. R. 1985. Conjectures on cognitive simplification in acquisition and divestment decision making. *Academy of Management Review,* 10: 287–295.

Duncan, R. B. 1972. Characteristics of organizational environments and perceived environmental uncertainty. *Administrative Science Quarterly,* 17: 313–327.

Duncan, R. B., & Weiss, A. 1979. Organizational learning: Implications for organizational design. In B. M. Staw (Ed.), *Research in organizational behavior,* vol. 1: 75–124. Greenwich, CT: JAI Press.

Durkheim, E. 1895/1938. *The rules of sociological method.* New York: Free Press.

Eden, C., Jones, S., Sims, D., & Smithin, T. 1981. The intersubjectivity of issues and issues of intersubjectivity. *Journal of Management Studies,* 18: 37–47.

El Sawy, O. A., Gomes, G. M., & Gonzalez, M. V. 1986. Preserving institutional memory: The management of history as an organizational resource. *Academy of Management Best Paper Proceedings,* 37: 118–122.

Feldman, M. S., & March, J. G. 1981. Information in organizations as signal and symbol. *Administrative Science Quarterly,* 26: 171–186.

Fiol, C. M., & Lyles, M. A. 1985. Organizational learning. *Academy of Management Review,* 10: 803–813

Fleck, L. 1938/1979. *Genesis and development of a scientific fact,* Chicago: University of Chicago Press.

Galbraith, J. R. 1977. *Organizational design.* Reading, MA: Addison-Wesley.

Halbwachs, M. 1950/1980. *The collective memory.* (F. J. Ditter, Jr. & V. Y. Ditter, Trans.) New York: Harper Colophon Books.

Hall, R. I. 1984. The natural logic of management policy making: Its implications for the survival of an organization. *Management Science,* 30: 905–927.

Hambrick, D. C., & Mason, P. A. 1984. Upper echelons: The organization as a reflection of its top managers. *Academy of Management Review,* 9: 193–206.

Hedberg, B. L. T., Nystrom, P. C., & Starbuck, W. H. 1976. Camping on seesaws: Prescriptions for a self-designing organization. *Administrative Science Quarterly,* 21: 41–65.

Huber, G. P. 1990. A theory of the effects of advanced information technologies on organizational design, intelligence, and decision making. *Academy of Management Review,* 15: 47–71.

Huber, G. P. 1991. Organizational learning: The contributing processes and the literatures. *Organizational Science,* forthcoming.

Jackson, S. E., & Dutton, J. E. 1988. Discerning threats and opportunities. *Administrative Science Quarterly,* 33: 370–387.

Janis, I. L., & Mann, I. 1977. *Decision making: A psychological analysis of conflict, choice, and commitment.* New York: Free Press.

Jarillo, J. C. 1988. On strategic networks. *Strategic Management Journal,* 9: 31–41.

Jelinek, M. 1979. *Institutionalizing innovation.* New York: Praeger.

Johnson, M. K., & Hasher, L. 1987. Human learning and memory. *Annual Review of Psychology,* 38: 631–668.

Kahneman, D. 1973. *Attention and effort.* Englewood Cliffs, NJ: Prentice-Hall.

Kantrow, A. M. 1987. *The constraints of corporate tradition.* New York: Harper & Row.

Kerr, S. 1975. On the folly of rewarding A, while hoping for B. *Academy of Management Journal,* 18: 769–783.

Kiesler, S., & Sproull, L. 1982. Managerial response to changing environments: Perspectives on problem sensing from social cognition. *Administrative Science Quarterly,* 27: 548–570.

Kotter, J. P., & Schlesinger, L. A. 1979. Choosing strategies for change. *Harvard Business Review,* 57: 106–114.

Krippendorff, K. 1975. Some principles of information storage and retrieval in society. *General Systems,* 20: 15–35.

Langer, E. J. 1983. *The psychology of control.* Beverly Hills, CA: Sage.

Larwood, L., & Whitaker, W. 1977. Managerial myopia: Self-serving biases in organizational planning. *Journal of Applied Psychology,* 62: 194–198.

Lawrence, P. R., & Lorsch, J. W. 1967. *Organization and environment.* Boston: Graduate School of Business Administration, Harvard University.

Loftus, G. R., & Loftus, E. F. 1976. *Human memory: The processing of information.* Hillsdale, NJ: Erlbaum.

March, J. G. 1972. Model bias in social action. *Review of Educational Research,* 44: 413–429.

March, J. G., & Olsen, J. P. 1975. The uncertainty of the past: Organizational learning under ambiguity. *European Journal of Political Research,* 3: 147–171.

March, J. G., & Olsen, J. P. 1976. *Ambiguity and choice in organizations.* Oslo: Universitets-forlaget.

March, J. G., & Sevon, G. 1984. Gossip, information and decision-making. In L. S. Sproull & J. P. Crecine (Eds.), *Advances in information processing in organizations,* vol. 1: 95–107. Hillsdale, NJ: Erlbaum.

March, J. G., & Simon, H. A. 1958. *Organizations.* New York: Wiley.

Marcus, A. A. 1988. Implementing externally induced innovations: A comparison of rule-bound and autonomous approaches. *Academy of Management Journal,* 31: 235–256.

Martin, J., Feldman, M. S., Hatch, M. J., & Sitkin, S. B. 1983. The uniqueness paradox in organizational stories. *Administrative Science Quarterly,* 28: 438–453.

Mason, R., & Mitroff, I. 1981. *Challenging strategic planning assumptions.* New York: Wiley.

Merton, R. 1968. *Social theory and social structure.* New York: Free Press.

Meyer, J., & Rowan, B. 1977. Institutionalized organizations: Formal structure as myth and ceremony. *American Journal of Sociology,* 83: 340–363.

Miles R. E. & Snow, C. C. 1986. Organizations: New concepts for new forms. *California Management Review,* 28(3): 62–73.

Miles, R. H., & Randolph, W. A. 1980. Influence of organizational learning styles on early development. In J. H. Kimberley & R. H. Miles (Eds.), *The organizational life cycle:* 44–82. San Francisco: Jossey-Bass.

Miller, D., & Friesen, P. H. 1980. Momentum and revolution in organizational adaptation. *Academy of Management Journal,* 23: 591–614.

Miller, D. T., & Ross, M. 1975. Self-serving biases in the attribution of causality: Fact or fiction? *Psychological Bulletin,* 82: 213–225.

Miller, G. A. 1956. The magic number seven plus or minus two: Some limits on our capacity for processing information. *Psychological Review,* 64: 81–97.

Morris, S. 1973. Stalled professionalism: The recruitment of railway officials in the United States. 1885–1940. *Business History Review,* 47: 317–334.

Morrow, P. C., & McElroy, J. C. 1981. Interior office design and visitor response: A constructive replication. *Journal of Applied Psychology,* 66: 646–650.

Murray, E. A. 1978. Strategic choice as a negotiated outcome. *Management Science,* 24: 960–972.

Neustadt, R. E., & May, E. R. 1986. *Thinking in time: The uses of history for decision makers.* New York: Free Press.

Newell, A., & Simon, H. 1972. *Human problem solving.* Englewood Cliffs, NJ: Prentice Hall.

Nisbett, R., & Ross, L. 1980. *Human inference: Strategies and shortcomings of social judgment.* Englewood Cliffs, NJ: Prentice-Hall.

Nystrom, P. C., & Starbuck, W. H. 1984. To avoid organizational crises, unlearn. *Organizational Dynamics,* 12: 53–65.

Oldham, G. R., & Rotchford, N. L. 1983. Relationships between office characteristics and employee reactions: A study of the physical environment. *Administrative Science Quarterly,* 28: 542–556.

O'Reilly, C. A. 1983. The use of information in organizational decision making: A model and some propositions. In L. L. Cummings & B. M. Staw (Eds.), *Research in organizational behavior,* vol. 5: 103–140. Greenwich, CT: JAI Press.

Ouchi, W. 1980. Markets, bureaucracies, and clans. *Administrative Science Quarterly,* 25: 129–141.

Park, S. H. 1990. *A framework for governance structure: An extension of the market and hierarchy paradigm.* Unpublished manuscript. Graduate School of Management. Eugene, OR: University of Oregon.

Perrow, C. 1972. *Complex organizations: A critical essay.* Glenview, IL: Scott, Foresman.

Perrow, C. 1979. *Organizational analysis: A sociological view.* Monterey, CA: Brooks/ Cole.

Pfeffer, J. 1981a. Management as symbolic action: The creation and maintenance of organizational paradigms. In L. L. Cummings & B. M. Staw (Eds.), *Research in organizational behavior,* vol. 3: 1–52. Greenwich, CT: JAI Press.

Pfeffer, J. 1981b. *Power in organizations.* Cambridge, MA: Ballinger.

Pfeffer, J. 1983. Organizational demography. In L. L. Cummings & B M. Staw (Eds.), *Research in organizational behavior,* vol. 5: Greenwich, CT: JAI Press.

Pinder, C. C., & Bourgeois, V. W. 1982. Controlling tropes in administrative science. *Administrative Science Quarterly,* 27: 641–652.

Pondy, L. R., & Mitroff, I. I. 1979. Beyond open systems models of organizations. In B. M. Staw (Ed.). *Research in organizational behavior,* vol. 1: 3–40. Greenwich, CT: JAI Press.

Popper, K. R. 1959. *The logic of scientific discovery.* New York: Basic Books.

Porter, M. E. 1980. *Competitive strategy: Techniques for analyzing industries and competitors.* New York: Free Press.

Posner, M. I. 1982. Cumulative development of attention theory. *American Psychologist,* 37: 168–179.

Prahalad, C. K., & Bettis, R. A. 1986. The dominant logic: A new linkage between diversity and performance. *Strategic Management Journal,* 7: 485–501.

Ranson, S., Hinings, B., & Greenwood, R. 1980. The structuring of organizational structures. *Administrative Science Quarterly,* 25: 1–17.

Ray, C. A. 1986. Corporate culture: The last frontier of control. *Journal of Management Studies,* 23: 287–297.

Reichers, A. E. 1985. A review and reconceptualization of organizational commitment. *Academy of Management Review,* 10: 465–476.

Richardson-Klavenn, A., & Biork, R. A. 1988. Measures of memory. *Annual Review of Psychology,* 39: 475–543.

Rubin, D. C. 1986. *Autobiographical memory.* Cambridge: Cambridge University Press.

Salancik, G. R. 1979. Field stimulations for organizational behavior research. *Administrative Science Quarterly,* 24: 638–649.

Sandelands, L. E., & Stablein, R. E. 1987. The concept of organization mind. In S. Bachrach & N. DiTomaso (Eds.). *Research in the sociology of organizations,* vol. 5: 135–162. Greenwich, CT: JAI Press.

Schank, R., & Abelson, R. 1977. *Scripts, plans, goals and understanding: An inquiry into human knowledge structures.* Hillsdale, NJ: Erlbaum.

Schein, E. H. 1984. Coming to a new awareness of organizational culture. *Sloan Management Review,* 25: 3–16.

Schon, D. A. 1983. *The reflective practitioner.* New York: Basic Books.

Schuman, H., & Scott, J. 1989. Generations and collective memories. *American Sociological Review,* 54: 359–381.

Shannon, C. E., & Weaver, W. 1949. *The mathematical theory of communications.* Urbana, IL. University of Illinois Press.

Shrivastava, P., & Schneider, S. 1984. Organizational frames of reference. *Human Relations.* 37: 795–807.

Simon, H. A. 1976. *Administrative behavior.* New York: Free Press.

Sims, H. P., & Gioia, D. A. 1986. *The thinking organization: Dynamics of organizational social cognition.* San Francisco: Jossey-Bass.

Smircich, L. 1983. Concepts of culture and organizational analysis. *Administrative Science Quarterly,* 28: 339–358.

Smith, G. D., & Steadman, L. E. 1981. Present value of corporate history. *Harvard Business Review,* 59: 164–173.

Smith, K. G., & Grimm, C. M. 1987. Environmental variation, strategic change and firm performance. A study of railroad deregulation. *Strategic Management Journal,* 8: 363–376.

Sommer, R. 1969. *Personal space.* Englewood Cliffs. NJ: Prentice-Hall.

Spradley, J. P. 1980. *Participant observation.* New York: Holt, Rinehart and Winston.

Sproutt, L. S. 1981. Beliefs in organizations. In P. C. Nystrom & W. H. Starbuck (Eds.), *Handbook of organizational design,* vol 2. 203 224. London: Oxford University Press.

Starbuck, W. H., Greve, A., & Hedberg, B. I. T. 1978. Responding to crisis. *Journal of Business Administration,* 9, 111–137.

Starbuck, W., & Hedberg, B. 1977. Saving an organization from a stagnating environment. In H. Thorelli (Ed.), *Strategy + structure = performance:* 249–258. Bloomington: Indiana University Press.

Taylor, F. W. 1923. *The principles of scientific management.* New York: Harper.

Taylor, S. E., & Crocker, J. 1981. Schematic basis of social information processing. In E. T. Higgins, C. P. Herman, & M. P. Zanna (Eds.), *Social cognition: The Ontario symposium,* vol. 1: 89–134. Hillsdale, NJ: Erlbaum.

Taylor, S. E., Crocker, J., & D'Agostino, J. 1978. Schematic bases of problem-solving. *Personality and Social Psychology Bulletin,* 4: 447–451.

Thompson, I. D. 1967. *Organizations in action.* New York: McGraw-Hill.

Tushman, M. L. & Anderson, P. 1986. Technological discontinuities and organizational environments. *Administrative Science Quarterly,* 31: 439–465.

Tushman, M. L., & Nadler, D. A. 1978 Information processing as an integrating concept in organizational design. *Academy of Management Review,* 3: 613–624.

Unason, G. R. Braunstein, D. N., & Hall, P. D. 1981. Managerial information processing: A research review. *Administrative Science Quarterly,* 26: 116–134.

Van Maanen, J., & Schein, E. H. 1979. Toward a theory of organizational socialization. In B. Staw (Ed.), *Research in organizational behavior,* vol. 1: 209–264. Greenwich, CT: JAI Press.

Vansina, J. 1985. *Oral tradition as history,* Madison: University of Wisconsin Press.

Walsh, J. P. 1988. Selectivity and selective perception: An investigation of managers belief structures and information processing. *Academy of Management Journal,* 31: 873–896.

Walsh, J. P., & Dewar, R. D. 1987. Formalization and the organizational life cycle. *Journal of Management Studies,* 24: 216–231.

Walsh, J. P., & Fahey, L. 1986. The role of negotiated belief structures in strategy making. *Journal of Management,* 12: 325–338.

Walsh, J. P. Henderson, C. M., & Deighton, I. 1988. Negotiated belief structures and decision performance: An empirical investigation. *Organizational Behavior and Human Decision Processes,* 42: 194–216.

Walsh, J. P., & Seward, J. K. 1990. On the efficiency of internal and external corporate control mechanisms. *Academy of Management Review,* 15: 421–458.

Weber, M. 1968. *Economy and society.* (G. Roth & C. Wittich. Trans.). Berkeley: University of California Press.

Weick, K. E. 1979a. *The social psychology of organizing,* Reading, MA: Addison-Wesley.

Weick, K. E. 1979b. Cognitive processes in organizations. In B. M. Staw (Ed.), *Research in organizational behavior,* vol. 1: 41–74. Greenwich, CT: JAI Press.

Weick, K. E., & Gilfillan, D. P. 1971. Fate of arbitrary traditions in a laboratory microculture. *Journal of Personality and Social Psychology,* 17: 179–191.

Wildavsky, A. 1979. *The politics of the budgetary process.* Boston: Little Brown.

Wilensky, H. L. 1967. *Organizational intelligence.* New York: Basic Books.

Wilkins, A. L. 1983. Organizational stories as symbols which control the organization. In L. R. Pondy, P. I. Frost, G. Morgan, & T. C. Dandridge (Eds.), *Organizational symbolism:* 81–92. Greenwich, CT: JAI Press.

Wilkins, A. L., & Bristow N. J. 1987. For successful organization culture, honor your past. *Academy of Management Executive,* 1: 221–229.

Wilkins, A. L., & Ouchi, W. 1983. Efficient cultures: Exploring the relationship between culture and organizational performance. *Administrative Science Quarterly,* 28: 468–481.

Wong, P. T. P., & Weiner, B. 1981. When people ask why questions and the neuristics of attributional search. *Journal of Personality and Social Psychology,* 40: 650–663.

Yates, B. 1983. *The decline and fall of the American automobile industry.* New York: Vintage Books.

Yates, J. 1990. For the record: The embodiment of organizational memory. 1850–1920. *Business and Economic History* (2nd Series), 19: 1–11.

10

Cosmos vs. Chaos: Sense and Nonsense in Electronic Contexts

Karl E. Weick

The growth of electronic information processing has changed organizations in profound ways. One unexpected change is that electronic processing has made it harder, not easier, to understand events that are represented on screens. As a result, job dissatisfaction in the 1990s may not center on issues of human relations. It may involve the even more fundamental issue of meaning: Employees can tolerate people problems longer than they can tolerate uncertainty about what's going on and what it means.

Representations of events normally hang together sensibly within the set of assumptions that give them life and constitute a "cosmos" rather than its opposite, a "chaos." Sudden losses of meaning that can occur when an event is represented electronically in an incomplete, cryptic form are what I call a "cosmology episode."

Representations in the electronic world can become chaotic for at least two reasons: The data in these representations are flawed, and the people who manage those flawed data have limited processing capacity. These two problems interact in a potentially deadly vicious circle. The data are flawed because they are incomplete; they contain only what can be collected and processed through machines. That excludes sensory information, feelings, intuitions, and context—all of which are necessary for an accurate perception of what is happening. Feelings, context, and sensory information are not soft-headed luxuries. They are ways of knowing that preserve properties of events not captured by machine-compatible information. To withhold these incompatible data is to handicap the observer. And therein lies the problem.

Reprinted, by permission of publisher, from ORGANIZATIONAL DYNAMICS Autumn 1985.

When people are forced to make judgments based on cryptic data, they can't resolve their puzzlement by comparing different versions of the event registered in different media. When comparison is not possible, people try to clear up their puzzlement by asking for more data. More data of the same kind clarify nothing, but what does happen is that more and more human-processing capacity is used up to keep track of the unconnected details.

As details build up and capacity is exceeded, the person is left with the question, What's going on here? That emotional question is often so disconcerting that perception narrows, and even less of a potential pattern is seen. This leads people to seek more information and to have less understanding, more emotional arousal, less complete perception and, finally, a cosmology episode.

When a person is able to connect the details and see what they might mean, processing capacity is restored. Meanings that can impose some sense on detail typically come from sources outside the electronic cosmos—sources such as metaphors, corporate culture, archetypes, myths, history. The electronic world makes sense only when people are able to reach outside that world for qualitatively different images that can flesh out cryptic representations. Managers who fail to cultivate and respect these added sources of meaning, and bring them to terminals, will make it impossible for people who work at screens to accurately diagnose the problems they are expected to solve.

This article provides a groundwork for this conclusion. After a brief discussion of how people make sense of the world when they are away from terminals, I will show how those same sense-making processes are disrupted when people return to the terminal. The problem at the terminal is that people no longer have access to data and actions by which they usually validate their observations. When confined to inputs that make invalidity inevitable, people understandably feel anxious. That's when cosmology episodes occur. I will conclude by suggesting what steps organizations can take to avoid such episodes.

Sense Making Away From Terminals

People use a variety of procedures to make sense of what happens around them, five of which are the focus of this analysis. To understand events, people (1) effectuate, (2) triangulate, (3) affiliate, (4) deliberate, and (5) consolidate.

Effectuating

People learn about events when they prod them to see what happens. To learn our way around a new job we try things to see what gets praised and what gets punished. To see what physical problem a patient has, a physician often starts a treatment, observes the response, and then makes a diagnosis. To discover what their foreign policy consists of, diplomats sometimes give speeches in which a variety of assertions are made. They then read editorial comments to learn what reporters think they "said," how the reporters reacted, and what should be preserved in subsequent speeches and policy statements.

People often say, "How can I know what I think until I see what I say?" People find out what's going on by first making something happen. Doing something is the key. Until I say something—anything—I can't be sure what I think or what is important or what my preferences are. I can't be sure what my goals are until I can observe the choices I made when I had some discretion over how to spend my time.

Action is a major tool through which we perceive and develop intuitions. Machines perform many operations that used to call for professional judgment—operations like reasoning, analyzing, gathering data, and remembering. Now perception and intuition are the major inputs that human beings can contribute when solving a problem with a computer. Since action is the major source of human perceptions and intuition, any assessment of the potential for sense making must pay close attention to action.

Triangulating

People learn about an event when they apply several different measures to it, each of which has a different set of flaws. When perceptions are confirmed by a series of measures whose imperfections vary, people have increased confidence in those perceptions or their conclusions about them. For example, committee reports, financial statements, and computer printouts are not sufficient by themselves to provide unequivocal data about the efficiency of operations. The conclusions from these data need to be checked against qualitatively different sources such as formal and informal field visits, exit interviews, mealtime conversations in the company cafeteria, complaints phoned to an 800 number, conversations with clients, and the speed with which internal memos are answered. These various "barometers," each of which presents its own unique problem of measurement, begin to converge on an interpretation. The key point is that the convergence involves qualitatively different measures, not simply increasingly detailed refinements, ratios, and comparisons within one set of measures. What survives in common among the several measures is something that is sensible rather than fanciful.

Affiliating

People learn about events when they compare what they see with what someone else sees and then negotiate some mutually acceptable version of what really happened. The highly symbolic character of most organizational life makes the construction of social reality necessary for stabilizing some version of "what is really happening."

People also affiliate when they want answers to specific questions. Herbert Simon explained how affiliation works by using this question as an example: "Do whales have spleens?" Suppose someone asked you that, what would you answer? Simon's reply was that he'd make five calls and by the time he got to the fifth one he'd know the answer. In each phone call he'd ask, "Who do you know who's the closest to being an expert on this topic?" He would call whoever was mentioned and would rapidly converge on the answer.

Deliberating

People learn about events through slow and careful reasoning during which they formulate ideas and reach conclusions. When the reasoning process is drawn out, partially formed connections are allowed to incubate and become clarified, irrelevancies are forgotten, later events are used to reinterpret earlier ones, and all of these processes are used to edit and simplify the initial mass of input. This reduction of input, or deliberation, takes time.

The activity of comprehending a speech is an example of how time can affect deliberation. If a speaker talks to an audience instead of reading a speech, then the speaker's mind works at the same speed as the listener's mind. Both are equally handicapped, and comprehension is high. If, however, a speaker reads a prepared text, the substance is more densely packed and is delivered at a speed that is faster than the listener's mind can work. The listener deliberates while the speaker accelerates, and comprehension decreases. Of course, we are talking about the speed of the mind, not the speed of the nervous system. Nervous systems can accelerate in response to environmental input from displays such as television or video-game screens. The only way to cope with this acceleration of activity in the nervous system is to stop thinking, because ideas cannot form, dissolve, and combine as fast as eye-hand coordination can make adjustments in response to computer displays. Mindless activity takes less time than mindful activity, and this difference can affect the kind and depth of sense one is able to construct within information systems.

Consolidating

People learn about events when they can put them in a context. The statement, "It is 30 degrees," is senseless until we know whether the context is Centigrade or Fahrenheit. An event means quite a different thing when it is seen as part of a cycle, part of a developmental sequence, random, predetermined, or in transition from one steady state to another.

The power of a context to synthesize and give meaning to scattered details can be seen in the current fascination with the "back to basics" movement. The diverse, unexplainable troubles people have right now are lumped into the diagnosis, "We've strayed from the basics." People think that if they go back to the basics (for example, Kenneth Blanchard's *The One Minute Manager*), their fortunes will improve. It is interesting that John Naisbitt's *Megatrends* has a more disorienting, less soothing message. According to Naisbitt, the basics themselves are changing. Naisbitt's view holds the prospect that events will become even more senseless.

To consolidate bits and pieces into a compact, sensible pattern frequently requires that one look beyond those bits and pieces to understand what they might mean. The pieces themselves generate only a limited context, frequently inadequate to understanding what is happening in the system, what its limitations are, or how to change it. That diagnosis has to be made outside the system and frequently involves a different order of logic. It is often the inability to move outside an information system, and see it as a self-contained but limited context, that makes it difficult to diagnose, improve, and supplement what is happening inside that system.

The famous paradox of Epimenides is an example of a problem in context. "Epimenides was a Cretan who said, 'Cretans always lie.'" The larger quotation becomes a classifier for the smaller, until the smaller quotation takes over and reclassifies the larger one to create contradiction. Gregory Bateson explains that when we ask:

> *"Could Epimenides be telling the truth?" The answer is: "If yes, then no,"
> and "If no, then yes." . . . If you present the Epimenides paradox to a computer, the answer will come out YES . . . NO . . . YES . . . NO . . . until the
> computer runs out of ink or energy or encounters some other ceiling.*

To avoid the paradox, you have to realize that a context in which classification used to be appropriate has become senseless. It is our inability to step outside, and invoke some context other than classification, that makes the situation senseless.

Consider a different problem. A dog is trained to bark whenever a circle appears and to paw the ground whenever an ellipse appears. If the correct response is made, the dog gets a reward. Now, begin to flatten the circle and fatten the ellipse, and watch what happens. As the two figures become more indistinguishable, the animal gets more agitated, makes more errors, and gets fewer rewards. Why? The animal persists in treating the context as one in which it is supposed to discriminate. When discrimination becomes impossible, the situation becomes senseless—but only because it continues to be treated as a problem requiring discrimination. If the animal moved to a different level of reasoning outside the system and saw that discrimination was only one of several contexts within which it could try to distinguish the look-alike ellipses and circles, then sense might be restored. If, for example, the context were seen instead as one that required guesswork, then there would be no problem. Reframing the situation as guesswork is possible only if you realize that many contexts are possible, not just the one in which your life is lived.

It is the very self-contained character of the electronic cosmos that tempts people, when data make less and less sense, to retain assumptions rather than move to different orders of reasoning. This error is especially apt to be made when information is defined only as that which can be collected and processed by machines. Different orders of meaning, those meanings that can impose new sense, can't be collected and processed by machines. The big danger is that these meanings will then be dismissed rather than seen as vehicles for resolving some of the senseless episodes generated by the assumptions inherent in machine processing.

Sense Making in Front of Terminals

People using information technologies are susceptible to cosmology episodes because they act less, compare less, socialize less, pause less, and consolidate less when they work at terminals than when they are away from them. As a result, the incidence of senselessness increases when they work with computer representations of events.

Action Deficiencies

The electronic cottage is a more difficult site for sense making than people may realize, because events are never confronted, prodded, or examined directly. People's knowledge of events is limited to the ways they are represented by machine and by the ways in which they can alter those machine representations. A crucial source of data—feedback generated by direct, personal action—is absent.

For example, Shoshana Zuboff describes what happens when a centralized "information interface," based on microprocessors, is placed between operators and machinery in a pulp mill. Operators no longer see directly what happens in pulp operations. They leave a world "in which things were immediately known, comprehensively sensed, and able to be acted upon directly" for a more distant world that requires a different response and different skills. What is surprising is the extent to which managers underestimate what is lost when action is restricted to one place. Zuboff quotes one manager as saying:

> The workers have an intuitive feel of what the process needs to be. Someone in the process will listen to things and that is their information. All of their senses are supplying data. But once they are in the control room, all they have to do is look at the screen. Things are concentrated right in front of you. You don't have sensory feedback. You have to draw inferences by watching the data, so you must understand the theory behind it. In the long run you would like people who can take data, trust them, and draw broad conclusions from them. They [workers] must be more scientific.

This manager makes several errors. "Things" are not in front of operators in the control room—symbols are. And symbols carry only partial information that needs to be verified by other means. Operators "don't have sensory feedback," but that's a problem, not a virtue, of technology. The display will substitute indirect for direct experience, because operators will have to "draw inferences" based on "the theory behind" the data. However, theories are just theories, and conjectures and inferences are shaky when based on partial data, tentative regularities, and flawed human induction. Operators are told to "take data . . . and draw broad conclusions from them," but the data are not of the operators' own choosing nor are they in a form that allows intuition to be part of the inferential process.

In the words of another of Zuboff's managers, "We are saying your intuition is no longer valuable. Now you must understand the whole process and the theory behind it." The irony is that intuition is the very means by which a person is able to know a whole process, because intuition incorporates action, thought, and feeling; automated controls do not.

An additional problem with terminal work is the fact that trial and error, perhaps the most reliable tool for learning, is stripped of much of its power. Trials within an information system are homogeneous and correlated. What is tried next depends on what was done before and is a slight variation of the last trial. For example, spreadsheets are the very essence of trial and error, or so it seems. People vary quantities that are acceptable within the spreadsheet program, but they do not vary programs, hardware, algorithms, databases, or the truthfulness of inputs. People vary what the program lets them vary and ignore everything else. Since programs do not have provisions to switch logics or abandon logics or selectively combine different logics, trials are correlated and they sample a restricted range of choices.

The more general point is that trial and error is most effective with a greater number of heterogeneous trials. That is why brainstorming groups often come up with solutions that no individual would have thought of before the discussion started. In these groups, suggestions are idiosyncratic and unconnected, but they sample a broader range of possibilities and improve the odds that someone will stumble onto a solution that lies outside traditional lines of thought.

Spreadsheets do not let people introduce whatever comes to mind or follow lines of thought that have arisen from previous comments or inputs to whatever conclusions these thoughts may lead. These constraints are action deficiencies, because they restrict the ways in which the target can be manipulated, which restricts what can be known about the target.

Comparison Deficiencies

Action is a major source of comparative data, which is one reason that the sedentary quality of information systems is so deadly. Moreover information systems do not give access to much of the data about a phenomenon or treat those data as noise. Not enough different perspectives are compared to improve accuracy. The illusion of accuracy can be created if people avoid comparison (triangulation), but in a dynamic, competitive, changing environment, illusions of accuracy are short-lived, and they fall apart without warning. Reliance on a single, uncontradicted data source can give people a feeling of omniscience, but because those data are flawed in unrecognized ways, they lead to nonadaptive action.

Visual illusions such as those depicted in Figure 10.1 are a metaphor for what happens when triangulation is ignored. The point of a visual illusion is that the eye can be tricked. But that is true only if you maintain a fixed eye position and do nothing but stare. If you tilt the illusion, view it along an edge, measure it, look at it from a different angle, or manipulate it, the illusion vanishes. As you manipulate the object, you add to the number of sensory impressions you initially had and therefore should run the risk of overload. Actually, however, you get clarity, because the several active operations give you a better sense of what is common among the several different kinds of information. One thing you discover is that the specific illusion that you saw when you did nothing disappears when you do something. Moving around an illusion is an exercise in triangulation because different perspectives are compared. Moving around is also an exercise in action that tells us about an object.

It is difficult to triangulate within a computer world because it's highly probable that the blindspots in the various alterations tried on a representation will be similar. For example, consider a simulated, three-dimensional computer design that represents bone fractures. The object is seen from several vantage points, but the program's assumptions are carried along with each view and are neither detected by the observer nor canceled by perspectives that make a different set of assumptions. Thus the system will keep making the same errors.

If you take a computer printout into the field and hold it alongside the event it is supposed to represent (for example, the behavior of a purchasing agent), the chances are good that the actual event will be noisier, less orderly, and more unique than is evidenced by the smoothed representation on the printout. Even though different kinds of potential error are inherent in a printout reading and a face-to-face observation, some similarities will be found when comparing these two perceptual modes. Those similarities are stable features of the observed phenomenon and are worth responding to. The differences between the two are the illusions (errors) inherent in any specific view of the world. What's important to remember is that if people stick to one view, their lives may be momentarily more soothing, but also become more susceptible to sudden jolts of disconfirmation.

Affiliation Deficiencies

Terminals are basically solitary settings. Christopher Lehmann-Haupt described computing as "quantified narcissism disguised as productive activity." Of course, computing is not always solitary; FAA air-traffic control systems assign two controllers to each "scope." But when the face-to-face, social character of sense making in information systems decreases, several problems can arise.

First, less opportunity exists to build a social reality, some consensus version of events as they unfold. Different people viewing the terminal display see differ-

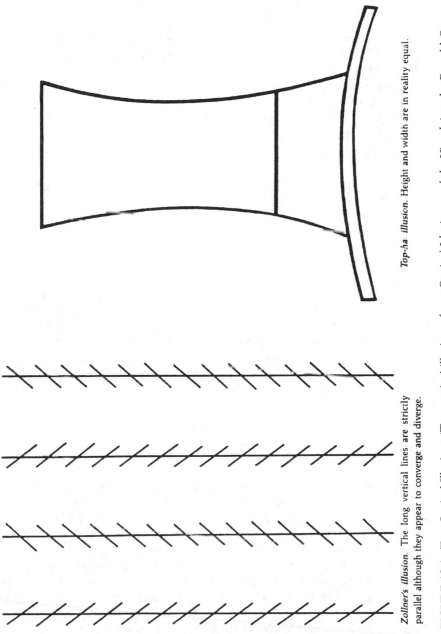

Top-ka illusion. Height and width are in reality equal.

Zollner's illusion. The long vertical lines are strictly parallel although they appear to converge and diverge.

FIGURE 10.1 Two Optical Illusions (Two optical illusions, from *Optical Illusions and the Visual Arts*, by Ronald C. Karraher and Jacqueline B. Thurston. Copyright © 1966 by Litton Educational Publications. All rights reserved.)

ent things, because they are influenced by different beliefs. There is a grain of truth in each of the different things that are "seen." As people work to build an interpretation they all can agree on, these grains of truth find their way into the final account and make that account more objective.

Cut off from this diversity and the negotiation process itself, the solitary person sees less of what there is to see. Even more troublesome, when a situation is ambiguous, is that invention of some version of reality is the only way to cope. When uncertainty is high, it's especially important to know what other people think, and what their analyses have in common with one's own.

A more subtle social issue in sense making is pointed out by Marion Kester's striking question: "If children are separated from their parents by hours of TV, from their playmates by video games, and from their teachers by teaching machines, where are they supposed to learn to be human?" A recent study of electronic mail in an open office found that people used terminals to communicate with the person in the next cubicle even when they could stand up, lean over the cubicle, and ask the person the same question face-to-face. Thus it would seem Kester's worry is not an idle one.

Extensive nonsocial interaction with a terminal can atrophy social skills. That becomes a problem when people confront an uncertain situation in which they have to construct a jointly acceptable version of reality. If they participate in such discussions with minimal social skills, the interaction may not last long enough or probe deeply enough to build a decent model that people can work with. If clumsy interactions distort social realities, then failure is inevitable. Working agreements about what is going on can make even the most incomplete electronic representations look coherent. This is so because consensual information fills in the gaps in electronic representations. However, when social skills are in short supply, those gaps may remain unfilled. That's when people begin asking, "What's going on here?"

Deliberation Deficiencies

Mander raises the interesting point that in an age of computers and information flow, the operative phrase may not be "small is beautiful," but rather "slow is beautiful." Deliberation takes time, yet that's the very thing that disappears when the velocity of information flow intensifies in information systems.

A more subtle problem with this acceleration is that computers operate close to the speed at which the stream of consciousness flows. This means that the whims and mixtures of feeling, thought, and images that flow through consciousness can be dumped into the analyzing process continuously. Not only does this increase demands on the person coming in afterward, who must deal with this kind of input; it also makes it harder to see priorities, preferences, and hierarchical structure and to separate the trivial from the important. The run-on sentences that have become a trademark of people writing with word processors exemplify this problem. As fast as images and possibilities bubble up, they are typed in and strung together with the conjunction *and,* which renders all images equally important. Most of what is typed is junk. But without discipline, self-editing, and deliberation, junk is left for someone else to wade through. The sheer volume and variety in an externalized stream of consciousness make it harder to separate figure from ground, which sets the stage for a cosmology episode.

Consolidation Deficiencies

When spontaneous material from stream of consciousness replaces deliberated thoughts and images based on data outside the information system, understanding becomes a problem. It is the very self-contained character of information systems that can undercut their value. Users fail to see that they need to reach outside the system for a different set of assumptions to understand what is happening inside the system. Herbert Simon explains that:

> *Whether a computer will contribute to the solution of an information-overload problem, or instead compound it, depends on the distribution of its own attention among four classes of activities: listening, storing, thinking, and speaking. A general design principle can be put as follows: An information-processing subsystem (a computer or new organization unit) will reduce the net demand on the rest of the organization's attention only if it absorbs more information previously received by others than it produces—that is, if it listens and thinks more than it speaks.*

But to register and absorb information (to listen and think), the sensor must be at least as complex as the information it is receiving and, often, information systems fall short. The sensor must go beyond mere enumeration if it is to synthesize detail. To go beyond detail is to move to higher levels of abstraction and to invoke alternative realities. At these higher levels, feeling informs thinking, imagination informs logic, and intuition informs sensation. Feeling, imagination, and intuition use vivid, compact images to order the details in a way that the system cannot. This is why metaphors that draw on our common culture, fairy tales, or archetypes ("This place is like a cathouse"; "Our agency is like the tale of Rumplestiltskin"; "Each quarter we live through the four seasons.") and novel labels or idioms (greenmail, golden parachutes, fast trackers), have such evocative power in linear systems. Each of these summarizing devices does three things: presents a compact summary of details, predicates characteristics that are difficult to name, and conveys a more vivid, multilevel image. All of these devices represent ways to absorb detail using logics that are qualitatively different from those contained within information systems.

Ways to Improve Sense Making

What is surprising is how many of the problems described here can be solved if people simply push back from their terminals and walk around. When people walk around they generate outcomes (effectuate), compare sources of information (triangulate), meet people and discover what they think (affiliate), slow down the pace of input (deliberate), and get a more global view of what is happening (consolidate).

Recent jokes about the invention of a new tool for word processing, which turns out to be a pencil, may be replaced by another joke about the new tool for managing called, "Pull the plug and go for a walk." The swiftness with which the idea of management-by-walking-around spread and the intensity with which people tout its benefits may be explained by the fact that many things that look like problems when they are viewed from a fixed position vanish when one changes position. Just as illusions disappear when you move them around or move around them, so too do problems disappear when they no longer are confined to one medium and one set of assumptions.

People who carry terminals into the field should be better problem solvers than are people who leave terminals at home, because people with terminals in the field are able to use different forms of data and test their hunches with triangulation.

A computer program can have action steps that ask people to leave the terminal, walk around, and come back, after which the program can ask them some questions. Imagine, for example, that a manager is trying to figure out whether there is a market for brand-name vegetables. He or she examines demographics and buying patterns and extrapolates trends; then the screen says, "Go walk through a supermarket for two hours and come back." (That same action step is appropriate for all kinds of related problems, from the question of whether you should purchase Conrail to what level inventories should be held at.)

The reason that the supermarket tour is appropriate for such diverse agendas is that it generates data that differ from those on the screen. The problem is seen in a different setting and thus is viewed differently: The supermarket is a place where people handle vegetables in distinctive ways, which might suggest what kinds of vegetable wrappers are appealing. The supermarket is a place stocked with items that could be shipped by rail, or perhaps these items could be handled efficiently only by other modes of transportation. Or perhaps the supermarket is seen as a place where stock moves directly from trucks to shelves, and just-in-time strategies are being used more widely than the person doing this exercise realized, so his or her own distribution needs to get more attention. With these vivid, nonmachine images in mind, the person returns to the terminal and sees its displays in a different light. The same notations take on different meanings, and more is seen.

While augmentation of sense making can occur if people become more mobile, other actions need to be taken as well. When any reorganization or change in information systems is contemplated, companies should systematically examine what those changes will do to action (effectuation), comparison (triangulation), interaction (affiliation), deliberation, and consolidation. A significant, permanent decrease in any of those five raises the likelihood that employees will know less about phenomena and will make more mistakes in managing them.

If any one of these five decline, local remedies are possible. If the potential for action drops, insert more breaks, longer breaks, or more interactive displays that allow for a wider variety of personal experiment or encourage the use of portable computing equipment. If the potential for comparison drops, make greater use of tie-ins between terminals and visual simulations of the phenomena being monitored, locate terminals closer to the events they control, or add other sensory modalities to the output from terminals. When interaction is lessened, assign two people to one terminal, have one person tell another what is being observed, set up teleconferencing and have operators' pictures continually visible in the corner of the display, or allow more intermixing of solitary work with group work.

When deliberation drops off, more time can be allocated for summarizing and thinking about information away from terminals, several people can be assigned to the same terminal so they are forced to spend some of their time thinking somewhere else, or processing can be slowed down to allow time to ponder what is displayed. Finally, when consolidation tapers off, people can read poetry, look at art, question assumptions, or engage in whatever activities will expose them to syntheses, theories, or generalizations that can put the inputs being considered into a new context.

The preceding analysis implies that overload is not really the problem with information systems. And indeed, confinement to a terminal is the problem, because it limits the variety of inputs, precludes comparison, and thus makes sense making more difficult. Overload occurs when you get too much of the same kind of information; ironically, if you increase the kinds of information you get, overload declines. In changing the quality of information about a phenomenon, one is able to see what stays constant and what changes. Impressions that change are method-specific. Impressions that don't are likely to be stable features that need to be dealt with. Since the common elements are fewer in number and better organized, they also make fewer demands on processing capacity. The key point is that overload can be reduced by moving around and thus getting a variety of inputs. As the number of vantage points increases, the amount of overload decreases.

A second implication of my analysis is that people and groups need to listen more and talk less. The value of an information system lies in what it withholds, as much as in what it gives. Listening and withholding require editing and categorizing—and these, in turn, require typologies, concepts, and ideas. The detail, specificity, and concreteness that can be achieved by information systems are worthless until patterns are imposed on them. Some of these patterns are inherent in the system itself, but most are found outside of it. People must listen for these patterns and, when they hear them in detail, transmit the pattern rather than the detail.

Third, not only do people need to listen—they need to edit. Job descriptions in the information organization need to specify each person's responsibility to absorb uncertainty and to transmit less than they receive. While there is always danger that people will edit out the wrong things, an even greater danger is that they will leave in too much, and thus paralyze themselves or those who come in after with too much detail. While electronic processing has the potential for everyone to check up on everyone else all the time, that kind of scrutiny will probably be infrequent because of the sheer quantity of work involved. It is more likely that faith and trust will become increasingly important as people become more dispersed, delegation is practiced more fully, and people come to depend on others to fill in their own limited, obsolete knowledge.

Finally, corporate culture takes on added importance in the context of the preceding arguments. Culture provides the framework within which cryptic data become meaningful. Current efforts to articulate culture may represent efforts to cope with intensified commitments to electronic processing, because it takes the former to understand the latter. Electronic organizations need to develop new respect for generalists, philosophers, and artists, because all three work with frameworks that provide context and meaning for the programs already in place.

CONCLUSION

Managers need to be just as attentive to meaning as they are to money. As organizations move more and more vigorously into electronic information-processing, they will increasingly bump up against the limits of human-processing capacity. The key to overcoming these limits is meaning, because it increases processing capacity.

And meanings that free up capacity usually originate outside the information-processing system in the form of different assumptions and contexts. Unless these qualitatively different kind of logic are developed, disseminated, and valued by the organization, people will find themselves increasingly unable to make sense of the products of information technology.

SELECTED BIBLIOGRAPHY

For further reading about sense making, see *The Social Psychology of Organizing,* by Karl E. Weick (Addison-Wesley, 1979). Gregory Bateson's work on logical types is *Mind and Nature* (E. P. Dutton, 1979).

Marion Kester's and Gerry Mander's comments about computers appear in the December 1984 issue of the *Whole Earth Review.* Another work that discusses the limitations of computers is *The Network Revolution,* by Jacques Vallee (And/Or Press, 1982).

For more on corporate culture as a source of meaning, see the September 1983 issue of *Administrative Science Quarterly.*

Herbert Simon's discussion of overload appears in M. Greenberger's book titled *Computers, Communications, and the Public Interest* (Johns Hopkins Press, 1971).

Christopher Lehmann-Haupt's view of computing may be found in his book review that appeared in the *New York Times* (October 3, 1984).

Finally, Shoshana Zuboff discusses human adaptation to automated factories in "Technologies That Informate" (in *Human Resource Management: Trends and Challenges,* edited by R. Walton and P. Lawrence, Harvard Business School Press, 1985).

11

Financial Risk and the Need for Superior Knowledge Management

Chris Marshall, Larry Prusak, David Shpilberg

Studies of recent failures of risk management suggest three underlying causes: dysfunctional culture, unmanaged organizational knowledge, and ineffective controls. The first and the last of these causes have been extensively discussed in the media. This article explores the importance of the second—knowledge management—as a more structured approach to: transferring knowledge to the business decision makers before it is needed, enabling the access of information as it is needed, and generating and testing new knowledge about the firm's changing risk management requirements.

A Series of Risk Management Failures

In the aftermath of recent risk management failures—such as at Baring Securities, Kidder Peabody, and Metallgesellschaft Refining & Marketing—many commentators are searching for common themes. It is becoming clear that such failures are not isolated incidents. Even a casual observer of the financial press could name other well-known organizations that have recently suffered risk management embarrassments: companies such as Proctor & Gamble, Gibson Greetings, Air Products and Chemicals, financial firms such as Paine Webber and Showa Bank, and public institutions such as Orange County and the State of Wisconsin.[1] What's really behind this spectacular series of losses? Some critics blame

---

[1] According to *Business Week* [October 16, 1995], P&G lost $195 million; Air Products, $105 million; Sandoz, $78 million; and Gibson Greetings, $23 million on derivative trades. Paine Webber has

the nature of the investment instruments themselves, demanding legislation to limit the use of derivatives. Many, resisting more government-imposed external controls, point to a need for improved internal controls for corporate and financial services' trading activities. Others believe the failures result from a misalignment of incentives within firms, encouraging individuals to assume risks with a personal upside but a corporate downside.

While acknowledging improved controls and incentives as elements of the solution, we believe the critics have missed the larger, strategic element that binds them: the way in which the knowledge of the organization is managed. In this article, we propose a framework for knowledge management that integrates the firm's culture, the skills of its employees, and their day-by-day actions into an effective risk management competence. Such a framework is long overdue—for both corporate treasuries and financial service firms. The problems at Barings, Kidder Peabody, and Metallgesellschaft illustrate only too vividly that while these firms were playing high-stakes games with their money, they were also mismanaging an even more valuable asset: their organizational knowledge. Many of the themes and lessons offered by their experience are equally applicable to other treasuries and financial service firms.

Consider the series of events at Metallgesellschaft Refining & Marketing (MGRM). There, traders in the corporate treasury pursued an innovative risk management approach that led to their taking large positions in derivatives (mostly oil futures contracts). As the exposure reached an uncomfortably high level, the subsidiary's supervisory board stepped in to cut the losses (at the same time removing all possibility of eventual recovery). Metallgesellschaft (MG), the parent company, had excellent knowledge resources at work, but apparently no effective means of transferring that knowledge across different parts of the organization.

Bad knowledge management was also the underlying problem at Kidder Peabody, where Joe Jett, a government securities trader, created $350 million in phantom profits from his manipulation of the firm's trading and accounting systems. Given Jett's reputation as a "rising star," no manager wanted to trust his or her own skepticism concerning Jett's trading. Kidder Peabody had a knowledge-hoarding culture at the trading level, and it depleted organizational knowledge at the management level. Compounding those problems, it had only limited and (as it turned out) easily sidestepped controls to check the almost inevitably dysfunctional consequences.

Like MG, Baring Securities suffered from a clash of cultures that led to an insufficient knowledge base in a critical area of its operations—a problem com-

spent $268 million to top up its short-term bond fund, which lost money after investing in derivatives, trying to boost its returns. Orange County's investment pool was reputed to have lost $1.7 billion, when their investments in inverse floaters went awry when interest rates began to creep up in 1994. The State of Wisconsin Investment Board is reputed to have lost $95 million this year in its use of structured derivatives.

pounded by Barings' failure to recognize and close that gap. Like Kidder Peabody, Barings' management was only too willing to assume infallibility on the part of a star performer, Nick Leeson. Ostensibly, Lesson was engaged in riskless arbitrage on the Japanese Nikkei equity index between different exchanges.[2] However, unknown to senior management, he parlayed this into highly risky volatility-based trades, the success of which was conditional on the stability of the Nikkei. Unfortunately, for Barings and for Leeson, in January 1994, the Nikkei fell suddenly, resulting in a $1.4 billion loss for Barings and the bankruptcy of one of the UK's oldest banks. No one questioned Leeson's trades until it was too late. Management hubris about the quality of its knowledge can only be limited by frequent testing and evaluation of the organization's supposed competence, in this case how the firm makes its money.

Ineptitude at Barings, MG, and Kidder Peabody in managing knowledge is an outrageous failing. What, after all, is their competitive advantage if not superior insight? We often see manufacturing firms discounting the role of knowledge in their strategies and operations, and we attribute their myopia to their technological cultures, which encourage a focus on physical assets such as raw materials, capital equipment, and inventory. But it is dismaying to see this in financial serv ices, given that, in a real sense, risk management *is* knowledge management.

What is Knowledge Management?

Before exploring how better knowledge management can drive better risk management, it is important to define some key terms. In particular, care must be taken to differentiate knowledge from its close cousin, information, and its more distant relative, data. Borrowing from the Western Rationalist and Empiricist traditions, knowledge is argued to be a set of justified beliefs. Information is the meaning that human beings assign to incoming data; Gregory Bateson described it as "those differences that make a difference."[3] Information affects knowledge by adding something to it or restructuring it.[4] Unlike data, both knowledge and information require an understanding of the socially defined context, where the knowledge and information came from, its embedded assumptions, and thus its importance and its limitations.[5]

It follows that the management of knowledge goes far beyond the storage and manipulation of data, or even of information. It is the attempt to recognize what is essentially a human asset buried in the minds of individuals, and leverage

---

[2]Such arbitrage is essentially riskless and involves buying futures contracts on one exchange and simultaneously selling them on another.

[3]G. Bateson, *Mind and Nature: A Necessary Unity* (New York, NY: Bantam Books, 1979).

[4]F. Machlup, *Knowledge: It's Creation, Distribution and Economic Significance: Volume I: Knowledge and Knowledge Production* (Princeton, NJ: Princeton University Press, 1984).

[5]P. Berger and T. Luckmann, *The Social Construction of Reality* (New York, NY: Doubleday, 1966).

it into an organizational asset that can be accessed and used by a broader set of individuals on whose decisions the firm depends. According to Sachiko Nonaka, a leading theorist in this area, knowledge management requires a commitment to "create new (task-related) knowledge, disseminate it throughout the organization and embody it in products, services and systems."[6]

There are at least seven things that can be done with knowledge at the organizational level: knowledge can be *generated* from internal operations or R&D groups; it can be *accessed* as it is needed from sources inside or outside the firm; knowledge can be *transferred* formally before it is utilized, through training, or informally, through on-the-job socialization; knowledge can be *represented* in the form of reports, graphs, and presentations, enabling easier access; after its validity is tested, knowledge can be *embedded* in processes, systems, and controls; and finally, these different knowledge processes can be *facilitated,* by the steady development of a culture, based on incentives and management leadership, that values, shares, and uses knowledge.

The Case for Knowledge Management

In industries as diverse as automotive manufacturing, chemical processing, electric utilities, and architectural engineering, firms are pursuing initiatives with the stated goal of generating, facilitating the transfer of, and improving the access to organizational knowledge:

- Hughes Space & Communications, the world's largest manufacturer of communications satellites, is busily constructing an internal "knowledge highway" to help its people avoid "reinventing the wheel" on highly complex, multi-year projects.
- BP, the huge energy concern, is reorganizing its global business around the knowledge, technologies, and processes associated with 88 major corporate assets. The new organization brings the right source of expertise rapidly to bear on problems and decisions around the world.
- Bechtel, the architectural engineering firm, has defined and implemented structured knowledge processes to ensure that its project teams bring to their design decision making all the benefit of discoveries made by other project teams past and present.
- Northeast Utilities, faced with post-deregulation upheaval in its industry, is re-engineering its fundamental work processes with a view to how they must be infused with new learning and be supported by cross-functional knowledge sharing.

[6]I. Nonaka and H. Takeuchi, *The Knowledge-Creating Company—How Japanese Companies Create the Dynamics of Innovation* (Oxford, UK: Oxford University Press, 1995).

Why the sudden emphasis on knowledge management? After all, haven't firms' greatest competitive assets always been the judgment and experience of their people? There are two basic answers: first, because organizational knowledge management is more necessary now than ever before; and second, because it is also more feasible.

Increasingly, senior executives are recognizing that knowledge and learning represent the preeminent source of sustainable advantage in a fast-moving, highly competitive world. They know it is no longer enough to leave critical knowledge sitting passively in the minds of individual employees. Workforce mobility, falling educational standards, and the rapid rate of business change mean that individuals can no longer be relied upon to provide consistent, comprehensive insight. Instead, the knowledge trapped within the employee base must be leveraged to the organizational level, where it can be accessed, synthesized, augmented, and deployed for the benefit of all. Organizations and individuals must learn rapidly and uniformly across different functions and levels of the organization. Yesterday's informal or tacit knowledge management techniques—the desktop, the hallway conversation, the memo, the trade show—are no longer sufficient in a period of radical change.

The Rise of Financial Risk Management

If knowledge management is of growing importance to every kind of business, its impact is perhaps most obvious in the financial services industry. This is because effective management of knowledge is key to managing risk. And the driving issue in both financial services and corporate treasuries today is risk management. Dennis Weatherstone, the former Chairman of J.P. Morgan, put it even more starkly when he said: "These days, the business of banking *is* risk management." Risk Management is ranked by CFOs as one of their most important concerns.[7] Why this emphasis? Accelerating technological change, more volatile markets, globalization, and deregulation have all led to increased uncertainty regarding underlying risk exposures facing all firms, both financial and nonfinancial.[8] In addition, leading practitioners' utilization of advances in financial theory, and a wider choice of hedging vehicles such as derivatives, have upped the competitive ante for all other players. Both trends translate to greater complexity, which if not managed appropriately, invariably leads to greater risk. Fundamentally, risk management is about managing the complexity inherent in the tradeoff between return and risk, through organizational knowledge, for the benefit of the firm's stakeholders.

---

[7]S. Waite Rawls and C. Smithson, "Strategic Risk Management," *Continental Bank Journal of Applied Corporate Finance*, 1 (1990).

[8]M. Miller, "Financial Innovation: Achievements and Prospects," *Japan and the World Economy*, 4 (1992).

Information Technology, Knowledge, and Risk Management

The dramatic spiral of financial innovation has been enabled by the extraordinary growth of high-speed, low-cost information technologies. Today, highly complex front and back office systems are the linchpin of any successful financial services organization and many large corporate treasuries. This complexity of operations (and hence of risk management) has been amplified by the competitive need for rapid response to changes in the market. According to Michael O'Gorman, European Operations and Systems Area Executive at Chase Manhattan in London:

> *If you want to be a market leader, particularly in a business like derivatives, you need to put enabling technology on people's desks. These new products are so complex—and the time you have before everyone else works out what you're doing and duplicates it is so short—that these machines are absolutely necessary.*[9]

While technology has amplified the potential of individual traders, it has also intensified the pressures on them to act rapidly. This poses a critical dilemma: if they take the time to study the investment opportunity thoroughly, the window of opportunity may slam shut; if they act with haste, the full implications, when they become clear, may be more than anticipated. Thus, information is both part of the risk management problem and part of the solution. According to Alan Sutherland, Senior Operating Officer at Salomon Brothers in London:

> *Banks have become major information repositories. Their success depends on that information, how fast they can access it . . . and on innovation—relating previously independent items.*[10]

But banks and treasuries are more than just databases. Risk management information is highly contextual; a report claiming that a firm's credit rating is "AA" must be interpreted in terms of the rating agency that produced it. "IBM," "International Business Machines," and "Big Blue" all denote the same entity, but woe betide any data entry clerk who enters the wrong one. According to one recent report, risk management executives estimated they spent 20–30% of their time *"understanding context or explaining it to others."*[11]

Information without knowledge of the context of the information is very dangerous. An increased emphasis on information demands a commensurate emphasis on knowledge. As the three cases outlined below make clear, risk manage-

---

[9]S. Brady, "How to Avoid an Upgrade," *Euromoney* (December 1992).
[10]Ibid.
[11]M. Siegel and D. Hart, "The Role of Information Systems in Risk Management," MIT IFSRC Report (1995).

ment is frequently not a problem of a lack of information, but rather a lack of knowledge with which to interpret its meaning.

Could Better Knowledge Management Have Helped?

Metallgesellschaft Refining & Marketing (MGRM)

MGRM's experience is perhaps the clearest example of a knowledge management failure. In 1992, MGRM, an American subsidiary of the German metals and services group Metallgesellschaft (MG), began selling long-term fixed-price contracts to supply fuel oil to its customers. To hedge itself against the risk of a price rise in fuel oil, MGRM purchased short-term oil futures on the New York Mercantile Exchange (NYMEX). But in late 1993, oil prices began to fall dramatically, hurting the value of the futures positions (but, simultaneously increasing the value of the underlying fixed price contracts). Margin calls from NYMEX to cover the shortfall in the value of the futures forced MGRM to pay as much as $50 million per month to the exchange. By the end of 1993, MGRM's supervisory board (made up of executives from its parent company and Deutsche Bank) had intervened and, against the wishes of the subsidiary's management, liquidated the futures positions, incurring more than $1 billion in losses.

There remains disagreement about the validity of using short-term instruments to hedge long-term risk. Some observers, including Nobel Prize-winning economist Merton Miller, argue that the Board's decision to liquidate the derivatives position contributed to the loss, making paper losses real.[12] Others, such as MG's senior management, argue that Miller's analysis ignores the significant costs of additional margin and the fact that the firm was rapidly becoming a target for speculators taking advantage of the firm's large futures position.

While the familiar "smoking gun" shows up in the form of derivatives trading, it is far from clear that the fuel-traders involved were ignorant of their risk, or were acting in anything but what they perceived to be the strategic interests of the firm. MGRM was innovative and sophisticated in its use of derivatives; one of their traders had even written a textbook on the subject. The very fact that argument continues in the academic community about the wisdom of MG's risk management approach makes it difficult to accuse either party of a lack of knowledge.

Whether the MG Supervisory Board did not understand the strategy, or simply disagreed with it, the failure seems to have been a lack of knowledge *transfer*—what the two management groups involved "knew" to be the best thing for the firm did not proceed from a common base of knowledge defined before these trades took place. That knowledge involved shared beliefs about the banks' ability to supply liquidity, its expectations of the future, the parent company's willingness

---

[12]M. Miller and C. Culp, "Metallgesellschaft and the Economics of Synthetic Storage," *Journal of Applied Corporate Finance* (Winter 1995).

to take on risk, the riskiness of the hedging strategy being employed, and the acceptable/probable payback horizon. Without that exchange of risk management knowledge describing the context of the trades, both parties were left to discover their basic knowledge differences far too late. In addition, different accounting standards in Germany and the U.S. seem to have exacerbated the problem, as German standards did not offset the fall in value of the hedge by the increase in value of the underlying contracts. A common understanding of accounting standards are but one example of the consistent procedures for knowledge-sharing between MGRM and its supervisory board that would have either illuminated the strategy for the Supervisory Board and won its support, or revealed to MGRM that it would ultimately not be supported if "the going got rough."

Better controls, on the other hand, would have had only a limited impact at MGRM. Controls affect actions—but not the underlying cultural assumptions and task knowledge guiding those actions. The knowledge management solution, stated most simply, is what one business commentator has called "management as conversation."[13] It is the idea that the "truth" (consisting of beliefs with greater validity) is more likely to emerge from a dialogue between contrary beliefs than in isolation.

Kidder Peabody

Kidder Peabody's experience demonstrates that what you don't know *can* hurt you. Joseph Jett was hired in 1991 to perform arbitrage between Treasury bonds and so-called Strips (Separate Trading of Registered Interest and Principal of Securities). Strips are bonds stripped of their coupon payments. Such arbitrage is essentially riskless and therefore would not show up on the firm's conventional market and credit risk management systems. Kidder did, however, made heavy use of a computerized expert system which *embedded* much of the knowledge about performing and valuing transactions in the bond market; it also automatically updated the firm's inventory and its Profit and Loss (P&L) statement. In keeping with different market conventions for Strips and bonds, the system valued the Strips temporarily lower than their associated bonds.[14] This difference was noted directly in the firm's P&L statement, which became the basis for assessing trader bonuses. By entering into forward transactions on the reconstituted Strips (effectively synthetic bonds), Jett was able to postpone almost indefinitely the moment at which the actual losses were recognized in the P&L, by racking up still larger positions in Strips and the reconstituted Strips. In 1992, Jett's trading profits were $32 million, a record unheard of at the Strips desk, and Jett's personal bonus was $2 million. The following year, Jett was made head of the trading desk and reported an even more remarkable $151 million in profits, and was rewarded with

---

[13]A. Webber, "What's So New About the New Economy?" *Harvard Business Review* (January/February 1993).

[14]Strips are valued at their net present value, while bonds are valued "ex-interest," i.e. without the interest accrued on the bond when sold.

a $12 million bonus and the Chairman's "Man of the Year" award. But the bubble was about to burst. By March 1994, Jett's positions included some $47 billion worth of Strips and $42 billion worth of reconstituted Strips. Finally, senior management began to investigate just how Jett was doing so well.

On April 17, 1994, Kidder Peabody announced that the head of Kidder's government trading desk, Joe Jett, had been inflating his own profits to the tune of $350 million. Eventually, an objective post mortem concluded that the false profits were allowed to grow over a period of two years due primarily to "lax oversight, as well as poor judgments and missed opportunities."[15]

Edward Cerullo, head of Kidder Peabody's fixed income division, enjoyed a reputation for recruiting some of the best traders in the industry. While knowledge *generation* doesn't seem to have been a problem for Kidder, knowledge *access* and *transfer* was. Information known to junior traders about Jett's activities was not accessed by senior managers. The details of Jett's mediocre track record prior to joining Kidder were not transferred to senior management. Nor was the knowledge of how to interpret Jett's bond position transferred to his immediate supervisor, who, unfortunately, repeatedly allocated more capital to Jett's use, despite the fact that he did not (and could not) understand how Jett was making money with the firm's capital. One reason for the lack of knowledge transfer was simply that Kidder management was blinded by Jett's apparent success, and their overconfidence led to an unwillingness to *test* the knowledge and skills of its employees and embedded in its systems. A recent article in *Institutional Investor* (March 1995) suggests that this blind use of embedded knowledge was critical:

> *Jett had been trained . . . to accept information from the computer screen and to act on it. If the computer got it wrong, he was going to get it wrong; and if the computer got it wrong in his favor, he would see no reason to ask questions, even if the thing got silly.*

Judicious testing of people and systems requires a managerial determination not to take historical results at face value; the means of obtaining the P&L is as important as its magnitude, if the firm is to avoid sacrificing long-term profits for the sake of short-term expediency.

There were also serious failures of knowledge *facilitation* at Kidder Peabody. Absent explicit management, knowledge access and transfer is possible only when employees voluntarily share their knowledge. This is rare in many trading firms where individuals compete against each other even more fiercely than they do against their competitors. *Investment Dealers Digest* quotes a typical attitude on the part of a trader: "Your ability to trade is your franchise. You're not interested in sharing how you make money." This attitude is strongly enforced by the reward system; a former Kidder Peabody trader explained that firms like Kidder

---

[15]Report of Inquiry into False Profits at Kidder, Peabody & Co., prepared by Davis Polk & Wardell, August 4, 1994.

"operate on P&L alone; your total sense of value, your total reputation, is in your P&L."[16] Cerullo, noted one observer, had "fostered a culture that rewarded the overly aggressive behavior of someone like Jett." This is not terribly surprising, given Cerullo's own background. In his early days, he was revered by associates as "the guy with a black box in the back room." A futures arbitrageur, he had a sophisticated knowledge of the mathematical underpinnings of the instruments—which no one else shared. While those skills had led to personal success, they may have had dysfunctional organizational consequences. Traders could easily ignore the rest of the organization and frequently chose not to share their trading strategies with accounting and control functions. By the time of the Jett incident, the problem was so pronounced that *Fortune* magazine speculated that "somewhere in the highly successful and celebrated General Electric [then the owner of Kidder Peabody] culture something is not right."[17]

The situation is repeated in many firms: while management may pay lip service to the value of cooperation and its ability to facilitate organizational knowledge, there is an underlying belief that performance is really driven by "lone rangers." And further, there is a belief that internal competition must be in place to attract these superstars—that only under-performers are attracted to cooperative environments, where they can be carried by the efforts of others. This is a dangerous attitude to perpetuate. While every firm wants to promote individual ambition and achievement, in today's complex, dynamic environment, individuals rarely have both the depth and breadth to act solely on their own knowledge. Even where such superior individuals exist, it would be folly for a firm to count on their continued performance. Such over-reliance backfires violently when an employee leaves, or even threatens to leave, the firm.

More explicit attention to knowledge management might have corrected another factor commonly cited for the failure of Kidder's internal systems of control: the elimination of middle management. Many firms are finding—post-downsizing, post-reengineering—that the middle managers who had seemed to be simply pushing paper, were in fact playing a valuable role in the transfer, access, and generation of knowledge. In their absence, new knowledge mechanisms can certainly be put in place—but they cannot be expected to spring up as naturally as their predecessors.

Baring Bank

Barings combines elements of both the Kidder and the MG debacles. At Barings, problems grew out of a cultural divide that led to an insufficient knowledge base in a critical area of its operations. The bank exacerbated this shortfall by overconfidence in its knowledge, and by failing to create adequate control systems to provide timely information to senior management.

[16]L. Maher, "Can Bonds Chief Cerullo Survive Kidder Scandal?" *Investment Dealers Digest*, May 2, 1994.
[17]T. Pare, "Jack Welch's Nightmare on Wall Street," *Fortune*, September 5, 1994.

Driven by a strong bull market, Barings' far eastern securities operations expanded rapidly throughout the late 1980s and early 1990s. In the rush, their formal systems of knowledge management and control seem to have been forgotten. Baring Securities' growth, from just fifteen employees in 1984 to over a thousand in 1991, also highlighted the long-standing cultural disparity between the Banks' two main constituencies, the merchant bankers of Baring Brothers, and the traders at Baring Securities. A former Barings securities trader, recalls "there was always an uneasy tension between Baring Brothers and Baring Securities. 'We're the Bankers', they seemed to say, 'heirs to 200 years of tradition, and you're the jumped-up guys from Liverpool.'"[18] There were also factions within the securities arm; like many trading organizations, Baring Securities, in the words of the official Bank of England report on Barings, "was a business led by its front office with poor lines of communication between its front and back offices." This in turn seems to have reflected the strictly limited respect held by the traders for senior back office management. One effect of all these divisions seems to have been that most executives cared more about protecting their own departments than about making the organization work as a whole. The clash came to a head in 1993, a period known within the firm as "the turbulence," when the merchant bankers effectively consolidated their control over the operations of Baring Securities. A new matrix organization structure was imposed whereby profit responsibility was on a product basis, but with local office management maintaining the office infrastructure (such as systems, controls, accounting, settlement, and administration). In Barings' more established far eastern securities operations in Hong Kong and Tokyo, the reorganization led to a series of personnel *transfers* that, according to one observer, left local management seriously weakened.[19]

Barings' London head office failed to recognize this knowledge deficit in its securities management. It assumed its merchant banking management knowledge was more than sufficient for understanding derivatives and that local talent could make up for any short-term shortfall. According to *The Economist,* Peter Baring, chairman of Baring Brothers, noted in October 1993: "Derivatives need to be well controlled and understood, but we believe we do that here."[20] Unfortunately, subsequent events proved him disastrously wrong. Confident of its knowledge, the firm was also passing up opportunities to *generate* new knowledge from outside the firm. For example, it chose not to join the International Swaps and Derivatives Association, through which it might have transferred knowledge about new developments in derivatives control. And while it received a list of recommendations on managing derivatives risk from the influential and respected "Group of Thirty" think tank,[21] it reportedly ignored many of them. Nor was such hubris limited to

[18]T. Shale, "Why Barings Was Doomed," *Euromoney* (March 1995).
[19]As reported by *Euromoney* at the time, "the pool of derivatives-based knowledge in the region virtually disappeared." *Euromoney* (March 1995).
[20]*The Economist,* "The Collapse of Barings," March 4, 1995.
[21]Group of Thirty, *Global Derivatives: Public Sector Responses* (1993).

strategic decisions. Baring Securities reportedly did not even own a copy of standard software used to verify margin accounts, a critical control mechanism for the
prevention of rigged reports.

Nick Leeson came to Barings as a settlements clerk in 1992. His earliest responsibility was implementing the local back office system. In the wake of early
success, he became both head trader and general manager for the Singapore office,
recruiting traders and back office staff. Soon after, he began aiding Barings' Tokyo
offices' arbitrage trading the Nikkei index between the Osaka Stock Exchange
and the Singapore exchange (SIMEX). Such arbitrage is theoretically riskless and
thus would not show up on any conventional risk management control system.
Leeson's arbitrage trading was phenomenal, coinciding with the Asian Bull market of 1993; net profits at Barings' Singapore office rose from $1.4 million in
1992, to $14 million in 1993, to more than $40 million in 1994. By the end of
1994, Leeson had earned $150 million for Barings Singapore. This was a major
source of revenues for Barings during this period. Naturally, this discouraged
questions, and little attempt seems to have been made to assess the reasonableness
of the profit. Historical performance was not analyzed or *tested* in depth, and
thus internal knowledge about derivatives trading was overestimated. After all,
Leeson's arbitrage trading was increasing everyone's bonuses. Despite suspicions
that Leeson was breaking his trading limits, senior management was all too willing to assume away any concerns about Lesson's arbitrage activities.

It now appears that since 1992, Leeson had been selling calls and puts on
Nikkei index futures. These deals, known as "straddles," make profits provided
the Nikkei index stays within a fairly narrow range. Using an unauthorized and
unreported account, he adjusted transaction prices so that profits would appear
on the authorized accounts, which were reported to the senior management, and
any losses would be hidden in the unauthorized account. While back office staff in
Singapore knew of the unreported account, they seem to have trusted Leeson's explanations that it was for a client wishing anonymity.

The month following the Kobe earthquake on January 17, 1994, saw the
Tokyo stock market plunge 1000 points, and with it the value of Leeson's straddles. In a last-ditch effort to shore up the flagging Nikkei, Leeson appears to have
spent February buying Nikkei futures, trying to move the market himself, engaged
in a "double or nothing" bet with the market. At one point, Barings through
Leeson, held over 50% of the open interest in the Nikkei. Ironically, although information about Barings' extraordinary position in the Nikkei was widespread in
the Singapore financial community, it was not accessible by the London head office for two reasons. First, internal controls did not produce adequate warning information since Leeson was in the preposterous position of overseeing both
trading and settlements for his office, and able to rig the reports to cover his
tracks. Second, Leeson's (multiple) direct superiors had little expertise in derivatives and thus could not override the inadequacies of the local control system.
Knowledgeable branch managers in the markets would have known what other
traders at other firms suspected; they would also have verified that Leeson's trades
matched real client accounts. It was this combination of poor controls and inadequate local knowledge that prevented management in London from knowing that

something was badly wrong until it was too late. And even when senior management did find out about the size of the positions, they steadfastly believed to the very end Leeson's explanation that they reflected an anonymous client buying Nikkei futures.

With Barings, we saw a deep schism between the securities and merchant banking divisions lead to a transfer of skilled senior managers in the securities area. Barings' most senior management became seduced by its misunderstood success in its Singapore operations, giving Leeson increased responsibility and capital, without imposing the risk controls that should go with it. In short, inadequate knowledge management was not the only thing that pushed Barings over the edge. But combined with a dysfunctional culture and weak control systems, what happened now appears to have been inevitable.

An Integrated Approach to the Problems of Risk Management

These three cases have broad lessons to teach, but extrapolating from them requires an understanding of the decision-making process employed by a typical trader. Traders gain much of their knowledge through shared experiences working on a desk or its back office, and this knowledge is reinforced through a long process of socialization within the firm's culture. They see what works, and what does not. Based on that knowledge and information from dynamic markets, traders make decisions about what to do, taking positions—constrained by controls—that affect the risk/return profile of the entire organization. Actions, therefore, follow from the individual's assumptions about what is good for him and the firm, as well as his own knowledge about the likely outcomes of those actions.

It follows that any attempt to solve risk management problems purely through improved controls or incentives misses the point. Management levers must act on at least three levels—influencing traders' assumptions, knowledge, and actions—since solving problems at one level will not solve the problems at other levels. Moreover, levers vary in the timing and extent of their resulting costs and benefits. Traditional control systems offer quick though limited payback, while knowledge management and cultural levers offer slower but much more substantial returns in the long term. The strategic challenge for firms is to manage the cost/benefit tradeoffs implicit in the implementation of these different levers, as it is only through a concerted effort to manage organizational knowledge that values and actions can be focused to serve the decision-making needs of both front-line traders and senior management. Table 11.1 outlines the relationship between traders' actions, their knowledge, and their underlying cultural assumptions, and specifies the management levers that can be used to influence each.

Traditional Control Systems

Based on a combination of interactive analytics and market knowledge, traders assess their expectations for a trade in terms of its P&L, its risks, and its

TABLE 11.1   Management Levers and Trading Behaviors

Management Lever	Effects on Traders	Implementation of Lever
Traditional Control Systems • Marked to Market P&L • Market and Credit Risk • Evaluation of risk/return tradeoff	Traders' actions (short term) • Pre-transaction Transaction Assessment • Transaction Execution • Post-transaction Management Reports	Interactive/Automated Analytics Dynamic Limits • Position • Risk • Capital Validation and Reconciliation Routine and Exception Reports
Levers for Knowledge Management • Transfer	Traders' knowledge (medium term) • Assessment of the past	Better training Hypermedia Decision Support Systems Expert Systems
• Access • Representation	• Understanding of the present	Integrated Data Architectures Knowledge Bases Balanced Scorecards EIS Visualization Multimedia
• Embedding • Testing		CASE tools Fifth Generation Software tools Independent Audits Worst case scenarios Process Perspective Re-engineering
• Generation	• Expectations of the future	Simulation Modeling Tools Groupware and E-Mail
Facilitating a knowledge culture	Traders' values and assumptions (long term)	Incentives Hiring Policies Leadership

effects on the rest of their portfolio. Transactions are also constrained by a system of limits imposed on a few quantifiable aspects of a trader's position.[22] After the transaction is cleared, front office records are reconciled and validated by the

---

[22]Examples might include the position's size, the capital allocated, the position's sensitivity to shifts in the market, or the credit rating of its counterparty.

back office. Routine reports by senior management then attempt to aggregate the tradeoff inherent in quantifiable elements such as P&L and market risk. Exception reports, at least in theory, should be produced if the limits prescribed earlier are broken, and they should attempt to describe specific cases—why, and to what extent, any limit rules have been broken. Aided by analytics, constrained by limits, and verified by reports, traders perform their trades, whether for a client account, to hedge some exposure (as in a corporate treasury), or according to some assumed market knowledge.

So why aren't controls sufficient? Many knowledgeable commentators have suggested that increased controls should be implemented by firms to limit the freedom of rogue traders like Joseph Jett and Nick Leeson. And it does seem absurd that any firm would allow a single trader to place its entire capital base at risk (as Barings did). But one must understand what a control system can and cannot do. Control systems can provide essential information to decision makers. But decision makers need knowledge to interpret that information. Information without knowledge is like pouring water into a sieve.

Essentially, controls automate or simplify human decision making. This is done by *embedding* knowledge into the controls—a good idea when that knowledge is reliable and robust. This is more likely the case when the inputs to, and outputs from the decision are clearly quantifiable, and where that clarity is in danger of being muddied by the biases, passions, and flawed interpretations associated with human knowledge. Controls enable traders and management to concentrate on the application of their knowledge to the detailed issues at hand. When controls are inadequate, as they were at Barings' Singapore office, information that might generate new knowledge of the trading environment is not gathered. This leads to declining awareness in management, and mounting hubris on the part of the knowledgeable, but isolated, trader. On the other hand, excessive controls also have dysfunctional consequences; an abundance of detail-oriented controls can quickly produce information overload for management, obstructing decision making. Knowledge *embedded* in controls is also often opaque (as in Kidder's trading expert system) and thus hard to modify to reflect changing circumstances (except through an explicit process of *testing*, something most firms do sporadically, if at all). An excess of control systems can also produce an illusion of control; hiding the very real risks that lie in those areas where much that is not quantifiable or constant must be factored into a decision, in which the onus is on good contextual knowledge to reduce the inevitable ambiguity.[23] Areas of ambiguity in risk management are legion, but invariably concern human resources (Kidder, Barings), model assumptions (MG, Kidder), as well as liquidity (MG), accounting (MG), credit, legal, data (Barings), and other operational risks (such as

---

[23]Peter Bernstein also emphasizes the importance of contextual ambiguity in risk management in his article "The New Religion of Risk Management" in the March/April 1996 issue of *Harvard Business Review*.

the combination of settlement and trading responsibility in Barings' Singapore Office).

The key to doing this effectively is not simply to impose an ever-growing list of internal and external controls to restrict the freedom of front-line traders. A plethora of controls will not help a trading operation if traders do not share contextual knowledge about their trades with their managers, or if traders operate with assumptions that differ from the equity holders of the firm. Barings was a case in point; a cultural divide gave rise to a knowledge deficit, which in turn provided the opportunity for rogue trades.

Rather than attempting to build every contingency into a trading limit or a new report, effort should be directed toward building a process by which knowledgeable judgment can be brought to bear on decisions rapidly, but in an *ad hoc* manner. Before the era of downsizing, it was the formal organization structure that allocated these decision rights. Today, some firms do this effectively through a carefully structured escalation process, whereby exceptions are highlighted (whether by middle management or information systems), and brought to the attention of knowledgeable management. Rather than an automatic response, the escalation triggers a dialogue among various responsible people who together decide, based on their collective knowledge of past experience and current exigencies, what action, if any, to take.

Making the decision is by no means the end of the story. Periodically, or by exception, firms must make the formulation of new controls an output of a broader knowledge process that explicitly and continually *tests* which parts of the business are generating new levels of ambiguity (and therefore new knowledge needs), what past experience can be embedded into controls, and whose knowledge should be brought to bear on exceptions. One problem apparent at both Kidder and Barings was that, as trading practice became more complex (and hence risk management became more central to daily decision making), no knowledge process was in place to update management's information requirements.

Levers for Knowledge Management

Now, largely enabled by developments in information technology, firms are discovering that knowledge management is more possible than ever before. In the context of risk management, a number of techniques are emerging:

Transferring Knowledge to Decision Makers

Transferring risk management knowledge is not simply a question of distributing informative reports; it also requires education and training to develop the knowledge to interpret the information. All firms subject trading personnel to training for purposes of licensing; those who truly value knowledge continue that process internally. This is more than allowing access to knowledge, it means actively teaching people and utilizing existing financial, management, and systems theory in the context of the firm's past experience with financial products, markets, and customers. It also means transferring knowledge about the rest of the organization, who knows what and who knows who. Nor is the transfer of knowledge ever completed, it must be both ongoing and cumulative to reflect the firm's changing context. This clearly did not happen at Metallgesellschaft. Such training must also be highly structured and focused. An attempt to cover the entire risk management domain in a single training course may actually be counterproductive if it buries the new and important knowledge under a mountain of the routine and habitual. Knowledge transfer should also be targeted to meet specific on-the-job needs. As Gary Gastineau of S.G. Warburg recently noted in an industry roundtable, "Everybody has to understand what they are doing."[24] Education must be distributed throughout the firm, otherwise it risks contributing to the complexity of the positions taken on by isolated expert traders. Supervisors should become more generalist, understanding in broad terms, the activities of all their subordinates. The risks of generalist supervisors are mitigated by the existence of accessible and embedded organizational knowledge. In an effort to secure ongoing transfer of knowledge, leading firms are closely following industry-wide initiatives such as the Securities Industry Continuing Education program, which provides detailed guidelines for members' initial and on-going training in compliance, regulatory, ethical, and sales issues.

Decision Support Systems (DSS), Expert Systems (ES), and Hypermedia tools, embedding the knowledge of more experienced executives, can also be used to transfer that knowledge to the less experienced. More generally, the development of all risk management tools should reflect this critical role of enabling knowledge transfer, "informating" the trader, rather than just attempting to automate.[25] Such information tools acknowledge the value of the trader's knowledge and thus the context of the information he uses, rather than trying to automate the decision making, which assumes that such a context is worthless. Nikko Securities put such a tool into operation. Their Options Trading Training System, initially designed for futures and options training, went on to become a full-fledged dealing support system.[26] The International Finance and Commodities Institute of Geneva is another leading developer of interactive training systems designed to enable such knowledge transfer.

Improving Accessibility to Existing Knowledge

Increasingly central to effective risk management is an integrated data architecture that enables access to information about ongoing trades, positions, risks,

---

[24]Management Roundtable, *International Finance and Commodities Institute* (March 1995).

[25]The critical differences between automating and informating using technology are described in Shoshana Zuboff, *In the Age of the Smart Machine: The Future of Work and Power* (New York, NY: Basic Books, 1988).

[26]D. Chorafas, *Treasury Operations and the Foreign Exchange Challenge* (New York, NY: John Wiley, 1992).

and business lines. One new application under development by Tandem Computers shows great promise for providing such wide-ranging access. It creates a data warehouse specifically designed to inform management about its portfolio risks, to which other systems have the responsibility of sending data. Such architectures utilize a wide variety of information types (reflecting a plethora of financial instruments) and draw upon global sources, provide timely updates, and house data in such a way that it can be "sliced and diced" in any number of ways. No such systems were available to Barings' London head office. Standardized definitions of products, customers, and markets are also essential if senior managers are not to be burdened with explaining the context of the definition rather than the specifics of the problem at hand. Some new risk management information architectures employ object-oriented technology to encapsulate procedural knowledge with data, allowing the rapid definition of new objects with inherited characteristics from previously defined objects. The traditional database then becomes a continuously evolving knowledge base, a centralized, easily accessible repository for the readily quantifiable elements of a firm's risk-related knowledge.

Better Representation of Knowledge

Knowledge must be represented in a form that is readily interpreted as useful information. There are two elements to this: the choice of information and its presentation. Good presentation is essential if the information and knowledge is going to be accessed. Visualization techniques, multi-media, and hyper-media have improved the presentation of risk management knowledge, providing greater ease of use and transparency. The choice of information to represent is more complex. In other industries, broad overviews of operations are described in so-called "balanced scorecards," in which a few critical performance factors are updated daily to support senior management decision making.[27] These factors include customer measures, internal business measures, financial measures, and innovation and learning measures. They can also be readily incorporated into Executive Information Systems (EIS) that summarize information generated throughout the business and allow it to be viewed in terms of these critical performance variables by manager, by desk, by client, or by product. The user can then "drill down" on these variables to a desired level of detail. An important new tool for the effective aggregation of financial information is J.P. Morgan's RiskMetrics™ daily estimates of asset volatilities and correlations. These grew out of J.P. Morgan's internal daily risk report and allow customers to represent their aggregate financial market risks over a given time period in a consistent and uniform fashion across major asset classes. RiskMetrics™ can be used in risk assessment, risk-based capital allocation, as well as performance evaluation. Furthermore, in an effort to make this knowledge testable, J.P. Morgan has made explicit the detailed methodology by which these volatilities and correlations are calculated.[28]

---

[27]R. Kaplan and D. Norton, "The Balanced Scorecard—Measures that Drive Performance," *Harvard Business Review* (January/February 1992).
[28]T. Guildiman, *RiskMetrics-Technical Document,* Morgan Guaranty Trust Company (1995).

Embedding Knowledge into Controls and Processes

According to writers such as Nonaka and Itami,[29] successful companies rapidly create, disseminate, and embed knowledge in new technologies and organizations. This knowledge then becomes an infrastructure for new knowledge, new assumptions, and new controls. It is the formalization of knowledge through embedding in existing controls and processes that allows the consolidation of previous knowledge gains. Spreadsheets, fifth-generation programming languages (5GLs), and Computer Aided Software Engineering (CASE) systems enable the rapid embedding of complex models into software. Some systems even assist with their own documentation. On the other hand, the trend towards distributed end-user development of systems (especially using spreadsheets in the Front Office) runs the risk of inadequate testing of the final system. Some estimates suggest that as many as 25% of these end-user systems have errors.[30] An additional challenge is to prevent such embedded knowledge being taken for granted, as it was in Kidder Peabody's expert system, and hence difficult to test and modify.

Testing Organizational Knowledge

After knowledge has been embedded into organizational systems and processes, it tends to become de-emphasized. Organizations, like individuals, forget, as the justifications for a particular process gets lost in the labyrinths of organizational history.[31] Effective organizational systems and processes require periodic testing of that embedded knowledge and the assumptions on which it is based. This can be done through rigorous audits by external, or at least independent internal, groups actively looking for cracks in the firm's knowledge infrastructure.

Testing of organizational risk management knowledge frequently begins with the quantitative models that underlie much of valuation and market risk management. Because financial models have a tendency to fall apart when the embedded contextual assumptions underlying them (such as continuity and liquidity) cease to hold, these must be made explicit, frequently tested, and revised if necessary. Information Systems can help organizations test their modeling and procedural knowledge. Some firms, for example, employ sophisticated *scenario analysis* and *stress tests* to assess the impact of major changes in their operating condition, thus heading off potential crises. Treasury groups at firms as diverse as 3M and Ciba Geigy use scenario-based tests of their portfolios, in which they try to stem the effects of adverse cash flow fluctuations.[32]

Testing must be both forward and backward looking. Testing of trading knowledge is based on a detailed understanding of how the firm actually performed in the past. Did it make money by taking on excessive risks? Without such

---

[29]H. Itami, *Mobilizing Invisible Assets* (Cambridge, MA: Harvard University Press, 1987).

[30]P. Cragg, "Spreadsheet Modeling Abuse: An Opportunity for OR?" *Journal of the Operational Research Society* (August 1993).

[31]K. Weick, *The Social Psychology of Organizing* (Reading, MA: Addison-Wesley, 1979).

[32]The Economist Intelligence Unit, "Risk Management Excellence," *The Economist* (1995).

a long backward look, firms are subject to a creeping overconfidence that, in the prescient words of the Kidder Peabody chairman at the time of the Jett scandal, Michael Carpenter, *"Can sink a firm in twenty four hours."*[33] Testing also looks to the future. It is invariably followed by redesign and reengineering, incremental and radical changes to alter the knowledge embedded in organizational controls and processes. It is virtually a truism in risk management that it requires a process-oriented Total Quality Management perspective, in which knowledge embedded in operational procedure is carefully and frequently tested. Fidelity is a good example of this; its "Project 20/20," focuses on managing firm-wide quality, knowledge, and technology.

Generating New Knowledge

Increasingly, the generation of "tacit" knowledge—that knowledge contained only within individuals' minds—is being targeted as a critical part of organizational knowledge.[34] Because it is so rooted in the experience of the individual, such knowledge is inherently hard to process and hard to transfer. Yet understanding the context of any piece of information invariably requires tacit knowledge. Generating such tacit knowledge can be enabled through traders' use of simulation and modeling tools. This allows them to gather a greater wealth of experience from which to develop their tacit knowledge without risking real resources.

But explicit knowledge at the level of the individual is not enough. Generating organizational knowledge invariably means converting the tacit knowledge of the individual into explicit knowledge accessible by all. The process by which this occurs is inherently social. It requires a shared context in which individuals can engage in a dialogue and create new perspectives. Then, through conflict and discussion, individuals are forced to question existing knowledge premises and thus generate new knowledge.

Information technology is most effective when it enables this social process. In essence, it replaces the middle managers who once served as a bridge between the visionary ideals of the top and the often chaotic reality of the front line business. It synthesizes the tacit knowledge of the traders, making it explicit and incorporating it into new products and services. Firms like Asea Brown Boveri are using groupware tools such as Lotus Notes™ in their treasury to revolutionize how individuals work together to produce new knowledge. Nations-Bank, for example, has designed a groupware-based forum called "Project Agora" in which non-structured discussion can take place among knowledge workers in various functions. Even electronic mail democratizes the nature of communication within organizations, encouraging the airing of contrary assumptions and the development of superior organizational knowledge.[35] Such communication tools might

---

[33]Securities Industry Association Annual Convention, December 1991.
[34]Nonaka, op. cit.
[35]L. Sproull and S. Kiesler, *Connections: New Ways of Working in the Networked Organization*

have made a difference at MG in making the assumptions of the parent company and subsidiary coincide. Consider Merck, widely recognized as a firm where the knowledge of skilled specialists in the Finance group is leveraged for the good of all its operational divisions. Finance staff are encouraged to go to the operating units and act proactively, taking the intuitions of good managers and quantifying them; thus generating new organizational knowledge, testable and accessible for the good of the entire firm.[36]

Knowledge tools, controls, and new organizational structures will go far to create a new culture in which informed decision making is valued, but explicit efforts to cultivate that culture are still needed. Knowledge and skills can never substitute for the motivation only an effective organizational culture can provide.

Facilitating a Knowledge Management Culture

Frequently proposed as the antidote to rogue trading is the revision of trading firms' competitive cultures, and specifically their incentive schemes (including the standard practice of paying huge bonuses to firm's top performers). Typically, a trader's remuneration package includes a bonus (millions in the case of star traders like Nick Leeson and Joseph Jett) based on how much revenue he earns for the firm. Moreover, firm's may recognize revenue at the beginning of the transaction rather than at the end. The worry, naturally, is that this creates a moral hazard encouraging traders to make short-term profits while passing longer-term risks to the firm.[37]

Some firms, notably Salomon Brothers, have tried to make traders behave more like the firm's equity holders, taking more of the risks in the bad times in return for more of the benefits in the good times. Not surprisingly, this has resulted in some top traders being poached by other firms. Absent a general industry change of attitudes towards incentive structure, it seems unlikely that many firms have the option of performing radical changes in incentives. Despite these constraints, incentives and other human resource practices remain broad levers to affect the cultural assumptions and beliefs used to inspire and direct the search for new opportunities. They are clumsy, but in the long term, highly effective. They provide the basic values, purpose, and direction for the organization, without which all organizations lose their innovative drive.

In particular, rewards and incentives signal what behaviors and outcomes are most valued by management. Are rewards, for example, determined by monitoring profit—or *risk-adjusted* profit? Where traders are compensated strictly based on the magnitude of profits (i.e., no limit to upside versus a compensation

(Cambridge, MA: MIT Press, 1991).

[36]J. Lewent and A. Kearney, "Identifying, Measuring and Hedging Currency Risk at Merck," in Donald Chew, ed., *The New Corporate Finance* (New York, NY: McGraw-Hill, 1993).

[37]E. Ludwig, "Lesson from Leeson," Risk, 8 (1995).

floor for the downside), it should not be surprising that knowledge accumulation and sharing are not valued. Compensation measures should also reflect the process by which traders contribute to the firm's P&L, through their own trades directly and also through their contributions to the firm's organizational knowledge. At one consulting firm, professionals are expected to document what they have learned about what works and doesn't work in client settings—and are partially compensated based on how often their documentation is accessed from a central knowledge repository. Similar incentives could be established among professionals in such a knowledge-intensive area as risk management. Management sends strong signals through its compensation policies; different roles are perceived of value according to their allocated compensation. As in Barings and Kidder Peabody, a key risk management issue for many firms in this regard is the differential between front-office and back-office compensation. The use of *transparent* knowledge-based qualitative compensation schemes can enable back and front office expertise to be better aligned, thereby both limiting operational risks and preventing the loss of critical back office talent.

But culture is more than just compensation, and it is responsive to influences other than paychecks. Management sends signals about what is important through its recruiting priorities, promotions, and possibly more than anything, through its own behavior. These deeply embedded cultural assumptions that result are significant; trading rooms differ by organization and by host country in what they consider acceptable levels of risk.[38] Cultural bravado and arrogance clearly play a role in the male-dominated world of trading.

Turning a culture around is far from easy. According to Ed Schein, a leading organizational psychologist, "The unique and essential function of leadership is the manipulation of culture . . . [the] leader needs both the vision and the ability to articulate it and enforce it."[39] Just consider the evolving role of the leader in effective risk management organizations. Several examples come to mind: Judy Lewent at Merck, Dennis Weatherstone at J.P. Morgan, and, despite recent controversy about aggressive tactics amongst its sales force, Charles Sanford at Bankers Trust. All have clearly made their vision for their firms explicit; Sanford has gone so far as to produce a document describing the future of the entire financial industry.[40] And finally, all of these leaders have parlayed their risk management visions into the major organizational changes that must inevitably accompany any comprehensive knowledge management effort.

[38]S. Zaheer, "Organizational Context and Risk Taking: A Study of Foreign Exchange Trading Rooms in the U.S. and Japan," MIT IFSRC Report 233-92S (1992).

[39]E. Schein, *Organizational Culture and Leadership: A Dynamic View* (San Francisco, CA: Jossey-Bass, 1986).

[40]C. Sanford, "Financial Markets in 2020," Federal Reserve Bank of Kansas City Economic Symposium in Jackson Hole, WY (1995).

Knowledge Management Requires Organizational Change

To be truly effective, knowledge management must be accompanied by organizational change. As a first step, financial services firms are setting up independent, centralized risk management organizations, composed of high-ranking staff representing various perspectives. The responsibilities of a dedicated risk management group should include:

- determining the required levels of trading and managerial knowledge with regard to risk management;
- enabling the centralized collection of that knowledge from sources internal and external;
- representation of current knowledge in documents, databases, and other clear and widely accessible formats;
- embedding of that knowledge in processes, policy, and control mechanisms;
- refinement and testing of that knowledge—for instance, by stress-testing the firm's existing models with worst-case scenarios;
- overseeing the transfer of knowledge and information to trading decision makers;
- overseeing the transfer of knowledge and information to the senior management monitoring the current state of risk management at the firm; and
- creation of an infrastructure to support all these activities.

What types of people should compose such a group? Almost certainly, it should include individuals drawn from cost accounting, operations, procurement, MIS, financial accounting, and legal.[41] The importance of contextual knowledge in risk management necessitates the extensive dialogue of both functional experts as well as more senior generalists.

As a staff function, the group must interface with the firm's Strategy group to set priorities; with the IT group to design appropriate information systems and databases; and with Human Resources to adapt hiring policies and incentive schemes to reflect risk-adjusted measures. The group should operate (although not maintain or design) global control systems setting capital, exposure, and stop-loss limits for traders. For the average trader, whose background and motivation do not make risk management the first instinct, such a group can provide a valuable filter for making clear the risk implications of actions. Exceptions to those limits should be noted and assessed by group staff, and remedial action should then be taken.

---

[41]D. Lessard and N. Nohria, "Rediscovering Functions in the MNC: The Role of Expertise in Firms' Responses to Shifting Exchange Rates," in C. A. Bartlett, Y. Doz, and G. Hedlund, eds., *Managing the Global Firm* (London, UK: Routledge, 1990).

The group should also report only to very senior management, perhaps directly to the CEO, and its independence should be scrupulously defended in the face of almost inevitable conflict. Similar groups have been formed at leading risk management firms such as Bankers Trust, and Citibank; the latter has taken steps toward establishing a centralized risk management function, putting in place a "process owner" who works with people across several related functions. Already, it has benefited from the integration of information from different areas, particularly in improving the netting process. Bankers Trust has leveraged its internal risk management group still further, and has begun selling its risk management information services to customers.

While the risk management group does not have the exclusive responsibility for creating new knowledge in the firm, it must act as an independent and highly knowledgeable internal auditor to review and ensure the integrity of the firm's existing risk management knowledge, as well as its controls and its evolving culture. As shown in Figure 11.1, it is important to see all of these knowledge management techniques as a whole, continually monitored by the risk management group.

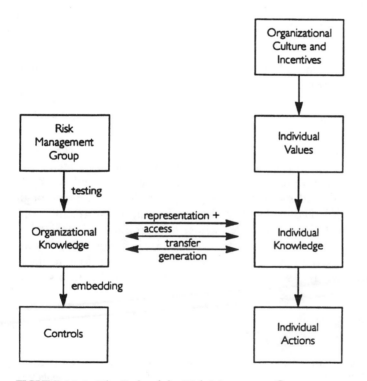

FIGURE 11.1 The Role of the Risk Managment Group

Improving Knowledge Management

The last word is far from in on the three cases of risk management failure described here. Not surprisingly, the first response to all three cases has been to focus on each firm's internal controls. With the benefit of hindsight, observers are incredulous that the misdeeds were not caught and corrected sooner. The standard charge is "failure to supervise" on the part of the rogue traders' superiors.

In fact, we would suggest that the main lesson from cases like MG, Kidder Peabody, and Barings, is that active knowledge management is essential for effective risk management. Moreover, traditional passive control systems can never be sufficient to provide adequate risk management. Too often, historical success (like that attributed to Joe Jett and Nick Leeson) skews the perception of internal knowledge, biases how new information is interpreted, and perhaps inevitably in the long term, produces disaster. To counter that potential for misinterpretation, the visionary executives must take on a larger goal. Rather than simply providing *ex post* checks against abuse, management must work positively to equip their employees for success. This means ensuring, through knowledge management, that:

- the firm understands what knowledge it has and seeks out the knowledge it needs;
- organizational knowledge is transferred to those who need it in their daily work;
- organizational knowledge is accessible to those who may need it as events warrant;
- new knowledge is rapidly generated and made accessible throughout the organization;
- controls are developed to embed the most reliable and robust knowledge;
- organizational knowledge is tested and validated periodically; and
- the firm facilitates knowledge management through its culture and incentives.

Equipping decision makers with the knowledge they need—and ensuring (through controls and incentives) that they use it—is the only way to deal with the new market context and the ever-increasing need for more speed, more flexibility, and more knowledgeable judgment. The challenge is to enable both front-line and senior management to apply knowledgeable judgment to their decisions by drawing on a knowledge base far broader than their own experience and intellect, in essence leveraging what composes the true value of a firm: its intangible knowledge, values, and controls.

Index

Health Care Research by Degrees

N. REID

Head of the School of Health and Social Sciences
Coventry University

OXFORD

BLACKWELL SCIENTIFIC PUBLICATIONS

LONDON EDINBURGH BOSTON

MELBOURNE PARIS BERLIN VIENNA

© 1993 Blackwell Scientific Publications

Blackwell Scientific Publications
Editorial Offices:
Osney Mead, Oxford, OX2 0EL
25 John Street, London WC1N 2BL
23 Ainslie Place, Edinburgh EH3 6AJ
238 Main Street, Cambridge,
  Massachusetts 02142, USA
54 University Street, Carlton,
  Victoria 3053, Australia

Other Editorial Offices:
Librairie Arnette SA
2, rue Casimir-Delavigne
75006 Paris
France

Blackwell Wissenschafts-Verlag
Meinekestrasse 4
D-1000 Berlin 15
Germany

Blackwell MZV
Feldgasse 13
A-1238 Wien
Austria

First published 1993

Set by Best-set Typesetter Ltd, Hong Kong
Printed and bound in Great Britain by
Hartnolls Ltd, Bodmin, Cornwall

DISTRIBUTORS
Marston Book Services Ltd
PO Box 87
Oxford OX2 0DT
(*Orders*: Tel: 0865 791155
       Fax: 0865 791927
       Telex: 837515)

USA
Blackwell Scientific Publications, Inc.
238 Main Street
Cambridge, MA 02142
(*Orders*: Tel: 800 759-6102
           617 225-0401)

Canada
Times Mirror Professional Publishing, Ltd
5240 Finch Avenue East
Scarborough, Ontario M1S 5A2
(*Orders*: Tel: 800 268-4178
           416 298-1588)

Australia
Blackwell Scientific Publications
Pty Ltd
54 University Street,
Carlton, Victoria 3053
(*Orders*: Tel: 03 347-5552)

British Library
Cataloguing in Publication Data
A Catalogue record for this book is
available from the British Library

ISBN 0-632-03466-1

Library of Congress Cataloging-in-Publication
Data
Reid, Norma G.
     Health care research by degrees/N. Reid.
         p. cm.
     Includes bibliographical references and
index.
     ISBN 0-632-03466-1
     1. Medicine – Research – Methodology.
2. Medicine – Research – Statistical
methods.   3. Medical care – Research –
Methodology.   4. Medical care – Research
– Statistical methods.   I. Title.
     R850.R45   1992
     362.1'072 – dc20
                                   92-28523
                                        CIP

MINITAB is a registered trademark of Minitab Inc, 3081 Enterprise Drive, State College,
PA 16801-2756 USA, tel. 814-238 3280, fax 814-238 4383. The author would like to acknowledge
their co-operation in the preparation of this book.

This book is dedicated to my husband
Derek
with love and gratitude

Contents

Foreword

'What on earth has statistics to do with health care?' you may ask, or you may be asked by those people to whom you describe the content of your course. 'Surely,' the questioner will continue, 'health care is about looking after people, real living individuals. You cannot treat them with tables of numbers and mathematics'.

The dryness of statistics, its remoteness from normal human activities and interests and the suspicion with which it is regarded are perpetual misconceptions of a subject that, when honestly and competently handled, is truly compassionate in its applications.

No two human beings are alike. This is a wonder of creation. Our differences make us the individuals we are. Take any single characteristic apart from the outline shape which classifies us as men or women – your height, your weight, your age, your fingerprint, your lung capacity – and you will find that you are not the same as the person standing next to you. Consider just a small set of characteristics. The combination of values that you carry make you unique. There is nobody else exactly like you.

It is this variability between individuals that makes people who don't understand statistics exclaim that you cannot apply statistical methods to medicine and other branches of human care. But when we are determined to discover every possible means of improving human welfare, of caring for the health of people, we quickly learn that statistical methods are powerful and essential.

The secret is to understand *variability*: first, that it exists; second, and this is *much* more difficult, its causes; and third, and this is *very* much more difficult, what to do about it.

Consider, for example, a simple clinical trial in which 40 patients are each prescribed one of two alternative treatments, which we shall call treatment A and treatment B. Some time later we examine these patients and record the following results:

	Treatment A	*Treatment B*	
Recovered	17	8	25
No better	3	12	15
	20	20	40

Now, if you examine this table, you may quickly conclude that treatment A is better than treatment B. But wait a minute. You can see that there were three patients who, given treatment A, did not recover. So why not? Were they not quite the same as those patients who did? Maybe not. Perhaps they were older, more feeble, or in a slightly worse condition at the start of the trial than those who did recover. Notice too, that there were eight patients who did recover when given treatment B, so it can't be all that bad, but there were also 12 who were no better. So clearly, for both treatments, there is a variability of response.

What if we did the trial again, would we get the same results? It's unlikely because, not only is there variability between the patients, but we shall have a different set of 40 patients all different from the first set.

So you will see that at least one reason for different responses to the two treatments is that people are variable. There may be other reasons too. For example, the prescribing doctor may think that one patient will do better with treatment A than with treatment B so, unless we guard against it in our management of the trial, we will get what is called an *allocation bias*.

Another reason for discovering different responses to the two treatments may be that the examining doctor, or the patient himself, may expect recovery with treatment A but not with treatment B. This leads to what is called *assessment bias*.

It may be, of course, that treatment A is truly better than treatment B, but we now have a problem because we understand that there may be several reasons why it only appears to be better. We need to tackle this problem because we care about people. We want to discover the best way to treat them. But the variability of people has led us into *uncertainty*. We have to cope with uncertainty.

There are ways of dealing with the problem: statistical ways. If you want to discover the best way of treating patients, who are ill, or of improving the lifestyle of other people who are not ill, but are in danger, as we all are, of becoming ill, then you must understand statistical methods. More broadly, you must understand and be able to use the research methods which embrace the statistical ones.

Much of health care is about uncertainty. Doctors, nurses, physiotherapists, and all other health care professionals, must be able to cope with uncertainty when they make decisions with respect to diagnosis and treatment. They must understand that symptoms, signs and tests are subject to variations of patients, physiological and pathological conditions, observer skills and experiences, and instrumental accuracy and precision. So, as a student, you must practise assembling, manipulating, presenting, interpreting and judging numerical data so that you can reach an understanding of the meanings of chance and probability associated with diagnosis, therapy and prognosis, never forgetting that *every* item of data represents a fact about a human individual who is as entitled to be as well and happy as any other.

If you remember that, statistics will not be a dry subject, but a compassionate one.

Perhaps in your daily work you will not, you think, be involved in research. So, if you don't see yourself becoming so involved, you may ask why you should learn about research methods and statistics.

Even in the most caring of interviews, of examinations and of treatments of individual patients, you are still a scientific observer, accumulating information and comparing experiences. Your success in this still depends on your understanding of change and variation in people that lead to uncertainty in how to care for them. Daily routine work will include the generation and recording of data on which health statistics are based. You must understand how those statistics will help you in your own work as well as in the management of all health services generally.

You will almost certainly participate at some time in clinical trials and other investigations such as social surveys. You must understand how these are designed and managed and how the resulting data are analysed and interpreted so that you can appreciate the need for conscientious participation and exact adherence to the protocols.

Then there is the literature. Reports of research are published so that health carers like you will learn quickly about results that will benefit you in your work. You can read these reports only if you have a good understanding of the statistical methods which pervade the literature. That understanding will also help you to judge whether or not the research has been well conceived, executed, or interpreted.

These are all good reasons for learning about research methods and statistics in health care. It is a difficult subject because it involves concepts that are, at first sight, strange. It is also difficult to write about because there are conceptual barriers to overcome. Norma Reid has tackled this task with sensitivity to the subject and sympathy for the student. She has written in practical terms and with reference to real situations. Her book is a companion to her classroom teaching and should be read at the pace of the course. When you have finished the course, I suggest that you read the book again. Then, two or three years after qualifying, read it again. It takes time, but eventually you will realize that the use of statistics has real merit in health care and is not so dull after all.

Tony Greenfield
Industrial Research Consultant.
Formerly, in the seventies, head of process computing and
statistics in the corporate research laboratories of British
Steel; and, in the eighties, professor of medical computing
and statistics at the Queen's University, Belfast.

Acknowledgements

I am indebted to Coventry University, and in particular its Vice-Chancellor, Dr Mike Goldstein, for making the writing of this book possible through a period of study leave. During this period I was seconded to the University of Ulster; my thanks are due to Professor Roger Ellis, Dean of the Faculty of Social and Health Sciences, and Ms Dorothy Whittington, Director of the Centre for Health and Social Research, for their hospitality and support. I am also deeply grateful to Miss Karen McCulloch, who typed the first draft, with whom, as always, it has been a pleasure to work. The transfer of the material and subsequent drafts were produced by Mrs Mandy Coult and Mrs Jane Lissaman, to whom I am indebted for their skill and patience.

Ms Lisa Field, my editor, has been an unfailing source of encouragement and advice and I greatly appreciated the opportunity to work with her.

Chapter 1
The Whys and Wherefores of Health Care Research

Why research?

Research is important and it can also be enjoyable. It engages the imagination, the emotion and the intellect. It is in some ways like detective work, starting with a problem, charting a way along a process of investigation, building up evidence, and moving towards conclusions. The end point of research may not be as neat as in a 'whodunnit'; but certain answers, and often another set of questions will emerge. The satisfactions are enormous. The sense of achievement in discovering a new thing, however small, is the great reward of research. If that new thing is an improvement in the treatment or care of a patient or client, the reward is even greater.

Beyond this personal satisfaction, however, there is a strong argument that *all* professional practice should be research-based and research-validated – because our patients and clients deserve care which has been demonstrated, through research, to be the best that can be given. It follows that the delivery of patient care, the planning, organization and management of the services and the education of those who provide that care should also be firmly based on well-researched practice. Within the role of every clinician, every manager and every educationalist in health, the need for research is plain: to ensure that our patients and clients are receiving the best possible care, to demonstrate that our services are cost effective and efficient and, not least, to ensure that we are educating the next generation of health professionals properly.

Research may not provide us with neat solutions or with certainties in responding to these challenges, but it greatly improves on the alternative – which is to go on doing what we have always done, or to do what we think is right and hope for the best.

As we move towards the next century, the commitment, vocationalism and experience which health professionals have always called upon, needs to be underpinned by a well-validated research base. This is not only in the interests of patients and clients, but will also ensure the survival of those same health care professions. As Etzioni put it as long ago as 1969, 'one of the characteristics of a profession is its ability to develop and validate a body of knowledge that is unique to itself'.

A key part of the process of carrying out research is acquiring a body of information which, when analysed, will in a concise way answer a question, solve a problem or at least tell us more about the topic under study. The information may come in a variety of forms: it may be in words, it may be in pictures, or via graphics (e.g. X-rays), or it may be in numbers. If it is in number form, we use two main tools to deal with it: statistics for the purposes of summarizing these numbers and possibly making some inferences from them, and a computer to lighten the burden of this process. The use of statistics and computers is an integral research skill: statistics and computing are means to an end, and that end is the taming of quantitative research data.

But other kinds of research data can be equally valuable. Numbers are not superior to words or graphics – just different. Depending on the circumstances, various kinds of information have their role and value. In the past health researchers have tended to take a more restricted view, putting all the emphasis on quantitative methods, and this, in my opinion, has unduly limited the scope and nature of what has been achieved. One reason for widening the scope of health research is that a merely quantitative approach can lead to preoccupation with questions of how and how much, the easy part; this leaves the harder less quantifiable questions of why and whether to be solved by others – usually by intuition, political acumen or some other kind of hunch. Another reason is believing firmly that an important part of future professional survival will depend on a willingness to dismantle artificial barriers and barricades – coined in the aphorism 'all professions are a conspiracy against the laity'. Researchers in health care must be willing and able to communicate their findings in language that the intelligent lay reader can understand. Jargon and algebraic formulae may both be smoke-screens, sometimes indeed clouding the researcher's own vision and obscuring the true nature of his or her findings.

The book will try to explain and show you how to use research methods with the aid of their close partners, statistics and computing. When you have read it, you too will be able to bandy jargon with the best of them – if you want to. But the book also aims to persuade you that the future lies not in mystification and mystique but in putting research and its findings at the service of the busy practitioner. In this way the gulf between research and practice, as identified by such writers as Taylor and Mitchell (1990), Alexander (1991) or Tammivaara and Shepar (1990) can be reduced. Above all, if you are about to join or rejoin one of the health care professions, I hope the book will help you to put your academic skills to practical use.

Professionalism and research

In striving for recognition, the emergent health care professions – nursing and health visiting, physiotherapy and occupational therapy

– have, not unnaturally tended to emphasize their individuality, distinguishing themselves from each other, or, even competing. This has manifested itself in research with a keen desire by each of the health care professions to develop their own unique body of knowledge. More recently there has been a growing perception of the need for all three professions to develop a basis of theory and practice which distinguishes them collectively from professions such as medicine.

But in research the concerns have generally been much narrower. Consider, for example, this declaration of policy by Charles Christiansen, founding editor of the *Occupational Therapy Journal* of Research (1981):

'The challenge of advancing our science may appear to be simply a matter of generating more research of higher calibre. A closer examination, however, reveals that the challenge is far greater than this; it involves the critical need to focus research efforts within the context of a united theoretical structure . . . It is worth noting here that our failure to meet the challenge of research may ultimately lead to our demise as a viable discipline'.

Nine years later, in reviewing the progress of occupational therapy research in the USA, Ottenbacher (1990) observed, in the same journal, that 'in a true profession the skills come from a clearly defined and well-developed knowledge base, generated largely by members of the discipline'.

Physiotherapists (called physical therapists in the USA) have also recently expressed support for a central theoretical base as the key to professional development. Tammivaara and Shepar (1990), observing that 'physical therapists are becoming increasingly aware of the importance of theory in physical therapy research and practice', conclude that 'as the theoretical base for physical therapy practice and research grows, so will physical therapy continue to develop as a distinct and socially valued profession'.

In nursing, too, Polit and Hungler (1989) noted that 'nursing scholars are increasingly calling for the development and use of theories that are unique to nursing' and argue that 'theories unique to nursing will help nurses to better conceptualize questions of special relevance to themselves and to define the difference between nursing and other disciplines'. They devote nearly a chapter to describing theories of nursing and insist that all nursing research must have a theoretical context, preferably from within nursing theory.

This book is based on different premises. First, that theory ought not to be plucked from the air, but based on practical utility and relevance, and that, in any event, many good research studies can be based solely on sound empirical investigation of clearly-stated hypotheses. Second, that an appropriate theory base for studies of health could often be drawn with advantage from other branches of the social and physical

sciences whose researchers have been there before, and that conversely it is unnecessarily limiting to confine health research to the
relatively narrow, recent and, perhaps, untested theory base within
particular health professions. It is greatly to be hoped that, as they
mature, the health care professions will feel relaxed enough to adopt
an eclectic research base, attributing the various methodologies to the
social and physical sciences from which they have evolved without
feeling the need to reinvent the wheel. In doing so, they can make a
much more distinctive collective impact by, for example, developing
research-led practice based on social models of health. This is an
approach so far neglected by the medical profession, and hence could
practically and effectively demonstrate the unique contribution of the
health care professions.

This is not an argument against theory. On the contrary: there is
nothing so practical as a good theory – but it has to be a good theory.
Good theories may well come from one health profession and the
developing theory of that profession will certainly be strengthened by
empirical research. But the future of the health professions will be
better served by wider horizons and shared theories.

The disciplinary roots of health research

In their search for academic credibility, researchers in the health
professions have tended to align themselves with scientific tradition.
Pratt (1989) comments, for instance, 'that science is a base for the
practice of physiotherapy seems not to be in question since a majority
of curriculum time is allocated to scientific subjects, anatomy and
physiology'. Yet he goes on to argue that 'it is becoming more and
more apparent that the response to an illness and, indeed, the origins
of the illness itself, may be at least partly accounted for in psychological terms'. This scientific orientation, of course, follows medical
precedents, which, though not to be rejected out of hand, may not
be an infallible model for emergent professions seeking to make a
distinctive contribution.

There are, of course, lively debates within what would be termed the
natural sciences and the social sciences. The latter are by no means
united in their views and draw on several philosophical traditions, as
Chapter 3 will show. However, many of the health care professionals
tend to ally themselves with the sciences – and hence a more medical
perspective – sometimes at the expense of a broader vision of developments in health care provision.

There are also some purely academic prejudices. Thus, Oyster,
Hanten and Horens (1987) in their book *Introduction to Research,
A Guide for the Health Science Professional* assert that 'the social
sciences, such as psychology and sociology, lag behind in the precision
with which purest research principles may be employed' and 'the
"hard" sciences, such as chemistry and physics, allow for a very close

adherence to the purest of research principles because very close control is possible with physical entities such as grams of sulphur'. While this is true, the health care sciences need to concern themselves with the problems of less easily-controlled human subjects, and cannot confine themselves to topics that can be studied through traditional scientific, experimental methods. Polit and Hungler (1989) devote a chapter to 'the scientific approach' in nursing research but they acknowledge that this has limitations, and advocate research methods from the social sciences as well. This book seeks to be open-minded and specifically rejects the view that research methods drawn from the social sciences are necessarily inferior. The historical and social background of the various health care professions – 'professions supplementary to medicine' as some of them are still sometimes called – has implanted in them attitudes different from those found in both academic and professional medical conventions. For tomorrow's world academic, professional and social considerations combine to suggest a new, more eclectic and less blinkered approach.

The shape of the book

In this chapter I have tried to suggest some of the reasons for doing research and some of the principles that should support it. The rest of the book will discuss ways of putting theory into practice.

Chapter 2 will develop a framework for carrying out research and explore its relationship to the philosophies of care prevalent within the health professions. It will present an overview of methodological approaches and their implications for models of health. Chapters 3 and 4 will then focus in more detail on research design and provide some detail on designs which are most commonly used in health research.

Chapters 5 to 8 will move to quantitative analysis and provide statistical and computing techniques for dealing with quantitative data. Chapter 5 deals with data preparation, Chapter 6 discusses techniques of descriptive analysis and Chapters 7 and 8 move on to inferential statistical analysis. In Chapter 9 analogous techniques of analysis are described for qualitative data.

Chapter 10 deals with the presentation of research findings, and provides guidelines for good practice in presenting oral and written research reports. The skills of evaluation are also described. All of the skills covered in this text come together at this point to provide a framework for evaluation of research – either of one's own research or of that published by others.

I hope, that at the end of it you will not only be better equipped to carry out research, but that you will understand its purpose better and enjoy it more. At the very least it is a part of your course in which you can direct your own study, choose your own topic, and perhaps discover something that no one has known before. Research can be a lonely business at times – just you and the apparent facts and it may be gloomy. Progress can be sporadic – for weeks you do not appear to be achieving anything tangible. But, then, suddenly, you move forward and all the misery is soon forgotten.

Until the next time, that is. The chances are that by the time you have successfully completed your first piece of research, you will have identified the next six studies which need to be done – and the chances are that you will want to do them. Research is a lifelong activity. As Mark Pattison (1875) put it, in 'Isaac Casaubon':

> In research the horizon recedes as we advance, and is no nearer at sixty than it was at twenty. As the power of endurance weakens with age, the urgency of the pursuit grows more intense . . . And research is always incomplete.

It can be fascinating, tantalizing, addictive and rewarding. If you are engaged in any of the health care professions or are about to be, then it is an essential tool of your trade. And the better you are at it, the more you are likely to enjoy it.

Discussion points

1. What are the reasons for carrying out research into health care?
2. Identify the main disciplinary influences in the curriculum for basic training in your profession. What are the implications of the basic curriculum (research training apart) as a preparation for research? Is it comprehensive? Is it adequate?
3. Does practice in your profession have a theoretical base? Does it matter? Should research in your profession always/sometimes/ never be based on theory of professional practice unique to your profession?
4. What characteristics do research and investigative journalism have in common and what are the key differences?

References

Alexander, M. (1989) Nursing Practitioners, Researchers, Teachers and Managers All Have The Same Goal. Guest Editorial. *Journal of Advanced Nursing*, **14**, 991–2.

Christiansen, C.H. (1981) Editorial: Toward resolution of crisis: Research requisites in occupational therapy. *The Occupational Therapy Journal of Research*, **1**, 116–24.

Etzioni, A. (Ed) (1969) *The Semi-Professions and Their Organizations*. Free Press, New York.

Ottenbacher, K. (1990) Editorial: Occupational Therapy Curricula and Practice: Skill Based or Knowledge Based. *The Occupational Therapy Journal of Research*, **10**, 7–11.

Oyster, C., Hanten, W. & Llorens, L. (1987) *Introduction to Research, A*

Guide for the Health Science Professional. J.B. Lippincott Company, Philadelphia.

Pattison, M. (1875) *Isaac Casaubon.* London.

Polit, D. & Hungler, B. (1989) *Essentials of Nursing Research,* 2nd edn. J.B. Lippincott Company, Philadelphia.

Pratt, J.W. (1989) Towards a Philosophy of Physiotherapy. *Physiotherapy,* **75**, 114–20.

Tammivaara, J. & Shepar, K. (1990) Theory: The Guide to Clinical Practice and Research. *Physical Therapy,* **70**, No. 9, September 1990.

Taylor, E. & Mitchell, M. (1990) Research Attitudes and Activity of Occupational Therapy Clinicians. *The American Journal of Occupational Therapy,* **44**, 350–55.

Chapter 2
Starting Out in Research

The mystique of research may lie in part in perceptions about its scale — those new to research often have an image of a multimillion-pound enterprise going on for many years, drawing on the newest and most sophisticated technology and employing a large team of very high-powered personnel. The myth is fortified by practicising health care professionals who tend to be self-deprecating about their research efforts and feel that it is all a bit amateur and not really proper research.

In fact both the small individual research project and the major study can be good or bad. All good research needs a framework — a set of stages, not necessarily chronological, which should be systematically addressed, whatever the scale of the project. These include:

- Choosing the topic and formulating the problem.
- Literature review and theory context.
- Setting aims, objectives or research hypotheses.
- Choice of methodological approach and design of the study.
- Resources, ethics, communications and access.
- Construction of instruments.
- Pilot study and data collection.
- Data preparation and analysis.
- Presentation of findings.
- Evaluation.

This research process is best thought of as a cycle, a circular process where, having worked through all the stages, you may well find yourself back at the beginning, rethinking the topic and formulation of the study. Or you might get to the funding stage and then be obliged to lower your sights to a much more modest undertaking because funding cannot be acquired. Each stage is interconnected with every other stage and may need to be reconsidered accordingly. It is helpful, however, in obtaining an overview of the process, to consider each stage independently.

Choosing the topic and formulating the problem

Most of us, in reflecting on our professional activity, have ideas about areas of research we would like to undertake. There are obvious advantages in choosing to carry out research on one of your own burning interests – nothing is more motivating or sustaining than the study of things dear to our hearts. But two potential problems should be kept in mind: if you feel strongly about your topic how can you ensure that no bias will inadvertently creep into your study? And is it really a manageable topic for a project which must be completed within, say, three to six months? It is not possible to find cures for cancer or solve the enigma of relationships between the health and medical professions within most student project time-scales.

In formulating your topic, you will almost always have to consider reducing the scale of your initial idea. If you want to work on a huge topic, the way to do this is to form an association with a professional research team – perhaps one of your tutors or lecturers can help you with this – with a view to identifying a manageable project within the research programme they are undertaking. Such a suggestion is usually very welcome as professional researchers often identify interesting areas of study which are tangential to their main remit, but are none-theless important and worth doing.

Relating your choice of topic to professional practice is always valuable and motivating. You should talk it through with professional colleagues at an early stage, however, and get a feel for issues of access, ethics and other practical considerations which you may need to examine in more detail at a later stage. You should also think about the scale of your study at this stage – is there a study population from which you can select a sample? How big should this sample be? Can you manage it in the time you have? Will there be funding implications?

It is no bad thing, as your thinking progresses, to write down as concise a description as you can of your proposal, thinking carefully about each word and its implication. For example, if the word 'pain' appears in your topic title, how will you define it and assess or measure it? Does every subject experience it in the same way? If not, how can you obtain standard measurements?

In addressing some of the myriad questions which will arise, you will be greatly helped by reviewing the relevant literature and theory.

Literature review and theory context

Reviewing the literature has a number of purposes:

- To find out the state of the art – has your study been done before? What is known already about this area of interest?
- To discover whether a theory exists to support your proposed study, or whether there are competing theories, one of which your study may support.
- To identify the various methodological approaches that have been applied to your area of study. You may want to write to an author

requesting a copy of the questionnaire that was used, if it looks as if it might be valuable in your work.

The best way to review literature is through a computer search. A variety of computerized indices are available and most libraries in higher education institutions will have purchased one or two of these, all of which operate on the same principle. The specification of key-words generates a list of all publications over a specified period in all of the journals covered by the index in question. The clue to this process is in the appropriate specification of keywords – too few keywords will generate thousands of references, which you can never hope to read. For example, you can imagine what would happen if you asked for all publications with the words 'health' and 'education' in the titles. If on the other hand you are too specific, you may not find anything at all. It is something of a hit-and-miss operation, but there is usually a helpful librarian who will advise you.

Examples of useful computerized indices in the UK are MEDLINE, which incorporates all of the constituent journals in Index Medicus and DHSSDATA which provides all DHSS publications. DIALOG includes almost 400 different databases including MEDLINE, which is also within DATASTAR. There may be a charge for a computer search – it can cost up to £50 per search – so you may need to rely on more old-fashioned means.

An alternative approach is to identify the best journals for your purpose and, working backwards in time, scan the contents lists for suitable papers. Among those journals widely read in the UK, are the *International Journal of Nursing Studies*, the *Journal of Advanced Nursing, Physiotherapy, Physiotherapy Practice*, or the *British Journal of Occupational Therapy*. The references in one or two relevant recent articles, will in turn provide you with a route for tracing backwards in time the sources of knowledge on your topic.

At this stage you should try to write a synopsis of the background to your study in order to concentrate your mind on essentials. You should also consult any experts who can assist you – your own tutor, perhaps, or someone else accessible to you, but do not be afraid to write to the established 'names' in the field. If you make clear your intention to acknowledge fully any help you receive, most researchers will be generous in sharing ideas or research materials with newcomers.

Having completed these first two stages, you should now be able to express your research problem within a short concise statement.

Stating aims, objectives and research hypotheses

Jargon is not confined to health research, and if you are not clear about the difference between aims and objectives you will not be alone in this. What matters is that you should set out, as succinctly as possible, what it is you hope to discover by your research and how you intend to set about it.

The purpose of the research can be expressed as a statement of aims or as a research hypothesis or both. For example, the aims of a study of the effect of a 12-hour shift system for nurses could be expressed as follows:

- The purpose of this study is to examine the impact of the 12-hour shift, as compared to traditional shift patterns, on the quantity and quality of patient care and on the attitudes of nursing staff. The study will aim to examine these effects in one health authority through detailed study within two hospitals.

A research hypothesis associated with this study might be:

- That the effect of the 12-hour shift, as compared with traditional shift patterns, in two hospitals in one health authority, is detrimental to the quality and quantity of patient care and the attitudes of nursing staff.

My own preference is for the more neutral statement of aims and purpose, but as you can see, both approaches contain the same information. If, however, you are working within a clear theoretical context, then the statement of a research hypothesis may be more meaningful.

Choice of methodological approach and design of the study

In carrying out health research the range of possible methodologies (the number of available research methods) is vast, stretching from classical experimental (scientific) method, through a variety of structured and semi-structured designs including clinical trials and surveys to ethnographic and qualitative approaches. All of these are valuable and have their place. Chapter 3 discusses the strengths and weaknesses of different approaches and provides some detail on the most commonly used designs in health research.

A practical factor to consider in undertaking a project as part of a course, is the resource implication of design choices. Qualitative research, for example, is most often an individual activity relying on the skills and judgement of the researcher. Techniques involving face-to-face surveys or observation may often require a team for the field-work, but may be less demanding intellectually. These techniques may be a wiser choice for a student project, where the student is to some extent training as a researcher; but if the need for a team implies payment there may be problems for the student in resourcing the project.

Resources, ethics, communications and access

You should be able to identify the resource implications of your study by the time you have reached the design stage, not just for those from whom you may seek support but also for yourself. Unless you have private means your greatest resource is your time – and you should consider carefully how much time you have. If you are a full-time student, what other study commitments do you have? If you are part-time, you must take account of the demands of your job and domestic commitments and be realistic about how much time you can give to your project. Whether it is full- or part-time, you should try to draw up a detailed timetable for each phase of your study before you commit yourself to it.

Do not forget the cost of travel in time and money. Unless your study is locally based, these costs (and your time commitment) can spiral very quickly. It is highly desirable that projects within courses be based locally, unless they can be done postally (e.g. through a postal questionnaire).

Students do not normally have time to seek external funding in any formal way, but you may be able to get assistance in kind, and you should find out in advance exactly what support may be available to you for the various tasks of typing, photocopying, production of study instruments and the project report. At all levels of research nowadays, however, word-processing skills are seen as the self-sufficient answer to many of these problems and an increasing number of students learn word-processing during their courses.

A quite different but equally important consideration is ethics. If your project is in any way – physically or emotionally – invasive and potentially affective to the physical or emotional status of a human subject, you must seek approval from a recognized ethical committee, operative in your study location. For a thoughtful discussion of ethical issues, Sim's (1989) paper on methodology and morality in physio-therapy research provides excellent advice and information for any health student. Some key issues are also covered by Cook (1976), including informed consent, providing information to participants and the rights of patients and clients in participating in research. Quite apart from the philosophical dimension of ethics, it is also a highly political area within health, with medical ethics dominant in the practice of ethical committees.

Many of these committees grind exceedingly slowly and sometimes too slowly to give clearance in time for a student project. It is worth checking out the local situation before committing yourself to a project which needs ethical approval. An increasing number of committees nowadays do schedule themselves to provide a service for student projects, or they delegate such authority to educational institutions.

A related issue is the extent to which the research results should be made available and on what terms – though such concerns tend to arise mainly when research is directly commissioned and paid for, which is relatively rare for student projects.

During the progress of the research you will need to communicate with various people about your study, and perhaps negotiate access, particularly if you want to do fieldwork outside your educational institution. Short letters explaining the purpose and remit of your study, and its likely demands on them should be given to study subjects. Letters should also be sent to any other professional staff who work in your study location, as well as their line managers. Protocol is particularly important in National Health Service (NHS) settings: you will need formal permission to carry out your study, and this can take a good deal of time, especially if your request for access has to be referred to a committee – so you should start early.

If you need further cooperation – perhaps from hospital-based professional staff – it is worth asking for a brief meeting to explain your needs. Even though your study may not directly involve local medical practitioners, it is advisable to ensure that they are fully informed about projects in their area.

You may be requested to give assurances of confidentiality either by those whom you are studying or by the officers of the institution in which your study is located. It is usual to provide such assurances in writing and to have available an account of the steps you intend to take to achieve confidentiality. The most usual techniques are the use of codes instead of names or the replacement of real names of people and places with imaginary names. Physical security of data and other research materials is also an important aspect of confidentiality. Not every project requires confidentiality, but if you do give assurances, it is essential that you can guarantee the promises made.

Construction of instruments

In this same period, you will need to be working on the construction or selection of your study instruments such as forms for recording data, questionnaires, attitude scales or physical equipment. Those from whom you seek ethical approval or access will sometimes wish to see copies of your material before giving their agreement to your project.

Chapter 3 discusses some widely-used techniques, but whatever kind of instrument you use, you should be able to defend its validity and reliability, a matter considered further in Chapter 4. Having drafted your instrument, it is often useful to try it out on a friend before proceeding to the pilot study.

Pilot study and data collection

The next stage is to carry out a pilot study in which the study instruments are tried out on a small group of subjects who meet the criteria for inclusion in your study – these pilot subjects should not then be included in the main study. The main purpose is to identify flaws in its design and to improve the instrument for the study proper. Tests for reliability and validity can sometimes also be carried out on the pilot data, providing that the instrument, as piloted, turns out to be sound.

In both the pilot and the main study, it is important to ensure that all documentation used in data collection is clearly labelled and dated, especially when codes rather than names are used to protect confidentiality. Data should be kept in a very secure place, not only for confidentiality, but because the effort of collecting data is often very substantial and it can be heart-breaking if precious data are lost or stolen. If possible, you should keep a secure copy of all data.

Electronic data collection is becoming increasingly popular. This usually entails the direct input of data onto a computer as they are collected. An example of this would be a telephone survey with respondents' answers being punched directly into a computer through a keyboard, or a piece of electronic equipment measuring some physiological parameter which transmits the result directly to a linked computer file. Such techniques not only save time, but reduce experimental error in the stage of transferring data from the collection source to the computer or other analysis source.

Data preparation and analysis

If automatic data input is not possible, you should prepare (code) the data and enter them into a computer. There are only two circumstances in which you should not use a computer to analyse research data: first, if the data are qualitative it may not be possible or helpful to computerize though software is now available for certain types of qualitative analysis such as Ethnograph, TAP (Text Analysis Package). Second, if the study is small-scale – fewer than 20 subjects and five variables – it may not be worth spending the time needed to prepare it for the computer. Chapters 5 to 8 deal in detail with the coding and analysis of quantitative data, and Chapter 9 covers qualitative analysis.

Whether you are using a computer or not, it is important to have thought through a plan of analysis in the early stages of formulating a study. The plan should not be left to emerge in an *ad hoc* way. Useful questions to ask include:

- What analysis is required to test the research hypotheses?
- Are the data at the appropriate level of measurement for the planned statistical tests? (If statistical advice is to be sought, this should be done at the design stage, before any data are collected.)

During the period of analysis, careful, neat and dated working notes should be kept. Computer output will probably be automatically dated, but it should also be filed in chronological order. You should throw away computer output containing mistakes, and file only that which is correct and which will contribute to the final report.

Presentation of findings

If your project is part of a course, the only requirement may be for you to provide a report for the educational institution concerned. It is good practice and good manners, however, to provide a short summary of your findings for anyone who has helped you in carrying out the research, and it may smooth the path for future students. Thank-you letters or cards may also be appreciated at this point.

Many courses now require an oral presentation of the research project as well as a written presentation. Chapter 10 covers in detail the skills required for oral and written presentations.

Although it is not normally expected that a student project will be of publication standard, exceptional projects are published, sometimes in collaboration with the academic supervisor. This is a different kind of presentation and must follow the guidelines set by the journal to which the paper is to be submitted. You should seek your supervisor's advice and help if you think your project may be good enough to publish.

Evaluation

At the end of the research cycle comes the important matter of evaluation. Constraints on your time and resources may have shaped the project you did, and you may well have ideas about how it could be developed in the future. But no research is ever perfect, and most of us can see, on reflection and with hindsight, that we could have done some part of it differently or better. This is an essential part of the learning process and many research teachers encourage students to produce a brief evaluation within the project presentation or report.

A key skill in developing the contribution of research to professional practice, is to evaluate other people's research and, where appropriate, apply it. The final chapter of this book discusses evaluation both of one's own research and of that of others.

The framework for research has now been described. It has been presented as a series of steps, but it is important to remember that the steps are interconnected. The framework can be conceptualized as a spiral aiming upwards, but with interaction both along and up and down the spiral, as illustrated in Fig. 2.1. Models apart, the process of research is no more – and no less – than a logical framework for problem solving. We used earlier the analogy of a 'whodunnit', but there is an analogy much closer to the day-to-day business of professional practice and we now need to consider this in some detail.

Care processes and research

Chapter 1 pointed out that a number of the health care professions, and nursing in particular, have been concerned in recent years to develop theory to underpin their professional practice. Before this, however, some of these professions had developed systematic frame-

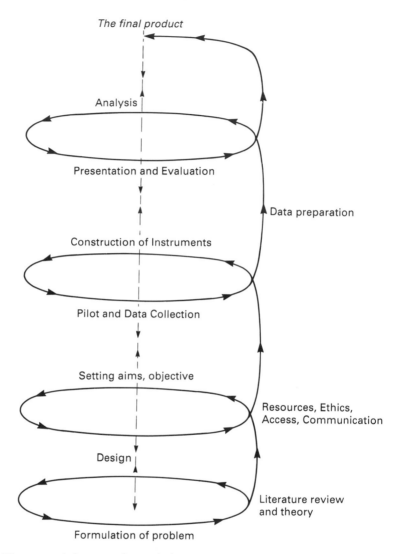

The final product

Analysis

Presentation and Evaluation

Data preparation

Construction of Instruments

Pilot and Data Collection

Setting aims, objective

Resources, Ethics,
Access, Communication

Design

Literature review
and theory

Formulation of problem

Fig. 2.1   The research framework: a spiral.

works for the delivery of care. These frameworks are conceptually very close to the framework for research described earlier.

The nursing process in particular has attracted great attention amongst researchers, but has also gained considerable credibility with practitioners: it is now standard practice in most UK hospitals and nursing documentation is often based on it. The nursing process is the underlying scheme which gives direction to nursing care. Most writers, including Stanton, Paul and Reeves (1980) agree that four phases or components are necessary: assessment; nursing diagnosis or identification of a problem; intervention or implementation; and evaluation. The process is continuous and cyclical so that, as a patient's episode of care progresses, there is reassessment and the cycle is repeated again, through to evaluation. The nursing process is generally recognized to be applicable within a variety of models or theories of nursing.

A very similar framework is recognized formally within occupational therapy and is termed 'the occupational therapy process'. Robertson (1988) described it as beginning with:

> 'a systematic collating of pertinent information, which may be collected by consulting case notes, conducting an interview, recording observations or using standardized or non-standardized tests. Following this initial data-gathering process, the information is summarized to identify a problem list which then enables the occupational therapist to design a treatment plan'. Robertson notes the comparability of this process to research.

Physiotherapy has not adopted the term 'physiotherapy process' but the same framework is recognized to underpin the delivery of physiotherapy care. Pratt (1989) observes, for example:

> 'Thus the individual patient's treatment may be seen in essence as a process of deductive reasoning (physiotherapy assessment), experiment (treatment – though it is not "experimental" in the sense of being previously untried or unpredictable) and induction (conclusion about the effects of the treatment). The observant and thoughtful practitioner may constantly re-examine the bases of her professional practice by such investigation and analysis'.

It can be seen then that the health professions in developing their philosophical framework for care have evolved processes which draw from and closely mirror the process of research. So far, however, there is little overt recognition of this vast common ground in the literature of any of the health professions – indeed the general impression given is that these frameworks have been independently developed.

If, however, the commonality of ideas in care processes described above is represented graphically, as in Fig. 2.2, a spiral of care processes in health care professions can be shown. By comparing this spiral with that of the research framework in Fig. 2.1, the strong analogies between the processes of care and research are easily identified.

The assessment stage equates to the formulation of a research problem, each process drawing upon existing evidence to obtain a clearer picture of what is needed. The diagnosis and care planning stage is comparable to the design stage of research and the setting of aims and objectives. Clinical intervention or implementation of care is likewise analogous to the data-collection stage of research, and in both pro-

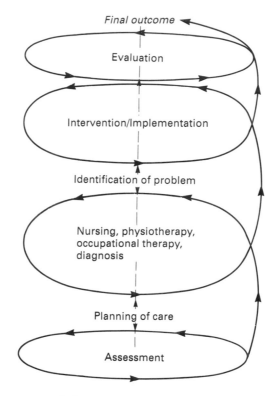

Fig. 2.2 The care process: a spiral.

cesses the final stage is evaluation. The spiral presentation of both processes represents progression up through stages, where you may, however, slide down the middle of the spiral to reconsider an earlier linked stage, or even begin the process again. In practice, the time-scale for the care process is, of course, very different from that of the average research project. But the conceptual similarities make a very powerful case for practice to be research based, not only in the short term, an idea which is already acknowledged in most health professions, but in the long term.

Discussion points

1. Choose a journal article from the best UK journal in your field. Identify the stages of the research framework. Were they all covered? If not, should they have been?
2. Choose an area of practice in your profession and identify a clinical procedure. Discuss a research framework for the investigation of the effectiveness of this procedure.

References

Cook, S.W. (1976) Ethical Issues in the Conduct of Research in Social Relations. In C. Selltiz, L. Wrightsman & S.W. Cook (eds) *Research Methods in Social Relations*. Holt-Saunders International Editions.

Pratt, J.W. (1989) Towards a Philosophy of Physiotherapy. *Physiotherapy*, Vol. 75, No. 2, 114–120.

Robertson, L. (1988) Qualitative Research Methods in Occupational Therapy. *British Journal of Occupational Therapy*, Vol. 51, No. 10, 344–6.

Sim, J. (1989) Methodology and Morality in Physiotherapy Research. *Physiotherapy*, Vol. 75, No. 4, 237–43.

Stanton, M., Paul, C. & Reeves, J. (1980) An Overview of the Nursing Process. In J. George (ed.) *Nursing Theories: the base for professional nursing practice*. Prentice-Hall International Editions.

Chapter 3
A Taxonomy of Research Designs

For students in the health care professions, a foray into research design must feel like being offered fifty-seven choices, all of them equally incomprehensible. The wide choice of research methods simply reflects, however, the eclectic disciplinary base of the health care professions. For in drawing from the traditional sciences and their evolution into medicine, and from psychology and sociology, the health professions are developing research tools that are based on an exceptionally wide range of methodological approaches.

This chapter will try to place these approaches within a taxonomy of research classifications that will help in understanding their contributions and their strengths and weaknesses relative to one another. But one thing must be borne in mind. Research is a creative activity and it is not possible or desirable to pigeon-hole every known technique. So within the taxonomy being developed, there will always be counter-examples. But this taxonomy is a fair representation of the main body of health research practice, and its purpose is to help health students to grapple with a very diffuse area of study, by providing some classifications and pathways.

Research traditions and three types of research

Underlying all research approaches, there are two main philosophical traditions. Positivism, sometimes called naturalism or the orthodox scientific approach, is the philosophical base of traditional scientific research, and consists of systematic investigation mounted within an objective reality and carried out in a controlled way. In contrast, the phenomenological tradition, sometimes called the interpretative approach, emphasizes the human experience as unique and self-determining and is based on the study of individuals as they create and shape their own experiences.

The philosophical assumptions of both scientific and social scientific research continue to generate heated debate – see, for example, Cook and Campbell (1979), or Yearley (1984). In particular, the positivistic approach has been heavily challenged in this century by ideas of Darwinian evolution and Einsteinian relativity, as well as by Freudian notions of rationalization. You may therefore find it helpful in moving towards a choice of research design to think about your project from

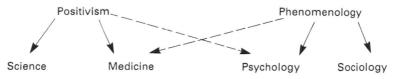

Fig. 3.1   Key disciplines contributing to health research and their philosophical bases.

perspectives which are both positivistic and phenomenological – this term, used in its broadest sense, encompasses a range of perspectives underpinning qualitative research.

These two traditions should not be seen as competing, but as complementary. The positivist approach makes excellent sense if your study concerns inanimate objects in laboratories. The validity of the phenomenological approach in the study of human emotions or attitudes is equally sound intuitively. Between these extreme examples lie a range of real life research problems which may be amenable to interpretation by one or other approach or, in the case of many health research problems, by both. The effect of a drug on a human being may well be amenable to experimental investigation in the scientific tradition – though, as we shall see, ethical issues will be critical – but the psycho-social effects of that same drug are likely to be better investigated using a phenomenological approach.

The first issue to address in research design is what your belief is about the philosophical foundation of your proposed project? The answer to this question will begin to move you along the road to choosing a methodology, because of the relationship of philosophical traditions to key disciplines which underpin health research. Figure 3.1 illustrates some of these relationships.

The four disciplines chosen to illustrate these issues are not, of course, as distinct in practice as they appear here. Medicine draws heavily on science and has evolved its own sciences; and sociology and psychology are often classified as social sciences. But there are identifiable bodies of research associated with these four areas. Scientific research draws clearly and probably exclusively on positivism as a base. Medical research also draws mainly from that tradition, but has a dotted line connecting it to phenomenology indicating that a minor influence in medical research comes from the phenomeno-logical tradition. In contrast, sociology is mainly influenced by the phenomenological tradition, as is psychology, though the latter also has a positivist tradition, mainly within experimental psychology.

By considering the appropriate philosophical basis for your project, you are veering towards one or other end of the disciplinary spectrum. This in turn influences your choice of research methodology because research methodologies have evolved around particular disciplines. There are three types of research design which pertain to the health

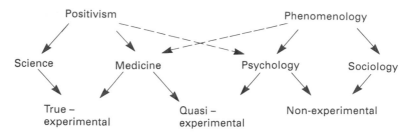

Fig. 3.2   Research methodologies and key disciplines in health research.

care professions: the true-experimental, the quasi-experimental and the non-experimental. Figure 3.2 shows the relationship of these to the key disciplines, and thus extends Fig. 3.1.

Experimental research offers the greater control of the research to the researcher, and the true-experimental approach has three characteristics: manipulation by the researcher of at least some of the study subjects, for example, by giving them a treatment or intervention; control over the experimental situation by the researcher; and giving every subject an equal chance of selection (randomization) in assigning study subjects to a control group or an experimental group. The quasi-experimental approach resembles the true experiment except that it either lacks the characteristic of randomization or else it lacks a control group. The non-experimental approach covers other kinds of research where manipulation is impossible or inappropriate and/or the true-experimental and quasi-experimental approaches are impractical or inappropriate.

We shall return to these three approaches and consider them, and their constituent research designs in more detail. At this point, their relationship with the key disciplines as illustrated in Fig. 3.2, will be further explored.

The true experiment is used by almost all scientific researchers, and is also widely used by medical researchers. The other occasional users of the true-experimental method are experimental psychologists. An example of the true experiment is the randomized controlled trial (RCT) where subjects are allocated randomly to control and experimental groups, and measurements are taken before and after an intervention.

The quasi-experimental method is used a good deal in medical research and by social scientists. An example of this would be a clinical trial in which a control group would not be ethically appropriate because it might deprive its members of an innovative treatment.

The non-experimental approach is the one most used by sociologists and is also widely used by other social scientists. Within this class of methods there are a wide range of research designs including surveys, observational studies (both participant and non-participant), ethnographic and anthropological studies, documentary studies and secondary analysis of data. These will be discussed in more detail later in this chapter.

Recognizing the links between key disciplines and research approaches, as shown in Fig. 3.2, helps to explain the prevalence of some research approaches within certain health professions and indicates the potential breadth of choice in methodology. Of the health care professions, physiotherapy and radiography are probably closest to the left-hand side of Fig. 3.2, being strongly oriented to the sciences in their initial curricula, and adopting a mainly medical health model. The influence of underlying models of health on methodology choice is often not appreciated, and indeed is often not explicitly recognized in teaching research to health students. In the same way that the philosophy of positivism is criticized for being reductionist (reducing human experience to only the few concepts under investigation), the medical model, at its most limiting, reduces the patient or client to the status of the afflicted body part.

This may be perfectly appropriate and acceptable for certain health research problems, but for many others, the class of techniques grouped towards the right hand side of Fig. 3.2 is more appropriate. In practice, nursing and occupational therapy – professions which are more committed to social models of health – tend to use non-experimental research methodologies much more often than physiotherapy or radiography. But the main determinant should always be the nature of the problem.

In summary, it is worth considering two issues at an early stage of your research: the appropriate philosophical base for your study and the health model underpinning your study. The consideration of these issues may lead you to either the left or to the right of Fig. 3.2. You should also be aware of disciplinary influences on your choice of category of methodology. The important thing is to be able to defend your choice of methodology and its philosophical implications, its implications for an underlying model of health and its disciplinary orientation with regard to the actual problem to be addressed.

Is the scientific approach 'purer'?

The historical dominance of the scientific approach is evident in most writings on health research. Even the labelling of the three main traditions implies that the true-experimental is the best, the quasi-experimental is the next best and if all else fails the non-experimental has to suffice. Many reputable texts perpetuate the view that the true experimental approach is 'pure' and the social science approach is less rigorous. For example, Oyster, Hanten and Llorens (1987) assert that their book on research for the health science professional 'presents formal scientific research principles. The ideal, naturally, would be to employ perfect techniques through every research project. This is not always (or even often) possible?'. They go on to praise the 'hard' sciences for their 'very close adherence to the purest of research principles' and then observe that 'the social sciences, such as psychology and sociology lag behind in the precision with which the purest research principles may be employed?'.

This does not bear examination. All research is prone to flaws and all forms of measurement contain error. In principle, there may be as much potential for error in any scientific measuring instrument, as there is in any technique of measurement used in social science. In both traditions absolute values are unknown and perhaps unknowable. Good practice in research seeks to control and reduce measurement error to a minimum. This is often easier in the true experimental situation, but not necessarily more successful. As the philosopher and scientist Bunge (1967) said: 'Science has not the monopoly of truth but only the monopoly of the means for checking truth and enhancing it'. The development of methods over the past two decades for enhancing rigour in the social sciences makes it possible to argue that science no longer has even this monopoly today.

The true-experimental approach does have clear advantages in well-defined and focused studies of cause and effect. The true-experimental design offers the most powerful tool for establishing cause and effect in these circumstances – but in health research such circumstances are relatively rare, so this class of designs is of more limited value in practice than might at first appear.

A major source of misunderstandings about 'hard' and 'soft' data and their relation to research methodologies, is sloppy thinking about quantitative and qualitative data. There is a widespread belief that the experimental approach produces only quantitative data (usually numbers) and the non-experimental approach produces qualitative data (usually words). It is mistaken. In theory both quantitative and qualitative data could be legitimately collected across the entire spectrum of research methods shown in Fig. 3.2. In practice it is unusual for the clinical trial to be measured qualitatively and few historical studies, for example, tend to be measured quantitatively, but, in principle, both research designs could use either quantitative or qualitative measurement or both. Equally, the survey, widely used by researchers in a range of disciplines, generally generates both quantitative and qualitative data.

Today, the best professional researchers in health increasingly regard these different traditions as complementary, not competing, and they use the term triangulation to describe the concurrent use of more than one approach to a research problem. Students with a limited time-scale for their projects will be unlikely to need or be able to manage more than one method, but your choice of methodology should recognize that all three approaches are of equal value.

Other fallacies with regard to research methods concern the validity and reliability of research. These topics are covered in the next chapter, but for present purposes, validity can be regarded as the extent to which the research is measuring what we think it is measuring; reliability refers to the stability of measurement. Some writers suggest that there are intrinsic differences among the three main methodological approaches (Fig. 3.2) in validity and reliability, whereas in fact the difference lies merely in the ease with which these characteristics can be assessed. It is much easier to devise ways of assessing validity and reliability in a true experiment than in a documentary investigation. But to go on to suggest that the true experiment is thus preferable is highly questionable. If the true experiment is the correct choice of method because of the philosophical basis of the project, its disciplinary orientation and its underlying model of health, then it is a bonus that validity and reliability may be relatively easy to assess. If the true experiment is not appropriate, then its general advantages are irrelevant.

The moral is: do not put the cart before the horse. Choose the most appropriate research design and then use every rigorous means possible to achieve validity and reliability.

Research designs in detail

The three main methodological approaches can now be discussed in more detail. Figure 3.3 shows a range of methods within each approach. Again this classification is one of convenience: it represents the main practice within health research but several of these constituent designs could, in theory, be used within more than one of the three approaches.

True-experimental	Quasi-experimental	Non-experimental
Randomized controlled trial (after only)	Non-equivalent controls	Survey
Randomized controlled (before and after)	Own controls (crossover, Latin square)	Observational
Solomon four	Cohort designs	Consultative
Factorial	Time-series designs	Historical
Matched pairs		Documentary
		Secondary analyses
		Case-studies

Fig. 3.3   Research designs within the three main approaches.

True-experimental designs

The purpose of the true experiment is almost always to establish cause and effect – or as it is more commonly put in health research, treatment/intervention and outcome. The true experiment has three characteristics:

Manipulation

In which the researcher does something to at least some of the study subjects. The variable, or factor, being manipulated through treatment or intervention is usually called the independent variable. The research outcome is often observed on the variable or factor which is affected, the dependent variable. For example, the dose of a blood-pressure drug is the independent variable affecting the subject's blood pressure, the dependent variable.

Control

In which the experiment is controlled by the researcher and the effect of the treatment on the study group (sometimes called the experimental group) is contrasted to that of a comparable control group which does not receive the treatment or intervention.

Randomization

In which study subjects are randomly allocated to the experimental or the control group, i.e. an objective process of allocation is used, not dependent on the decision of the researcher or the study subject. Chapter 4 describes how this is done. A number of research designs within the true-experimental approach will now be examined.

In using these research designs, it is advisable to consider the criteria which render a subject eligible for the trial. You may, for example want to exclude very young and very old people, so you might state that all subjects should be aged 18 to 65. It is also advisable to set criteria for any other variable which might skew your trial such as, for example, health status. For example, in studying blood pressure, you may want to exclude people who are very hypertensive and deal with those within a defined range of blood pressures. Or you may wish to exclude people with coterminous medical problems which could mask or confuse the effects of the trial. People may exclude themselves, of course, and this as well as other ethical issues will be discussed later.

Randomized controlled trial (after only)

This is the simplest form of clinical trial within the true-experimental category. It involves the random assignment of the study subjects to an experimental group and a control group. Fixed criteria will have determined their entry to the trial. The treatment or intervention under trial is then given to the experimental group, and the control group either receive a standard treatment or a placebo treatment (one which appears in its outward administration the same as the experimental treatment, but which has no clinical effect, e.g. a dummy pill). The dependent variable is measured in both groups and the effect of the treatment or intervention thus determined. For example, a new blood-pressure drug could be given to the experimental group, a standard drug given to the control group and the blood pressures of both groups then compared.

The main technical concern about this kind of trial lies in ensuring that the two groups are really comparable at the start of the trial. If the randomization has achieved its purpose this should be the case; but randomization is not always effective. This design, because it measures the 'after only' effect, assumes that the randomization achieved comparability of groups.

Randomized controlled trial (before and after)

This trial is very similar to the after-only type but it deals formally with the issues of the initial comparability of groups by taking measurements of the dependent variable before instituting the intervention. In this way the initial comparability of the groups can be measured; otherwise the trial operates in the same way as for the after-only trial, by comparing the values of the dependent variable for the control and experimental groups after the treatment or intervention has occurred.

A possible technical flaw in this design is that pre-testing may influence the results of the treatment or intervention and thus contaminate the experiment.

Solomon four group design

The Solomonic wisdom of this trial consists in its combining the after-only randomized controlled trial (RCT), and the before-and-after RCT to produce a four-group design. Subjects are allocated randomly to four groups, two of which are observed before the treatment/intervention, which is given to one and not to the other; the other two are measured only after the treatment/intervention, which is given to one and not to the other. This design overcomes the areas of possible technical concern with the two previous designs, though the use of four groups obviously becomes relatively time-consuming and expensive.

Matched pairs design

The matched pairs design is conceptually close to the RCT designs. It takes a different approach to achieve comparability of experimental and control groups by constructing each from pairs of subjects who are matched in specified ways. One subject from the pair goes into the experimental group and the other goes into the control group and this allocation is made randomly.

Subjects are matched on variables which are not directly under study but might affect the experiment. For example in the study of a new blood-pressure drug, we might match for age and sex, both of which are known to affect blood pressure. Matching for sex is straightforward, but for continuous variables like age, a band for matching should be defined. It may not be easy to find a match of age exactly 47, but if a match is defined as within the band 45–50, it may be more feasible. However it becomes difficult in practice to match on more than three variables.

This is a powerful design which, if analysed appropriately, removes a good deal of the variation among subjects which can cloud the results of a trial.

Factorial designs

So far we have considered experiments where only one factor, the independent variable, is being manipulated at a time. In many research problems we want to look at two or three factors simultaneously. The factorial design enables the researcher to isolate the individual effects of each factor and the effect of their interaction with each other. A hypothetical example might involve a study of the effects of a drug and a weight-reducing diet on blood pressure. Three different doses of the drug and the presence and absence of the diet might be included in the experiment, shown in Table 3.1.

Table 3.1   Design for a 2 × 3 factorial experiment.

		Dietary Regime	
		Reducing Diet (A)	Normal (B)
Drug	Level 1	Level 1, Diet A	Level 1, Diet B
Dosage	Level 2	Level 2, Diet A	Level 2, Diet B
	Level 3	Level 3, Diet A	Level 3, Diet B

Each of the six experimental groups in Table 3.1 would have the combination of drug and diet regime described. This is called a 2 × 3 factorial experiment with two levels of the diet and three levels of the drug. This design can be extended to cope with three or more simultaneous factors. Whilst there is not always an identifiable control group in the same sense as for the RCT designs, the control characteristic is achieved through the comparisons which are possible through this design – which may, however, include a placebo or standard treatment.

These five designs constitute probably the most commonly used and potentially valuable designs for health research, in the true-experimental category. There are others – research design is a creative activity and every day new variations are developed.

Strengths and limitations of true-experimental designs

The main strength of the true experiment is its power to establish causality. In a laboratory context, where the study is of inanimate objects, there is no doubt that these methods are very powerful. But they have some serious limitations in the context of health research in natural settings with human subjects.

We noted earlier that models of health were an important consideration in choosing a research design. The true experiment is most effective within a medical model. If, for example, you consider hypertension within a social model of health, all kinds of confounding factors come into play – such as social class or socio-economic status – in explaining cause and effect. The true-experimental approach is best used for physically oriented investigations which are very well-defined and focused.

Many writers have noted ethical concerns about the use of these methods in health research. In essence they centre round the morality of withholding the experimental treatment or intervention from the control group, or withholding the standard treatment from the experimental group. Are subjects receiving less-than-optimal treatment as a result?

Most authors advise that it must be ethically possible to give both the experimental and the control group any of the treatments involved. There must therefore be no a priori suspicion that any treatment could harm a subject, nor that any treatment is a priori *known* to be superior. It is usual to compare new interventions or treatments against standard interventions or treatments. Sim (1989) provides a comprehensive account of ethical issues relating to the use of RCTs in physiotherapy research, and his analysis holds good for any health professional using this method.

Another concern about the use of RCT is the contamination of results through awareness on the part of the researcher or the subject of the nature of the study. The Hawthorne Effect, where study subjects' performance is affected because they are aware of being under observation, is a well-established phenomenon. This is often overcome in RCTs by using a double-blind approach where neither the researcher nor the subject knows whether the subject has been in the experimental or the control group at the point of measuring the outcome of the intervention. This approach raises further ethical questions, however, about the level of information involved in informed consent, and can be difficult to arrange in practice.

A final limitation of the true-experimental approach in health research is that many key variables in health simply cannot be manipulated – for example, social class, blood type and age. Sometimes a variable can, in theory, be manipulated, but it may be unethical to do so – asking an experimental group to take up smoking in order to examine its physiological effects would not be acceptable. So in practice, many health research problems cannot, for pragmatic, ethical or technical reasons be addressed through the true experiment. But for those problems which do fit the conditions for the true experiment, it is a valuable and powerful class of design, particularly in clinical research.

Quasi-experimental designs

The form of the quasi-experimental design looks very similar to that of the true experiment but lacks either the characteristic of randomisation or of control.

Trials with non-equivalent controls

When randomization is not or cannot be used to construct the experimental and control groups, there is a danger that the groups are not equivalent or comparable. This often arises in health research in natural settings. Say, for example, that you wished to evaluate the effect of a new shift system on the staff of a hospital. Since all the staff will have been put on the new shift, you will need to find a similar group of staff elsewhere not on this shift system for the purposes of comparison. This design functions best when pre-test measures are made to establish comparability of the groups on key variables, before the intervention or treatment takes place for the experimental group. Provided that initial comparability is established, this design is almost as rigorous as the before-and-after RCT, even though it has not been possible to randomize it.

Trials where the group is its own control

These designs do not use separate experimental and control groups – rather, the subjects effectively act as their own controls. This design is very effective in removing variation to do with individual subject differences. By comparing before and after measures for the same subject, it can be assumed that most things stay the same – age, weight, social class, blood type – other than the feature(s) under study. The problem in this design is to do with knock-on effects, since the subjects receive more than one treatment, being subjected to both the placebo or standard intervention and to the experimental intervention(s).

The design is best used when there are no such knock-on effects. But even then, causality is harder to establish through this design than through a randomized controlled trial. With the own-control design, it is difficult to be certain that some factor other than the experimental factor is not responsible for the effects observed. In the blood-pressure example an apparent improved blood-pressure level on the new drug could be due to some other factor, perhaps a social or psychological factor, prevalent at the same time.

Provided such concerns can be taken into account, it is a useful design. One variant is the cross-over design. Here, half the subjects first have the experimental treatment, the rest having the standard or placebo treatment; they each then cross over to the other treatment. The latin square design simply extends this principle to three or more treatments or interventions. Hamilton (1974) provides detail of cross-over and latin square designs.

Cohort designs

Cohort designs are a variant on the non-equivalent control design where the control group is another group with similar characteristics. For example, in a study of the effects of a new curriculum on health students, a previous group on the old curriculum could be used to compare with the next group on the new curriculum. The strength of this design again depends on the extent to which the groups are similar in key characteristics – in this example, they would need to be of comparable educational entry-level, age and previous relevant experience.

There are various other types of quasi-experimental design – for example, the interrupted time-series design, useful when the effect of an intervention changes over time; and regression-discontinuity designs, where assignment of subjects to groups is based on some pre-intervention measure. A comprehensive account of quasi-experimental designs and their analysis is provided by Cook and Campbell (1979).

At this point, three other designs should be briefly described; these, though falling technically into the category of quasi-experiments, are weak designs and therefore not recommended. The first uses non-equivalent groups with no pre-testing; the second uses only one group (with no control) and no randomization, and only post-test observations are taken; the third uses one experimental group with both pre- and post-testing. All of these designs are open to many interpretations and are inadequate in trying to establish causality. Cook and Campbell (1979) label these as pre-experimental designs and recommend their use only in establishing preliminary hypotheses.

Strengths and limitations of quasi-experiments

Quasi-experiments are often the most useful designs in those aspects of health research where the true experiment cannot be used for practical or ethical reasons. If carefully conducted, the quasi-experiment offers comparable rigour. It is, however, less powerful than the true experiment in establishing causality. Interpreting the quasi-experiment must be undertaken with caution as there can be alternative explanations for observed effects which are external to the intervention carried out.

The quasi-experiment design also raises many ethical problems. While it overcomes some ethical objections to the RCT in certain circumstances, there is no point in jumping from the frying pan into the fire. Designs where subjects are their own controls raise the question of whether it is ever morally right to remove a successful treatment in order to institute another, perhaps less successful one.

A major strength of quasi-experimental designs in health care research is their suitability for use in natural settings. They thus provide an attractive blend of objective rigour and subjective reality to a research study.

Non-experimental designs

There remain a vast spectrum of research designs, all widely used with the social sciences and highly appropriate for many health research problems, particularly within a social model of health (though badly served by the label 'non-experimental'). In non-experimental research there is no manipulation of variables by the researcher, so that the issue of control, so central to other types of design, does not arise: the study is carried out in natural settings and phenomena are observed as they occur. Non-experimental research is carried out when variables cannot or should not be manipulated, but it may be used when causality is being studied or in projects which are purely or largely descriptive.

Studies of causality in the non-experimental tradition are called *ex post facto* (deriving from the fact), since the cause being investigated occurred in the past. If the effect has also happened in the past the study is called retrospective; if the effect will occur (or not) in the future the study is called prospective; and if the study is not concerned with cause and effect, but provides an informative account, it is known as descriptive.

Some of the most commonly-used research methods in non-experimental research are surveys, observation, consultation, historical-documentary and secondary data analysis.

Surveys

Surveys are very widely used particularly in exploring attitudes and behaviours. A survey can be conducted through either face-to-face interviews or postal questionnaires. In both cases the wording, formulation and presentation of questions are critical to the rigour of the technique. For a comprehensive account of the techniques of designing surveys, it is hard to better the classic text by Moser and Kalton (1972).

Face-to-face interviews require special skills, are time-consuming, and may sometimes make undue demands on the patience of both the interviewer and the interviewee. Their strength is in the opportunity they provide to probe vague responses, and to follow up unexpected or interesting ones. Response rates are usually good, as respondents are more likely to accede to a face-to-face request for cooperation than a written one. A skilled researcher can use an interview to note other factors about the environment of the respondent – housing, for example – which may provide useful supporting information. There are considerable methodological benefits in one person doing all the interviewing as this eliminates possibe bias from different interviewers. For student projects, however, the time required may be excessive.

The postal survey is one of the cheapest methods of research and is very suitable for many – though not all – health topics. Questions must be fairly straightforward as the researcher is not present to elucidate. The main weakness is that response rates tend to be low but this can be overcome by such strategies as follow-up questionnaires. The postal survey is manageable, fairly quick and not costly and for these reasons is an excellent choice of method for a student research project. An increasingly popular alternative is the telephone survey, which is the fastest technique of all for data collection, but can be correspondingly imprecise.

Observation

Observational designs are invaluable in carrying out clinical research in natural settings. There are two forms: participant and non-participant observation. The first is when the researcher is part of the group of people being studied. Typically, participant observers use qualitative methods to record events and behaviour in great detail but in a necessarily unstructured way. The non-participant observer is present in the role of researcher and tends to record information in a more structured fashion, but to get less of it. However, in principle both qualitative and quantitative data may be collected within any observational technique.

There are sometimes concerns about the possible lack of objectivity of the participant observer, who may become emotionally involved and thus biased about events or people; or who may not be able to sample representatively the events and behaviours being observed. Against that, is the potential depth and quality of the information provided and the insights that may be obtained by a skilled and sympathetic researcher. It is the major method of data collection in qualitative research and has considerable credibility in that tradition. For a fuller discussion of participant observation techniques see Polit and Hungler (1989).

Non-participant observation, if based on a well-validated and reliable instrument, provides a sound method of observing clinical practice and is thus widely used in health research. For a fuller treatment of this topic too see Polit and Hungler (1989). A particularly useful technique is activity analysis (Reid, 1986) which enables the researcher to obtain a continuous, representative profile of activity in a health care setting.

Consultative methods

Consultative methods use either written or verbal communication with subjects to assist the construction of policy or the evaluation of policy or events. The processes are usually iterative, consisting of continuing interaction between the researcher and the study participants. An example of such methods is the Delphi technique (Reid, 1989), which has considerable potential for eliciting professional consensus on a range of issues. A fuller description of the Delphi method appears in Chapter 9.

Historical-documentary methods

More literary and descriptive methods are used to investigate past events, and their value will depend on the extent and quality of the acquisition and analysis of relevant information. Primary sources include documents, relics and oral testimony or written firsthand accounts. Secondary sources provide information about the topic but are not based on direct knowledge or experience. In this method, authenticity – sometimes called external criticism – is important; as is the researcher's evaluation of the intrinsic value of the material, the internal criticism.

Secondary data analysis

The analysis of secondary data is the easiest design of all, since someone else has already done the hard work! It is included here because it can be a very sound way of investigating a topic within a limited time-scale, provided you do not claim originality for the entire effort. In particular, students can benefit from secondary analysis of data collected by their lecturers. As long as the formulation, aims and objectives of the project are themselves original, there is no reason not to test hypotheses through secondary data and then proceed to original analyses and draw new conclusions.

Strengths and limitations of non-experimental designs

Non-experimental designs are particularly valuable in studies which explore social dimensions of health, as they enable the investigation of social phenomena in natural settings. This type of design also tends to raise fewer difficult ethical issues than the experimental designs, and may thus provide ethically acceptable ways of studying human subjects, when this is otherwise difficult to achieve.

Non-experimental designs are powerful for descriptive studies and have particular strengths in the investigation of qualitative issues and in research with the aim of generating hypotheses. They are less valuable when the main purpose is to establish cause and effect.

Terminology

Finally, you will find terms used by various writers to mean different things. The case-study, for example, to a management student, may mean the story of a particular firm, or an episode in its history; but in health research it is an observational design carried out in a specific location, using either participant or non-participant observation. It usually occurs within a non-experimental design, but could be used in an experimental design as well. Similarly, the longitudinal study and the cross-sectional study generally fall within the non-experimental *ex post facto* category. The longitudinal study follows the study subject over a period of time, and data are collected periodically, whereas the cross-sectional study requires a single collection of data at one particular point.

Figure 3.1 offers a working taxonomy of research design types – with the caveat that they represent the main practices within health research and would not hold good for every single study ever done. Its purpose is simply to help you to narrow down and focus your search for a suitable research design. The suggested strategy is that you should first consider philosophical underpinnings and models of health. For example, are you going to manipulate a variable or observe things as they happen; can you randomize and control? Addressing questions like these should lead you to choose one of the three categories of design in Table 3.1. You should then consider each method within the chosen category. It is then down to judgement and preference. If you follow this process you should then be able to defend logically the choice of design for your particular research problem.

Discussion points

1. Choose a published research paper in a journal in your professional area. Identify the implicit or explicit model of health, the category of research design used and evaluate the appropriateness of the design of the problem.
2. As a hypothetical exercise, consider the use of different categories of design in the evaluation of professional practice.

References

Bunge, M. (1967) Scientific Research I: The Search for System. *Studies in the Foundation, Methodology and Philosophy of Science*, Vol. 3, Springer-Verlag, New York.

Cook, T.D. & Campbell, D.T. (1979) *Quasi-Experimentation, Design and Analysis for Field Settings*. Houghton Mifflin Company, Boston.

Hamilton, M. (1974) *Methodology of Clinical Research*, Churchill Livingstone, Edinburgh and London.

Moser, C. & Kalton, G. (1972) *Survey Methods in Social Investigation.* Heinemann, London.

Oyster, C., Hanten, W. & Llorens, L. (1987) *Introduction to Research, A Guide for the Health Science Professional.* J. B. Lippincott Company, Philadelphia.

Polit, D. & Hungler, B. (1989) *Essentials of Nursing Research, 2nd Edn.* J. B. Lippincott Company, Philadelphia.

Reid, N. (1986) *Wards in Chancery? Nursing Training in the Clinical Area.* Royal College of Nursing, London.

Reid, N. (1989) The Delphi Technique – its contribution to the evaluation of professional practice. In R. Ellis (ed.) *Professional Confidence and Quality Assurance in the Caring Professions.* Croom Helm, London.

Sim, J. (1989) Methodology and Morality in Physiotherapy Research. *Physiotherapy,* **75**, No. 4, 237–43.

Yearley, S. (1984) *Science and Sociological Practice.* Open University Press, Milton Keynes.

Chapter 4
Techniques of Research Design

This chapter describes some techniques which are central to a wide range of experimental designs. Randomization is a key strategy in meeting the conditions of a true experiment; it is also used in quasi experiments, and it is a fundamental requirement of probability sampling which can underpin any of the research designs we have discussed. The chapter will go on to consider ways of measuring validity and reliability. By assessing validity and reliability we can evaluate the design of a study and form judgements about the value of the study instruments.

Randomization

There are at least two reasons for the use of randomization in research design. The first is to ensure that subjects involved in the research are representative of a wider population of subjects who might have been involved. In its most basic form, simple random sampling, those chosen to participate are selected in a way which gives all possible subjects an equal chance of selection. The second reason for randomization is to ensure that subjects assigned to different groups are comparable and that subjects have an equal chance of being assigned to any group.

There are a number of ways of achieving randomization. If the purpose is to select a sample of subjects for a study from a bigger set of possible subjects (the study population), you obviously first need a list of that total set of subjects. It might be all the patients in a hospital or all the clients within a case-load over a year, or all the qualified professional staff in the UK, or all patients with a particular condition who are admitted to a unit over the previous year. If this list is kept on a computer, then randomization may also be done by computer.

If the population list is not on a computer, it should be numbered sequentially e.g. the first patient on the list is 01, the next 02 and so on until the final patient is labelled number 90, for example. Random number tables are now needed. These are available in most statistical tables e.g. Neave (1989). Table 4.1 displays part of the table of random digits provided by Neave (1989).

You then stab blindly at the page to pinpoint a starting number. Let us say you hit the number circled in Table 4.1. Proceeding from there

Table 4.1   Random digits (taken from Neave, 1989).

7 1993	2 4053	40677	75150	51292
3 5496	5 8987	29194	25288	83687
4 0588	⑥3015	06872	56579	25469
[3]9643	4 2119	18649	83509	85186
8 2926	7 8554	90463	25440	81318

in any direction – we will choose to go across the line to the right – the first few two digit numbers are 63, 01, 50, 68, 72, 56, 57, 92, 54, 69, 39, 64, etc. So you build up the sample by choosing the 63rd, 1st, 50th, etc., until the required sample size is reached.

This method produces a simple random sample, but the process of randomization underpins all types of probability sampling. It constitutes good practice in obtaining a sample which represents the underlying population from which it was selected, and also guards against any human bias in that selection. It cannot, however, guarantee that a sample is representative.

Another use of randomization is in assigning subjects to groups. If only two groups are involved, a control group and an experimental group, subjects may be assigned by tossing a coin – heads to the control group, tails to the experimental group, or vice versa. (It is advisable to test the coin for possible bias first – an uneven weight distribution will bias a coin.) For three or more groups, random number tables should be used. For example, if you have 60 subjects to assign to three groups, label them sequentially one through to 60. Then stab at the page of random digits to find a starting point. Let us say you hit the number in the box in Table 4.1. The 39th subject is allocated to the first group, the 64th to the second group, the 34th to the third group, the 21st to the first group, 19th to the second, 18th to the third and so on. If a number greater than 60 occurs in the random digits, disregard it and move on to the next two digit number. In both examples given, samples of size less than 100 were illustrated. For samples of size three figures, read the random digits in groups of three.

The technique of randomization ensures that no human bias affects the selection of study subjects or their allocation to groups; however, the technique is not foolproof. It can still happen, for example, that by chance your control group is all male and your experimental group is all female. If this matters, you may need to re-randomize. The general rule is that you should review the situation if there is a concentration of any variable in one group which affects markedly the variable under study. Either re-randomize or use a matched-pairs design, matching for the affecting variable, randomly allocating one of each pair to each group.

Sampling

Sampling can be used in a whole variety of research designs: to select those entering a randomized clinical trial, to select study groups within quasi-experiments, to select samples for surveys or to select topics or events for observation. There are two kinds of sampling: non-probability sampling and probability sampling.

A sample needs to be representative of the population from which it is drawn, so that having studied the sample, the researcher can make inferences about the whole population. This can best be achieved through probability sampling, where a listing of the whole population is available and every member has a known chance of being selected. In practice, acquiring population lists (called sampling frames) can be time-consuming and difficult. All kinds of issues about confidentiality and anonymity can arise in health research, and the researcher's life has not been made easier by the Data Protection Act (1984) which places constraints on the uses to which computerized information may be put. The laudable intention of the Act is to protect individual rights, but it can incidentally impede the researcher who wants access to information for research purposes. For these practical reasons, probability sampling may be difficult or impossible to achieve within the timescale of a student project, so two methods of non-probability sampling will be described.

Convenience sampling

This consists of selecting study subjects convenient to the researcher. These may be colleagues, patients, friends or neighbours. The underlying population is unknown and the clear limitation of this method is that no inferences may be legitimately made beyond the subjects studied. You may be able, however, to note characteristics of the convenience sample and compare these with known demographic information, such as census data or hospital statistics. In this way, it may be possible to make some case for generalizing the results of the study beyond the study group, but care must be taken not to over-claim.

Quota sampling

This is based on specifying certain characteristics in the subjects sought and then choosing the first available subjects who meet that specification. For example, you might specify five men aged 40–59 in each social class, and five women aged 40–59 in each social class. This method is widely used in market research and in opinion polls. At its best, it can be representative of the underlying population, if the specification is very detailed and based on knowledge of the demography of the population. But inferences cannot be made about the underlying population with any confidence.

Both convenience sampling and quota sampling have their place in student projects, and provided their limitations are understood and explained, they provide a practical way of selecting a sample when time is limited. However it is better to use one of the various methods of probability sampling described below, if you can.

Simple random sampling

This seeks to ensure that each member of the population has an equal chance of selection. The technique of randomization described earlier is the best way to carry out simple random sampling. However, as we have seen, it is not a perfect technique in that some biases may still occur. For example, the sample may have 70% men and 30% women whereas the population had 50% of each gender. This may not matter in some studies, but, if it does, a more complex technique should be used.

Stratified random sampling

This ensures proportionate representation in the sample of key variables which are chosen because they markedly affect the main study variable or variables. For example, in a study of blood pressure, age would be an important variable to take into account across study groups, or in selecting the sample. What you would need to do is to section or stratify the population in terms of age and to sample proportionally from each age band. Thus if 25% of the population are under 30, a quarter of the sample might be selected from this stratum, and so on. It is possible to stratify on more than one variable but it does become very complex as the number of variables increases.

Cluster sampling

This is used to obtain concentrated study units. For example, a simple random sample of 1,000 patients in hospitals in a regional health authority could involve dozens of hospitals and the negotiation of access and, indeed, travel time and costs could be impossible to achieve within a limited time-scale. An alternative would be to identify clusters – in this case, hospitals, randomly sample a small number of these and select all or a sample of the patients within the selected hospitals.

The chosen method of probability sampling has many implications for analysis. Even apparently straightforward statistics like means can become more complex to calculate if stratified sampling or cluster sampling have been used. Simple random sampling, in contrast, leads to a fairly straightforward analysis, at least in terms of summary statistics. Cochrane (1977) provides a comprehensive account of the mathematical implications of sampling choices and gives details of analytical techniques, although less mathematically oriented readers may prefer Barnett (1974).

Reliability

A measuring instrument is reliable if it is accurate and if it measures in a stable and consistent way. This is easiest to visualize within experimentation where, for example, a sphygmomanometer should provide both an accurate measure of blood pressure and one which does not vary in its readings through some mechanical defect. But reliability is also needed in attitude scales and a variety of other psychometric measurements. Indeed reliability is important across the range of research designs.

Test/retest reliability

This measures the stability of the instrument. The same subjects are tested twice and the results compared. If the second test is carried out immediately after the first, in identical conditions, this establishes whether measurement is stable or otherwise. If the nature of what is being tested is such that subject measurements are likely to remain stable over time (e.g. personality, blood type), then the test/retest can also be used to establish stability over time. Test/retest reliability is assessed through the calculation of the correlation between the two sets of readings. Chapter 8 gives an account of how the calculation is done.

The method is unsuitable if the factor being tested may change over time (e.g. weight, opinions). A further problem lies in possible contamination of the retest by the process of the original test. For example, in an attitude survey, pondering on the test items may shift a subject's attitude, so that a different attitude is being measured at the retest stage.

A number of tests of reliability exist for attitude scales which have been constructed by selection of test items from a pool of items, such as scales which measure job satisfaction by asking respondents to tick a point on a five point scale ranging from 'strongly agree' to 'strongly disagree'.

Alternate-form reliability is based on the construction of an alternate set of items from the same pool of items and giving subjects both scales. The correlation coefficient calculated as shown in Chapter 8, indicates both stability and the consistency of response to the two forms.

Split-half reliability establishes the internal consistency of a scale, by splitting the scale into two comparable halves and calculating the correlation coefficient. Care must be taken in choosing the two halves, to ensure that they are really comparable.

If further assurance of internal consistency and homogeneity of a scale are required more elaborate measures of reliability may be calculated. The Kuder-Richardson procedure examines performance of subjects on each test item and produces a correlation coefficient which is equivalent to the mean of all split-half coefficients, resulting from different splits. The Kuder-Richardson Formula 20, as it is known, is designed for test items requiring binary (two-category) responses; but it has also been generalized in the Cronbach alpha reliability coefficient. For a full account of these measures, Anastasi (1976) is recommended.

Another facet of reliability is the consistency with which different interviewers carry out interviews based on a questionnaire. This is called inter-rater reliability. You are unlikely to need to test this on a student project, where the best approach is to use only one interviewer – yourself. But if a team of interviewers is used, training can increase inter-rater reliability and it can be measured with a fair degree of sophistication. See, for example, O'Muircheartaigh and Payne (1977).

The measurement and establishment of reliability is regarded as essential in true experiments and quasi experiments, and is also widely practised in such non-experimental designs as surveys and observational techniques. It is employed less in qualitative research such as case studies and ethnographic studies, a point to which we shall return. First, however, we need to consider the related topic of validity.

Validity

If a technique is not reliable, it is certainly not valid; but that does not mean that just because it is reliable, it acquires validity. Indeed, research is concerned with various types of validity that may need to be checked out.

Content validity

This refers to the extent to which the research instrument adequately represents the topic under investigation. There should not, for example, be undue attention to one aspect of the topic in relation to others. This often occurs through over-emphasis on things that are easiest to measure. For example, a study of risk factors in heart disease might concentrate too much on smoking, nutrition and alcohol intake – which are relatively easy to measure – at the expense of stress, which is very difficult to measure. Sometimes such biases are easy to spot, but in the end content validity is based on judgement, and cannot be measured empirically. The important thing is that you should be able to defend the content validity of your own research by rational argument.

Face validity

This simply means that the research instrument appears valid to those who are its subjects or administrators. Some researchers place a low value on face validity as a criterion because it is subjective. Here it is simply argued that in health research face validity, though not sufficient, is valuable, if the purpose of the research is to influence practice or policy. The findings of research are much more likely to be adopted in professional practice if the methodology is well thought of by the profession.

Criterion validity

In this, by contrast, the validity of a research instrument is checked against some external criterion. For example, an instrument designed to assess learner performance in a clinical setting could be checked against the results of the students' next formal assessment.

If the chosen criterion is available at the same time as the test, it is said to establish *concurrent validity*. If the criterion is applied some time after the test it is called *predictive validity*. The main difficulty in practice is finding a relevant criterion which is itself reliable and valid. Once a criterion is established, however, validity can be measured by correlating the test score and the criterion score.

Construct validity

This refers to the validity of a research instrument which aims to measure a construct, i.e. an abstraction inferred from situations, events or behaviour such as happiness, job satisfaction or pain. Construct validation requires the gradual accumulation of information from a variety of sources: the theoretical basis of the construct may need to be explored to find relationships with other constructs or criteria. Hence, the establishment of construct validity can be circuitous and indirect.

There are other kinds of validity but these are rarely useful in health research. For a fuller account of validity and how to measure it, Anastasi (1976) is recommended.

Reliability and validity in qualitative research

Issues of validity and reliability tend to have received less attention in the non-experimental tradition, but there is one technique, known as triangulation, that can help. The process is conceptually close to the various techniques for the establishment of validity and reliability. It can include the use of multiple-data sources in a study; the use of multiple investigations to collect, analyse and interpret a single set of data; the use of multiple theory perspectives to interpret a set of data; and the use of multiple methodologies to address a single problem. For a further discussion see Polit and Hungler (1989).

Ready-made instruments

Reliability and validity are important if you are designing a new research instrument, but there is no need to re-invent the wheel. It may be that you can negotiate permission to use an instrument developed and validated by another researcher. Or you may use a standard instrument like the General Health Questionnaire (Goldberg, 1978) or the Maslach Burnout Inventory (Maslach and Jackson, 1981) which can be bought. Within the limited time-scale for a student project, indeed, there may be benefits in adopting someone else's instrument and devoting more of your time to the analysis.

Three case studies

Guidelines for good research design can often be derived from case studies. Three have been selected here to represent a range of health research applications and a range of methodologies. They constitute a convenient sample of recently published studies. They have not been chosen because they are especially good or bad, but because of their potential for illustrating good practice in research design. It should be emphasized that the author claims no expert knowledge in the fields of research involved, and that the comments are made purely from a methodological point of view.

Having first read the published article to which each of the case studies refers, you may wish to consider the following questions before reading the case studies:

- What category of research design has been used?
- Why use this type of design for this topic?
- Was sampling used and, if so, was it appropriate?
- Did the design meet the study objectives?
- Were the study measures valid and reliable?
- What are the strengths of the design?

(1)   A quasi-experimental study in nursing

Prompted voiding therapy for urinary incontinence in aged female nursing home residents.
N. Creason, J. Grybowski, S. Burgener, C. Whippo, S. Yeo, B. Richardson. *Journal of Advanced Nursing*, 1989, **14**, 120–6.

The study concerns the effect of two nursing interventions, prompted voiding and socialization on incontinence. Prompted voiding involved asking patients at regular intervals if they needed to void and, if so, providing help in toileting. Socialization consisted of a two to three-minute 'contact of a social nature' each hour, with no mention of voiding or toileting unless in response to the patient expressing a need or desire to use the lavatory.

It was carried out at four nursing homes with 288, 240, 102 and 100 beds respectively. The study subjects were 85 female residents, 65 years-old or more who had been incontinent for two weeks or longer and were without indwelling catheters.

A quasi-experimental design was used in assigning these 85 subjects to three groups, a control group, and two experimental groups, one for prompted voiding and one for socialization. All patients were assessed for functional capacity including mobility, self-care, cognitive status and a complete history and physical evaluation. The interventions were then instituted for two weeks. Regular 24-hour observation of continence patterns was undertaken for all 85 patients in these two weeks. Data were then evaluated. Nursing home staff and the researchers together developed individual care plans based on these data. Residents with continence patterns were then approached with the appropriate experimental treatment based on their voiding pattern. After four weeks, individual care plans had been developed for all the residents and data were then collected for a further two weeks.

The analysis first compared the pre-intervention measures for the three groups. Both the percentage of times incontinent and the functional assessment showed differences between the experimental groups. The socialization group had patients being incontinent for lower percentages of time; this group also scored significantly higher on the functional assessment, and was significantly younger. The comparison of incontinence episodes after the interventions showed the socialization group scored lowest by some way, with the prompted voiding group next and the control group with the highest level of incontinence. The statistical analysis suggested that these differences were significant.

The discussion in the paper recognized weaknesses in design and concluded that 'the improvement of residents in the prompted voiding group by weeks four and five suggests prompted voiding therapy can be useful in decreasing incontinence'; and that 'it is not possible to comment on the usefulness of the socialization intervention'. The conclusions are therefore heavily qualified and very cautious.

Why use a quasi-experimental design for this topic?

The study used a clinical trial, including a control group, the treatment variable was manipulated to provide two experimental groups, but randomization was not carried out. Had this been done, this would have been a true experiment. The authors offer an explicit reason for not randomizing: 'random assignment to experimental groups was not done due to control problems associated with monitoring different experimental methods on one unit'.

While this is helpful as an indication of a practical constraint on randomization, the word unit is ambiguous. Does it mean hospital? If so, this means that there was only one group per hospital (and therefore the fourth hospital used for the pilot?) which is a serious design flaw in that the effects of the treatment and of the location are confounded and cannot be separated. If unit on the other hand means a ward, or group of wards, similar although less serious, confounding effects could be present. It is a weakness of the study that no explanation of the distribution of subjects across hospitals and groups is provided making evaluation of the design difficult.

The decision not to randomize is understandable, because in principle randomization could have resulted in the need to brief all staff on all three treatment regimes. An alternative might have been to use only one hospital and select 85 subjects; thus only the staff of one hospital would need to be briefed. Perhaps, however the problem would still arise, in that the delivery of three regimes could overload any individual staff member with instructions and tasks. In this case it might have been better to carry out a single-intervention study and use randomization.

The problems resulting from not randomizing are only too evident in the analysis, which demonstrates that the groups were not, in fact, equivalent on key attributes. This is always the risk of using non-equivalent control groups. It is to the authors' credit that they recognize this flaw, report it unequivocally and tread very softly in their conclusions.

Was the sampling appropriate?

Eighty-five subjects were included in the study from four hospitals with 730 beds. A strength of the study is the specification of criteria for subjects entering the trial: over 65 years-old; incontinent for at least two weeks; and no indwelling catheter. But unfortunately it is not stated whether the total of 85 subjects met these criteria or whether the 85 were selected from a larger group who met the criteria.

Purposive sampling was used to allocate the 85 subjects to three groups. This type of sampling is in essence convenience sampling, but the researcher subjectively tries to balance the groups on certain characteristics. We are told nothing about how the purposive sampling was done, or on what basis – and in fact the technique more resembles purposive allocation than sampling and is a weak method. All kinds of bias may have resulted but the reader cannot judge this on the information provided.

Did the design meet the study objectives?

The report posed three research questions, which will be considered in turn.

Does prompted voiding and/or socialization affect the ability of aged female nursing-home residents to achieve urinary continence?

It is not exactly clear how the design was intended to answer this question. The literature review acknowledges that socialization is an inevitable part of a prompted voiding intervention but is not clear whether this is the assumption behind the design. If it is, the design is attempting to distinguish between a control group receiving no intervention; a group receiving prompted voiding including socialization; and a group receiving socialization only. By comparing the latter two groups the effect of prompted voiding could be isolated. The problem here is that this design will only meet the study objective if socialization remains the same in the latter two groups. But evidence of this does not emerge from the description of what was done – there is no mention of social interaction in the prompted voiding intervention, in contrast to the description of the socialization intervention. A further problem is that different people with different personalities and talents for socialization delivered the interventions to the two groups.

An alternative interpretation of the design is that the effect of socialization should be measured by comparing the control group and the socialization group. The effect of prompted voiding would emerge from comparing the control group and the prompted voiding group. But this design would mean that socialization would have to be absent from the prompted voiding group, and the authors themselves noted in their literature review that this could not occur in practice. In fact, any benefit of prompted voiding, they observed, could be due to socialization.

It is doubtful therefore, whichever of these interpretations was intended, that the study design could have answered this first question. A further concern is the inevitable amount of socialization which the control group received – they must have been spoken to – when the study design implicitly assumes this group had no socialization.

What are the functional and cognitive parameters related to urinary incontinence in aged female nursing home residents?

This question could only be answered by comparing incontinent subjects with similar continent subjects. This is recognized by the authors in their discussion. The observed correlations within the study subjects between incontinence and age, cognition and functional ability could be spurious. This research question could not be answered through the research design used.

Can patterns of continence/incontinence be identified and used in planning care?

The design accommodated this question in that relevant data were produced and a professional judgement then made about care planning. This is probably best seen as a secondary objective.

A related concern is, however, that the paper appears to suggest that some subjects were moved mid-study to a different group if their voiding pattern suggested that another experimental treatment would best meet their needs. This may be a misunderstanding of the published account, which is not easy to follow at this point. But if this is a correct reading of what was done, it would invalidate the entire project since it violates fundamentally the design principles of the quasi-experimental design.

Were the study measures valid and reliable?

The measures of the dependent variable were 'wet/dry', 'toileted or not', and a record of the amount of voiding as small, medium or large. The validity of these measures seems beyond question and the reliability of the 'wet/dry', 'toileted or not' measures is likely to be high. However, the reliability of the subjective measure of amount of voiding as small, medium or large, would need to be established. No comment is provided on any testing of reliability within the paper.

What are the strengths of the design?

A number of fundamental criticisms have been noted – some of them, however, with the caveat that the paper is not always clear in its account of the methodology. The strong feature of the paper is that the authors have themselves identified some weaknesses and have been very cautious in drawing conclusions. They have contributed to understanding the practical problems involved in carrying out research in this area and have encouraged others to develop their ideas in further research.

It is always easier to be critical of a study than to provide alternative suggestions, and this study concerns a topic which is particularly difficult to investigate. There were also serious practical constraints on the conduct of the study. Without fuller information about the study setting, it is difficult to arrive at conclusions about alternative ways in which this research could have been done. But some residual questions need to be addressed:

- Can socialization really be manipulated experimentally? Can it ever be entirely withdrawn within a control group and can it be sufficiently controlled within experimental groups?
- Could this topic have been studied through a non-experimental approach?
- Could randomization have been used within a single-intervention clinical trial? Would the practical implications of randomization, in requiring staff to administer two regimes be insuperable?
- Is the subjective measurement of voiding as small, medium or large a reliable measure? How could its reliability be tested, and should this have been reported?

(2)   A non-experimental study in occupational therapy

Qualitative methods in occupational therapy research: an application.

Susan Cook-Merrill. *Occupational Therapy Journal of Research*, 1985, Vol. 5, No. 4, pp. 209–22.

This paper presents an overview of qualitative research methods, and an analysis of the relationship between qualitative and quantitative approaches in social and cultural research. It also presents a brief discussion of reliability, validity and researcher objectivity in qualitative research. A strong case is made for the value of qualitative research methods in occupational therapy.

An application of qualitative research in occupational therapy was carried out in investigating the role of occupational therapy in the treatment of juvenile arthritis. As a practising therapist, the author had identified an apparent mismatch between the objectives of the occupational therapy service and the perception of its value by her adolescent clients. The purpose of the study was to obtain an insider view of the condition by describing the subjects' functional performance of daily occupations and their use of time; and by describing patterns of behaviour and their relationship to development in adolescence; and by describing each subject's feelings about his or her life quality. It was hoped that further research questions would be generated and that the understanding of the use of qualitative research methods in occupational therapy might be enhanced.

Four subjects were used, two with juvenile arthritis (JA) and two without any form of chronic disability. The subjects were matched for age, socio-economic status and geographic location. The instruments used relied on the process of triangulation to strengthen validity and reliability and to allow judgments about the quality of the data to be made. Four instruments were used: two semi-structured interviews, one an activity-performance-and-effectiveness interview (APEI), the other a behavioural-patterns interview (BPI); a time-log; and lastly participant observation in the subject's environment.

The APEI described the subjects' self-maintenance activities and basic functional skills. It was evaluated for interrater reliability, and content validity, and then used in interviewing the subject and subject's mother together. There was also some observation to supplement the interview material. The BPI was used in a one-to-one interview with the subject alone, away from family and friends, to reduce distortion on issues pertaining to feelings and relationships. Reliability was tested by comparison of these data with those gathered in other parts of the study, and content validity was obtained prior to the study proper.

The time-log was kept by the subject for 24 hours and entailed recording of all activities in terms of feelings, reasons for activities, and who assisted or participated in the activities. The author also observed each subject for 10–14 hours over a two-week period. These observations were made in the home and elsewhere.

The four approaches to data collection generated some 100 pages of data on each subject. Analysis of data began as the first data were collected and any questions raised were pursued with subjects at the next meeting. Categories were then generated into which data were classified. This was done independently by the researcher and a colleague and the results synthesized. About 30 categories were identified for each subject; case studies were then written and the four subjects compared.

Although the researcher had posed some research questions at the beginning of the study, she had difficulty in answering them directly from the case material. She concluded that this was because the original questions were based on what she thought the data might reveal, and did not take account of the categories which had emerged from the research. The conclusion of the project was a statement of questions to be pursued in the next cycle of the process, then using both quantitative and qualitative methods.

Why use a non-experimental design for this topic?

The author makes a succinct case for this choice of design. Very little was known about this topic and almost no research had been done on the insider view of juvenile arthritis – how the adolescent *felt* about it. Feelings and emotions are clearly not amenable to manipulation or experimentation so a non-experimental design was needed. Within this class of designs the author chose a highly qualitative case-study approach; which makes good sense, given the complexities and sensitivity of the subject. Another reason for choosing this method-ology was that the purpose of the research was to understand the condition better in order to generate further hypotheses for research. Qualitative research is much the best way to do this kind of study.

Does the design meet the study objectives?

The author posed some questions at the beginning of the paper and those questions could be considered as objectives. As the analysis developed, it was found that these objectives did not easily fit the natural structure of the data. This is a facet of qualitative research which is important to recognize – the study is dynamic in a way in which experimental research may not be: as the qualitative study progresses, its direction may change. Of course a broad statement of purpose, as in this research, can guide the design and analysis, but the detailed outcomes may not always be specified in advance. This study met its general purpose, but not in the detailed way in which the author had a priori expected.

Was the sampling appropriate?

The study did not use formal sampling and was clearly designed as a case study. The report states explicitly that no attempt was made to generalize beyond the study subjects. It is interesting, however, that matching was used to standardize some unwanted sources of variation in the four subjects, i.e. – for age, socio-economic status and geo-graphical location. This is an effective use of a technique more usually employed within experimental research.

Were the study measures valid and reliable?

The author, recognizing that validity and reliability are key issues in qualitative research, cites triangulation as a major strategy in improving validity and reliability in her study. The APEI instrument was tested for both validity and reliability before use. One concern is, however, that it was used in the presence of both subject and mother, even though for the other instrument to investigate feelings it was recognized that the presence of another person could cause distortion. It is arguable also that subjects could distort their account of functional ability – perhaps to protect a parent from unpalatable information, or to assert independence – so there may be some loss of reliability in the APEI. It may be, however, that the concurrent observational checks were adequate protection against this.

The BPI was tested for validity and reliability and administered to subjects on their own. The time-log is described without any account of validity or reliability. Such techniques are, in effect, time-sampling methods and do raise questions about how representative, valid and reliable the information is. There is no justification of the observations made by the researcher in terms of validity or reliability, but triangulation is a possible defence.

What are the strengths of this design?

This study represents good practice in the use of the qualitative case study in non-experimental research. The topic is highly suitable for this kind of methodology, and in fact could hardly be studied effectively in any other way. A particular strength is its rigour – using matched subjects and testing most of the study instruments for validity and reliability. The study design enabled the researcher to meet her overall purpose of illuminating this area of knowledge and generating further hypotheses.

(3) A true-experimental study in physiotherapy

A double-blind clinical trial of low-power, pulsed shortwave therapy in the treatment of a soft-tissue injury.
A.T. Barker, P.S. Barlow, J. Porter, M.E. Smith, S. Clifton, L. Andrews, W.J. O'Dowd. *Physiotherapy*, December 1985, Vol. 71, No. 12, 500–504.
This study investigated the non-thermal effect of a low power pulsed electromagnetic energy system, the Therafield Beta system, on soft tissue injuries. A double-blind clinical trial was used, with the machine randomly providing the active treatment or being disabled to provide a control. Neither patient nor physiotherapist could tell whether the machine was in the active or control mode – this was established retrospectively from the patient code.

Patients were of either sex, aged between 16 and 65 and had suffered a lateral ligament sprain of the ankle within the previous 36 hours. They were referred to the physiotherapist from casualty and entered the trial if they were willing to participate and if they met the following criteria:

(1) Radiographs showed that no bone damage had occurred.
(2) Neither ankle had been injured in the previous nine months.
(3) There were no other current conditions affecting the feet, ankles or gait.
(4) There were no open wounds or skin infections in the lower limbs or feet.
(5) Severe vascular disease was not present.
(6) The patient was not pregnant.
(7) The patient did not wear a pacemaker.
(8) The patient was not taking anti-inflammatory or anti-coagulation drugs.
(9) The patient had signed a consent form.

The intervention was carried out on days one, two and three, and patients were assessed before and after the intervention on day one, after the intervention on days two and three and again on days eight and fifteen. All patients received the same general medical treatment besides the randomly chosen intervention. The assessment consisted of measures of: movement range, using a goniometer; gait, using an electronic walkway; pain, using a subjective assessment scale; and swelling, using water displacement.

Eighty-two patients met the admission criteria during a five-month period; eight dropped out and two were subsequently found to have bone fractures. The paper reports that 73 entered the trial, 34 in the experimental group and 39 in the control group.

Data were analysed by carrying out t-tests to compare mean values for the two groups at the six assessment points on each of the seven assessment measures. No significant results were found and it was concluded that the manufacturers' claims for the efficacy of this treatment for soft tissue injuries remain unproven.

Why use a true-experimental design for this topic?

There seems little argument that the true experiment is the obvious design for a study of a physical treatment of a physical injury. The treatment variable could be easily and accurately manipulated. Randomization was achieved in an ingenious way by building a mechanism into the treatment machine, and the researchers were able to control the experiment in a clinical laboratory setting. The only caveat – one which applies to almost every health use of clinical trials – is that the study is based on a medical health model. Even in the most obviously physical disorders, psycho-social and social factors can affect healing and therefore some of the effects observed could be due to other such factors. This study and most similar ones would benefit from the use of some supplementary social or psychosocial assessment of patients during the study period. Randomization produced groups with fairly comparable age and sex distributions. If it had not done so, age could have biased the results as possibly could gender – given that weight, for example, could be an indirect factor affecting healing.

Does the design meet the study objectives?

Again the use of a medical/physical model of health comes into the reckoning. If this model is accepted as adequate, then the design is appropriate. The trial was carried out in exemplary fashion, and the design, of itself, cannot be faulted.

The statistical analysis does, however, raise some questions. In this particular study there is reference to non-parametric tests having been also carried out but not reported because the 'p' values were larger than those obtained from the t-tests. This does not inspire confidence. It is not good statistical practice to carry out both parametric and non-parametric tests (see Chapter 7). One or other is appropriate for the data, depending on the distribution of the outcome measures. This report makes no mention of the distribution of its outcome measures, although there are obvious complications since most of them are ratios.

The conclusion is that the design was correct, in theory, to meet the study objectives and was well executed. But the analysis may be technically flawed and thus the study objectives may not have been met entirely.

Was the sampling appropriate?

The 82 patients who met the criteria over a five-month period are described in terms of age and sex. No information is given on the extent to which they are typical patients – is it the case, for example, that almost twice as many men as women sustain this type of injury? Some comment on the population of such patients, drawn perhaps from hospital records, would have strengthened the claims of the study to be more generally applicable.

There were then eight patients who dropped out and two who were withdrawn because of previously undetected bone fractures. This should have left 72 patients in the study, but the report is based on 73 patients. An extra one has been acquired somehow!

The randomization was done using a device within the treatment machine. This clever strategy overcomes an often cited problem in health research of making the control and experimental treatments look the same. The randomization was appropriately carried out.

Were the study measures valid and reliable?

There is no discussion whatever of validity and reliability of the measures used, and this must be considered a weakness. Tests of reliability for these instruments could be easily devised and would be important in establishing the accuracy of measurements. Validity is probably less of a problem for measures of movement range, gait and swelling, but the validity of the pain measurement would need to be justified.

What are the strengths of this design?

This is an exemplary study of a clinical trial of a physical treatment for a physical injury. The randomization method was laudable; the selection criteria were explicit and appropriate; a double-blind approach was used; and in every respect the conduct of the trial was excellent. The study conclusions are carefully stated and follow from the results provided. However, the statistical analysis and the lack of checks on reliability should be noted, as these may cast doubt on the study findings.

These three studies cover the three main categories of research design and offer examples of both good and less good practice in research design in order to illustrate the theoretical material in the previous chapter.

It may be appropriate to add that the authors cited are among the small minority in their professions who are carrying out and publishing research, and to that extent they are pioneers. It must also be acknowledged that it is much easier to be an armchair critic than to do something! It is a rare piece of published research which is not flawed in some way. This apart, these comments are offered, not as criticism for its own sake but as ways of helping new researchers into good habits, and encouraging the stringent self-analysis which is the essential starting point for all of us.

Discussion points

1. Choose a published research study in your area of interest and evaluate the work which was done to establish the validity and reliability of the study instruments.
2. Consider the proposition that validity and reliability will always necessarily be weaker within non-experimental research as compared to true-experimental research.

References

Anastasi, A. (1976) *Psychological Testing*. MacMillan, New York.

Barnett, V. (1974) *Elements of Sampling Theory*. English Universities Press, London.

Cochrane, W.G. (1977) *Sampling Techniques*. Wiley, New York.

Data Protection Act (1984) Office of the Data Protection Registrar, Wilmslow.

Goldberg, D.P. (1978) *Manual of the General Health Questionnaire*. NFER-Nelson, Windsor.

Maslach, C. & Jackson, S. (1981) The Measurement of Experienced Burnout. *Journal of Occupational Behaviour*, **2**, 99–113.

Neave, H. (1989) *Elementary Statistics Tables*. George Allen and Unwin, London.

O'Muircheartaigh, C. & Payne, C. (1977) *The Analysis of Survey Data, Vols 1 and 2*. Wiley, New York.

Chapter 5
Preparing Data for Analysis

There are many kinds of data including both words and numbers. In principle, almost any kind of data can be used in any research design: it is not true that qualitative data can only be collected in case studies, for example, or that only quantitative data are appropriate for scientifically based methods. There is no reason why a clinical trial should not be evaluated qualitatively or the case-study variables measured quantitatively. In practice, however, quantitative methods tend to be used to a greater extent within true experiments and quasi-experiments; and, conversely qualitative methods occur mainly within non-experimental designs. In terms of the taxonomy of research designs featured in Fig. 3.3, qualitative measures tend to be used more as you move towards the right of the diagram, and quantitative measures as you move to the left.

The collection of data may be highly structured, consisting of a predefined set of measurements carried out in exactly the same way for all study subjects. Or it may be unstructured, allowing the research study to take a natural course which is not prescribed in advance. A related question is the extent to which the researcher interacts with the study subjects. In non-experimental research, the researcher may interact with the subjects to the extent that he or she becomes part of the study. Participant observation and ethnographic methods are examples of this. In contrast, the researcher takes a strictly neutral non-interactive role in clinical trials or in non-participant observation.

Quantitative data either come in the form of numbers or can be easily transformed into numbers. Qualitative data tend to come in words – usually narrative – but may also be subsequently structured and transferred into numerical codes. In classifying data, the key attribute is the level of measurement, which determines in turn the pathways of analysis that can be legitimately carried out.

Levels of measurement

The lowest level of measurement is nominal. At this level subjects are assigned to categories e.g. by speciality, where the categories might be surgical, medical, geriatric and pediatric, or by sex, where the categories are male and female. There is no hierarchical relationship between these categories, they are simply different from each other.

Ordinal measurement

The next level of measurement is ordinal, where the subjects are assigned to ranked categories (grade) which might include student, staff nurse, or sister. There is now a clear hierarchy across the categories, but the distance between the categories is unspecified and not necessarily equal. For example, the distance between the student and staff nurse categories may be less than, the same as, or more than, the distance between the staff nurse and sister categories.

Interval measurement

In interval level measurement, the subjects can be placed in ordered categories and the distance between each category is known. An example would be temperature measured on the Fahrenheit scale where 60°F is 20° hotter than 40°F and 20° cooler than 80°F. The interval scale does not have a true zero, but, like Fahrenheit, an arbitrary zero − you cannot have no temperature. Thus we should not say that 60°F is twice as hot as 30°F, but that it is 30°F hotter.

Ratio measurement

Ratio level measurement is the highest level of measurement, having all the attributes of interval level measurement and a true zero. Examples are height and weight. Measurements of this type enable statements like: 'He is twice as tall now as he was five years ago'.

The level of measurement critically limits the statistical analysis which can be legitimately carried out, a topic which is considered in detail in Chapters 6, 7 and 8. For this reason, it is a useful exercise in designing a research study to note the level of measurement of every variable at the design stage, and then consider the planned statistical analysis. These chapters describe techniques of data analysis and denote the required levels of measurement for each technique.

Levels of measurement can be manipulated downwards. If a variable is nominal, then, of course, nothing more can be done. But if it is ordinal, for example, it can be aggregated to become nominal. Table 5.1, adapted from Polit and Hungler (1989), takes the variable pulse and moves it down through the four levels of measurement.

The first column shows the pulse rates of eight subjects as directly measured. These are ratio level measurements, with Leroy's pulse rate, for example, almost twice as fast as Ali's and Anita's pulse rate 50% faster than Ali's pulse rate. The second column converts these to interval level measurements, setting an arbitrary zero at the lowest pulse rate, Ali's, and calculating everyone else's pulse rate from that base. Thus Anita is 25 points higher than Ali and 21 points lower than Leroy, but the absolute values are not available at this level of measurement.

The third column simply orders the pulse rates to obtain ordinal scores from the lowest, Ali, with a score of one, to the highest, Leroy, with a score of eight. Note that the relative differences between

Table 5.1 Sample data showing levels of measurement.

Name	Ratio	Interval	Ordinal	Nominal
Bill	64	14	3	1
Sarita	58	8	2	1
Leroy	96	46	8	2
Anita	75	25	6	2
Ali	50	0	1	1
Zeta	74	24	5	2
David	77	27	7	2
Sinead	67	17	4	1

subjects disappear at this level of measurement. The final column creates categories, giving a score of one if the pulse rate is below average and a score of two if the pulse rate is above average. This level of measurement loses the order between subjects.

In general, it is good statistical practice to use all of the information available in data and since moving down the levels of measurement leads to loss of information, this is almost never advisable. In fact, having collected data at ratio level, it is highly unlikely that you would wish to manipulate its level of measurement downwards: higher levels of measurement facilitate parametric statistical tests of the kind described in Chapters 7 and 8, and these are the most powerful tests available. The important thing is to make sure that you collect data at a high enough level to make possible the statistical analysis you wish to carry out.

Suppose, for instance, you are collecting information about people's ages. Exact age in years is ratio-level measurement, but not every respondent may wish to reveal his or her age to you. People will more readily tick an age band – for example 30–45 – and this will give you ordinal measurement. The decision in this case will emerge from weighing your needs for analysis against the ease of obtaining responses to different formulations of the question.

Discrete and continuous variables

In research, each piece of data collected is called a variable, meaning simply that it varies for different subjects. In health science research, people are different in most of the things you will wish to measure, so height, weight, blood group, religion, health status are all variables. All variables are either discrete or continuous. For example, the number of children in a family might be three or four but it cannnot be 3.5, so this variable takes discrete values. On the other hand, height might be 2 m or 2.3 m or anything in between, so height is a continuous variable. The analysis of discrete and continuous variables differs somewhat in practice, as we shall see in Chapter 6. So it is important to identify for each of your research variables whether it is discrete or continuous.

Data preparation

The techniques of data collection will vary depending on the type of design, the role of the researcher and the nature of the data. The techniques of collecting data have been briefly discussed earlier in this chapter, and very full treatments of this topic appear elsewhere (see, for example, Polit and Hungler, 1989). Less attention has been given to the preparation of data for analysis and, where appropriate, the input of data into a computer.

Not all data need preparation for analysis and not all data should be analysed by computer. Generally, the kinds of data which emerge from true experiments and quasi-experimental design are quantitative and more often than not at ratio level. Such data require minimal extra preparation before being fed into a computer or analysed by other means.

Qualitative information from case studies in the non-experimental tradition may not require numerical analysis. It may be analysed from narrative, in a narrative style. On the other hand, many such studies are analysed by identifying categories and classifying narrative material within these categories. This is nominal level measurement. If qualitative data so measured are to be analysed by computer, numerical codes must be assigned to the categories; but it should be remembered that these codes are merely numerical labels, and they have no real numerical meaning. For example, if males are coded '1' and females coded '2', the labels '1' and '2' have no meaning as numbers, they merely indicate that there are two different categories.

Most other non-experimental research designs yield data at a variety of levels of measurement: it is a rare survey, for example, which does not require two or more levels of measurement and usually the collection of qualitative data as well. This information will generally require preparation before it can be fed into a computer.

When should a computer be used? Provided that the study is quantitative in its focus, the decision should depend on the scale of the study. Within a student project it can be a marginal decision since data should be kept within manageable – and analysable – limits. But the skills acquired in analysing data through a computer may well justify the time devoted to feeding data into the system; and the gains in analysis time are substantial, even with small datasets. As a rough rule of thumb, a study with more than 20 subjects and more than five quantitative variables is likely to benefit from the use of a computer in analysis. You should take into account the nature of the data, the proposed analysis and the scale of the study, and when in doubt, you should consult a statistician. More often than not it is the case that research studies in health benefit from analysis through a computer.

For Office
Use Only
1 2
0 1

1. In which hospital do you work? (please tick)

   Hilltown ⸺ 3/1
   Lowtown ⸺ 3/1
   Hightown ⸺ 3/3
   Rivertown ⸺ 3/4
   Downtown ⸺ 3/5

2. For how many years and months have you been qualified?

   ⸺ years   4 5 6
   ⸺ months

3. In which institution did you train? _____ 7 8

4. Was your training: (please tick)

   very satisfactory? ⸺ 9/1
   satisfactory? ⸺ 9/2
   neither satisfactory
   nor unsatisfactory? ⸺ 9/3
   unsatisfactory? ⸺ 9/4
   very unsatisfactory? ⸺ 9/5

5. Please briefly describe the chief benefit you derived from your training:

   10 11

   _____
   _____
   _____

6. Please rate your training in terms of the following: (tick the appropriate column)

	very good	good	neither good nor bad	bad	very bad	
Teaching of clinical skills						12
Teaching of theory skills						13
Teaching of analytical skills						14
Teaching of skills in numeracy						15
Teaching of skills in literacy						16
Teaching of high professional standards						17

THANK YOU FOR YOUR COOPERATION

Fig. 5.1 Training survey.

If you decide to use a computer, ratio or interval level data, which mainly emerge from true and quasi-experimental designs, need no further preparation, other than dealing with missing values (see subsequent discussion in this chapter). Ordinal data and nominal data may need to be assigned numerical codes or labels before they can be entered into the computer. Qualitative data may need to be categorized and then treated as nominal. Surveys use most of these types of data, so here is a hypothetical survey with comments about levels of measurement and about how the data should be presented and prepared.

This survey is a postal questionnaire about initial training for a health profession. The layout is shown in Fig. 5.1. The training survey questionnaire is intended to illustrate coding and data preparation techniques rather than exemplary questionnaire design, though it is hoped that there are no glaring inadequacies. For guidance on questionnaire design, Moser and Kalton (1972) is a classic text. In Fig. 5.1 the right hand column, headed 'For Office Use Only', is for the insertion of computer codes by the researcher after the questionnaire has been returned. Most computers operate on a grid system where each row of data can take up to a locally specified maximum of characters, one in each box. In this example only 17 boxes are needed, but in a real life questionnaire, several rows, each of many characters, might be needed for each subject. The first two boxes in the right hand column contain a serial number to identify the respondent: this particular example is for respondent number 01.

The next questionnaire would be labelled 02 and so on. Two boxes have been allocated as this survey is being sent to fewer than 100 subjects. The serial number is normally placed on the form before it is distributed, and it can then be used in conjunction with a confidential master-list of names and addresses to follow-up non-responders. The serial number is written in the first two boxes which are labelled '1' and '2' above (see start of the office-use-only section of the training survey). In the questionnaire itself the first question asks the subject to tick the hospital in which he or she works. This is a closed question – only the five hospitals within the study area are listed. The tick is placed close to the margin with codes just the other side. The response to this question goes in column three (you can imagine a box here) and, depending on the answer ticked, either a 1, 2, 3, 4 or 5 will be entered into the computer. The advantage of this style of coding is that, if a data preparation service is used, they can punch via a keyboard directly into a computer from this question as answered by the respondent. No subsequent coding – called 'postcoding' – is needed. Note also that had there been ten or more hospitals within the study area, two boxes would have been necessary, to allow two digit codes, e.g. 01, 02, . . . 10, 11, 12.

The second question asks how many years and months the subject has been qualified. Three boxes, 4, 5, and 6, are provided so that the researcher may calculate the months as a decimal of a year and place the answer in these boxes. For example, 12 years and 6 months will be entered as 12.5 – the decimal point can go in the same box as the 5. Take care if the number of years is nine or less to put a zero in the 'tens' box. For example, 4 years and 5 months would be entered as 04.4.

The third question asks where the subject trained. In theory, they may have trained at any one of 40 training establishments in the UK, or even abroad. They cannot all be listed on the questionnaire, so this is left as an open question which must be postcoded by the researcher. This is done by assigning a unique number to each training institution cited e.g. Newcastle school is 01, so every time this school is cited the code 01 is assigned; Birmingham is 02; Coventry is 03 and so on. Two boxes 7 and 8, are included in the margin, and the researcher enters the appropriate code each time a school is cited. The researcher must keep a master list of code numbers assigned – often called a codebook – and make sure that consistent codes are assigned consistently for all subjects.

The fourth question, like question one, provides a five-point scale for the response so that no postcoding is needed. This layout should always be used where possible to reduce the task of postcoding, but it can obviously only be used for simple closed questions. The response goes in column 9 which can be imagined as a box.

Question five seeks a qualitative response in narrative form. The researcher might decide to write a narrative report based on all the responses, in which case no codes or computer boxes would be required at all. But the more usual way of dealing with such information is to categorize the narratives in nominal form, numbering each according to the responses given. This may mean guessing how many categories might emerge, and thus how many boxes are needed. The two boxes 10 and 11 shown here will allow up to 99 categories – more than enough in any meaningful taxonomy!

Question six represents a more complex tabular format often used in questionnaires, particularly with attitude scales or statements. For this, scale-codes need to be assigned to each response category e.g. very good = 5, good = 4, neither good nor bad = 3, bad = 2, very bad = 1. Each element in the question has its own box, one of columns 12 to 17, in which the code number is placed. This question thus requires postcoding.

The six questions in this training survey represent a range of levels of measurement and one of them is qualitative. Questions one and four require no postcoding, questions two and six require postcoding but of an automatic and fast kind, the codes being predetermined, but questions three and five require some time in assigning codes – particularly question five where judgements are needed about the data. For this reason, questions in the format of three and five should be kept to a minimum, particularly if time is constrained.

The stage of data preparation is the time to deal with missing values.

These can occur because a subject does not wish to answer a question in a survey, or because the question is not applicable, or because the subject does not know the answer. Missing values can also occur, especially in experimental research, through instrument failure, a subject failing to return for a repeat measurement, or researcher error. The key point is that if you are using a computer to analyse data, missing values need a code. If the relevant box or column is simply left blank the computer may read it as the number zero. Hence a person who had not wished to reveal his or her age would be recorded as having an age of zero. Missing values should be given a unique code, which cannot otherwise occur – 9, 99 or 999 are often used, with 9 then not being permitted as a response code. This can be hazardous with ratio-level data. If 99 is used as a missing value code for age, you cannot then deal with a subject aged 99 in your study. If you have a possible 99-year-old subject you could also easily have one aged 100, so the answer is to use three columns or boxes for your age code and use 999 for missing values – this should be safe enough!

It is sometimes useful, particularly in social surveys, to distinguish between different kinds of missing value e.g. refusal to answer, question not applicable, answer not known. In this case several different missing value codes will be needed.

Using a computer

Once you have made the decision to use a computer for your research it is not enough simply to put the data in and wait for it to come out on the other side, as if from a magic box. Some knowledge of how computers operate and what they can and cannot do will help you prepare your data properly and also hold your own with computer professionals and with eight-year-old children who know all about these things.

Data may be entered into a computer by you, operating a keyboard at a terminal; or it may be entered by a specialist data preparation officer who ensures that the processed material is stored in a computer file to which the researcher has access through a keyboard at a computer terminal.

Computers operate through a combination of hardware and software. Hardware is the term given – in the pleasant way computer experts seek to demystify these fiendishly complex devices – to all of the computer's electronic and mechanical parts and processes (the microchips and so forth). Software is what they call the sets of instructions, or array of programs, that are needed to drive the hardware.

A computer system has three basic elements: a central processor which can perform operations according to the programs fed into it; a storage device, or memory to record the results; and devices to put data into this memory store and to extract it from the store at a time and in a form convenient to the user (input and output devices).

There are two kinds of computer. Mainframe computers, which have great storage capacity and can perform many operations simultaneously, are favoured by large organizations, because they allow many users to have access to these giants through terminals plugged into the mainframe. Personal computers offer their more limited, but still considerable, capacity for the exclusive use of individuals or smaller groups. Programs fed into the personal computer on disks, send and receive instructions through a keyboard: the screen then shows the results in whole or in part and, if required, further instructions. In both personal and mainframe computers output is also made available in tangible form through a printer.

Most computers can be driven by a wide range of different software programs, which can usually be purchased commercially. For instance, you can buy packages that will instruct the computer to behave as a word-processor or as a data analyst.

The procedures for using a software package are the same whether you are working on a mainframe or a personal computer. But it may take a little longer on a mainframe as 200 other people may be making simultaneous demands on it. The only difference between your operation of the mainframe and the personal computer is gaining access to the system.

Think of the mainframe computer as a large house. All authorized computer users have access to this house and they may all want to store private information in it. They may then want to go into a variety of rooms within the house and to use the specialist facilities. They will need different software packages for this but first they have to get through the front door. The key to this first move is a username and a password. These are allocated by the authorized guardians of the computer, such as the computer centre or computer service within the organization. They must be kept secret, because they not only let you through the front door but also allow access to a personal 'strong box' called a directory in the front hall. In this directory you can safely store all your data and research results. Once you have opened the front door by typing in your username and password, all you have to do is to give the system command (which you can find out from your computer centre) and you can open your directory whenever you want and check out what is in there.

The information in your directory has to be stored in files, each of which has to be labelled systematically and recorded. These files may contain raw data as collected, or results that the computer has calculated according to instructions. Various systems commands enable manipulation of the information in your directory. You can list the names of the files to serve as an index, available on command, of the range of information you have in your directory. You can list the detailed contents of any individual file; you can change or edit the material in the files; and you can ask for a printed copy – usually called a hard copy – of any file.

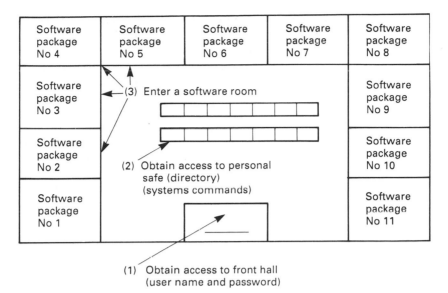

Software package No 4	Software package No 5	Software package No 6	Software package No 7	Software package No 8
Software package No 3	(3) Enter a software room			Software package No 9
Software package No 2	(2) Obtain access to personal safe (directory) (systems commands)			Software package No 10
Software package No 1				Software package No 11

(1) Obtain access to front hall
(user name and password)

Fig. 5.2 Using a mainframe computer.

Your first task as a mainframe computer user with access to a terminal is to contact your computer centre and obtain a username and password and a set of instructions for the basic systems commands for the particular computer. You are then ready to switch on your terminal and to familiarize yourself with your keyboard. This looks like a type-writer keyboard but with extra keys for numbers, letters and symbols such as asterisks. Identify the important ones before you start – the 'delete' key is a crucial one! The 'return' key signifies that you have completed one operation and if you press it you will be invited to give another command. The shift key and space bar operate in the same way as on a typewriter. Time spent studying instruction books and handouts from the computer centre, or practising typing skills, will be well repaid.

Once you have mastered the process of entering the system with your username and password, often called logging on, and have learned how to inspect and manipulate what is stored in your direc-tory, you will be able to move to the next stage. This involves using a software package. The mainframe computer user simply specifies the name of the required package and follows the instructions it contains. You can stop at any point, instruct the computer to put all your workings in a file and save it until you are ready to start again; when you have finished using the package that file will be stored in your directory. You can call for the list of files in your directory and check that it is complete. Figure 5.2 uses the analogy of a house with rooms to illustrate these processes.

Life is simpler in many respects for the personal computer (PC) user at this point. Only one person uses it at a time and he or she has personal disks, usually small and circular like compact disks, on which to record the material. Disks are purchased commercially. The software package which drives the computer can also be purchased commercially, and also comes on disk. The PC user simply switches on the machine, inserts a work disk and a software disk and gets to work. At the end of the session the results can be stored permanently on the work disk, and printed, if required, and the disk can be removed and kept safe by the researcher. No usernames or passwords are needed because the issue of security does not arise. But you have to take great care not to expunge your work accidentally or to fall victim of a power cut.

Entering data into the computer

The first time you gain access to a mainframe computer there will be nothing at all in your directory unless it has been put there at your request by a data preparation service. This service should include entering your data on a file, agreeing a name for the file with you and storing the file in your directory when you first log on. You may also use a data preparation service to prepare a disk for you to load onto your PC.

It may be, however, that your first task on logging on to the computer will be to enter your own basic data. Using systems commands on a mainframe, you can type data into a file of your own creation which can then be stored in your directory. On a PC you can type your data on to a new disk and store it there. You should obtain local advice on the systems commands if you use a mainframe. Similarly there will be a handbook or instruction disk for your personal computer. However, different software packages do this in slightly different ways requiring differences in the format used to enter the data.

The layout process illustrated earlier in this chapter for the hypothetical training survey should meet the needs of most packages – but you should check this out with your local computer centre at the design stage. There are many statistical packages on the market. The two most widely-used in educational and academic circles are SPSS (Statistical Package for the Social Sciences, 1975) and MINITAB. SPSS is mainly suitable for survey data and it has particular advantages in large scale studies. For student projects, however the use of MINITAB is recommended.

The first advantage of MINITAB for this purpose is that it was designed as a teaching package, so the student develops skills and knowledge in the course of using the package. Second, MINITAB is an interactive package, which means that as you give an instruction it is carried out immediately and displayed on the screen for your inspection. You can therefore see exactly what is happening and react to it at each stage of your analysis as it happens. Third, the principle on which MINITAB is designed is that of exploratory data analysis (EDA), which means that you get close to your data, get a feel for it and find your own pathway of analysis based on a real understanding of the data. Fourth, the commands within MINITAB are simple, couched in ordinary language and short. The use of MINITAB is increasing rapidly and the program is available for use either with a mainframe or personal computer.

Another strength of MINITAB is that the accompanying documentation is well-expressed and statistically sound – which is not always the case with computer manuals. The MINITAB manual by Ryan, Joiner and Ryan (1985) is highly recommended. Within the scope of the present study, it is possible to give only a small sample of the range of commands available within the programme chosen to illustrate various methods of analysis in health research.

How to use MINITAB

MINITAB stores data by placing each variable into a column. The first variable goes into a column called C1, the second goes in C2, the third in C3 and so on. The total number of columns varies depending on the capacity of the computer you are using, but usually hundreds are available, many more than needed by any one research project. A column may be as wide as the variable. For example, if the first variable is a two-digit variable, C1 is two characters wide, if it is a five-digit variable, C1 is five characters wide.

Let us now construct a set of hypothetical research results from the survey used earlier in this chapter. Table 5.2 shows the results from surveying 30 subjects.

The codes used were shown earlier on the survey schedule and are summarized in the form of a codebook in Table 5.3.

Having loaded the MINITAB package on to your PC or having obtained access to your mainframe and then typed the word MINITAB you should now have on your screen the following:

MTB >

All lines of MINITAB begin in this way which simply means that the machine is now primed to expect a command.

Data from the training survey can now be entered, one variable at a time. Type the following command:

SET C1

and then press 'return'. The machine will respond:

DATA >

thus indicating that it is ready to receive data. Then type in each hospital code, leaving a space between each. When you have finished press the return button. It will respond:

Table 5.2   Research data from training survey.

	C1	C2	C3	C4	C5	C6	C7	C8	C9	C10	C11
1	1	7.4	12	5	7	1	4	3	3	2	1
2	3	9.8	4	2	1	2	5	1	3	1	5
3	3	10.2	3	4	9	4	4	5	4	1	1
4	3	9.1	3	2	8	3	4	5	9	1	1
5	3	12.5	1	4	4	4	5	4	4	4	1
6	5	6.3	11	2	12	1	1	1	4	5	2
7	1	10.6	6	3	2	1	4	5	4	1	2
8	2	6.1	11	2	12	2	2	5	5	2	1
9	1	8.9	13	5	4	2	1	2	5	2	1
10	4	9.2	7	1	11	2	2	4	1	1	1
11	1	4.7	7	3	5	3	4	5	4	1	1
12	4	4.0	6	3	2	1	4	2	4	1	4
13	5	16.3	3	3	11	1	4	4	4	5	4
14	4	8.5	6	2	2	1	4	2	5	2	1
15	9	4.6	8	4	1	1	1	1	1	1	4
16	1	14.9	13	1	1	2	4	2	4	1	2
17	5	1.5	9	4	6	4	5	4	5	3	1
18	1	10.4	5	2	5	3	4	5	5	1	2
19	2	99.9	5	3	8	1	4	5	5	2	1
20	5	10.8	7	4	99	4	5	3	4	1	1
21	5	1.6	13	5	8	4	5	4	4	3	4
22	2	10.7	2	5	12	2	5	4	4	4	1
23	1	1.8	10	4	8	1	1	4	4	3	3
24	2	9.5	11	4	3	2	4	4	5	1	1
25	4	11.2	7	2	10	2	1	1	4	1	5
26	2	10.3	13	2	11	1	5	4	5	1	1
27	2	10.6	12	3	3	4	5	2	1	2	4
28	3	13.4	13	4	1	1	1	5	2	1	3
29	2	10.9	1	1	5	3	5	5	3	2	1
30	1	12.0	10	2	8	1	4	1	5	1	1

C1 – hospital, C2 – years qualified, C3 – training institution, C4 – satisfaction with training, C5 – view of training, C6–C11 – training scores

DATA >

and you type in END and press return.

The first variable, hospital, is now in C1 and you can inspect it by typing: PRINT C1 and return to obtain printouts. Repeat this for all eleven variables from the study. At this point inspect them all at once, to see the structure of MINITAB by typing: PRINT C1–C11 and return.

The screen cannot show all 30 subjects, or cases, at once so it will print a screenful at a time, usually about 20 rows, and will ask you:

CONTINUE Y/N? (Yes or No?).

Then type in: Y and press return to see the remaining cases on the screen.

Table 5.3 Codebook for the training survey.

Column in MINITAB	Name of Variable	Codes used
C1	Hospital	1 = Hilltown; 2 = Lowtown; 3 = Hightown; 4 = Rivertown; 5 = Downtown
C2	Years qualified	as recorded
C3	Training institution	13 different institutions cited which were labelled 01–13
C4	Satisfaction with training	1 = very satisfactory; 2 = satisfactory; 3 = neither satisfactory nor unsatisfactory; 4 = unsatisfactory; 5 = very unsatisfactory
C5	View of training	12 different views were cited which were labelled 01–12
C6–C11	Training scores	1 = very good; 2 = good; 3 = neither good nor bad; 4 = bad; 5 = very bad

The data are now within MINITAB. But if you want to preserve the data for posterity or for future analysis you must take care to instruct the computer accordingly before you end this MINITAB session. This is done by saving the data into a file. You choose a name for the data-file – usually eight characters or fewer. In this instance let us choose the name 'TSDATA', short for training survey data. This can be preserved by typing SAVE 'TSDATA' and pressing the return key. Note that within MINITAB the data-file must have inverted commas around it.

The command SAVE 'TSDATA' will store your data in a file and place that file in your directory. It will also name your file TSDATA.MTW within your directory to indicate that it is a **MINITAB** work file. Once you have 40–50 files created through different software you will find this a useful device.

You can now end this MINITAB session by typing STOP and pressing the return key. At this point you simply switch off your PC or, if using a mainframe use a simple system command to log out. To return to the earlier analogy, this is like leaving the house and locking it.

This completes the procedure for entering data through MINITAB and illustrates also how to enter and leave the package. The alternative way of getting data into MINITAB is to have it punched into a computer file in your directory by a data preparation service. There is then another procedure within MINITAB called the READ command (Ryan, Joiner and Ryan, 1985, pp 351–3) whereby you can read the data into the MINITAB columns C1–C11. Once the data are in MINITAB they should be saved as before using the SAVE command. Once the data are safely stored in the computer, the analysis can then begin.

Discussion points

1. As an exercise, find a group of colleagues or fellow students who are willing to complete the training survey in this chapter. Pool your data and then prepare them for computer analysis.
2. Obtain samples of output from your computer centre, displaying a couple of software packages – perhaps SPSS and MINITAB. Discuss the strengths and weaknesses of each in the context of communicating research results to a lay audience.

References

Joiner, R.B. & Ryan, T. (1985) *Minitab Handbook*, 2nd edn, PWS Publishers, Duxbury Press, Boston.

Nie, N. *et al.* (1975) *Statistical Package for the Social Sciences*. McGraw-Hill, New York.

Polit, D. & Hungler, B. (1989) *Essentials of Nursing Research*, 2nd edn, J.B. Lippincott Company, Philadelphia.

Chapter 6
Quantitative Analysis: descriptive statistics

In analysing quantitative data it is a good idea to start with a descriptive analysis, which is a good way for the researcher to get a feel for the data. But the results of descriptive analysis may also be invaluable in a research report, by giving the reader a picture of the form and structure of the data and some idea of the scale and variation of the research. But before undertaking any analysis at all, some preliminary tasks are essential.

Missing values, cleaning and validating

Chapter 5 discussed the why and how of coding missing values. Inspection of the training survey data (Table 5.1) reveals that there are four missing values: in row 15 of C1, hospital; in row 19 of C2, years qualified; in row 20 of C5, view of training; and in row 4 of C9, teaching of numeracy. Note the missing value codes of 9 for C1 (a one-digit code); 99.9 for C2; 99 for C5; and 9 for C9. It is now necessary to tell the software programme that 9 is not a real value in these cases, but denotes missing data. Table 6.1 shows how to do this in MINITAB. First go into MINITAB and retrieve your saved data by typing:

MINITAB

RETRIEVE 'TSDATA'

PRINT C1–C11

Table 6.1   Denoting missing values in MINITAB.

MTB > code (9)	to '*' in C1, put back in C1
MTB > code (99.9)	to '*' in C2, put back in C2
MTB > code (99)	to '*' in C5, put back in C5
MTB > code (9)	to '*' in C9, put back in C9

This set of commands will result in the printing of an asterisk where each missing value has been. MINITAB uses the asterisk to denote missing values. The command:

PRINT C1–C11

will provide from screen a printout of the data set with all the missing values denoted by asterisks. This is shown in Table 6.2.

Table 6.2   Training survey data with missing values denoted.

ROW	C1	C2	C3	C4	C5	C6	C7	C8	C9	C10	C11
1	1	7.4	12	5	7	1	4	3	3	2	1
2	3	9.8	4	2	1	2	5	1	3	1	5
3	3	10.2	3	4	9	4	4	5	4	1	1
4	3	9.1	3	2	8	3	4	5	*	1	1
5	3	12.5	1	4	4	4	5	4	4	4	1
6	5	6.3	11	2	12	1	1	1	4	5	2
7	1	10.6	6	3	2	1	4	5	4	1	2
8	2	6.1	11	2	12	2	2	5	5	2	1
9	1	8.9	13	5	4	2	1	2	5	2	1
10	4	9.2	7	1	11	2	2	4	1	1	1
11	1	4.7	7	3	5	3	4	5	4	1	1
12	4	4.0	6	3	2	1	4	2	4	1	4
13	5	16.3	3	3	11	1	4	4	4	5	4
14	4	8.5	6	2	2	1	4	2	5	2	1
15	*	4.6	8	4	1	1	1	1	1	1	4
16	1	14.9	13	1	1	2	4	2	4	1	2
17	5	1.5	9	4	6	4	5	4	5	3	1
18	1	10.4	5	2	5	3	4	5	5	1	2
19	2	*	5	3	8	1	4	5	5	2	1
20	5	10.8	7	4	*	4	5	3	4	1	1
21	5	1.6	13	5	8	4	5	4	4	3	4
22	2	10.7	2	5	12	2	5	4	4	4	1
23	1	1.8	10	4	8	1	1	4	4	3	3
24	2	9.5	11	4	3	2	4	4	5	1	1
25	4	11.2	7	2	10	2	1	1	4	1	5
26	2	10.3	13	2	11	1	5	4	5	1	1
27	2	10.6	12	3	3	4	5	2	1	2	4
28	3	13.4	13	4	1	1	1	5	2	1	3
29	2	10.9	1	1	5	3	5	5	3	2	1
30	1	12.0	10	2	8	1	4	1	5	1	1

MTB > SAVE 'TSDATA'
Worksheet saved into file: TSDATA.MTW
MTB > STOP

To store this version of the data type

SAVE 'TSDATA'

To end this MINITAB session type STOP and press the return key; you may then inspect your directory or log out.

Error can creep in at a number of stages in empirical research, however carefully the work is undertaken, and you may need to clean or validate your data. It is impossible to detect, let alone remove, all sources of error, but it may be helpful to describe a few obvious ones which can be highlighted, using the MINITAB package. The procedures are different for discrete and for continuous variables.

For discrete variables (all in the training survey data set, except C2) the command:

TALLY C5

will list each value that C5 takes and the frequency with which that value occurs. 'View of training' (C5) should only take values between 1 and 12, so you can see at a glance whether this is so. Table 6.3 provides some sample outputs.

Table 6.3 Using the tally command to clean data.
MTB > TALLY C5

C5	Count
1	4
2	3
3	2
4	2
5	3
6	1
7	1
8	5
9	1
10	1
11	3
12	3
N =	29
* =	1

This technique should be applied in turn to all of the discrete variables. The closest equivalent technique for continuous variables is to ask MINITAB to draw a histogram. We will return to the histogram in more detail later in this chapter, but for now, Table 6.4 demonstrates some sample output. By inspecting the histogram, illegal values may be identified by observing the range of the data. Note that MINITAB prints the midpoint of each range, e.g. the midpoint of the range 1–3 is 2, and so on.

The identification of illegal values in any of the variables may have arisen from a coding, transcription or data-entering error. The correct values may often be easily identified by returning to the sheets on which data were originally recorded. If the correct values cannot be ascertained the value should be denoted as missing. If, however, the correct values are available, the data should be edited: this can involve

Table 6.4   Histogram of C2, years qualified in service.

MTB > histogram C2
Histogram of C2   N = 29   N* = 1

Midpoint	Count	
2	3	***
4	3	***
6	2	**
8	3	***
10	12	************
12	3	***
14	2	**
16	1	*

N.B. If a value falls on a group boundary, it is assigned to the higher interval of the two whose dividing boundary it falls on e.g. 9.0 years would go in the group 9–11 (midpoint 10).

changing data, deleting data or inserting data. Table 6.5 provides some commands which will change the data in Table 6.2 and then change it back to the form in which it appears in Table 6.2.

Any eventual changes in your data set must then be recorded and stored again if you want them to be preserved for later use. This is done, as before, by typing SAVE 'TSDATA'. Facilities for changing, deleting and inserting (illustrated in Table 6.5) are also invaluable at the stage of entering data; though if a mistake is identified immediately, and before the return key has been pressed, the delete key is the easiest way to deal with it.

It is very useful to be able to keep a record of all work done within MINITAB as there is then no need to take notes from the screen. Everything that appears on the screen will be stored if you insert the following command as soon as you go into MINITAB:

OUTFILE 'RESULTS1'

From this point onwards, everything which appears on your screen will be stored in a file called RESULTS1. When you finish your MINITAB session, type STOP and you can then list the contents of your directory. This will include a file called RESULTS1. It may have an added identifier such as RESULTS1.LIS, to indicate that it is a work file, which distinguishes it from files ending in .MTW, which are saved data files.

You can print RESULTS1 using a system command on a mainframe computer. For all analysis which follows, it is advisable to use the OUTFILE facility. The only snag is that it will contain your mistakes as well as your successes, so it is a good idea to go through it as soon as you have printed it and put a red line through any parts which did not work out.

Table 6.5 Changing, deleting and inserting.

MTB > LET C2 (11) = 25.4
MTB > PRINT C2

C2

7.4	9.8	10.2	9.1	12.5	6.3	10.6	6.1	8.9	9.2	25.4
4.0	16.3	8.5	4.6	14.9	1.5	10.4	*	10.8	1.6	10.7
1.8	9.5	11.2	10.3	10.6	13.4	10.9	12.0			

MTB > LET C2 (11) = 4.7
MTB > PRINT C2

C2

7.4	9.8	10.2	9.1	12.5	6.3	10.6	6.1	8.9	9.2	4.7
4.0	16.3	8.5	4.6	14.9	1.5	10.4	*	10.8	1.6	10.7
1.8	9.5	11.2	10.3	10.6	13.4	10.9	12.0			

MTB > DELETE 16, C6
MTB > PRINT C6

C6

| 1 | 2 | 4 | 3 | 4 | 1 | 1 | 2 | 2 | 2 | 3 | 1 | 1 | 1 | 1 |
| 4 | 3 | 1 | 4 | 4 | 2 | 1 | 2 | 2 | 1 | 4 | 1 | 3 | 1 | |

MTB > insert between rows 15 and 16 of C6
DATA > 2
DATA > END
MTB > PRINT C6

C6

| 1 | 2 | 4 | 3 | 4 | 1 | 1 | 2 | 2 | 2 | 3 | 1 | 1 | 1 | 1 |
| 2 | 4 | 3 | 1 | 4 | 4 | 2 | 1 | 2 | 2 | 1 | 4 | 1 | 3 | 1 |

Descriptive analysis: a strategy

The main reason why people have problems in making sense of numerical research information is that there is too much of it. Raw data, uninterpreted, may convey almost nothing, even in small-scale projects with few variables and a limited number of subjects or cases. The purpose of descriptive statistics is to translate raw data into

Table 6.6   A framework for descriptive statistical analysis.

RAW DATA	$\longrightarrow$	PICTORIAL OR GRAPHICAL REPRESENTATION	$\longrightarrow$	SUMMARY STATISTICS

data

frequency distribution
- histogram
- dotplot
- stem and leaf
- pie chart

measure of location –
mean or median
measure of scatter –
standard deviation
or semi-inter-
quartile range

$\longleftarrow$ all levels of measurement $\longrightarrow\!\!\times\!\!\longleftarrow$ ratio and interval $\longrightarrow$
(occasionally ordinal)

digestible, communicative pieces of information; hence the alternative term, summary statistics. You can use the framework illustrated in Table 6.6, to analyse quantitative data, whatever research design has been used, or whatever subsequent analysis is intended.

Starting with raw data, the data as collected are usually in the form of a data matrix as in Table 5.1. The first stage is to try to make sense of the raw data through pictures or graphs. This can best be done by using the frequency distribution for each variable: this is the frequency with which each value of a variable appears in a data set. This is precisely the information that the TALLY command provides for discrete variables, as displayed in Table 6.3. It can be used pictorially in a variety of ways including histograms, dotplots, stem and leaf diagrams and pie-charts, all of which provide summary information at a glance (see the following section for more detail). As the Chinese proverb has it, one picture is worth a thousand words, so you should use graphical presentation whenever possible, especially for a lay audience.

Next you should calculate two summary statistics for each variable – one measure of location and one measure of scatter. This stage applies to interval and ratio level data only. Measures of location are intended to give a numerical estimate of the central value of the variable and a mean or a median (not both) should suffice. Other measures of location occasionally used include the mode: this is the value occurring most frequently. In general this is not recommended as a measure of location as it can be misleading, particularly if distributions are irregularly shaped. For most variables, a mean or a median convey the best summary information. You should also give a measure of scatter – also known as variation or dispersion – for each variable. This should be either a standard deviation, if you are using the mean, or a semi-inter-quartile range, (SIQR) if you are using the median.

To summarize briefly, for each variable there should first be graphical representation based on the frequency distribution; then, for interval- and ratio-level variables, the calculation of two summary statistics, a measure of location and a measure of scatter should be provided.

Pictorial and graphical representation

Most graphs and pictures relating to individual variables are based on the frequency distribution of the variable. This consists of each value of the variable and the frequency with which each value appears in the data set. For example, the frequency distributions for C1 (hospital), and C5 (view of training) are shown in Table 6.7. Being frequency distributions of variables, these can be established through MINITAB using the command:

TALLY C1,C5

Table 6.7 Frequency distributions for hospital and view of training.

Hospital		View of Training	
Value	Frequency	Value	Frequency
1(Hilltown)	8	1	4
2(Lowtown)	7	2	3
3(Hightown)	5	3	2
4(Rivertown)	4	4	2
5(Downtown)	5	5	3
	29*	6	1
		7	1
		8	5
* One missing value		9	1
		10	1
		11	3
		12	3
			29*

* One missing value

Similar frequency tables may be drawn up for all the other discrete variables in the training survey data set.

For continuous variables like C2 (years qualified), you will have to group data into suitable intervals before you can draw up a frequency distribution. The choice of interval is a matter for the researcher, but it should be such as to help, not hinder drawing a histogram to show the shape of the distribution. You may not get this right first time; as an

Table   6.8   Frequency   distribution   for   yearrs
qualified.

Range of Values	Frequency
1.05– 3.05	3
3.05– 5.05	3
5.05– 7.05	2
7.05– 9.05	3
9.05–11.05	12
11.05–13.05	3
13.05–15.05	2
15.05–17.05	1

exercise you may like to try presenting C2 (years qualified), in such a form, with or without the aid of Table 6.8 which shows suitable groups and the frequency of values in each. This procedure may be achieved using MINITAB by the command HISTOGRAM C2.

Having obtained frequency distribution tables of both discrete and continuous variables, the next step is to plot them. For either discrete or continuous variables the histogram may be drawn in MINITAB. Table 6.9 shows samples of histograms from the training survey data.

For C1, hospital, the histogram plots the data exactly as laid out in the frequency distribution table (Table 6.7). C5 (view of training), provides a rather erratic histogram, as might be expected given the arbitrary assignment of codes to views. For C1 and C5, the number labelled midpoint by MINITAB is actually the discrete value, these being discrete variables. (MINITAB uses the same layout for histograms of discrete and continuous variables).

For continuous variables such as C2, the midpoint printed is at the centre of the interval. The intervals used here are 1–3, 3–5, 5–7, 7–9, 9–11, 11–13, 13–15, 15–17. In the manual frequency distribution shown in Table 6.8, slightly different intervals were used to avoid the problem of a value occurring exactly on a boundary. MINITAB deals with this by placing boundary values in the higher interval. But, as you can see by comparing Tables 6.8 and 6.9, the results are the same. You will find that MINITAB prints histograms on their sides, compared to those in many textbooks, but this need not matter provided that the histogram is clearly labelled. Similarly, MINITAB presents data in rows of asterisks instead of the lines or boxes conventionally used; these are matters of presentation not substance.

An alternative presentation for discrete variables is the dotplot. Table 6.10 provides some examples; these are achieved by typing:

DOTPLOT C1

As you can see the dotplot, although very similar to the histogram tends to be more spread out and thus less suitable for revealing the

Table 6.9 Histogram of C1, C2, C5.

Histogram of C1	N = 29	N* = 1
Midpoint	Count	
1	8	********
2	7	*******
3	5	*****
4	4	****
5	5	*****

Histogram of C2	N = 29	N* = 1
Midpoint	Count	
2	3	***
4	3	***
6	2	**
8	3	***
10	12	************
12	3	***
14	2	**
16	1	*

Histogram of C5	N = 29	N* = 1
Midpoint	Count	
1	4	****
2	3	***
3	2	**
4	2	**
5	3	***
6	1	*
7	1	*
8	5	*****
10	1	*
11	3	***
12	3	***

shape of the frequency distribution for a continuous variable. For discrete variables, the two methods are almost identical, except that the dotplot shows frequency on the y axis and the histogram on the x axis.

As a refinement of the dotplot command in these examples, there are two extra subcommands (which can also be used with the command HISTOGRAM). A semicolon after any MINITAB command indicates that subcommands are to follow. This is acknowledged by the

Table 6.10   Dotplots of C1, C6, C7.

```
MTB  > dotplot C1;
SUBC > increment = 1;
SUBC > START = 1.
```

Points missing or out of range

```
  :                 .
  :            :             .
  :            :         :          :          .
  :            :         :          :          :
  + ·········· + ······· + ······· + ······ +−C1
 1.0          2.0       3.0        4.0        5.0
```

```
MTB  > dotplot C6;
SUBC > increment = 1;
SUBC > START = 1.
```

```
  :
  :
  :            :
  :            :         :
  :            :         :          :
  :            :         :          :
  + ·········· + ······· + ······· +−C6
 1.0          2.0       3.0        4.0
```

```
MTB  > dotplot C7;
SUBC > increment = 1;
SUBC > START = 1.
```

```
                                     :          .
                                     :          :
  :                                  :          :
  :            :                     :          :
  + ·········· + ······· + ······· + ······ +−C7
 1.0          2.0       3.0        4.0        5.0
```

message SUBC >. The subcommand, INCREMENT = 1, tells the package that you want plots at intervals of 1 and the subcommand, START = 1, tells the package that you want to start at the value 1. The final subcommand ends with a full stop to indicate that there are no further subcommands to come. This facility allows you to manipulate the scale of a dotplot or histogram and, in the latter case, enables easy manipulation of the groups selected to provide the histogram you want.

Another increasingly popular graph is the stem-and-leaf diagram.

Table 6.11   Stem-and-leaf diagram of C2.

MTB > STEM-AND-LEAF C2	
Stem-and-leaf diagram of C2	N = 29
Leaf unit = 1.0	N* = 1

3	0 111
3	0
6	0 444
9	0 667
(6)	0 889999
14	1 000000001
5	1 223
2	1 4
1	1 6

This splits each value into a stem (which might be the 'tens') and a leaf (which might be the 'units'). Table 6.11 shows a stem-and-leaf diagram for C2 (years qualified).

Each value is split into its tens and units. The values below 10 have a stem of 0 and the leaves appear as integers: so the three ones represent the values 1.5, 1.6 and 1.8 and so on. The values of 10 and above have a stem of 1 and a leaf of the units so that the final value 16, represents the value 16.3. Whilst the decimal point is lost in this illustration of the technique, it has the general advantage of displaying frequency using the actual values.

Last but not least comes the pie-chart. In this widely-used graphic system the frequency distribution count is converted to degrees of a circle; it is presented as a cook's eye-view of a circular pie carved up into slices showing individual values or ranges. For a discrete variable such as C1 (hospital), a pie chart would be drawn as shown in Table 6.12. Similarly pie charts could be produced for continuous variables, with slices of the pie representing each range or group chosen.

Table 6.12   Pie-chart of C1.

Value	Frequency	Degrees
1	8	99[*]
2	7	87
3	5	62
4	4	50
5	5	62
	29	360

[*] e.g. $\dfrac{8}{29} \times 360 = 99$

Analysis through pictorial and graphical representation is suitable and desirable for all levels of measurement. In fact it is the end point of analysis for nominal and ordinal data, to which more sophisticated summary statistical techniques should not normally be applied. For this, as well as higher levels of measurement, however, diagrams and pictures give useful visual information about the frequency distribution. Histogram and dotplots also provide information about the shape of the distribution, which can be significant at the next stage of analysis, the calculation of summary statistics.

Summary statistics

We have noted earlier that for each variable measured at the ratio or interval level, two summary statistics should be calculated, a measure of location and a measure of scatter. A useful working rule is as follows: if the frequency distribution is symmetrical, use the mean as the measure of location and its partner, the standard deviation, as the measure of scatter; if the frequency distribution is assymetrical, use the median as the measure of location and its partner, the semi-inter-quartile range (SIQR), to measure scatter.

The mean is the sum of all observations divided by the number of observations. The median is the central value (or the average of two central values) when data are placed in order.

The following simple sums illustrate the calculation of each:

For the numbers 4, 7, 3, 6, 8:

$$\text{the mean} = \frac{\Sigma x}{n} = \frac{4 + 7 + 3 + 6 + 8}{5} \qquad = 5.6$$

the median: 3, 4, 6, 7, 8 $\qquad\qquad = 6$
(n = odd)

For the numbers 4, 7, 3, 6, 8, 10:

$$\text{the mean} = \frac{\Sigma x}{n} = \frac{4 + 7 + 3 + 6 + 8 + 10}{6} = 6.3$$

the median: 3, 4, 6, 7, 8, 10 $\qquad\qquad = 6.5$
(n = even)

If a distribution is perfectly symmetrical, the mean and the median will be the same; e.g. for the numbers 2, 4, 6, 8, 10:

$$\text{the mean} = \frac{2 + 4 + 6 + 8 + 10}{5} \qquad = 6$$

the median: 2, 4, 6, 8, 10 $\qquad\qquad = 6$

However, at the next stage of analysis much more powerful tech-niques can be based on the mean (and the standard deviation,) and they should therefore normally be used as summary statistics for sym-metrical distributions.

In contrast, the median is a much better measure of location for skewed distributions. To illustrate this, we can create an artificial highly skewed distribution by replacing the final observation, 10, in the previous example, with the value 30, and recalculate, for example:

for the numbers 2, 4, 6, 8, 30:

$$\text{the mean} = \frac{2 + 4 + 6 + 8 + 30}{5} = 10$$

the median: 2, 4, 6, 8, 30 $\qquad = 6$

Note how the single abnormal value which creates the skew has the effect of pulling the mean up to 10. Note also how poor a measure of location this mean now is — bigger than 80% of the values. The median, in contrast, has remained unaffected and still provides a sound measure of location. For this reason, the median is the appropriate measure of location for assymetrical or skewed distributions, and its partner, the semi-inter-quartile range the correct measure of scatter. Means or medians and their partners may be used appropriately for ratio and interval level data. They should never be used with nominal data, where numerical values are mere labels, not real numbers, and they should be used with care and only in some circumstances with

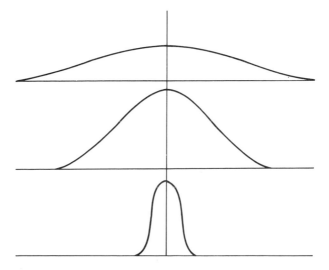

Fig. 6.1 Three different distributions with identical measures of location

ordinal data. Before illustrating this, however, we need to go a bit more deeply into the measurement of scatter.

A measure of location is not sufficient to describe a distribution. In the three figures in Fig. 6.1, for instance, the three distributions shown are self-evidently very different, but have the same measure of location.

What makes the difference in Fig. 6.1 is the scatter. If the distribution is symmetrical this should be measured by the standard deviation. The standard deviation may be thought of as the average distance of the data from the mean. This average distance is squared up early in the calculation and squared down through taking the square root at the end. For a less formal explanation of this formula, see Reid and Boore (1987). The calculation of the standard deviation is best illustrated through a simple example for the numbers 4, 7, 3, 6 and 8:

$$
\begin{array}{cc}
x & x^2 \\
4 & 16 \\
7 & 49 \\
3 & 9 \\
6 & 36 \\
8 & 64 \\
\hline
\Sigma x = 28 & \Sigma x^2 = 174
\end{array}
$$

$$
\begin{aligned}
\text{Standard deviation} &= \sqrt{\dfrac{\Sigma x^2 - \dfrac{(\Sigma x)^2}{n}}{n - 1}} \\[2ex]
&= \sqrt{\dfrac{174 - \dfrac{28^2}{5}}{4}} \\[2ex]
&= \sqrt{\dfrac{174 - 156.8}{4}} \\[2ex]
&= \sqrt{\dfrac{17.2}{4}} \\[2ex]
&= \sqrt{4.3} \\[1ex]
&= 2.074
\end{aligned}
$$

For an asymmetrical distribution the best measure of scatter is the semi-inter-quartile range. This is the partner of the median, that value which comes at the mid point of the ordered data and which divides the ordered data into two equal halves.

We can go on to identify *quartiles* which divide the data on similar principles into four areas as shown in Fig. 6.2.

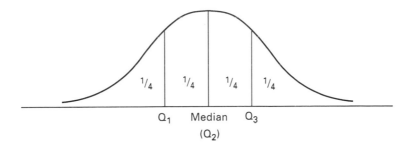

Fig. 6.2 Sample distribution showing quartiles

The lower quartile, Q_1, cuts off the bottom quarter of the values, the median, Q_2, halves the data, and the upper quartile, Q_3, cuts off the top quarter of the values. The SIQR is $\frac{1}{2}(Q_3 - Q_1)$. A simple example would be:

raw data: 4, 6, 7, 9, 2, 3, 5, 1
ordered data: 1, 2, 3, 4, 5, 6, 7, 9

$$Q_1 \quad Q_2 \quad Q_3$$

Of the eight values, Q_1 cuts off the bottom two at 2.5, the mean of 2 and 3; the median, Q_2, is 4.5; and Q_3 cuts off the top two values at 6.5, the mean of 6 and 7. Having calculated the quartiles, $Q_1 = 2.5$ and $Q_3 = 6.5$, the SIQR is easily computed by subtracting Q_1 from Q_3 and dividing by two. So:

$$SIQR = \tfrac{1}{2}(6.5 - 2.5) = 2$$

Calculating these summary statistics is not enough. They have to be used judiciously. The tedium of calculation can be lessened by using one simple MINITAB command to print summary statistics but the time saved should be used to try to avoid indiscriminate reporting of them.

To obtain summary statistics using MINITAB, C2 from the training survey data will be used. C2 is a ratio level variable denoting the number of years qualified. The command and output are:

MTB > DESCRIBE C2

	N	N*	MEAN	MEDIAN	TRMEAN	STDEV	SEMEAN	MIN	MAX	Q_1	Q_3
C2	29	1	8.890	9.800	8.889	3.772	0.700	1.50	16.3	6.20	10.85

Here N is the sample size; N* is the number of missing values for that variable; the mean and median are as shown; the TRMEAN is obtained by disregarding the top and bottom 5% of values and averaging the central 90% (thus avoiding extreme values). The STDEV is the standard deviation; and the SEMEAN is the standard error of the mean, which is the term given to the standard deviation of the mean and is calculated by dividing S(STDEV) by $\sqrt{N}$ (see Chapter 7, single sample t-tests). MIN and MAX give the minimum and maximum values and Q_1 and Q_3 are the lower and upper quartiles.

You now need to consider the shape of the distribution of C2 (see Table 6.9) and choose one measure of location and one measure of scatter. Table 6.9 suggests a fairly symmetrical distribution so the mean and standard deviation might be appropriate. But if you have doubts about whether it is sufficiently symmetrical, a safer option would be to use the median and to calculate the SIQR $= \frac{1}{2} (Q_3 - Q_1) = 2.325$. C2 presents a fairly difficult problem in terms of symmetry, but the right decision will usually be much more obvious.

As to the rest of the training survey data, C1 (hospital), C3 (training institution) and C5 (view of training) are nominal variables: under no circumstances should the 'describe' function be used, nor should any summary statistics be calculated. A simple reporting of the percentage in each category should be the extent of the descriptive statistical analysis. A subcommand of the TALLY command will do this. The command and subcommand are:

TALLY C1,C3,C5;
ALL.

In Table 6.13, the frequency in numbers (COUNT) and the frequency as a percentage (PERCENT) are shown. These counts and percentages, perhaps displayed by a pie-chart or other graphical device, are as far as you should go in the direction of descriptive statistics for a nominal variable.

Ordinal variables such as C4 and C6 and C6–C12 in the training survey data set require individual consideration. C4 and C6–C12 all use five-point scales. In such cases, the mean or median may be used as a measure of location, but the notion of scatter has little meaning when only five values can be taken by these variables. Indeed, purists might recommend treating them in the same way as nominal variables. While it may be acceptable to report a measure of location, even looking at it liberally, it makes no sense to base measurement of scatter on five-point scales, and as a working rule, ordinal variables should have ten or more values to make measures of scatter meaningful. In most cases it is best to use only the median with discrete data of this kind because it will reflect an actual value whereas the mean calculated to the nearest decimal place may be something (like a fraction of a child) that does not occur in practice. So the safe strategy is to use the TALLY function and simply report percentages in each category, and if you want to report measures of location also, use the DESCRIBE function.

Table 6.13 Summarizing nominal variables C1, C3, C5.

MTB > TALLY C1, C3, C5
SUBC > ALL

C1	Count	CUMCNT	PERCENT	CUMPCT
1	8	8	27.59	27.59
2	7	15	24.14	51.72
3	5	20	17.24	68.97
4	4	24	13.79	82.76
5	5	29	17.24	100.00
N =	29			

* = 1

C3	Count	CUMCNT	PERCENT	CUMPCT
1	2	2	6.67	6.67
2	1	3	3.33	10.00
3	3	6	10.00	20.00
4	1	7	3.33	23.33
5	2	9	6.67	30.00
6	3	12	10.00	40.00
7	4	16	13.33	53.33
8	1	17	3.33	56.67
9	1	18	3.33	60.00
10	2	20	6.67	66.67
11	3	23	10.00	76.67
12	2	25	6.67	83.33
13	5	30	16.67	100.00
N =	30			

C5	Count	CUMCNT	PERCENT	CUMPCT
1	4	4	13.79	13.79
2	3	7	10.34	24.14
3	2	9	6.90	31.03
4	2	11	6.90	37.93
5	3	14	10.34	48.28
6	1	15	3.45	51.72
7	1	16	3.45	55.17
8	5	21	17.24	72.41
9	1	22	3.45	75.86
10	1	23	3.45	79.31
11	3	26	10.34	89.66
12	3	29	10.34	100.00
N =	29			

* = 1

Table 6.14 The cumulative distribution function for C2.

```
MTB  > SET C11
DATA > 3 5 7 9 11 13 15 17
DATA > END
MTB  > SET C12
DATA > 3 6 8 11 23 26 28 29
DATA > END
MTB  > PLOT C12, C11
```

```
        ─
C12  30  +                                                    *
        ─
        ─                                               *
        ─
        ─                                         *
        ─
        ─                                   *
        ─
     20  +
        ─
        ─
        ─
        ─
        ─
        ─                         *
        ─
     10  +
        ─
        ─                   *
        ─
        ─            *
        ─
        ─     *
        ─  *
        ─
      0  +
         ................+.............+.............+.............+.............+........... C11
                        5.0          7.5          10.0         12.5         15.0
```

*= 1

A graphical method for estimating the median and SIQR

You can also estimate the median and its partner the SIQR by plotting the cumulative distribution function. The cumulative frequency of a variable is the frequency of that value plus the frequency of all smaller values. The CUMCNT column in Table 6.13 shows this for C1, C3 and C5, and the CUMPCT column expresses it as a percentage.

To estimate the median of a continuous variable like C2, the upper end of each interval is plotted against the cumulative frequency. The MINITAB commands and the resultant plot are shown in Table 6.14.

Draw a line through the points shown in Fig. 6.14. This is a graph of the cumulative distribution function (CDF). Along the x-axis are the values of C2 and along the y-axis are its cumulative frequencies. Since the cumulative frequency of the median, Q_2, is 14.5 (half of the total cumulative frequency), by drawing across from the y-axis at 14.5, and then down to the x-axis, you can obtain an estimate of the median. (This is about 9, compared to the exact value of 9.8 obtained using the DESCRIBE function).

Similarly, by drawing across from the cumulative frequency of 7.25 (a quarter of the total), Q_1 can be estimated, and by drawing across from 21.75 (three quarters of the total) Q_3 can be estimated from the graph. This approximate method gives values of 6.2 for Q_1, and 10.4 for Q_3 – quite close to the MINITAB DESCRIBE values displayed earlier. In practice, though the exact results from the DESCRIBE function give greater accuracy, the CDF is valuable in itself as a graphical way of describing the data.

Descriptive analysis, in whatever form it is undertaken, can be fundamental to the ultimate success of a piece of research and a great help to the researcher and to those he or she wishes to inform and influence. For the researcher it may bring insights and understanding that will inform and improve later, more sophisticated or more detailed analysis. But it may also inspire valuable perceptions in sponsors, practitioners or other researchers that uplift and encourage or deter intuitive, political or prejudiced enquires in the same general area.

It should be added that researchers can sometimes over-analyse their raw data, not always to the advantage of the reports they produce. Statistical appendices can sometimes add to the bulk of a presentation without adding to its quality. If the researcher strives to embody them in his or her findings, the result can be an indigestible medley, merely confirming the prejudices of lay observers.

Starting out on a research project is like embarking on a journey. The main routes should be planned in advance, according to well-tried and declared methods, with a view to reaching an end point by a specified time. The plan should allow for contingencies, and even occasional detours, but its success should not be measured by quantitative or qualitative analyses of how the journey proceeded. Indeed these criteria are usually relevant only in relation to failure, a circumstance in which however impressive the accompanying statistics may be, they should not be allowed to cloud the issue.

Discussion point

1. Obtain a copy of a standard questionnaire – perhaps the General Health Questionnaire or the General Household Survey (see Goldberg, D.P. (1978) *Manual of the General Health Questionnaire*, NFER–Nelson, Windsor). Identify the level of measurement of some of the variables, reflect on the likely shape of the distribution and consider what summary statistics might be appropriate.

Reference

Reid, N. & Boore, J. (1987) *Research Methods and Statistics in Health Care.* Edward Arnold.

Chapter 7
Quantitative Analysis: One- and Two-Sample Tests

Descriptive statistical analysis is intended to summarize and describe the data actually collected. This may be extremely valuable, but it gives information only about subjects within the study. But the study objectives will often require more than simple description. They may require the investigation of cause-and-effect, exploration of differences between groups, or analysis of the status of subjects before and after an intervention. In investigating these more complex questions, it will often be important to be able to generalize from the results of the study subjects to a wider population. This process of generalization is called statistical inference: that is, making inferences about a wider population from a randomly-chosen study sample. This is done through tests of significance, which take a variety of forms, depending on the nature of the hypothesis being tested.

The logic of significance tests

All significance tests are based on the same logic, which can be explained as follows.

(1) Set up a null hypothesis (NH) (a statement of null effect) and an alternative hypothesis (AH).
(2) Collect relevant data.
(3) Calculate the probability of observing these data if the null hypothesis were true. This is done by calculating a test statistic.
(4) If the probability of observing these data, if the null hypothesis were true, is high, accept the null hypothesis. If not, reject it and accept the alternative hypothesis. In accepting a null hypothesis, no assertion about the truth of that hypothesis is being made; rather, there is no significant evidence against it, therefore it stands and we accept it. In accepting the alternative hypothesis there is equally no assertion of its truth, merely a recognition of significant evidence against the null hypothesis and therefore the alternative hypothesis stands.

It is important to make a correct statement of the null hypothesis, and to understand clearly the distinction between a research hypothesis and a null hypothesis. For example, a study of the social science content of courses in physiotherapy and nursing could be posed in terms of the following hypotheses:

(1) There is no difference in the social science content of physio-therapy and nursing courses (NH).
(2) There is a difference in the social science content of physiotherapy and nursing courses (AH).
(3) The social science content of nursing courses is greater than that of physiotherapy courses (AH).
(4) The social science content of physiotherapy courses is greater than that of nursing courses (AH).

Any of these statements could be legitimate research hypotheses, but only the first is a null hypothesis, being a statement of null effect.

The second, third and fourth statements provide a choice of alternative hypotheses. Statement (2) hypothesizes a difference in social science content, but does not assert in which direction this difference operates: i.e. this statement could be true if either physiotherapy or nursing had the greater social science content. This statement, if chosen as the alternative hypothesis, would therefore lead to a two-tailed test. Statements (3) and (4) specify the direction of the difference; so either of these chosen as the alternative hypothesis leads to a one-tailed test. The alternative hypothesis is stated at the beginning of the research analysis. Its form will determine whether the test is one-tailed or two-tailed, which in turn affects the final stage in a significance test, when a decision is made about the acceptance or rejection of the null hypothesis.

A significance level should be specified for each statistical test. This attaches a probability of error to the rejection of the null hypothesis. Conventionally, the level chosen is 5%; if the null hypothesis is rejected, it means that there is a less-than 5% chance of observing these data if the null hypothesis were true. This is a fundamental issue in significance testing, which is not a black and white process and cannot establish anything with certainty. The conclusion is either that there is no significant evidence against the null hypothesis, in which case, it is accepted; or that there is significant evidence against it, in which case it is rejected at the 5% level.

The MINITAB package will provide, for every statistical test, the probability of the data being observed if the null hypothesis is true. If that probability (usually presented in the form p = some decimal) is greater than 0.05, the null hypothesis is accepted. If p is less than 0.05, the null hypothesis is rejected at the 5% level and the alternative hypothesis is accepted. If p is less than 0.01, rejection is at the 1% level i.e. the NH is rejected with a 1% probability of error; and if p is less than 0.001, rejection is at the 0.1% level.

These levels are conventions. The critical point normally chosen for rejection of a null hypothesis is 5%, and if there is even stronger evidence for rejection, these are conventionally reported at 1% or 0.1%. But you may choose other more stringent rejection levels. If, for example, an intervention with potentially serious consequences were being tested, 5% might well be considered too high an error level; then the critical rejection level could be set as low as seemed appropriate. You must state explicitly the significance level being used in a test.

These principles and the four logical steps apply to all statistical tests. The form of the null hypothesis can, however, vary a good deal, and the mechanics of calculating the test statistic depend on the particular kind of test being used. The next section will describe a number of widely-used statistical tests and illustrate their use with MINITAB. Hypothetical data will be used which can be entered into MINITAB using the SET command described earlier. These data may be saved, if required, using the SAVE command.

Some widely-used tests

First, one-sample tests will be described: these generally test hypotheses about the mean or the median of the population from which the sample comes. Then two-sample tests will be described: these test hypotheses about the difference between the population means or medians of the two samples.

In the next chapter, tests for association or correlation between two variables will be introduced. For all of these hypotheses, two kinds of test will be discussed: non-parametric tests which require no assumptions about the data distribution; and the more powerful parametric tests, which may only be legitimately used when the data meet the distributional assumptions required.

Table 7.1 classifies the statistical tests to be covered in this chapter. This classification is based on two underlying questions:

(1) What is the form of the null hypothesis to be tested – an NH concerning a single mean or median? Or an NH concerning two means or medians?
(2) Does the distribution of the data suggest a parametric or a non-parametric test? Is it continuous, bell-shaped, symmetrical? Or is it discrete?

For each test, Table 7.1 indicates the lowest level of measurement which is required. For example, t-tests require at least interval-level measurement, which means they can be done on interval- or-ratio level data, but not on nominal or ordinal data. For tests concerning population means and medians, it is essential that the samples are representative of the populations from which they are drawn. This

Table 7.1 Classification of statistical tests.

	SUBJECT OF THE NULL HYPOTHESIS	
	Single mean/median	Two means/medians
Parametric	One-sample t-test (interval)	Paired t-test (interval) Independent t-test (interval)
Non-Parametric	One-sample sign test (nominal) One sample Wilcoxon test (ordinal)	Two-sample sign test (nominal) Two-sample Wilcoxon test (ordinal) Two-sample Mann Whitney test (ordinal)

means that probability sampling must be correctly used in selecting the sample. The importance of this cannot be overstated as the process of statistical inference fundamentally depends on the representativeness of the sample selected.

The normal distribution

All the parametric tests in Table 7.1 require the data to follow the normal (or Gaussian) distribution. While these tests are fairly robust (i.e. it is permissible to depart to some extent from the distributional requirements), some characteristics of the normal distribution should be present if they are to be correctly used. As a rule-of-thumb, the data should be continuous, bell-shaped and symmetrical if a test based on the normal distribution is to be used. Otherwise, a non-parametric test should be used. However, non-parametric tests are less powerful than parametric tests, so it may be preferable to transform the data into a normal distribution so that a parametric technique may be used. Appendix A shows how to transform distributions using MINITAB.

Before embarking on any statistical test, the distribution(s) of the data should be studied to establish whether a parametric or non-parametric test is to be used. Then, depending on the form of the null hypothesis, a test may be chosen from Table 7.1.

Single mean/median tests

The single sample t-test is a parametric test which assumes that the data are normally distributed. The population variance (i.e. the square of the standard deviation) or standard deviation is not known in this example. This will be demonstrated on the variable C2 (years qualified), in the training survey data set. The null hypothesis that these data come from a population with a mean of seven years qualified will be tested. This might be done because national statistics show a mean of seven years qualified and you want to test how your data compare with the national distribution. The test is shown below in its four steps:

Step 1: N.H.: $\mu = 7$

A.H.: $\mu \neq 7$

(μ denotes the population mean)

Step 2: Data are as listed in Chapter 5, Table 1, C2.

Step 3: Calculation of test statistic.

$$t = \frac{\bar{x} - \mu}{s/\sqrt{n}}$$

$$t = \frac{8.89 - 7}{3.772/\sqrt{29}}$$

$$= 2.70$$

where $\bar{x}$ is the sample mean s is the sample standard deviation and n is the sample size.

Step 4: The probability of observing this result if the NH is true is established manually by comparing this calculated t-value with the tabulated t-value with $n - 1$ degrees of freedom so that $t_{28,5\%} = 2.0484$ (Neave, 1989, p20, column 2). (The appropriate tabulated t-value has associated degrees of freedom which depend on the sample size and the way in which the test statistic has been calculated. In the case of the single sample t-test the appropriate t-value has $n - 1$ degrees of freedom.)

Since the calculated t is larger than the tabulated t, you can reject the NH at the 5% level, and accept the AH. The conclusion is that the sample does not belong to a population with a mean of seven years qualified. This test can be done on MINITAB as follows:

RETRIEVE 'TSDATA'

Then type TTEST 7 C2. The printout this will result in is displayed in Table 7.2.

Note that in this example a two-tailed test was carried out, with an alternative hypothesis of $\mu \neq 7$. A one-tailed test with data drawn from a population with a mean greater than seven is carried out as follows:

Step 1: N.H.: $\mu = 7$

A.H.: $\mu > 7$

Step 2: Data as before

Table 7.2 **The single sample t-test (population variance unknown).**

	N	MEAN	STDEV	SE MEAN	T	P VALUE
		MTB > T-test 7 C2				
		Test of MU = 7.000 VS MU NE 7.000				
C2	29	8.890	3.772	0.700	2.70	0.012

Table 7.3 **The single sample t-test (one-tail, population variance unknown).**

	N	MEAN	STDEV	SE MEAN	T	P VALUE
		MTB > T-test 7 C2				
		SUBC > alt 1				
		Test of MU = 7.000 VS MU GT 7.000				
C2	29	8.890	3.772	0.700	2.70	0.0058

Step 3: $t = \dfrac{8.89 - 7}{3.772/\sqrt{29}} = 2.70$

Step 4: The Neave (1989) statistical tables are again consulted but this time the appropriate table for a one-tailed 5% test is used (see p. 20, column 1). The calculated value is larger than the tabulated value of 1.7011, so the null hypothesis is rejected and the alternative hypothesis is accepted.

Please note that for Step 1 some statisticians take the view that in a one-tailed test of this form the NH should include the 'less-than' i.e. $\mu \leq 7$. This is an area of continuing debate in this subject. The present text is based on the premise that the one-tailed test should only be used when the less-than possibility can be a priori demonstrably excluded, and thus the NH for one-tailed tests includes only the equal sign. All one-tailed tests in this book are handled in this way.

The one-tailed test is done in MINITAB by using a subcommand as follows:

TTEST 7 C2;

ALT 1.

The MINITAB procedures in Tables 7.2 and 7.3 provide the sample size, mean, standard deviation and the value of the calculated t-statistic. The mean of a variable itself has a distribution – if you think of drawing many samples and calculating the mean of each, you will see that these means will themselves have a mean and a standard deviation. The standard deviation of the means is called the standard error of the mean (called SEMEAN in MINITAB) and is, in fact, the bottom line of the t-statistic, $s/\sqrt{n}$. You will see SEMEAN on the MINITAB output in Tables 7.2 and 7.3.

The p value printed by MINITAB gives the exact probability of observing the data if the null hypothesis were true. This can simply be compared with the chosen level of significance to obtain the result at step four. Thus, using MINITAB precludes the need to use statistical tables. For the two-tailed example (see Table 7.3), p = 0.012 so you could safely reject at the 5% level; but the p value is not small enough to reject more strongly at the 1% level. So the conclusion would be to reject at 5% – the same result as obtained by using Neave's tables. For the one-tailed example, p = 0.0058, so it is certainly legitimate to reject at 5% and further to reject at 1% in this case: the conclusion is to reject at the 1% level.

Having rejected the null hypothesis that the sample comes from a population with a mean of seven, what can be said about the population from which it comes? A confidence interval can be constructed for its population mean. It is 95% certain that its population mean lies within:

$$\bar{x} \pm \frac{t\sigma}{\sqrt{n}}$$

(where $\bar{x}$ is the sample mean; σ is the standard deviation (in practice, where σ is not known, use s, the sample standard deviation); n is the sample size; and t has n − 1 degrees of freedom and is at 5% level (Neave, p. 20)

$$8.89 \pm \frac{2.0518 \times 3.772}{\sqrt{29}}$$

8.89 ± 1.435

$7.455, 10.325$

Note that the value 7, which was tested, lies outside this range and hence the rejection of the NH at the 5% level. Thus the calculation of a confidence interval and the testing of a specified hypothesis are analogous statistical procedures.

For a 95% confidence interval, when the population standard deviation is unknown, Table 7.4 provides a MINITAB output.

The previous procedures assumed that the population variance or standard deviation was unknown. If it is known, then the standard deviation of the sample (s in the test statistic), is replaced by σ, (sigma)

Table 7.4   95 % confidence interval, variance unknown.

	N	MEAN	STDEV	SE MEAN	95 PERCENT CI
		MTB > t interval 95 PERCENT, C2			
C2	29	8.890	3.772	0.700	(7.455, 10.325)

the population standard deviation and the tabulated t-value is 1.96 for a two-tailed test, irrespective of the sample size, so the NH is rejected if a figure larger than 1.96 is calculated.

This can be done in MINITAB with the command (for a known standard deviation of 8) of:

ZTEST MU = 7 SIGMA = 8 C2

This will give a p value of 0.20 which leads to an acceptance of the NH. Similarly, if the standard deviation is known, the confidence interval formula replaces s with the known σ, and the t becomes 1.96, whatever the sample size. The MINITAB command for this is:

ZINTERVAL 95 PERCENT SIGMA = 8 C2

The output is given in Table 7.5 below.

If, however, the data do not meet the normal assumptions required for the preceding techniques, a non-parametric technique should be used. If you have done a descriptive analysis at an earlier stage you should have chosen a median as a measure of location, if the data distribution is assymetric. Non-parametric tests in this chapter are concerned with the median of the underlying population.

Table 7.5   95 % confidence interval, variance unknown.

	N	MEAN	STDEV	SE MEAN	95 PERCENT CI
		MTB > Z interval 95 PERCENT sigma = 8, C2			
		The assumed sigma = 8.00			
C2	29	8.89	3.77	1.49	(5.97, 11.81)

The sign test

This makes no assumptions whatsoever about the distribution of the data. It will be demonstrated on a set of data showing lengths of service (in years) for 30 nurses. Table 7.6 displays the data and a histogram. The distribution is heavily skewed, so a non-parametric test is advisable.

Table 7.6   Data and histogram of length of service.

MTB > print C1

C1

12.9020	2.4913	0.8662	1.1392	0.9685	1.3276	4.6573
1.1560	4.9653	0.5611	13.1706	1.4857	12.3496	4.7444
2.9316	2.4448	6.0116	1.9555	4.5976	4.1250	0.3797
9.2684	8.5081	3.7509	2.8984	5.3261	2.4389	9.2303
4.5314	5.4975					

MTB > histogram C1

Histogram of C1   N = 30

Midpoint	Count	
0	1	*
1	7	*******
2	4	****
3	2	**
4	2	**
5	7	*******
6	1	*
7	0	
8	0	
9	3	***
10	0	
11	0	
12	1	*
13	2	**

MTB > histogram C1
SUBC > increment = 2

Histogram of C1   N = 30

Midpoint	Count	
0.00	4	****
2.00	10	**********
4.00	7	*******
6.00	3	***
8.00	1	*
10.00	2	**
12.00	2	**
14.00	1	*

The steps in carrying out a sign test are as follows:

Step 1: N.H.: The data come from a population with a median of
5 : $\eta = 5$
A.H.: $\eta \neq 5$ (two-tailed)

Step 2: Collect data – See Table 7.6.

Step 3: For each observation, assign a '+' if it is above 5, a '−' if it is below 5 and a 'o' if it is exactly 5. Then count the number of plus signs and the number of minus signs. The smaller of these is the test statistic, S.
Number of pluses = 9
Number of minuses = 21. Number of 'o' = 0 = > S = 9.

Step 4: Identify the degrees of freedom* which equal the sample size minus any 'o' values. (Like the tabulated t and all test statistics, the tabulated S values are presented with associated degrees of freedom which depend on the sample size and the way in which the particular test statistic is calculated.)

$$n = 30$$

Consult Neave (1989) p.29 for the critical value of 9. If the tablulated value is less than or equal to the calculated S value, reject the NH. In this case S = 9 so reject NH at the 5% level and conclude that the data do not come from a population with a median of 5.

Note that in a sign test, small values of S reject the NH, whereas in a t test, large values of t reject the NH. Table 7.7 shows how to do this test in MINITAB.

The MINITAB package prints the exact probability of observing the data under the NH, and this being less than 0.05, the NH is rejected. This precludes the need to use statistical tables as in step four above. Table 7.8 shows a one-tailed test of the same NH with the AH $\eta < 5$.

The Wilcoxon test provides a half-way house between the t-test, which requires normal assumptions and the sign test which makes no assumptions whatever about the data. The Wilcoxon test should be used when the distribution is approximately symmetrical, but it need not be normal. Table 7.9 displays data from a five-inch long-scale with extreme opposition to a move to degree level initial education at one end, and strong support at the other end. Subjects placed a mark along this five-inch scale and the distance of this mark from the left-end point was measured; a histogram for 20 subjects is shown in Table 7.9.

The steps in the Wilcoxon test are:

Step 1: N.H.: the data come from a population with a median of three, $\eta = 3$ (see note about one-tailed t-tests).
A.H.: $\eta < 3$ (one-tailed)

Table 7.7 Sign test (two-tailed) in MINITAB.

			MTB > s-test 5 C1			
			Sign test of median = 5.000 versus NE 5.000			
	N	Below	Equal	Above	P-value	Median
C1	30	21	0	9	0.0428	3.938

Table 7.8 One-tailed sign test.

			MTB > s-test 5 C1; SUBC > ALT −1.			
			Sign test of median = 5.000 versus LT 5.000			
	N	Below	Equal	Above	P-value	Median
C1	30	21	0	9	0.0214	3.938

Table 7.9 Data and histogram for attitude scale.

			MTB > print C2			
			C2			
2.84109	2.69411	2.27705	2.59171	3.88024	3.84201	4.30648
1.89908	2.77183	2.31795	3.13904	2.09435	2.76580	3.25188
3.25539	2.75364	3.23566	3.09002	2.83412	3.62020	

MTB > histogram C2

Histogram of C2		N = 20
Midpoint	Count	
2.0	2	**
2.4	3	***
2.8	6	******
3.2	5	*****
3.6	1	*
4.0	2	**
4.4	1	*

Step 2: Collect data – see Table 7.9.
Step 3: (a) Subtract 3 from each observation (3 being the value
of the population median cited in the N.H.);
(b) take the absolute values;
(c) rank the absolute values;
(d) assign the original sign (plus or minus) from stage (a);
(e) sum the ranks with plus signs and sum the ranks with
minus signs and the smaller is W, the test statistic.
Now carrying out (a) to (e):
(a) −0.15891   −0.30589   −0.72295   −0.40829
    −1.10092   −0.22817   −0.68205   0.13904
     0.25539   −0.24636   0.23566   0.09002

     0.88024   0.84201   1.30648
    −0.90565   −0.23420   0.25188
    −0.16588   0.62020
(b) and carrying out (c) and (d):
    −3   −11 −15 −12 +17 +16   +20
    −19   −5   −14 +2   −18 −6   +9
    +10   −8   +7   +1   −4   +13
(e) Sum of pluses = 95
    Sum of minuses = 115
    So W = 95
Step 4: Find a critical value by looking up tabulated values of W
(Neave, 1989, p.29) for n = 20 (no values dropped), so
that:

$$W_{20,5\%} - 60 \quad \text{(one-tailed)}$$

Since the calculated value is larger, accept the NH. Note
that, as in the sign test, large calculated values of the test
statistic accept the NH, small values reject (in contrast to
the t-test which is the other way around).

Table 7.10 shows this test done through MINITAB. MINITAB prints
the exact probability of observing these data under the NH (0.361) and
since this is greater than 0.05, the NH is accepted. MINITAB precludes
the need to look up statistical tables at step four.

In these tests for single samples, concerning hypotheses about
means and medians, for normally distributed data, the t-test should be
used, for symmetrical but non-normal data the Wilcoxon can be used,
and the sign test may be used with any kind of distribution. This stage
of analysis should follow logically from descriptive analysis. It is point-
less to produce means and standard deviations as summary statistics
and then to test hypotheses about medians. If you have chosen means
and standard deviations, the same logic should lead you to a t-test.

Table 7.10   The Wilcoxon test (one-tailed) in MINITAB.

MTB > w-test 3 C2;
SUBC > alt − 1.

Test of median = 3.000 versus median LT 3.000

	N	N for test	Wilcoxon statistic	P-value	Estimated median
C2	20	20	95.0	0.361	2.963
			6.00 3	***	
2.84109	2.69411	2.27705	2.59171	3.88024	3.84201	4.30648

Two sample mean/median tests: comparing two means or medians

In this set of tests the null hypothesis takes the form: $\mu_1 = \mu_2$, where the two samples are from populations with the same mean; or $\eta_1 = \eta_2$, where the two samples are from populations with the same median. The parametric tests are first the paired t-test, where there are pairs of observations for each study unit and second the independent t-test where two independent samples have been drawn. These tests require that both variables are normally distributed and that the population variances are equal. In both these tests the NH is that the two population means are the same, i.e. $\mu_1 = \mu_2$. The non-parametric tests are based on the NH that the two samples come from populations with the same median. The Wilcoxon two-sample test requires that both samples are fairly symmetrical – but not necessarily normal – and the two-sample sign test makes no distributional assumptions.

The paired t-test is designed for two samples which are pairs of readings on the same units. For example, in a clinical trial there could be readings of diastolic blood pressure before and after an intervention for a set of ten subjects. Table 7.12 shows a set of data from such a trial, with histograms of the before- (first sample) and after- (second sample) data.

Table 7.11 shows that the first subject had a before reading of 98 and an after reading of 91, the second subject improved from 98 to 81 and so on. The distributions are both normal. The paired t-test is carried out as follows:

Step 1: N.H.: there is no difference in the population means of the two samples, i.e. $\mu_1 = \mu_2$;
A.H.: the population mean of the second sample is lower than that of the first, i.e. $\mu_1 > \mu_2$.

Table 7.11   Data and histograms for paired t-test.

MTB > PRINT C1

				C1						
98	98	90	102	101	105	118	105	94	107	102
113	106	95	102	103	93	92	105	100	92	97
97	95	108	110	87	95	84	102			

MTB > PRINT C2

				C2						
91	81	87	63	91	92	77	75	82	84	94
74	87	79	82	85	93	87	70	65	107	88
78	74	87	96	84	90	90	102			

MTB > histogram C1

Histogram of C1   N = 30

Midpoint	Count	
85	2	**
90	3	***
95	7	*******
100	8	********
105	6	******
110	2	**
115	1	*
120	1	*

MTB > histogram C2

Histogram of C2   N = 30

Midpoint	Count	
65	2	**
70	1	*
75	4	****
80	5	*****
85	7	*******
90	6	******
95	3	***
100	1	*
105	1	*

Step 2: Collect data – see Table 7.11.

Step 3: Subtract each pair of observations and calculate the mean and standard deviation of the differences (for details of the following calculations, see Chapter 6):

Differences: 7, 17, 3, 39, 10, 13, 41, 20, 12, 23, 8, 39, 19, 16, 20, 18, 0, 5, 35, 35, −15, 9, 19, 21, 21, 14, 3, 5, −6, 0

$$\text{mean, } \bar{d} \qquad \frac{\Sigma d}{n} = \frac{461}{30} = 15.37$$

$$\text{S.D., S,} \quad \frac{\Sigma d^2 - (\Sigma d)^2}{n-1} = 13.80$$

$$\text{The test statistic } t = \frac{\bar{d}}{s/\sqrt{n}} = \frac{15.37}{13.80/\sqrt{30}} = 6.10$$

Step 4: Statistical tables (e.g. Neave, 1989, p.20) should be consulted to obtain a critical value for t with 29 degrees of freedom at the 5% level (one-tailed) $t_{29,5\%} = 1.6991$. Since the calculated t is larger the NH is rejected and the conclusion is that the population mean of the second sample is less than that of the first i.e. the intervention has been effective in reducing diastolic blood pressure.

Because this test is based on the difference between each pair of readings, it is in effect the same test as the single sample t-test. Table 7.12 shows how this test is done in MINITAB.

Table 7.12   The paired t-test in MINITAB.

```
MTB  > LET C3 = C1 - C2
MTB  > t-test 0 C3
SUBC > alt 1
```

Test of MU = 0.00 VS MU GT 0.00

	N	MEAN	STDEV	SE MEAN	T	P VALUE
C3	30	15.37	13.80	2.52	6.10	0.0000

MINITAB prints the exact probability of observing these data if the NH were true – in this case the value of 0.0000 indicates that p is very small indeed. It is substantially less than 0.05 so the NH is rejected at the 5% and 1% levels (p being less than 0.01) and at the 0.1% level (p being less than 0.001). MINITAB, as always, precludes the need for statistical tables to be consulted.

A confidence interval may be attached to the difference between the two means. This enables a statement to be made of 95% confidence that the mean population difference lies between two values. This may be done through MINITAB as shown in Table 7.13.

Table 7.13   95 PERCENT confidence interval for difference between means.

MTB > t-interval 95, C3

	N	Mean	STDEV	SE MEAN	95 PERCENT CI
C3	30	15.37	13.80	2.52	(10.21, 20.52)

This result supports confidence at the 95% level in at least an average 10-point improvement in diastolic blood pressure and perhaps as much as a 20-point improvement.

The two-sample independent t-test

This is used when two independent samples have been drawn from normal distributions with equal variances or standard deviations, and we want to test the hypothesis that there is no difference between the population means. For example, we might want to compare the systolic blood pressures of men and women. Table 7.14 provides a sample of diastolic pressures for 20 women and 30 men.

The steps in the two sample t-test are as follows:

Step 1: N.H.: the two samples are from the same population i.e. there is no difference in the population means i.e.
$$\mu_1 = \mu_2$$
A.H.: $\mu_1 \neq \mu_2$ (two-tailed)

Step 2: Collect data – see Table 7.14.

Step 3: The test statistic is given by:

$$t = \frac{\bar{x}_1 - \bar{x}_2}{Sp\sqrt{\dfrac{1}{n_1} + \dfrac{1}{n_2}}}$$

where $\bar{x}_1$ is mean of first sample, $\bar{x}_2$ is mean of second sample, n_1 is size of first sample, n_2 is size of second sample and where the pooled variance (which may be thought of as the joint variance of the two samples)

$$Sp^2 = \frac{(n_1 - 1)s_1^2 + (n_2 - 1)s_2^2}{n_1 + n_2 - 2}$$

where s_1 is the standard deviation of first sample and s_2 is standard deviation of second sample.
For the data in Table 7.4:

$$\bar{x}_1 = 80.6, \ \bar{x}_2 = 79.13, \ n_1 = 40, \ n_2 = 30$$
$$s_1 = 16.27, \ s_2 = 15.52$$

(For methods of calculation, see Chapter 6)

$$\text{So} \quad Sp^2 = \frac{39 \times 16.27^2 + 29 \times 15.52^2}{40 + 30 - 2}$$

$$= \frac{10322.803 + 6985.2416}{68}$$

$$= 254.54477$$

Table 7.14 Data and histograms for independent t-test.

C1										
73	69	90	74	68	67	43	80	102	85	88
99	70	92	93	98	78	83	86	82	62	71
78	63	115	66	44	69	121	94	96	78	78
78	87	72	68	106	71	77				

MTB > histogram C1

Histogram of C1		N = 40
Midpoint	Count	
40	2	**
50	0	
60	2	**
70	11	***********
80	10	**********
90	8	********
100	4	****
110	1	*
120	2	**

MTB > PRINT C2

C2										
110	87	73	61	89	53	87	79	88	83	76
83	115	73	77	111	74	56	85	47	85	76
78	71	89	73	89	68	70	68			

MTB > histogram C2

Histogram of C2		N = 30
Midpoint	Count	
50	2	**
60	2	**
70	8	********
80	7	*******
90	8	********
100	0	
110	2	**
120	1	*

$$t = \frac{80.6 - 79.13}{15.95\sqrt{\dfrac{1}{40} + \dfrac{1}{30}}} = \frac{1.47}{15.95 \times 0.2415} = 0.38$$

Step 4: Consult statistical tables for t with 68 ($n_1 + n_2 - 2$) degrees of freedom at the 5% level (two-tailed) (Neave, 1981, p. 20). The tabulated value is approximately 1.995, so the NH is accepted since the calculated value is smaller. (All parametric tests accept the NH on small calculated values and reject it on large ones – the opposite is true for non-parametric tests). The conclusion is that there is no difference in the diastolic blood pressure of men and women.

Table 7.15 shows this test on MINITAB.

Table 7.15 Independent t-test using MINITAB.

MTB > two-sample t-test C1, C2;
SUBC > pooled.

Two-sample t-test for C1 vs C2

	N	MEAN	STDEV	SE MEAN
C1	40	80.6	16.3	2.57
C2	30	79.1	15.5	2.83

95 PERCENT CI for MU C1 – MU C2: (–6.225, 9.158)
T-test MU C1 = MU C2 (vs NE): T = 0.38 P = 0.70
DF = 68
Pooled STDEV = 16.0

The probability of observing these data under the NH, p = 0.70 is high and much higher than 0.05, so the NH is accepted. Tables need not be used if the test is done through MINITAB. The confidence interval for the difference between the population means is also given. Note that zero lies in the interval as it always will when a NH of $\mu_1 = \mu_2$ is accepted.

If you have any suspicion that the variances of your two samples are not equal, MINITAB provides an alternative and preferable form of this test. For details of the algebra see Joiner, Ryan and Joiner (1985). Table 7.16 displays the output.

For the data used (Table 7.14) the variances were in fact equal, the result in Table 7.16 is very similar to that in Table 7.15, but had the

Table 7.16 Independent t-test when variances may be unequal.

MTB > two-sample t test C1, C2

Two-sample t-test for C1 vs C2

	N	MEAN	STDEV	SE MEAN
C1	40	80.6	16.3	2.57
C2	30	79.1	15.5	2.83

95 PERCENT CI for MU C1 − MU C2: (−6.182, 9.115)
T-test MU C1 = MU C2 (vs NE): T = 0.38   P = 0.70
DF = 64

variances been unequal, the procedures in Table 7.16 would be advisable and preferable.

Turning to non-parametric tests, both the two-sample sign test and the two-sample Wilcoxon test are used for paired data (equivalent to the parametric paired t-test). The sign test makes no assumptions about the distribution of the data, while the Wilcoxon test requires symmetrical but not necessarily normal data.

The sign test

This is applied here to paired samples of data consisting of the length of service in the first and second post held by 30 occupational therapists.

Table 7.17 displays the data and the histograms.

Step 1: N.H.: the two samples come from populations with the same median, $\eta_1 = \eta_2$
A.H.: $\eta_1 < \eta_2$

Step 2: Collect data – see Table 7.17.

Step 3: For each subject subtract the first of the paired data from the second to obtain 30 differences. Count up how many are positive, and how many are negative. The smaller of these is the test statistic, S.
The signs of the differences are:
+ − − + + − + − + + − + + + − + + + + − + +
− + + + + + + +
There are 22 pluses and 8 minuses so S = 8.

Step 4: Compare this calculated value against tabulated critical values (Neave, 1989, p. 29). For 30 degrees of freedom at the 5% level for a one-tailed test, the critical value is 10, so the NH is rejected. (Non-parametric tests reject the NH on small values.)

Table 7.17 Data and histograms for two-sample sign test.

C1						
0.0789	3.0998	11.0735	4.9658	2.2393	3.3325	3.7108
1.3211	1.6143	0.1389	3.7000	2.2625	0.6022	0.1899
3.6943	0.1069	0.9010	4.7800	0.2069	10.3863	0.8912
3.8563	1.0302	1.4006	1.0954	1.8243	4.6877	0.3435
0.0561	1.0168					

MTB > histogram C1

Histogram of C1		N = 30
Midpoint	Count	
0	7	******
1	8	*******
2	4	****
3	2	**
4	4	****
5	3	***
6	0	
7	0	
8	0	
9	0	
10	1	x
11	1	*

MTB > print C2

C2						
1.1471	1.2255	2.8928	5.7836	2.3264	1.7075	7.6011
0.5059	1.8784	4.4082	1.2976	6.8273	1.0249	5.1923
1.9078	3.5250	6.3981	5.0248	1.6563	2.1880	8.0970
5.8685	0.9586	1.5719	3.5088	13.0886	5.0362	0.8290
6.1989	7.6575					

MTB > histogram C2

Histogram of C2		N = 30
Midpoint	Count	
1	7	******
2	7	*******
3	1	*
4	3	***
5	3	***
6	4	****
7	1	*
8	3	***
9	0	
10	0	
11	0	
12	0	
13	1	*

Table 7.18 Two-sample sign test using MINITAB.

		MTB > LET C3 = C2 − C1				
		MTB > s-test 0 C3;				
		SUBC > alt = 1.				

Sign test of median = 0.00000 versus GT 0.00000

	N	Below	Equal	Above	P-value	Median
C3	30	8	0	22	0.0081	0.6516

Table 7.18 shows how to do this test using MINITAB.

Note that MINITAB provides the exact probability of observing these data under the NH, 0.0081, which being less than 0.05 rejects the NH.

For symmetrical, but not necessarily normal data, the Wilcoxon two-sample test provides an alternative way to test whether the population medians of two samples of paired data are the same. The data in the following example come from a five-point scale with the categories 'strongly disagree', 'agree', 'neither agree nor disagree', 'disagree' and 'strongly agree'. The subjects tick one of five categories in response to a statement. Thirty subjects were tested before and after a course to find out their views about the desirability of inclusion of curriculum areas within initial training. Table 7.19 shows the results for one curriculum area and histograms of the before and after data.

The steps in the Wilcoxon test are as follows:

Step 1: N.H.: The two samples come from populations with the same median ($\eta_1 = \eta_2$)

A.H.: $\eta_1 \neq \eta_2$ (two-tailed)

Step 2: Collect data – see Table 7.19.

Step 3: For each pair, subtract the value in the second sample from that in the first sample to obtain a set of differences:

1, 2, 2, −1, 2, 0, 0, 1, 0, 0, 0, −1, 0, −2, 0, 1, 3, 0, −1, −1, 1, −1, −2, 3, 4, 0, −1, 0, 0, 0

From here the test is effectively the same as the single sample Wilcoxon (the two-sample paired t-test also reduces in this way to a single sample t-test on the differences between the pairs). Ties – zero differences – are dropped, giving an effective sample size of 18. The absolute values are then ranked, tied ranks share the available ranks and the sign of the original difference is assigned. The ten values '1' share the ranks 1−10, so each receives the average rank 5.5. The values '2' share the five ranks 11, 12, 13, 14, 15, so each has the average rank of 13, the values '3' share two ranks, 16 and 17,

Table 7.19 Data and histograms for two-sample Wilcoxon test.

MTB > print C3

C3

5	3	3	1	3	2	3	5	2	4	5	1	5	1	3
2	5	4	3	3	3	3	2	4	5	3	2	5	2	4

MTB > print C4

C4

4	1	1	2	1	2	3	4	2	4	5	2	5	3	3
1	2	4	4	4	2	4	4	1	1	3	3	5	2	4

MTB > histogram C3
Histogram of C3 N = 30

Midpoint	Count	
1	3	***
2	6	******
3	10	**********
4	4	****
5	7	*******

MTB > histogram C4
Histogram of C4 N = 30

Midpoint	Count	
1	6	******
2	7	*******
3	5	*****
4	9	*********
5	3	***

each being ranked at 16.5 and the value 4 is ranked 18.
By then assigning a plus or minus sign, according to the
original difference the signed ranks are:
5.5, 13, 13, −5.5, 13, 5.5, −5.5, −13, 5.5, 16.5, −5.5,
−5.5, 5.5, −5.5, −13, 16.5, 18, −5.5
Sum of positive ranks = 112
Sum of negative ranks = 59, so W = 59.
Step 4: By consulting statistical tables (Neave, 1989, p. 29) the
critical value for n = 18 at the 5% level (two-tailed) is 40.

Table 7.20　The two-sample Wilcoxon test using MINITAB.

MTB > LET C5 = C3 − C4
MTB > PRINT C5

C5

| 1 | 2 | 2 | −1 | 2 | 0 | 0 | 1 | 0 | 0 | 0 | −1 | 0 | −2 | 0 |
| 1 | 3 | 0 | −1 | −1 | 1 | −1 | −2 | 3 | 4 | 0 | −1 | 0 | 0 | 0 |

MTB > W-test 0, C5

Test of median = 0.000000 versus median NE 0.000000

	N	N for test	Wilcoxon statistic	P-value	Estimated median
C5	30	18	112.0	0.258	0.000E + 00

Since the calculated value of W is larger, the NH is accepted and it is concluded that there is no evidence of a difference. Table 7.20 shows how this test is done in MINITAB.

Note that MINITAB prints the larger of the sums of ranks rather than the smaller (W = 59) but the test is done in exactly the way shown above and the exact p value of 0.258 indicates that the NH should be accepted.

For independent samples, the non-parametric test which compares two medians is the Mann-Whitney test. Table 7.21 illustrates data for this test in the comparison of the body mass index (BMI) for men and women. The BMI for an individual is the ratio of weight (kg) to height squared (m^2). Because the distribution of complex indices can be difficult to establish, non-parametric tests can be valuable in such circumstances. Table 7.21 displays the data and histogram for 27 men and 20 women.

The steps in the test are as follows:

Step 1: NH: The two samples are from popualtions with the same median: $\eta_1 = \eta_2$
AH: $\eta_1 \neq \eta_2$ (two-tailed)
Step 2: Collect data − see Table 7.21.
Step 3: The data from both samples are ordered, but the identity of the sample is retained. The ranks for the first and second samples are added (R_1 and R_2) and two calculations are then done.

Table 7.21 Data and histograms for Mann-Whitney test.

				MTB > PRINT C6				
				C6				
29.42	29.53	21.09	23.52	18.82	21.50	26.04	29.49	27.25
24.63	26.86	26.23	19.45	21.14	25.22	18.66	15.94	25.11
23.77	28.87	24.32	21.44	26.19	26.23	22.41	31.15	26.71

MTB > histogram C6
Histogram of C6 N = 27

Midpoint	Count	
16	1	*
18	2	**
20	1	*
22	5	*****
24	4	****
26	8	********
28	2	**
30	3	***
32	1	*

MTB > print C7

			C7					
21.21	29.36	28.79	26.03	29.45	22.36	30.37	30.67	25.68
22.92	30.32	23.92	26.59	27.61	30.01	26.49	22.23	24.86
21.03	25.30							

MTB > histogram C7
Histogram of C7 N = 20

Midpoint	Count	
21	2	**
22	2	**
23	1	*
24	1	*
25	2	**
26	3	***
27	1	*
28	1	*
29	3	***
30	3	***
31	1	*

Table 7.22   Ranked data for the Mann-Whitney test.

Sample 1	Rank	Sample 2	Rank
29.42	39	21.21	8
29.53	42	29.36	38
21.09	6	28.79	36
23.52	15	26.03	25
18.82	3	29.45	40
21.50	10	22.36	12
26.04	26	30.37	45
29.49	41	20.67	46
27.25	34	25.68	24
24.63	19	22.92	14
26.86	33	30.32	44
26.23	28.5	23.92	17
19.45	4	26.59	31
21.14	7	27.61	35
25.22	22	30.01	43
18.66	2	26.49	30
15.94	1	22.23	11
25.11	21	24.86	20
23.77	16	21.03	5
28.87	37	25.30	23
24.32	18		547
21.44	9		
26.19	27		
26.23	28.5		
22.41	13		
31.15	47		
26.71	32		
	581		

$$n_1 n_2 + \frac{n_1(n_1 + 1)}{2} - R_1$$

where n_1 = size of first sample

$$n_1 n_2 + \frac{n_2(n_2 + 1)}{2} - R_2$$

where n_2 = size of second sample, and the smaller is the test statistic, U.

Ranked data for the Mann Whitny test are shown in Table 7.22. Note that when two results were the same, they shared ranks 28 and 29 and were each given a rank of 28.5.

$$n_1 n_2 + \frac{n_1(n_1 + 1)}{2} - R_1$$

$$= 27 \times 20 + \frac{27 \times 28}{2} - 581 = 337$$

$$n_1 n_2 + \frac{n_2(n_2 + 1)}{2} - R_2 - 27 \times 20 + \frac{20 \times 21}{2}$$

$$- 547 = 203$$

So $U = 203$

Step 4: Comparing this calculated value of U against the tabulated critical value (Neave, 1989, p. 35), U (27 and 20 respectively) at the 5% level is 178. So, becaused the calculated U is larger than the critical value, the NH is accepted and the conclusion is that there is no difference in the BMI of men and women.

Table 7.23 shows this test done through MINITAB. Note that MINITAB prints the column total of 581, rather than the test statistic, U, and also provides an exact p-value (p = 0.1525) and a confidence interval.

Table 7.23   The Mann-Whitney test using MINITAB.

MTB > Mann-Whitney C6, C7

Mann-Whitney confidence interval and test

| C6 | N = 27 | Median = 25.110 |
| C7 | N = 20 | Median = 26.260 |

Point estimate for ETA1 − ETA2 is −1.520
95.1 PERCENT CI for ETA1 − ETA2 is (−4.090, 0.410)
W = 581.0
Test of ETA1 = ETA2 vs ETA1 NE ETA2 is significant at 0.1525. The test is significant at 0.1525 (adjusted for ties)
Cannot reject at alpha = 0.05

All of the tests listed in Table 7.1 have now been described in detail. In making a discerning choice of test the form of the null hypothesis and the distribution of the data should inform the decision. Whilst the detail of the calculation of test statistics has varied from one test to another, the logic underlying every test is the same. This logic also applies to tests of null hypotheses about correlation and association, which are described in the next chapter.

Discussion points

1. If it has not been possible to use probability sampling, is there any point in carrying out significance tests?
2. Computers are unhelpful in assisting people to understand data because they encourage an uncritical attitude to data.

References

Neave, H. (1989) *Elementary Statistics Tables*. George Allen and Unwin, London.

Ryan, B., Joiner, B. & Ryan, T. (1985) *Minitab Handbook*, 2nd edn, PWS Publishers, Duxbury Press, Boston.

Chapter 8
Quantitative Analysis: Association and Correlation

The concept of association or correlation refers to the extent to which two variables are related to each other. In Chapter 6 the use of summary statistics for individual variables was described. In Chapter 7 tests were carried out on hypotheses concerning the sizes of means and medians, both for individual variables (single-sample tests) and for pairs of variables (two sample tests). Association and correlation, or measuring the relatedness of two variables, may be described through the calculation of a correlation coefficient; their strength may also be tested using hypothesis tests based on the logic described in Chapter 7. In this chapter, the use of the correlation coefficient as a descriptive statistic will first be explained and some significance tests will then be discussed.

The correlation coefficient is a measure of linear correlation. It should be used only when the relationship being measured is clearly linear rather than, say, quadratic or cubic. This can be established by drawing a graph of the two variables. It is recommended that the correlation coefficient should never be calculated unless a graph (called a scattergram) of the two variables has first been drawn and linearity thus demonstrated.

Correlation coefficients take values between minus one and plus one. A plus sign indicates positive correlation i.e. as the values of one variable increase or decrease so do the values of the other. Positive correlation indicates that the values change in the same direction. Negative correlation indicates that the values change in the opposite direction i.e. as the values of one variable increase, those of the other variable decrease or vice versa. Table 8.1 shows typical scattergrams.

The size of the correlation coefficient indicates the strength of the correlation. Zero indicates no correlation; plus one indicates total positive correlation (all of the points would lie on a perfect upward straight line); and minus one indicates perfect negative correlation (all the points would lie on a perfect downward straight line).

Depending on the distribution of the data, parametric or non-parametric techniques should be selected both in measuring correlation or association and in testing their strength. Table 8.2 summarizes the techniques described in this chapter.

Table 8.1   Typical scattergrams.

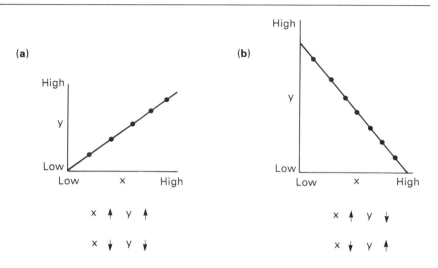

Table 8.2   Correlation for statistical tests of correlation and association.

	Subject of the null hypothesis association/correlation
Parametric	Pearson product moment correlation (interval)
Non-parametric	Spearman correlation (ordinal) Chi-square Test (nominal)

The Pearson product moment correlation coefficient

The Pearson product moment correlation coefficient is designed for use on normally distributed variables. Table 8.3 provides data on two test scores for each of 20 students, the first sample being a set of theory test scores marked out of 20; and the second sample being a set of clinical practice scores, marked out of 40. Table 8.3 displays the data and individual histograms.

The calculation of the Pearson correlation coefficient is through the formula:

$$r = \frac{\Sigma xy - \dfrac{\Sigma x \Sigma y}{n}}{\sqrt{\Sigma x^2 - \dfrac{(\Sigma x)^2}{n}} \; \sqrt{\Sigma y^2 - \dfrac{(\Sigma y)^2}{n}}}$$

Table 8.3 Data and histograms for correlation coefficient.

						Print C1						
						C1						
10	14	15	12	8	5	13	11	7	17	12	10	13
7	9	11	15	17	11	10						

MTB > histogram C1
Histogram of C1 N = 20

Midpoint	Count	
5	1	*
6	0	
7	2	**
8	1	*
9	1	*
10	3	x x x
11	3	***
12	2	**
13	2	**
14	1	*
15	2	**
16	0	
17	2	**

MTB > print C2

						C2						
16	24	22	20	12	8	22	18	12	30	20	13	22
10	15	18	26	29	18	17						

MTB > histogram C2
Histogram of C2 N = 20

Midpoint	Count	
8	1	*
10	1	*
12	2	**
14	1	*
16	2	**
18	4	****
20	2	x x
22	3	***
24	1	*
26	1	*
28	0	
30	2	**

The calculation is best done manually by setting out the data in columns:
so:

x	y	x^2	y^2	xy
10	16	100	256	160
14	24	196	576	336
15	22	225	484	330
12	20	144	400	240
8	12	64	144	96
5	8	25	64	40
13	22	169	484	286
11	18	121	324	198
7	12	49	144	84
17	30	289	900	510
12	20	144	400	240
10	13	100	169	130
13	22	169	484	286
7	10	49	100	70
9	15	81	225	135
11	18	121	324	198
15	26	225	676	390
17	29	289	841	493
11	18	121	324	198
10	17	100	289	170
$\Sigma x = 227$	$\Sigma y = 372$	$\Sigma x^2 = 2781$	$\Sigma y^2 = 7608$	$\Sigma xy = 4590$

$$\text{So: } r = \frac{4590 - \dfrac{227 \times 372}{20}}{\sqrt{2781 - \dfrac{227^2}{20}} \ \sqrt{7608 - \dfrac{372^2}{20}}}$$

$$= \frac{367.8}{14.302 \times 26.245}$$

$$= 0.980$$

This Pearson correlation of 0.980 indicates a strong positive correlation between the two sets of marks. Table 8.4 shows how MINITAB draws a scattergram and calculates the Pearson correlation coefficient.

With a correlation of 0.980, it is hardly necessary to test for significance; but in general it is advisable to do so, since the significance of a correlation coefficient depends on sample size. To test a Pearson correlation coefficient, use the following:

Step 1: N.H.: There is no correlation $r = 0$
A.H.: $r > 0$ (one-tailed)

Table 8.4 Correlation coefficient and scattergram using MINITAB.

MTB > plot C1 C2

```
                 -                                                     *  *
                 -
C1    16.0       +
                 -
                 -                                    *          *
                 -                                        *
                 -                                  2
      12.0       +                          2
                 -                      3
                 -              *      *  *
                 -
                 -        *
       8.0       +      *
                 -   *    *
                 -
                 -
                 - *
                 + ---- + ---- + ---- + ---- + ---- + ---- C2
                8.0    12.0    16.0    20.0    24.0    28.0
```

MTB > corr C1 C2
Correlation of C1 and C2 = 0.980

Step 2: Calculate r from above calculation;

$$r = 0.980$$

$$\text{calculate } t = r\sqrt{\frac{n-2}{1-r^2}}$$

$$= 20.984$$

where n is the number of subjects

Compare this with a critical value of 1.64 for a one tailed test. Since the calculated value is larger, the NH is rejected and the conclusion is that there is significant correlation.

The Spearman ranked correlation coefficient

The equivalent non-parametric technique is to calculate the Spearman ranked correlation coefficient. The following data come from the ranking of a set of 12 students on placement; the first sample are the clinical supervisor's ranking and the second sample are the academic tutor's ranking. Table 8.5 displays the data. Because these samples are small, a scattergram has not been drawn, but this is recommended for real data.

Table 8.5   Data for Spearman correlation coefficient.

MTB	>	set C6
DATA	>	2 6 5 1 10 9 8 3 4 12 7 11
DATA	>	end
MTB	>	set C7
DATA	>	3 4 2 1 8 11 10 6 7 12 5 9
DATA	>	end

The Spearman coefficient is calculated by first obtaining the difference (d) between each pair of observations, squaring that difference (d^2) and adding up the squares (Σd^2).

C6	C7	d	d^2
2	3	−1	1
6	4	2	4
5	2	3	9
1	1	0	0
10	8	2	4
9	11	−2	4
8	10	−2	4
3	6	−3	9
4	7	−3	9
12	12	0	0
7	5	2	4
11	9	2	4

$$\Sigma d^2 = 52$$

The Spearman correlation coefficient, r_s, is then given by

$$r_s = 1 - \frac{6\Sigma d^2}{n^3 - n}$$

where n is number of pairs

$$= 1 - \frac{6 \times 52}{1728 - 12} = 1 - \frac{312}{1716} = 1 - 0.18 = 0.82$$

Table 8.6 shows how this calculation is done in MINITAB. To test the significance of the Spearman correlation coefficient, a NH of $r_s = 0$ against an alternative of $r_s > 0$ may be tested by comparing the calculated r_s to a tabulated critical value (Neave, 1989, p. 40) for n =

Table 8.6 Spearman correlation coefficient using MINITAB.

MTB > let C8 = C6 − C7
MTB > print C8

___

C8

___

| −1 | 2 | 3 | 0 | 2 | −2 | −2 | −3 | −3 | 0 | 2 | 2 |

MTB > let C9 = C8 * C8
MTB > print C9

___

C9

___

| 1 | 4 | 9 | 0 | 4 | 4 | 4 | 9 | 9 | 0 | 4 | 4 |

MTB > sum C9
SUM = 52.000
MTB > let C10 = 1 − 6 * 52/(12 * 12 * 12 − 12)
MTB > print C10

___

C10

___

0.818182

12, 5% level, one tailed. This value is 0.5035; so, having a larger calculated value, the NH is rejected and the conclusion is that there is significant correlation between the two sets of rankings.

The Chi-square test

The Chi-square test is designed to establish whether there is an association between two variables. Data must be nominal or ordinal; if data were collected at interval or ratio level, it is usually possible to rearrange into ordinal or nominal categories. A table of the two variables can then be set up, which is called a contingency table. The chi-square test is based on the contingency table. It compares the values observed in the contingency table with the values that would be expected if the NH of no association were true. It is important to scrutinize these expected values before proceeding with the test and to establish that first, no expected value is less than one; and second, that less than 20% of cells have expected values less than five. If either of these occurs the chi-square becomes invalid and an alternative test should be used. Siegel (1956) provides alternatives.

To illustrate this, the training survey data can be used to investigate

Table 8.7   Training survey, recoding and contingency table.

MTB   > code (1 : 8)1 (8.1 : 17)2 C2, put in C12
MTB   > table C1, C12;
SUBC > Chi-square 2.

Rows	C1	Columns	C12
	1	2	ALL
1	3	5	8
	2.29	5.71	8.00
2	1	5	6
	1.71	4.29	6.00
3	0	5	5
	1.43	3.57	5.00
4	1	3	4
	1.14	2.86	4.00
5	3	2	5
	1.43	3.57	5.00
	1	2	ALL
ALL	8	20	28
	8.00	20.00	28.00

Chi-square = 5.174 with DF = 4
Cell contents – COUNT EXP FREQ

the relationship between hospital (C1) and years qualified (C2). C1 is a nominal variable already in categories, but C2 is a ratio level, so it must be recoded into categories. Because there are only 30 cases, C2 will be recoded into just two categories, 8 years and under (recoded to the value 1) and over 8 years (recoded to the value 2). Table 8.7 shows how to do this in MINITAB and obtain a contingency table.

In Table 8.7, the observed value (0) and, beneath it, the expected value (E) are printed for each cell of the contingency table. The expected value is obtained by:

$$E = \frac{\text{row total} \times \text{column total}}{\text{grand total}}$$

So, for example, for the first cell with an observed value of 3, the expected value is:

$$\frac{8 \times 8}{28} = 2.29$$

Three subjects were observed in category 1 (8 years or fewer qualified, and hospital 1), and we would have expected 2.29 if the NH is true. However, note that almost all of the 10 cells have expected values of less than five. These data are invalid for a chi-square test – but note that MINITAB has nonetheless printed a result. This is an example of the need for thought and vigilance when using computer packages.

Turning to another example: a set of research results about the gender of nurses working in different settings, Table 8.8 displays the data in a contingency table. Expected values, calculated as described earlier, are in brackets next to each observed value.

Table 8.8 Data for Chi-square test.

Setting	Gender		Row totals
	Male	Female	
Hospital	15(24)	45(36)	60
Community	5(16)	35(24)	40
Education	25(20)	25(30)	50
Administration	35(20)	15(30)	50
Column totals	80	120	200

The steps in the chi square test are:

Step 1: NH: There is no association between gender and setting
AH: There is an association
Step 2: Collect data – see Table 8.8
Step 3: Calculate $\Sigma \dfrac{(O - E)^2}{E}$

$$= \frac{(15 - 24)^2}{24} + \frac{(5 - 16)^2}{16} + \frac{(25 - 20)^2}{20} + \frac{(35 - 20)^2}{20}$$

$$+ \frac{(45 - 36)^2}{36} + \frac{(35 - 24)^2}{24} + \frac{(25 - 30)^2}{30}$$

$$+ \frac{(50 - 30)^2}{30}$$

$$= 3.375 + 7.563 + 1.25 + 11.25 + 2.25 + 5.042 + 0.833 + 7.5$$

$$= 39.063$$

This is the test statistic, called the chi-square statistic.
Step 4: The degrees of freedom are the product of the number of rows in the table minus one and the number of columns in the table minus one – in this case $3 \times 1 = 3$.

By looking up tables (Neave, 1989, p. 21) the critical value for 3 degrees of freedom at the 5% level may be found. The value is 7.815, so having a larger calculated value, the NH is rejected and the conclusion is that there is an association between gender and setting.

Table 8.9 shows how to do this test using MINITAB.

Table 8.9   Chi-square test using MINITAB.

```
MTB  > read C20 – C21
DATA > 15, 45
DATA > 5, 35
DATA > 25, 25
DATA > 35, 15
DATA > end 4 rows read
```

```
MTB > Chi-square C20 – C21
```

Expected counts are printed below observed counts

	C20	C21	Total
1	15	45	60
	24.00	36.00	
2	5	35	40
	16.00	24.00	
3	25	25	50
	20.00	30.00	
4	35	15	50
	20.00	30.00	
Total	80	120	200

Chi-square =   3.375 + 2.250 +
              7.563 + 5.042 +
              1.250 + 0.833 +
              11.250 + 7.500 = 39.062
df = 3

If the Chi-square test is invalid owing to small expected values in some cells, it is permissible to create fewer categories by amalgamating some cells, provided the data are at least at ordinal level and the resulting categories have some meaning. If this does not solve the problem, or if data are nominal, alternative tests must be sought.

There is a special case formula for the 2×2 chi-square, where each variable has only two categories. The test statistic should be

$$x^2 = \frac{N\left[|ad - bc| - \frac{N}{2} \right]^2}{ABCD}$$

where the 2×2 contingency table is:

a	b	D
c	d	C
A	B	N

Otherwise, steps 1, 2 and 4 are as described for the 4×2 example given.

A very important caveat for this class of methods for investigating association and correlation is that they can never prove cause and effect, and should not be used for this purpose. X and Y may be associated or correlated with each other but could both be caused by Z, which is correlated with them both. Equally, caution should be used in interpreting correlation – even when it appears highly significant, it may be spurious. There would, for example, be a strong positive correlation between the incidence of mental illness and sales of micro-wave ovens, both having increased markedly in recent decades. No one would be likely to infer causation in such a case, but when intuition suggests that a correlation may, in fact, represent cause and effect, the dangers are greater.

Discussion points

1. Can cause and effect ever be established with reasonable con-fidence in health research? What designs and which statistical tests are most helpful in this?
2. Identify some variables which occur in your day-to-day life which you think are correlated with each other. Could this correlation be spurious?

References

Neave, H. (1989) *Elementary Statistics Tables*. George Allen and Unwin, London.

Siegel, S. (1956) *Non-parametric Statistics for the Behavioural Sciences*. McGraw-Hill, Kogakusha Ltd.

Chapter 9
Analysing Qualitative Data

Qualitative approaches to research in health can be enormously valuable either as stand-alone methodologies or as supplements to more structured quantitative approaches. Many qualitative analyses, by imposing a structure on the data, can indeed develop into a quantitative form; the techniques of descriptive statistical analysis covered in Chapter 6 may be applied, taking care to note the level of measurement.

There may be a particular advantage in using qualitative methods, especially in a new area of study about which little is known. It is often not possible to use structured methods until there is some knowledge and understanding of a topic, and the early pioneering work may well be done best through qualitative methods. The hypothesis generation is best achieved in this way: the example described in Chapter 4 (Merrill, 1985) had as a main objective the identification of hypotheses for further study. In exploring concepts underlying data, the use of grounded theory (Glaser and Strauss, 1967) is becoming more common in health research. In this, rather than specifying hypotheses in advance, theory is elucidated by being grounded within the data and being exposed through the analysis.

Another great strength of qualitative data is their capacity to illuminate a research area. Cause and effect is most convincingly established through experimental and, almost always, quantitative methods; but the explanation and interpretation of causal relationships is much more likely to come from qualitative information. Hence qualitative and quantitative information can supplement each other. The face validity of quantitative research can be very low – many health professionals are unenthusiastic about number-crunching approaches to issues that concern caring for people. The use of qualitative material to illustrate and illuminate numbers or percentages can help offset this.

There are no set methods of analysis for qualitative data. It is not possible to produce a list of methods or a taxonomy of approaches. Indeed it is the very essence of the qualitative approach to let the path of the analysis emerge from the process of analysis. Even when the researcher specifies in advance a form for the analysis, it often happens that the data emerge in a different form and a new approach emerges (see Merrill, 1985).

Qualitative data almost always take the form of words – historical

documents, policy documents, letters, taped interviews, taped conversations or fieldnotes, for example. This usually means that there will
be a huge amount of material. The sheer volume of data produced by
most qualitative projects can make the analysis very time-consuming.
This is why qualitative questions are kept to a minimum in surveys.
Even a small qualitative project is likely to generate a mass of material
and every word must be read, re-read and considered carefully.

It is also difficult to provide examples of qualitative analysis because
to place the example in context, a mass of material would be needed.
Also the relationship of each part of the data to the rest is crucial.
There is no equivalent process to that of focusing attention on one
variable within a survey in order to illustrate a typical method.

Quantifying qualitative analysis

There is continuing debate about the extent to which qualitative data
should be quantified. Some argue that qualitative methods are superior
in preserving the flavour of the data and are more likely to lead to
sound inferences. The counter-argument is that by quantifying the
data, objectivity is better served, and that the principles of statistical
inference, and a range of powerful statistical techniques can then be
applied, if a sampling approach has been used. Some writers stress the
complementarity of quantitative and qualitative methods. There is much
to be said for the viewpoint of Holsti (1969) who argues that 'it is by
moving back and forth between these approaches that the investigator
is most likely to gain insight into the meaning of his data'.

The term 'content analysis' is used to describe a class of techniques
for dealing with qualitative data. To illustrate some of its uses, hypothetical sets of results will be considered. The source of the data is all
editorials over a two-year period in a physiotherapy journal, a nursing
journal and an occupational therapy journal – a total of 24 editorials
from each journal.

The first approach within content analysis is to identify themes and
then count the number of times each theme is mentioned in each
journal. The results are shown in Table 9.1.

The assumption behind this technique is that the frequency with
which a theme is mentioned is significant; and that the more frequently
it is mentioned the more important it is to the writer. This is debatable,
but of course it would be possible to proceed from Table 9.1 to test for
differences between the professional journals and to examine in more
detail the significance of the attention to individual themes.

A second technique within content analysis also concerns themes;
but here the presence or absence of the theme is recorded rather than
its frequency of mention. So, whether a theme is mentioned once or
ten times, it is simply recorded as having been mentioned. Table 9.2
gives an example of this approach.

Those who object to quantification of qualitative data tend to prefer

Table 9.1   Content analysis frequency count.

Theme	Journals of:		
	Physiotherapy	Nursing	Occupational Therapy
	(N = 24)	(N = 24)	(N = 24)
General management versus professional management	15(37.5%)	25(50.0%)	5(12.5%)
Interprofessional collaboration	1(2.5%)	5(10.0%)	10(25.0%)
Clinical developments or issues	16(40.0%)	5(10.0%)	20(50.0%)
Educational developments or issues	8(20.0%)	15(30.0%)	5(12.5%)
Total	40	50	40

Table 9.2   Presence or absence of themes.

Theme	Journals of:		
	Physiotherapy	Nursing	Occupational Therapy
	(N = 24)	(N = 24)	(N = 24)
General management versus professional management	10	20	2
Interprofessional collaboration	1	3	8
Clinical developments or issues	12	2	9
Educational developments or issues	8	15	1
Total	31	40	20

this second approach to the frequency approach, but their general preference is to analyse the narrative discursively. This can be done within each document. For example, the major theme of each individual editorial could be identified and a report then written from this set of themes. Alternatively, themes could be identified a priori and the editorial material sorted into these themes; the analysis would then be built around the taxonomy of themes. This latter approach probably allows most power to the data themselves and is thus preferred by ethnomethodologists and by those opposed to quantification.

Content analysis provides one of the main methodological traditions within qualitative research. There is, however, increasing interest in a method called the Delphi technique, which is a way of obtaining a consensus of opinion from a panel of experts. This method is of particular value in health research in eliciting professional judgements.

The Delphi technique

The Delphi technique (named after Apollo's Delphic oracle) is a method for the systematic collection and aggregation of informed judgements from a group of experts on specific questions or issues. The key characteristic of the technique is that it involves a consultative process in which each member of a panel presents his or her views to all other members anonymously and by post. The objective of the method is to obtain a consensus of opinion.

A panel of experts is chosen and structured information and questions are then posted to each member. The returns are analysed and the consensus extracted. A second round is then carried out where the panel members are invited to reconsider their initial views in the light of the collated views of all of the panel in the first round. The returns are then analysed and the consensus extracted. This process is repeated until a satisfactory consensus has been obtained.

It is generally recognized that there are three main types of Delphi technique: the numeric, the policy and the historic. Strauss and Zeigler (1975) state that the goal of the numeric Delphi is to specify a single or minimum range of numeric estimates or forecasts on a problem; and the goal of the policy Delphi is to define a range of answers or alternatives to a current or anticipated policy problem. They believe that the goal of the historic Delphi is to explain the range of issues that fostered a specific decision; or to identify the range of possible alternatives that could have been poised against a certain past decision. Secondary goals or objectives, according to Turoff (1970), are these:

- To explore or expose underlying assumptions or information leading to different judgements.
- To seek out information in order to generate a consensus of judgement on the part of the respondent group.
- To correlate informed judgements on a topic spanning a wide range of disciplines.
- To educate the respondent group as to the diverse and interrelated aspects of the topic.

Strauss and Zeigler (1975) identified six characteristics that are common to all Delphi exercises. These are:

- All Delphis use panels of experts for obtaining information or data.
- All Delphis are conducted in writing, using sequential questionnaires interspersed with summarized information.

- All Delphis systematically attempt to produce a consensus of opinion divergence.
- All Delphis guarantee anonymity of both the panel members and their statements.
- All Delphis use iteration and controlled feedback.
- All Delphis are conducted in a series of rounds, between which a summary of the results of the previous round is communicated to, and evaluated by, panel members.

Applications of the Delphi technique

The Delphi technique is one of the spin-offs of defence research. The method was developed in the USA in the early 1950s in a study by the Rand corporation of the likely targets and impact of a Russian bombing campaign. Interest in the method was mainly within the defence industry until 1964 when it was applied to technological forecasting. Academics discovered the method more recently, but it is being used increasingly and its value in health research has become widely recognized.

Until recently the use of the Delphi technique in health research was relatively infrequent. But the publications cited over the last ten years in MEDLINE, one of the main computer databases in health research, demonstrate a wide range of applications and suggest that the method is highly flexible and adaptable to a variety of problems.

For example, it has been used successfully in diverse areas of clinical medical research in drawing together new developments in treatments and interventions. Its potential in such studies is obvious for all the health care professions, where clinical advances so often occur in isolation, or through responding to local patient needs. The Delphi technique can draw together the ideas and achievements of people who live far apart and thus assist evaluation and dissemination of clinical advances. It has also been used to evaluate the development of particular services for clients and patients and has been used to tackle administrative and managerial problems within health services. A novel use of the method has been in devolving budgets for social services to the field level workers.

Policy Delphis have been used to predict future events and developments in nursing. Within education, the Delphi technique has been used to develop educational strategies for meeting anticipated changes in educational needs, in response to developments within the nursing service. An intriguing use of the method is in curriculum development, where it has been successfully used within dietetics, surgery and medicine.

The technique has been used less in the evaluation of professional practice, but its potential here is considerable. Reid (1989) gives a detailed account of its use in the assessment of nurse learners in clinical settings and cites some examples published elsewhere. The Delphi could become the primary research methodology in the evaluation of professional competence, an area of research which has been fraught with methodological difficulties.

In general there is reason to believe that of all qualitative research methods, the Delphi will become the most widely used in health research in the coming decade. Reid (1989) provides a critical review of the method and a case study.

Analysing the Delphi

The numeric Delphi produces quantitative data and the establishing of the consensus at each round consists simply of a descriptive statistical analysis as described fully in Chapter 6. Techniques of qualitative analysis are needed for the analysis of a policy or historic Delphi and the usual approach is to select one of the methods within content analysis as described earlier in this chapter. For example, at any round of a Delphi, all of the returns would first be read to identify the range of opinions. A percentage of panel members supporting that opinion would then be calculated, and this would constitute the feedback for the next round. Note that although the method of analysis is qualitative the end result could be quantitative. A purely qualitative alternative would be to summarize discursively the responses of one round and provide some verbal indication of the relative popularity of different opinions.

It should be noted that the Delphi method is one of the cheapest research methods available. It is, however, relatively time consuming: there is a delay between each posting and the responses; reminders may be needed to urge non-responders to comply; and the analysis, particularly of qualitative material, can require a lot of time.

The main criticism of the Delphi lies in the way in which it is often implemented. Many published studies display poor selection criteria in the choice of panel, poor response rates and thus dangers of response bias, and conclusions which do not appear to follow from the Delphi process. Reid (1989) provides a detailed critique of the method and suggests that it would greatly benefit from the application of the principles of good practice in survey methods. The main limitations are not inherent in the method itself, but in lack of rigour in the implementation. Provided that the researcher has time to complete all the stages in the Delphi, and is careful in its implementation, the method has a good deal to offer in health research.

A case study of qualitative analysis

In considering qualitative methods of analysis, it has been necessary to confine the description to principles and guidelines, since the approach does not lend itself easily to selection of small-scale examples to illustrate techniques. The best way to obtain a feel for the nuts and bolts of qualitative analysis is to read some published studies in the journals and then request some of the source material from the researcher.

Kielhofner (1981) gives an account of an exemplary qualitative study of the experiences of deinstitutionalized adults. His paper also provides substantial quotation from the primary research materials. It reports a three-year ethnographic study of 69 deinstitutionalized so-called retarded persons in which occupational therapists and social scientists observed subjects in their everyday environments. Field notes, interviews and videotape data were collected. The aim of the study was to examine the daily lives and the social and physical environment of the subjects.

The analytical approach was known as the heuristic method (Glaser and Strauss, 1967). Kielhofner defines a heuristic method as a declaration with a statement of plausibility attached to it. It implies that evidence-to-date suggests the truth of the statement and directs the researcher to look for further instances that either verify or contradict the statement. The data generated by the study are used to refine, develop and respecify the heuristic method. It may be thought of as a research hypothesis which changes through an iterative process as the study findings become available.

In Kielhofner's study, the researchers first met in a series of sessions to generate the preliminary data categories. Each of these was associated with one or more 'heuristics' which would be used to develop and test inferences related to the category. An example was that the so-called retarded persons experienced time in daily life differently from most cultural members and held notions about the passage of time that were different from those of mainstream culture. Further, it was specified that these 'retarded' persons would show different attitudes towards such practices as scheduling and goal-setting and would demonstrate quite different temporal patterns. Data were then used, as they became available, to test the accuracy of these heuristics. As data accumulated, the category heuristics would be adjusted as was appropriate. Finally the researchers examined all the relevant categories of data, examining their relationship and mutual patterns.

The analysis of this study could be described as a dynamic version of some class of content analysis. It illustrates well that qualitative analysis can be done within a more flexible and adaptable framework than quantitative analysis. This is its great strength. Many problems in health research can only be tackled meaningfully through such techniques.

Discussion points

1. Consider how the Delphi technique could be used to evaluate professional practice in your area of work.
2. In what circumstances are qualitative methods most valuable?

References

Glaser, B. & Strauss, A. (1967) *The Discovery of Grounded Theory*. Aldine, New York.

Holsti, O. (1969) *Content Analysis for the Social Sciences and Humanities*. Addison-Wesley Publishing Company, 235.

Kielhofner, G. (1981) An Ethnographic Study of Deinstitutionalized Adults: their community settings and daily life experiences. *Occupational Therapy Journal of Research*, Vol. 2, 125–42.

Merrill, S.C. (1985) Qualitative methods in occupational therapy research: an application. *Occupational Therapy Journal of Research*, Vol. 5, No. 4, 209–22.

Reid, N. (1989) The Delphi Technique: its Contribution to the Evaluation of Professional Practice. In R. Ellis (ed.) *Professional Competence and Quality Assurance in the Caring Professions*, Chapman & Hall.

Chapter 10
Presentation and Evaluation

Presentation

The central feature of the researcher's presentation is usually a written report. Research reports may be written to serve a variety of purposes: to meet the requirements of an examined course, to publish findings in an academic journal, or to provide feedback to those who have assisted in the research or who may benefit from being made aware of the findings. It is highly unlikely that the same version would be appropriate for these different purposes. It may be necessary to write up the piece of work in several different ways to meet the needs of different audiences. So the first task is to define the readership and then to be clear about the objectives of the written report.

If the report is to meet course requirements the main readers are likely to be one or more academic staff and one or more external examiners. You should establish who these people are – or, at least, what their academic and professional backgrounds are. It may be, for example, that one of the external examiners is a sociologist or a physiologist with no health qualification. In this case it might be necessary to explain terms which would not require elucidation if only professional qualified examiners read the work. Equally, an examiner appointed for expertise in a health profession will not necessarily have the same level of theoretical knowledge of the social or physical sciences as someone qualified to post doctoral level in one of these disciplines. You must therefore take account of the diversity of expertise in your readers.

The audience for articles in research journals tends to be less diverse and you can generally assume that you are communicating with other academics. Similarly a report for professional colleagues is likely to be more concerned with the implications of the study for professional practice.

Not only the content and style but also the objectives of reports can be affected by the audience. If the report is for an examined course the first objective is to pass; so the first essential in preparing such a report is to study any guidelines provided that may indicate what the examiners are seeking. If no guidelines have been provided the course leader may be able to help you. You should, of course, have taken account of these guidelines during your project work, but it is especially important to remind yourself of the ground rules when writing the final report.

If the written paper is for an academic journal, the journal will have its own set of guidelines – usually provided at the back or front of all issues. And naturally, since your objective is to achieve publication and communicate your work to the academic community, you should adhere closely to the journal house-style and rules.

If you are writing for professional peers, in-house perhaps, your aim might be to provide feedback in return for assistance in a project. This is good manners and should be offered on that ground alone; but it may also give you an opportunity to share the ideas in your research with professional colleagues. It is important to consider such factors as the seniority, educational background and research experience of your readers.

Writing style

Whatever the readership, a written research report should be lucid, accurate and if possible interesting. Clarity requires first of all that the writer really understands the material. The use of words like 'clearly' or phrases like 'it is clear that' rarely add much. On the contrary they are often tell-tale signs of the author's uncertainty about the content. The key to clarity is to write short simple sentences. People often feel that because research is a serious and weighty business the writing style must be portentous and must sound learned. The likelier result is pomposity and obfuscation. Crisp, simple, logical sentences are much the best aid to clarity. Precision is the most important quality of the researcher, and this usually leads to a conservative use of language since the important thing is not to over-claim or exaggerate.

Accuracy is essential in a research report, and it requires absolute honesty. There is no point in trying to conceal awkward facts: an astute reader will sense any attempt at concealment and the entire study may then be discredited. In a research report you must be able to stand on every word. There is no room for unsubstantiated assertions, unattributed declarations or general speculation. Even statements of opinion should be limited and confined to a discussion section where it is obvious that what is offered is opinion, not established fact.

Internal consistency is essential. Those who referee research reports for publication will usually first check for internal consistency – and it is surprising how often the writer contradicts his or her own 'facts'. Tables of figures which do not add up to the totals given may be the result of a typing error, but they reflect badly on the author, whose responsibility it is to proof-read the final version. Assertions should be referenced. For example: 'increasing numbers of qualified nurses are leaving the NHS' is an assertion. If it is not supported by a referenced source it must be made clear that it is based solely on the opinion of the author. Conversely, it is essential to attribute to others any of their ideas or findings that you cite.

In seeking to write an interesting research report, try to avoid sensationalism. Research reports are not the place for 'purple' prose. Even if you feel strongly about an issue, you should avoid emotive adjectives, exclamation marks and journalistic devices. If your results are dramatic, they will speak for themselves. Qualitative research materials can be an invaluable way of adding interest to a research report. Direct quotation of a relevant kind can catch the reader's attention, form a bond between the writer and the reader and illuminate the text. The use of diagrams, graphs and pictures can also enhance the interest of a research report and can be used to break up the text into manageable chunks. The graphics technology available now is an enormous help: attractive graphs can be easily produced on a computer to provide a professional-looking finish.

Grammar, punctuation and spelling

In the past twenty years there has been great controversy in the British educational system about the teaching of grammar, punctuation and spelling. We have gone from the orthodoxy of a highly systematized approach based on rote-learning and rules, to a more liberal, or some would say, slapdash view based on creativity and self-expression. Whatever the merits of the second approach for general purposes, it is not recommended in writing research reports. You may not be able to achieve perfect spelling, punctuation and grammar but you should try. It is beyond the remit of this book to provide detailed guidance on these topics, but there are many excellent texts ranging from standard works like Fowler, H.W. (1983), Fowler, H.W. and Fowler F.G. (1970), Gowers (1986), Partridge (1973) and Vallins (1979); to more utilitarian efforts like Birley (1991). As can be seen from the dates, several of these have stood the test of time, while others take on board more contemporary literacy issues.

For those who have difficulty with spelling, the advent of spell-checkers within most computer-based word-processing packages is a considerable benefit. These checkers will detect wrongly spelled words provided the wrong spelling is not another correctly spelled word (for example, if 'there' is incorrectly typed as 'their' the package will not detect any error). More generally, the use of word-processors greatly improves the presentation of a research report.

Non-sexist and non-racist language

One of the unmistakeable improvements in modern writing style is the reduction in terms that might, wittingly or otherwise, give offence on religious or racist grounds. There has been slightly less progress with regard to sexist language, but the tide is beginning to turn. It is assumed that readers of this book would wish to avoid sexist language from conviction. It takes only a little effort to write in a way which displays no gender bias. Whatever your personal view, many journals and publishers now insist on this, and even if they do not, prudence suggests neutral use of language, for there is no doubt that many people, both women and men, feel strongly about this and may be offended by insensitivity. It is equally important, of course, to ensure that you do not use language pejoratively about people with a disability or any form of social or physical disadvantage.

Planning the report

For a written document longer than a page or so, it is advisable to devise a framework or writing plan in advance of beginning to write. This plan could consist of chapter and section headings or just a set of notes about content which could later be ordered into a logical sequence.

In working towards research publications, you will almost certainly have produced interim working papers. For example, a literature review can be written up provisionally at an early stage, and a methods section can be written as soon as the study is designed. It may then be possible, particularly on a word-processor, to shape these working papers into the final report.

Organization of the research report

Writing is, of course, a highly individual pursuit, but the writing of research reports does require a certain degree of uniformity. There will have to be a title, probably an abstract, and an introduction which covers the relevant literature, policy or local background and theoretical context. A section on design and methods will normally be required followed by a results section and a discussion. For the purposes of this discussion it is assumed that the report will contain the following:

- A title page.
- An abstract.
- Literature review.
- Background material (e.g. policy/theory).
- Aims and objectives or hypotheses.
- Design and methods.
- Results.
- Discussion.
- References.
- Appendices.

Title page

This should state the title of the research study, the names of the authors and their institutions. These should all be centred and usually in block capitals. The first author in the list of authors is generally taken to be the correspondent for the study if it is published in a journal; so, if one of the other authors is to be the correspondent, this should be indicated in a footnote. For multiple authored papers, the order of the authors is decided amongst themselves. Sometimes it is alphabetic, but this can be seen to be unfair to people with surnames like Yates, particularly if there are several publications and Yates is always last. Many researchers identify the order of authors to reflect the balance of contributions to that piece of work. If the contributions are equal, authors may be rotated on subsequent papers, or decided by drawing lots.

The abstract

This is a brief summary of the research, often between 100 and 200 words. It should convey the subject of the research, the methods and the main conclusions. It is important to portray an accurate picture of the study as many readers of journals will decide on the basis of the abstract whether or not to read the entire paper.

The literature review

Though this may have been done early in the study, it should be revised once the study findings are known. You will have a much better insight into the topic by then; you may want to be kinder or harsher in your judgements; or you may want to change the general emphasis of the initial literature review to illustrate better the points that have emerged from your study.

Within the literature review – and at various other points of the research report – you will wish to cite the findings or ideas of other authors. This can sometimes be done within a sentence:

> Bloggs (1981) found that retention of qualified physiotherapists was not a consequence of the initial educational experience of these staff . . .

Or it can be done by citing the source at the end of a sentence:

> Initial educational experiences are not thought to affect the retention of qualified physiotherapists (Bloggs, 1972).

When there are several authors, they should all be listed at the first citation; subsequently they can be cited as associates of the main author as in:

> Bloggs et al. (1986) supported this view.

If there are an exceptional number of authors – more than five – it is acceptable to use the 'Bloggs *et al.*' format, even for the first citation. However all the authors should be listed in the references. All the references cited in the text should be listed at the end of the research report.

Political context

Besides the literature background to your study, there may well be a political or policy context which needs to be described, or there may be a local impetus to your study. You should bear in mind any assurances you have given about confidentiality – it is possible to identify locations inadvertently in describing the background to your study.

Aims and objectives

You will have produced statements of aims and objectives and/or research hypotheses early in your study, but at this point it may be an idea to consider whether you have stuck to them. It is remarkable how many published papers include explicit statements of objectives which are demonstrably not met by the research as published.

Design and methods

The design and methods should also have been written in draft form at the appropriate stage of the work. The better your drafting, the less you will now have to do. You may wish to add diagrams, which can be very helpful in communicating your design to the reader. You should also include any work you did on reliability and validity; or cite your sources if these checks were done by another researcher.

Depending on the nature of the study, it may also be useful to describe the process of data collection at this point. Do not be afraid to draw attention to any practical difficulties you had as an aid to any future researchers in your field. In one study managed by the present author it was reported that the fieldwork involved over 200,000 miles of car travel. This sparked a lively correspondence with other researchers who had been contemplating similar studies.

This may also be the most appropriate place to describe your pilot studies and to discuss the ethical implications, if any, of your project.

Results

The results section is arguably the most important in the report. It may well constitute at least half the total content, so it will probably need to be subdivided. You may do this in terms of the stages of analysis, or perhaps by identifying a number of themes. High-quality computer graphics will enhance this section considerably – many of those described and illustrated in Chapter 6 would be suitable. Decisions will be needed about the number of tables and figures and their location. Try to balance tables and text: nothing is more daunting – or boring – than

23 consecutive tables with minimal commentary. If it is necessary to use a lot of tabular material, it may be best to put it in appendices; though the counter argument is that it is irritating for the reader to have to flick forwards and backwards to integrate related material. Diagrams are often a more interesting alternative to tables especially if you vary the types of diagram used.

Statistical tests

Any statistical tests should be reported by quoting the value of the test statistic, the degrees of freedom and the p-value. For example:

'A paired t-test was carried out to test the null hypothesis that the population means were equal. No significant difference was found $(t = 0.326, df = 25, p = 0.61)$'.

If an exact value of p is not available and conventional statistical tables are used, the result would be: $(t = 0.236, df = 25, p > 0.05)$. The results section should not provide a full discussion of findings, but it should report them, drawing attention to points of interest.

Discussion

The discussion of the results should come in the next section which may be more discursive in style. The section should draw some appropriate conclusions and make appropriate recommendations for policy or practice. Some researchers – particularly those with social science backgrounds – go deeply into the implications of their work and make detailed recommendations. As a statistician the present author has tended to leave this to those with responsibility for the implementation of policy or the delivery of care, believing that her role is to inform the decision-maker but not to influence the decision directly. It is an interesting issue and one on which all authors should consider their position before writing a discussion. For one reason or another, discussion sections usually conclude by identifying the need for further research. This may be a relatively painless way of drawing attention to the limitations of the original study, but in any event if there are substantial limitations they are best declared and discussed.

References

Finally, there should be a list of references. There are a number of acceptable formats, so you should check whether your publisher, tutor or whoever prefers any particular one. If your research project is within a course you are likely to have been taught a method of citation and you should of course use this. For general purposes the method used in this book is widely accepted, and a perusal of its list of references will illustrate the following conventions.

An article in a journal is cited by listing surname, initial (for each author with a comma separating authors), year of publication in brackets, title of paper, name of journal, volume number, journal issue number and page numbers. For example:

'Todd, C., Reid, N. & Robinson, G. (1989) The quality of nursing care under eight-hour and twelve-hour shifts: a repeated measures study. International Journal of Nursing Studies, 26, 4, 359–368'.

Some publishers require the name of the journal and the volume number to be underlined. Books are cited by listing the surname and initial of the author or authors, the year of publication in brackets, the title of the book, which edition it is (if appropriate), the name and location of the publisher and the number of pages. For example:

'Goldstone, L. (1983) Understanding Medical Statistics. William Heinemann Medical Books Limited, London, pp. 191'.

Some publishers will require the title to be underlined. A contribution to a book edited by one or more authors would be worded as follows:

'Mortimer, A.J. (1981) Effects of ultrasound on membrane physiology. In: Proceedings of the International Symposium on Therapeutic Ultrasound, editors: A. Mortimer & N. Lee. Canadian Physiotherapy Association, Winnipeg'.

For reports made to government departments and similar bodies the format is:

'Reid, N. & McClean, S. (1990) The Limbo Report, Report to the Department of Health and Social Services. DHSS, Belfast'.

The guidelines provided in this book are, in the experience of the author, widely accepted as good practice in writing research reports. But every research report is different in its objectivity and also its audience. The sections suggested for inclusion in research reports are not intended to be exhaustive. It is not unusual, for example, to have a page of acknowledgements of assistance. This would come after the title paper and would include those who have helped with funding, resources, access, fieldwork, analysis and general academic, professional or personal support. You may also wish to include some appendices at the end of your report or paper. There may be other sections which would be necessary for your particular report. The golden rule is to be led by the person or persons for whom the report is intended.

Oral reports

Most researchers have occasion to present their work orally and many courses now require an oral presentation of the project as well as a written report.

The oral report differs from the written report in style, detail and length, but the key points to consider remain the nature of the audience and your objectives with that audience. You need to be aware of the nature of their academic background, their status and seniority and their level of interest in your presentation. Are they conscripts or volunteers? Will they a priori be looking forward to hearing your report or is there some unease or even hostility?

Your objectives in making an oral report may be to share your findings, to communicate with professional and academic colleagues, or they may be more honestly expressed as wishing to impress the audience, either because your talk is being formally assessed in some way, or because you hope to enhance your reputation and standing with the audience.

There is an old teaching maxim which goes: 'Tell 'em what you're going to tell 'em; tell 'em; and tell 'em what you've told 'em'.

This is good advice if you have time. You may be allocated a small amount of time – perhaps as little as ten minutes – and you must make the most of it. You may simply have to 'tell 'em'. If your oral report is a supplement to a written report, do not try to repeat everything that is in the written report. Select a small number of themes and arrange your talk around them. However much time you have do not feel obliged to tell the audience every last thing that you know about the topic. It is a good idea to save some material if there is to be a discussion or a question-and-answer session.

Some audiences are easily bored, so the use of audio-visual aids is recommended not only to provide a periodic change of focus but to illustrate better the points you wish to make. Both slides and overhead acetates are widely used, but the object of the exercise will be defeated if they are not of high quality. There is nothing worse than sloppily handwritten overheads which the audience can barely read. If you cannot achieve high quality, do not use slides at all. Slides must be clearly labelled, neatly laid out and not overladen with information; colour can be used to good effect. Nowadays videos are increasingly used to support oral presentations and these require even higher standards.

Beware of handing out written materials at the beginning of your talk or part way through it. Some of the audience will immediately start to read, others will be distracted by rustling pages and you will lose your grip on the situation. Written handouts should be issued at the end of the talk. But it is a good idea to tell the audience that you will be distributing a handout as this will remove their need for taking notes and you are more likely to have their undivided attention.

Style and presentation

While all lecturing is to some extent a performance, your own style and personality must largely determine your approach. A relatively informal style is generally appropriate and if you can inject some humour into the session this is always helpful. If you amuse an audience they will let you get away with almost anything. But the humour must be relevant – there is no point in going into a stand-up comic routine if the jokes do not in some way help to make the points you want to communicate.

It is best not to read from a prepared text. Such an approach is understandable in a nervous and inexperienced speaker, but the effect is almost always boring and stilted. A good compromise between reading a prepared speech and a totally *ad lib* approach is to use little cards with cues which lead you through the talk. Slides are also valuable cues for the speaker.

Most inexperienced speakers – and not a few experienced ones – tend to talk too fast. If you can arrange to listen to yourself on video or close circuit television or even on tape, this can be a most useful (if uncomfortable) opportunity to assess your diction and mannerisms in private. Trying to alter your accent is not usually a good idea. The important thing is to speak slowly and clearly. It may be necessary to project your voice fairly positively to reach every corner of a large auditorium.

Finally, your appearance is obviously important. You will want to be clean and tidy but it is equally important that you feel comfortable. Lecture rooms and theatres can be very hot, so it may be wise to check this in advance and dress accordingly. It is advisable to look smart but haute couture is not necessary and you may take the view that you do not want your appearance to attract attention away from what you have to say.

If possible you should check the room before your lecture for the appropriateness of the seating – do you want to lecture rows of people or chat to a more intimate circle? Check that the audio visual aids work and are correctly placed and, if possible, do a dry run of your talk in front of a critical but kindly friend or colleague.

Evaluation

In presenting your own research, or considering the work of others, you should not neglect the important stage of evaluation. As has been noted throughout this book it is a rare piece of research that is not flawed in some way. Furthermore every completed piece of work may provide new information which will increase understanding and knowledge of the topic. This new information may be negative, perhaps related to the enormous practical and methodological difficulties encountered; or it may constitute a significant advance.

It is essential for the researcher to acquire the skills to evaluate his or her own work as well as the work of others. The fundamental purpose of research into health care issues is to advance knowledge with a view to providing better care for patients and clients. The researchers themselves make an enormous contribution, but it is generally for others to evaluate that research and decide whether or not to make changes or innovations based on its findings.

This process takes place at many levels within the health care professions. Research on national staffing issues and resourcing is constantly being evaluated by the senior civil servants who plan and manage the services. Research on transfers of services from hospital to community needs to be weighed by those who are responsible for district and regional services. Researchers constantly evaluate the work of other researchers, usually through literature reviews. Clinical research is the day-to-day concern of those who directly deliver care to patients and clients. There is thus a strong argument that every nurse, physiotherapist, occupational therapist or radiographer should be able to evaluate research that is relevant to his or her practice.

To evaluate research it is not necessary to be a researcher: you do not need to be a carpenter to know if a table is soundly constructed. But you should respect the carpenter's skills. Evaluation of research must be balanced, identifying both strengths and weaknesses. Too often it is seen as a negative fault-finding exercise and the effect can be counter-productive.

Researchers are wise if they do not get too twitchy about the process. Even the best piece of research is unlikely to achieve perfection and very few single pieces of work become the definitive statement on a topic. The frontiers of knowledge are more often pushed back through the collective efforts of many researchers, often over a long period. Balanced evaluation is the best way to contribute to that process, pointing out the positive features and the potential flaws.

Evaluation must be done sympathetically and the stages in the process of research, described in detail in Chapter 2, will be used to illustrate a sound framework.

The title

The title should reflect accurately the content of the report or article. Since it may attract, discourage or even mislead potential readers, it is important that it conveys the essence of the piece. It is not, however, necessarily a pointer to the quality of the research *per se*. Useful questions are:

(1) Is the title an accurate reflection of the content?
(2) Is it concise and arresting, serious, catchpenny, vague or woolly?

Background – literature review

The review of the literature should be relevant, up-to-date and comprehensive. It should include sound academic sources and may also include material from the popular ones such as magazines. There should not be an over-reliance on articles which constitute mere opinion: well founded research evidence must provide the core. There should not be an overemphasis on secondary sources.

It is most important that the review represents a thoughtful analysis of the field, not just a collection of quotations and conclusions. It should include all published points of view, not just those which support the views of the authors. Some relevant questions are:

- Is the review comprehensive?
- Is it discriminating or does it contain irrelevant sources?
- Is it up-to-date?
- Is there enough sound research-based evidence?
- Is the use of secondary sources excessive?
- Has the author appraised the material critically?
- Is the selection of sources even-handed?

Other background (policy and theory)

This section may cover national or local policy perspectives or it may provide a theoretical context for the study. Whatever the nature of the content, you should, having read it, be able to make a judgement about whether the study needed to be done, and you should be clear about the rationale behind it. If a theory context is given, it should be relevant and helpful. A contrived theoretical background is almost always evident since this leads to a lack of integration at the later stages of the study, with, for example, almost no mention of the theory at the discussion stage. Useful questions include:

- Is the rationale clear and explicit?
- Is the policy background well-presented?
- Is the theory background relevant; and adequate but not excessive?
- Does the impetus for the study emerge?

Formulation of the research question

There should be a concise statement of the purpose of the study. This should include either a statement of aims, and/or objectives, or research hypotheses – or all of these. It should then be possible to form a view about the scope and manageability of the study. Questions might include:

- Is the research question well-formulated?
- Are aims, objectives and/or research hypotheses clearly stated?
- Is the study too ambitious or too limited?

Design and methods

In Chapter 4 three detailed examples were provided of evaluation of research designs and methods. In summary, the key issue is the choice of design type for the particular research question. There should be some justification by the author of the use of a true-experimental, quasi-experimental or non-experimental design and of the particular choice of design within these categories. The chosen design should be capable of meeting the study objectives in theory and should have done so in practice. Constructs should have been appropriately defined and, if borrowed from other studies, their value in those studies should be indicated.

The decisions made about use of sampling should be clearly stated and justified. If sampling was used, the method should be fully described and should be related to the generalizability of results. The sample size should be large enough to sustain the statistical analyses. If questionnaires are used, response rates should be reported along with comment on and, if necessary, investigation of response bias. The study instruments should be clearly described with assurances about reliability and validity and with either confirming sources or original establishment of these properties. Some useful questions include:

- Why use this category of design for this topic?
- Why use this particular design within that category?
- Does the design meet the study objectives?
- Was sampling appropriate? Why?
- Is the sampling method adequately described?
- Are any limitations of sampling recognized?
- Are the study measures reliable and valid?
- What are the main strengths and weaknesses?

Resources, ethics, communications and access

In evaluating the scope of the research, it is important to take into account the resources that were available. If resource constraints affected the conduct of the research, the writer ought to point this out. On the other hand, it would be unreasonable to criticize elements of the research if the researcher had no alternative because of resource shortages.

The ethical implications of the study and whether ethical approval was sought and given, should be stated by the researcher. In commenting on this, irrespective of the outcome it should be remembered that the operation of local ethical committees can be idiosyncratic. If the research required negotiation of access to clinical or other faculties, this should be described briefly and any difficulties noted. A brief account should also be given of communications needed to facilitate the project. Questions might include:

- Were there any resource constraints and were optimal strategies developed?
- Does the research have ethical implications and how were these handled?

- Was access properly negotiated?
- Are communications adequately described?

Data collection and analysis

The account given of the methods of data collection should demon-strate that the study was carried out as designed. There should be no introduction of bias through the modes used or personnel employed in data collection. The analysis should follow a plan emanating from the study objectives. It should be well-organized and logical and the chosen path should be evident.

The inferential statistical analyses should be based on clearly-stated null hypotheses and should be appropriate for the nature of the data. The use of attractive diagrams and tables is desirable and the inclusion of material should be thoughtful. Too much material with too little structure can make a results section very difficult to follow. Questions might include:

- Was data collection appropriately carried out?
- Was the integrity of the design preserved during data collection?
- Does the results section follow a plan?
- Are the statistical analyses well-presented and correctly done?
- Is the results section well organized?
- Is the amount of tabular and graphical material appropriate and helpful?
- Does the analysis relate directly to the study objectives?
- Are all the data presented or is there a selection? If the latter, why?
- Do the findings support the author's predictions?

Discussion

This section will provide the researcher's commentary on the findings and probably some conclusions or recommendations. These should follow directly from the study findings, not constitute some leap into the unknown based only loosely on the preceding study. The study data must justify the conclusions and recommendations, and the dis-cussion should demonstrate that the study objectives have been met. There should not be exaggerated claims about the study's contribution – on the contrary a statement of its limitations is often more helpful at this point. Any discussion of generalizability of results should tally with the statistical methods adopted. Almost all studies should be able to demonstrate their relevance to some aspect of professional activity and this should be part of the discussions. Some useful questions are:

- Does the discussion follow logically from the results?
- Is the tone modest and restrained or is there a tendency to over-claim?
- Have the study objectives been met?

- Are the conclusions neat and lucidly expressed?
- Is the author aware of the study's limitations?

References
These should be in an acceptable format and should be accurately cited so that any one can be located by the reader. They should be consistent with the text. Questions might be:

- Are the references in the correct format?
- Are they correct in detail?
- Do they correspond with the text?

Having worked through these stages of the research publication, some general questions can now be posed:

(1) Are standards of grammar, punctuation and spelling acceptable?
(2) Is the style of writing acceptable?
(3) Is the study important within the field of study?
(4) Does it contribute to professional practice in any sphere?
(5) Was it worth doing?
(6) Does it build logically on previous work in the field – is it the obvious next step or is it premature?
(7) Is it either over-ambitious or too limited?
(8) Is the level of detail sufficient, too little or too great?
(9) Is the presentation well-organized?

Finally, in evaluating your own or other people's work, it is worth asking at each stage what alternative choices there might have been; and, if you can think of a better approach, offering it. This is the essence of constructive criticism. So at the end, as at the beginning, we keep always in mind why we do research in the first place. Perhaps, fundamentally, because we are curious, and want to know more. Perhaps also because we find it exciting and enjoyable. But, beyond this, we do research in the health care professions to find more and better ways of caring for our fellow citizens. For all of these reasons we surely must strive to achieve the highest possible standards. That is why you should not only be a researcher but should make the extra effort to become a good researcher. I hope this book will help you, if only in a small way, to take at least a few steps along the road to excellence.

Discussion points

1. The researcher's role is to inform policy-makers, but not to influence policy or practice directly. Do you agree?
2. Draw up a marking scheme for the assessment of:
   (i) a written report;

(ii) an oral report;

indicating your criteria for both of these in detail and the marks available.

References

Birley, D.S. (1991) *Putting it in Writing*. University of Ulster.

Fowler, H.W. (1983) *A dictionary of modern English usage, 2nd edn with corrections revised by Ernest Gowers*. Oxford University Press.

Fowler, H.W. & Fowler, F.G. (1970) *The King's English, 3rd edn*. Clarendon Press, Oxford.

Gowers, F. (1986) *The complete plain words*. Revised edn by Sidney Greenbaum & Janet Whitcut. HMSO, London.

Partridge, E. (1973) *Usage and abusage, a guide to good English*, reprinted with revisions. Penguin, Harmondsworth in association with Hamish Hamilton.

Vallins, G.H. (1979) *Good English*. Pan, London.

Appendix A

Transformations using MINITAB

Transformations can be done easily through MINITAB. In practice, transformations are generally used to obtain a symmetrical distribution when data are continuous but the distribution is skewed. There are many ways in which this can be done, but the most commonly used

Table A1   Transformations.

MTB > histogram of C1 N = 100

Midpoint	Count	
0	27	******************************
2	26	**************************
4	15	***************
6	10	**********
8	7	*******
10	6	******
12	1	*
14	4	****
16	2	**
18	2	**

MTB > let C2 = $\sqrt{(C1)}$
MTB > histogram C2

Histogram of C2 N = 100

Midpoint	Count	
0.5	16	****************
1.0	20	********************
1.5	17	*****************
2.0	15	***************
2.5	13	*************
3.0	8	********
3.5	7	*******
4.0	2	**
4.5	2	**

```
MTB > let C3 = log t (C1)
MTB > histogram C3
```

Histogram of C3 N = 100

Midpoint	Count	
−1.0	2	**
−0.8	1	*
−0.6	3	***
−0.4	6	******
−0.2	8	********
0.0	10	**********
0.2	10	**********
0.4	13	*************
0.6	15	***************
0.8	14	**************
1.0	9	*********
1.2	9	*********

```
MTB > let C4 = −1/C1
MTB > histogram C4
```

Histogram of C4 N = 100
Each * represents 2 obs.

Midpoint	Count	
−12	1	*
−11	1	*
−10	0	
−9	0	
−8	0	
−7	0	
−6	1	*
−5	0	
−4	1	*
−3	6	***
−2	8	****
−1	22	**********
0	60	******************************

are by taking the square root of the data, by taking logarithms and by taking the negative reciprocal. The weakest of these is the square root transformation; the logarithm is stronger and the negative reciprocal is the strongest. This may be observed from the above set of transformations done on MINITAB (see Table A1).

The data indicate lengths of service of physiotherapists. First the histogram is printed to display the skewed distribution. To replicate this distribution, type:

RANDOM 100 OBS INTO C1;

CAUCHY 4

Then the square root transformation is done by typing:

LET C2 = SQRT(C1)

and the histogram is printed.

The distribution is less skewed now, though still markedly askew. The next strongest transformation is applied by typing:

LET C3 = LOGT(C1)

The histogram is now fairly symmetrical and, if anything, slightly skewed in the other direction.

Finally, the negative reciprocal is done by typing:

LET C4 = −1/C1

and printing the histogram which is now highly skewed in the opposite direction to the original data. Of the three transformations, the logarithm works best in this case and parametric techniques can now be applied to those data. Transformations are hit-and-miss techniques; it is a question of trying several and finding one which works.

Appendix B

Some introductory epidemiological terms and methods

A number of standard indices are used in health research to summarise such events as deaths, births and illnesses. In this appendix some brief definitions and methods are provided.

Births

The crude birth rate is the number of live births occurring in a period per 1000 population. For example the birth rate for Lapland in 1975 might be 23 per 1000. If birth rates must be compared from one place to another, or from one year to another, you should check that the populations are demographically comparable. A relatively high number of elderly people (beyond child-bearing age) could give rise to an underestimate of the birth rate. For comparative purposes it is best to use the fertility rate.

The *fertility rate* is the number of live births occurring in a period per 1000 women of child-bearing age. It is essential, for comparative purposes, to ensure that the definition of child-bearing age is consistent. A more specific measure is the age specific fertility rate which is the number of live births occurring in a period per 1000 women within the specified age band.

Deaths

The crude death rate is the number of deaths per 1000 population in a given period. This index is also dependent upon the demography of the constituent population, and in this case, a relatively high proportion of older people – or, indeed a relatively high proportion of men or women – could give rise to an inflated estimate of the death rate. This may be overcome by calculating age specific death rates or sex specific death rates, and both age and sex may be standardized by calculating age specific rates separately for each sex.

The standardized mortality rate (SMR) is the mortality rate for a given population over a given period, relative to a standard against which it is compared. If, for example, the mortality rate of a base year is set at 100, the standardized mortality rate ten years later might be 120 which would indicate a 20% increase in the rate. The SMR may also be standardized for age and sex as described earlier.

A variety of death rates are used for specific groups of people and for particular causes of death. For example, government statistics routinely report perinatal and neonatal mortality rates and a range of mortality rates for particular diseases.

Mortality statistics can also be used to calculate the expectancy of life. This is done by examining retrospectively the death rates at each age for a population. By applying these rates to a new living cohort, the number of deaths each year can be predicted. The number of years lived at any given age is the number of survivors plus half the number who are expected to die at that age – on the assumption that the deaths are timed equally throughout that year. By repeating this calculation for each age, it is then possible, for any given age to calculate the total years of life which can be expected in future years. This number is averaged over the survivors at that age to give a mean life expectancy. These calculations are usually presented in a *life table* which shows for each age where death can occur: the number of survivors at the beginning of that year (x), the expected number of deaths in that year (y), the total years lived in that year $\left(x + \dfrac{y}{2}\right)$, the total years of life expected beyond that year (the total of $x + \dfrac{y}{2}$ for all subsequent years), which can be written as:

$$\sum_{\substack{\text{all} \\ \text{subsequent} \\ \text{years}}} x + \frac{y}{2}$$

And finally the mean life expectancy which is:

$$\frac{1}{x} \text{ times } \sum_{\substack{\text{all} \\ \text{subsequent} \\ \text{years}}} x + \frac{y}{2}$$

Illnesses

Morbidity statistics are difficult to obtain since morbidity is recorded only for a limited number of diseases. Otherwise the collection of morbidity data tends to be idiosyncratic and local and there are enormous difficulties in obtaining standardized information which can be used comparatively.

The incidence rate for a disease is the number of new cases in a specified period per hundred population. The prevalence rate is the number of cases in existence at a particular point in time per hundred population.

Index